PUBLIC AND INTERNATIONAL ECONOMICS

Also by Ali M. El-Agraa

BRITAIN WITHIN THE EUROPEAN COMMUNITY (*editor*)
INTERNATIONAL ECONOMIC INTEGRATION (*editor*)
INTERNATIONAL TRADE
JAPAN'S TRADE FRICTIONS
PROTECTION, COOPERATION, INTEGRATION AND DEVELOPMENT (*editor*)
THEORY OF CUSTOMS UNIONS (*with A. J. Jones*)
THE ECONOMICS OF THE EUROPEAN COMMUNITY (*editor*)
THE THEORY AND MEASUREMENT OF INTERNATIONAL ECONOMIC INTEGRATION
THE THEORY OF INTERNATIONAL TRADE
TRADE THEORY AND POLICY

Public and International Economics

Essays in Honour of Professor Hirofumi Shibata

Edited by

Ali M. El-Agraa
Professor of International Economics and European/American Economies
Fukuoka University, Japan

Assisted by

Toshihiro Ihori
Associate Professor of Economics
Tokyo University, Japan

150th YEAR
M

St. Martin's Press

First published in Great Britain 1993 by
THE MACMILLAN PRESS LTD
Houndmills, Basingstoke, Hampshire RG21 2XS
and London
Companies and representatives
throughout the world

A catalogue record for this book is available
from the British Library.

ISBN 0–333–58583–6

Printed in Great Britain by
Ipswich Book Co Ltd
Ipswich, Suffolk

First published in the United States of America 1993 by
Scholarly and Reference Division,
ST. MARTIN'S PRESS, INC.,
175 Fifth Avenue,
New York, N.Y. 10010

ISBN 0–312–09721–2

Library of Congress Cataloging-in-Publication Data
Public and international economics : essays in honour of Professor Hirofumi Shibata / edited by Ali M. El-Agraa ; assisted by Toshihiro Ihori.
p. cm.
Includes bibliographical references and index.
ISBN 0–312–09721–2
1. Finance, Public. 2. Welfare economics. 3. International trade. I. Shibata, Hirofumi, 1929– . II. El-Agraa, A. M. III. Ihori, Toshihiro, 1952–
HJ141.P77 1993
336—dc20 93–18908
CIP

Contents

Preface and Acknowledgements

Professor Hirofumi Shibata was born in Fujisawa in Kanagawa Prefecture, Japan. Fujisawa lies to the south of Tokyo, and from there, one can command a magnificent view of the majestic Mount Fuji ('Fujisan' in Japanese) throughout most of the year. Fujisan is unique in that, on a clear day, because of its impressive height, it can also be viewed from other parts of Japan. Hence, it is a constant reminder to all Japanese to aim high by trying their utmost irrespective of their natural limitations; a slogan well ingrained in their education system where effort is paramount and talent is nothing more than an insignificant headstart. Also, the grip of Fujisan's beauty ensures that Japanese never forget where their heart really belongs, which is why they never feel at ease anywhere else. No wonder, Fujisan seems to dominate every aspect of Japanese life.

These manifestations of Fujisan are clearly reflected in the life of Professor Shibata. After graduating from Kobe University, he joined the Ministry of Finance by passing its rigorous selection examination. To be with the Ministry would normally be the ultimate in the aspirations of a Japanese graduate, but not for Professor Shibata. Six years later he left Japan (in 1959) to study for his MA at McGill University in Canada, through a Canada Council Fellowship, a much needed scholarship due to the economic poverty of Japan in those days! Not only did he succesfully negotiate his degree, but also part of his dissertation was published in the American Economic Review (in 1968) to become the celebrated article on the 'equivalence of tariffs and quotas'. Then, through a Research Fellowship from the International Economic Integration Programme, he moved to Columbia University (in 1962) to work on his PhD, which he received in 1965. His thesis was published in the classic two volumes edited by Professor Carl Shoup entitled Fiscal Harmonisation in Common Markets (in 1967), a work still much quoted by those specializing in the branch of International Economics referred to as International Economic Integration. After that, he returned to Canada as an Assistant, later to become an Associate Professor of Economics with Queen's University. He was then recruited for the Department of Economics in the newly-established York University in Britain, where he started as a Senior Lecturer and was later promoted to Reader in Economics (in 1971). During that period, he joined the Department of Economics in the University of Maryland at Park College as a Visiting Associate Professor (in 1970). His, and his founding colleagues', contribution to the Department of Economics at York University no doubt can explain the high ranking of that department in Britain today. He then joined the United Nations in New York as a Senior Economist with the Department of Economic and Social Affairs in 1972, but during the same year he departed to assume the responsibility of a full Professor of Economics with the University of Kentucky. However, in 1977, after almost two decades away from the grip of Fujisan, he finally succumbed by returning to Japan as Professor of Economics with Osaka University, one of the top seven national universities of Japan, the so-called Impirial Colleges.

A glance at his short personal history and publications, with are set out in Chapter 1, will clearly show that, although he could not escape the grip of Fujisan, Professor Shibata has continued his very close relationships with the outside world both through visiting professorships and consultancies. Moreover, contrary to Japanese tradition, he has sought publication of his academic works in internationally acclaimed and refereed journals. The quality of these papers has been so high as to warrant his entry, from the first edition, in the Blaug/Sturges Who's Who in Economics.

In the previous paragraph I mentioned that it runs against Japanese tradition for Japanese academics to publish their work in foreign journals. Indeed, this is still largely the case since most research articles tend to be published in domestic (own faculty) unrefereed journals. The rationale for this is that academics are supposed to be personally responsible for the quality of their work and that those who seek information regarding such publications can always consult the various guide journals and libraries providing it. Moreover, most Japanese scholars were, and a large number still are, almost completely incompetent in English (and other foreign languages), hence the chore of having to translate their papers for submission to journals which they themselves largely ignored, or read at a turtle's pace, was an unforgivable waste of time. Furthermore, there are those Japanese who would claim that the fact that a growing number of Japanese have become internationally known and respected largely because of the validity of their work in English is a clear indication of the quality of the reasearch published only in Japanese since those who are internationally acclaimed do not seem to stand out within

Japan itself. Moreover, there is also the concern that both the refereeing processs and the referees may not be all that objective, particularly so when specialists try hard to suppress any work that does not follow the bandwagon in terms of either topicality or methodology; otherwise why do international journals insist on anonymous refereeing! Finally, this Japanese tradition could simply be due to the high respect for age and learning: an academic is respected simply because he is in the profession and the older he gets the deeper his thoughts become, hence the more respect is afforded to him.

In short, there are arguments both for and against this Japanese tradition, but in the context of Professor Shibata, he has tried to promote a nice balance between the two conflicting viewpoints: he has continued to publish in both Japanese and English and in both domestic and international journals. However, he has tried to do more than just that. In Japan, there is also a strong tradition of making appointments only through personal knowledge and contact with the candidates. This has come to mean that professors appoint only their own graduate students or, what amounts to the same thing, those recommended by the professor who supervised them during their doctorate courses, hence also those recommended by their ex-postgraduate students. This linkage is facilitated through that unique Japanese educational institution called the 'professor's seminar' and the hierarchical nature of the society. The latter accords great respect to age and the former, which can be simplified to mean teaching by example where the professor is like a parent who guides the students both academically and socially, ensures that the parental relationship lasts for ever, hence the appointments procedure just described.

This procedure has sometimes resulted in almost every member of the same department having the same academic slant. For example, until very recently, it was well-known that one had to be a Marxist to stand a chance of joining the Faculty of Economics at the University of Tokyo. Similar things do happen in distinguished universities in the West, but not to the same extent; however, this is not the occasion to go into these matters. What is important for my purposes is that the Faculty of Economics in Osaka University has been following a different path since its members not only pursue diverse topics and approach them through different methodologies, but they also come from a wide spectrum of the profession. Morever, the Faculty's domestic journal, the Osaka Economic Papers, is both refereed and listed in the Journal of Economic Literature. Professor Shibata and his colleagues must be accredited with the uniqueness and academic distinction of their Faculty.

Because of all of the above, I felt that Professor Shibata's formal retirement from Osaka University should not go unnoticed by the outside world. He has been honoured in a special issue of the Osaka Economic Papers by a group of distinguished academics, both from Japan and other countries, but the circulation of that journal is too limited to reach the sort of audience that is familiar with Professor Shibata's work; hence my decision to publish this book. I have selected and edited the most appropriate papers and notes from that issue for the Festschrift, but I hope this will not offend the other contributors to that issue: space limitations and the chosen theme have guided me in my selection.

The book begins with a chapter on the personal history and publications of Professor Hirofumi Shibata. This is followed by three chapters, written in a non-technical style, covering the interesting topics of the value of freedom of choice, by Sir Alan Peacock, the institutional management of 'free riders' and common property resources, by Professor Roumasset, and some methodological issues in the use of cost-benefit analysis in health care, by Professor Williams. Then come five technical chapters, by Professors Culyer, Kohn, Negishi, Suzumura and Saposnik, on various aspects of equity and efficiency in resource allocation. The following chapter, a non-technical one on the international harmonization of taxes, by Professor Shoup, is appropriately followed by five technical chapters on different taxation issues, by Professors Bird, Hatta, Wiseman/Posnet, Georgakopoulos/Hitiris and Ihori. Next are eight chapters, by Professors Benveniste/Boyd/Greenbaum, Olson, Takayama, Hamada, Onitsuka, and McGuire, and Drs Tanzi (IMF) and Panagariya (World Bank), which can be classified as international macroeconomic in nature; these deal with: bank capital regulation; collective choice and microeconomic approach to macroeconomics; the 'Fisher effect' and the long term structure of interest rates; investment demand; the political economy of the choice of an exchange rate regime; savings, economic growth and the balance of payments; factor migration, trade and welfare under the threat of commercial policy; and the pattern of factor migration between the North and South. The final four chapters, by Professors Sato, Drysdale, Hindley and El-Agraa, tackle the topical issues of Japan's land prices, VERs, the extension of 'EC 1992' to EC public utilities, and Asia-Pacific cooperation. Therefore, this is a unique collection covering a wide range of topics in public and international economics, written by leading authorities to honour a distinguished professional colleague, and a personal friend who has taught in universities in Canada, the USA and Japan, who has worked for the IMF and United Nations, and whose research is widely quoted.

This is the appropriate place to thank the editors of the Osaka Economic Papers for copyright permission to publish edited versions of the papers in that issue. In this context, I would also like to express my sincere gratitude to Professor Toshihiro Ihori not only for his willingness to act as Assistant Editor for the Festschrift and the effort he put into the preparation of the special issue of the Osaka Economic Papers, but also for providing the subject index.

This is also the occasion to thank all the chosen contributors for their notes and articles, their enthusiasm for the venture and their cooperation with me during the editing process. I do hope that the final result is to their liking.

Moreover, I would like to express my special gratitude to Professor Masahiro Abiru of the Faculty of Economics at Fukuoka University for all his efforts in persuading me to persevere with the type-setting wordprocessing system which enabled me to achieve this excellent product.

Finally, and most importantly, since this is a tribute to Professor Shibata, I would like to take this opportunity to wish him a happy active retirement. Active, since he will be moving to a private university in Kyoto: the retirement age for Japanese national universities is much lower than for those employed in the private sector.

ALI M. EL-AGRAA

Notes on the Contributors

Larry Benveniste is Professor of Finance, Department of Finance, Boston College School of Management, Northwestern University, USA.

Richard M. Bird is Professor of Economics, Department of Economics, Toronto University, Canada.

John Boyd is Research Officer, Federal Reserve Bank of Minneapolis, and University of Minnesota, USA.

Anthony J. Culyer is Professor of Economics and Head, Department of Economics and Related Studies, York University, UK.

Peter Drysdale is Professor and Executive Director, Economics Division, Australia-Japan Research Centre, Research School of Pacific Studies, Australian National University, Australia.

Ali M. El-Agraa is Professor of International Economics, and European and American Economies, Faculty of Commerce, Fukuoka University, Japan.

Theodore A. Georgakopoulos is Professor of Economics and Chairman, Department of International and European Economic Studies, Athens University of Economics and Business, Greece.

Stuart I. Greenbaum is Norman Strunk Distinguished Professor of Financial Institutions and Director, Banking Research Centre, J. L. Kellogg Graduate School of Management, Northwestern University, USA.

Koichi Hamada is Professor of Economics, Department of Economics, Economic Growth Centre, Yale University, USA.

Tatsuo Hatta is Professor of Economics, Institute of Social and Economics Research, Osaka University, Japan.

Brian Hindley is Professor of Economics, London School of Economics, London University, UK.

Theodore Hitiris is Senior Lecturer, Department of Economics and Related Studies, York University, UK.

Toshihiro Ihori is Associate Professor of Economics, Faculty of Economics, University of Tokyo, Japan.

Robert E. Kohn is Professor Emeritus of Economics, Department of Economics, Southern Illinois University at Edwardsville, USA.

Martin C. McGuire is Clifford S. Heinz Professor for the Economics of Global Peace and Security, University of California, Irvine, USA.

Takashi Negishi is Professor of Economics, Faculty of Economics, University of Tokyo, Japan.

Mancur Olson is Distinguished Professor of Economics, University of Maryland at College Park, and Chair, Center on Institutional Reform and the Informal Sector (IRIS), USA.

Yusuke Onitsuka is Professor of Economics, Department of Social and International Relations, College of Arts and Sciences, University of Tokyo, Japan.

Arvind Panagariya is a Senior Economist in the Trade Policy Division of the World Bank's Country Economics Department and is Professor of Economics, University of Maryland at College Park, USA.

Alan Peacock is Research Professor in Public Finance, Heriot-Watt University.

John Posnett is Senior Lecturer in Economics, Department of Economics and Related Studies, York University, UK.

James A. Roumasset is Professor of Economics, Department of Economics, University of Hawaii at Manoa, USA.

Rubin Saposnik is Professor of Economics, Georgia State University, USA.

Kazuo Sato is Professor of Economics, Department of Economics, Rutgers University, USA.

Carl S. Shoup is McVickar Professor Emeritus of Political Economy, Columbia University, USA.

Kotaro Suzumura is Professor of Economic Systems Analysis, the Institute of Economic Research, Hitotsubashi University, and Editor, *Journal of Japanese and International Economies*, Japan.

Akira Takayama is Vandeveer Professor of Economics, Department of Economics, Southern Illinois University at Carbondale, USA.

Vito Tanzi is Director, Fiscal Affairs Department, International Monetary Fund, USA.

Alan Williams is Professor of Economics, Department of Economics and Related Studies, York University, UK.

Jack Wiseman was Professor Emeritus of Economics, Department of Economics and Related Studies, York University, UK.

Professor Hirofumi Shibata

1 Personal History and Publications of Hirofumi Shibata

Ali M. El-Agraa

PERSONAL HISTORY

1. 1929: Born in Fujisawa City, Kanagawa Prefecture, Japan on 27 September.
2. 1953: Graduated from Kobe University of Economics (now Kobe University), Japan.
3. 1953: Passed a national examination for the senior level career government officials and appointed as an officer in the Ministry of Finance, Japan.
4. 1958: Nominated as a grantee of a Fulbright Travel Fellowship to participate in the International Program in Taxation, Havard University, but opted for a Canada Council Fellowship.
5. 1959: Received a two-year Canada Council Fellowship to study at the Faculty of Graduate Studies and Research, McGill University, Montreal, Canada.
6. 1962: Received his Master of Arts Degree (in Economics) from McGill University. The title of the dissertation was: *The Japanese Voluntary Export Control*, a part of which, 'On the equivalence of tariffs and quotas', was published in the *American Economic Review*, vol. 58, March, 1968.
7. 1962: Received a three-year Research Fellowship from the International Economic Integration Program, Columbia University, New York, and enrolled in the Graduate School of Arts and Sciences, Columbia University.
8. 1965: Received his Doctor of Philosophy Degree (in Economics) from Columbia University. The title of the thesis was: *A Theory of Economic Unions: Comparative Analysis of Customs Unions, Free Trade Areas and Tax Unions*. It was published in *Fiscal Harmonization in Common Markets* (Columbia University Press, 1971), edited by C. S. Shoup.

Major career

1. 1965: Appointed Assistant Professor of Economics, Queen's University, Kingston, Ontario, Canada.
2. 1967: Promoted to Associate Professor of Economics, Queen's University.
3. 1969: Appointed Senior Lecturer in Economics, The University of York, York, Britain.
4. 1970: Visiting Associate Professor, Department of Economics, The University of Maryland, College Park, Maryland.
5. 1971: Promoted to Reader in Economics, The University of York, Britain.
6. 1972: Appointed Senior Economist, Department of Economics and Social Affairs, United Nations, New York.
7. 1972: Appointed Professor of Economics, the University of Kentucky, Lexington, USA.
8. 1977: Appointed Professor of Economics, Osaka University, Japan.
9. 1983: Listed in the first edition of *Who's Who in Economics: a Biographical Dictionary of Major Economists, 1700–1981*, edited by Mark Blaug and Paul Sturges (MIT Press). 2nd. Edition, 1988.
10. 1985: Elected Member of the Executive Board, Osaka University.
11. 1988: Invited Visiting Scholar, Fiscal Affairs Department, International Monetary Fund, Washington, DC.
12. 1989: Visiting Professor, Department of Economics, the University of Maryland, College Park, Maryland.
13. 1989: Elected Dean, Faculty of Economics and Director of the Graduate School of Economics, Osaka University.

Other positions held

1. 1966: Consultant, Department of Finance, Government of Canada, Ottawa.
2. 1967: Research Economist, Private Planning Association of Canada, Montreal.
3. 1968: Consultant, Department of Economics and Social Affairs, United Nations, New York.
4. 1971: External Graduate Programme Adviser, Centro De Economia E Financas, Instituto Gulbenkian De Ciência, Fundacão Calouste Gulbenkian, Lisbon, Portugal.

5. 1972: Consultant, the Urban Institute, Washington, DC.
6. 1991: Member, the Gakujutsu Shigikai (The Academic Council), Japanese Government.

Responsibilities for learned societies

1. 1977–1982: Executive Editor, *Growth and Change: a Journal of Regional Development.*
2. 1983–: Member of the Board of Advisory Editors, *Public Finance/Finances Publiques: International Quarterly Journal.*
3. 1989–: Member of the Board of Advisory Editors, *Kokyo Sentaku no Kenkyu* (Studies in Public Choice).
4. 1987–: Member of the Board of Management, International Institute of Public Finance.
5. 1990–: Member of the Executive Board, Japan Society of Research and Information on Public and Cooperative Economy.

PUBLICATIONS

Books and monographs in English

1. (1967) 'The theory of economic unions: a comparative analysis of customs unions, free trade areas and tax unions', in Carl S. Shoup (ed.), *Fiscal Harmonization in Common Markets, Vol. I: Theory* (New York: Columbia University Press).
2. (1967) 'Tax harmonization in the European Free Trade Association', in Carl S. Shoup (ed.), *Fiscal Harmonization in Common Markets, Vol. II: Practice* (New York: Columbia University Press).
3. (1968) (with H. G. Johnson and P. Wonnacott), *Harmonization of National Economic Policies Under Free Trade* (Toronto: the University of Toronto Press).
4. (1969), *Fiscal Harmonization Under Freer Trade: Principles and Their Applications to a Canada-US Free Trade Area* (Toronto: the University of Toronto Press).
5. (1985) (editor and author with P. Drysdale), *Federalism and Resource Development: the Australian Case* (London: Allen & Unwin).

Articles in English

1. (1968) 'On the equivalence of tariffs and quotas', *American Economic Review*, vol. 58.
2. (1968) 'The tax mix', in *Report of Proceedings of the Twentieth Tax Conference of the Canadian Tax Foundation* (Toronto: Canadian Tax Foundation).
3. (1969) 'On Watkin's taxes and tax harmonization in Central America', *Canadian Journal of Economics*, vol. 2.
4. (1970) 'The taxation of capital gains: a comment', *Canadian Journal of Economics*, vol. 3.
5. (1971) 'A bargaining model of the pure theory of public expenditure', *Journal of Political Economy*, vol. 79.
6. (1971) 'Abstract of a bargaining model of the pure theory of public expenditure', *Journal of Economic Literature*, vol. 9.
7. (1972) 'A theory of free trade areas', in P. Robson (ed.), *Penguin Modern Economics Readings: International Economic Integration* (Baltimore: Penguin Books Inc.)
8. (1972) 'Pareto optimality, trade and the Pigovian corrective tax', *Economica*, vol. 39.
9. (1972) 'Joint production, externality and public goods', in R. M. Bird and J. Head (eds.), *Modern Fiscal Issues* (Toronto: The University of Toronto Press).
10. (1973) 'Public goods, increasing cost, and monopsony: comment', *Journal of Political Economy*, vol. 81.
11. (1974) 'Pareto optimality and gains-from-trade: a further elucidation', *Economica*, vol. 31.
12. (1974) 'Zoning as an externality controlling method' (Center for Real Estate and Land Use Analysis: University of Kentucky).
13. (1976) (with Aiko Shibata) 'Economics of permanent employment system in Japan: a risk aversion theory' (Center for Labor Research: University of Kentucky).
14. (1977) 'What is the optimal control of pollution?', *Osaka Economic papers*, vol. 27.
15. (1979) 'A theory of group consumption and group formation', *Public Finance/Finances Publiques*, no. 3.
16. (1981) 'The choice of fiscal measures against external diseconomies'. *Osaka Economic Papers*, vol. 31.
17. (1982) 'Economic analysis of indirect democracy', *Osaka Economic Papers*, vol. 32.
18. (1982) 'Fiscal measures against pollutions: are effluent taxes and

abatement subsidies equivalent?', *Discussion Paper*, no. 32 (Faculty of Economics: Osaka University).

19. (1983) 'Fiscal measures against pollution: are effluent taxes and abatement subsidies equivalent?', in D. Biehl, K. W. Roskamp and W. F. Stolper (eds.), *Public Finance and Economic Growth* (Proceedings of the 37th congress of the International Institute of Public Finance) (Detroit: Wayne State University Press).
20. (1983) 'The energy crises and Japanese response', *Resources and Energy*, vol. 5.
21. (1983) 'Rational of the representation democracy: a model of skewed representation', *Osaka Economic Papers*, vol. 31.
22. (1983) (with S. Winrich) 'Control of pollution when the offended defend themselves', *Economica*, vol. 50.
23. (1984) Review of G. S. Tolley, P. E. Graves and A. S. Cohen (eds.), *Environmental Policy: Air Quality, Journal of American Statistical Association*, vol. 79.
24. (1984) 'Economics of representative democracy: a model of skewed representation', in H. Hanusch (ed.), *Public Finance and the Quest for Efficiency* (Proceedings of the 38th congress of the International Institute of Public Finance) (Detroit: Wayne State University Press).
25. (1984) 'The optimal Pigovian tax policies reconsidered', *Osaka Economic Papers*, vol. 34.
26. (1985) 'Financing and the politics of financing public pension plans: an analysis and proposal for reform', in G. Terny and A. J. Culyer (eds.), *Public Finance and Social Policy* (Proceedings of the 39th congress of International Institute of Public Finance) (Detroit: Wayne State University Press).
27. (1986) (with Yoko Kimura) 'Are budget deficits the cause of growth in government expenditures?', in B. P. Herber (ed.), *Public Finance and Public Debt* (Proceedings of the 40th congress of International Institute of Public Finance) (Detroit: Wayne State University Press).
28. (1986) 'Security expenditures versus protection of domestic industries: a neglected dimension of international trade theory', *Osaka Economic Papers*, vol. 35.
29. (1986) 'Macro-micro linkages in energy conservation: the Japanese experiences', in W. James (ed.), *Energy Conservation in the Asian Region* (Tokyo: Asian Productivity Organization; Honolulu: East–West Center, Resource Systems Institute).
30. (1986) (with M. C. McGuire) 'An economic analysis of inter-

dependence between trade and security in the US–Japan partnership', *Japan–US Symposium on the Special Project on US–Japan Economic and Trade Relations* (Tokyo: Japan–US Educational Commission; the Fullbright Commission).

31. (1987) (with A. Shibata) 'Rent redistribution through provision of public goods', in A. M. El-Agraa (ed.), *Protection, Cooperation, Integration and Development* (London: Macmillan).
32. (1987) (with Yoko Kimura) 'Government debt and growth in public spending: reply', *Public Finance/Finances Publiques*, vol. 42.
33. (1987) 'The relative impact of income and consumption taxes', *IMF Working Papers* (Washington, DC: International Monetary Fund).
34. (1987) 'Stockpilling vs. industrial protection as a defense against possible disruptions in international commerce', *Economics and National Security Working Papers* (Maryland: University of Maryland).
35. (1988) 'A workable method of finding Pareto-optimal supply of public goods', *Public Choice Workshop Discussion Papers* (Maryland: University of Maryland).
36. (1988) 'General nonconvexities with externalities', *Osaka Economic Papers*, vol. 36.
37. (1989) 'Merit goods and public choice: the case of higher education: comment', *Public Finance/Finances Publiques*, vol. 43.
38. (1989) 'Impact of "voluntary export control" on the exporter's economy: a theory and the case of the Japanese automobile industry', a paper presented at the International Conference of Political Economy of Export Restraint Arrangements, organized by The Trade Policy Research Centre, London and Washington, DC. Also printed in *Osaka University Department of Economics Discussion Papers* in 1990 and in *Pacific Economic Papers*, no. 202 (Canberra: Australia–Japan Research Centre, Australian National University).
39. (1990) 'On the bilateral control of externalities', in M. Neumann (ed.), *Public Finance and the Performance of Enterprises* (Proceedings of the 43rd congress of the International Institute of Public Finance) (Detroit: Wayne State University Press).
40. (1990) 'The restricted origin principle revisited', *Osaka Economic Papers*, vol. 40.
41. (1991) (with Arvind Panagariya) 'Defense expenditure, international trade and welfare in general equilibrium', *Osaka Uni-*

versity Department of Economics Discussion Papers, no. 103.

42. (1992) (with M. C. McGuire) 'Protection of domestic industries vs. defense against trade disruptions: some neglected dimensions', *Osaka University Department of Economics Discussion Papers*, no. 122.

Books in Japanese

1. (1989) (with A. Shibata), *Kokyo Keizaigaku* (Public Economics) (Tokyo: Toyo Keizai Shinposha).
2. (1989) (with A. Shibata), *Shoup's Shougen* (translation of C. S. Shoup's, *Tax Mission to Japan: 1949–1950)* (Tokyo: Zeimu-Keiri Kyokai).

Articles in Japanese

1. (1981) 'Kogaiboushi no zaiseishochi no sentaku: osenzei ka osenyokusei hoshokin ka' (the choice of pollution control methods: taxes or subsides), *Osaka Economic Papers*, vol. 31.
2. (1981) 'Kansetsu minshusei no keizai bunseki' (economic analysis of indirect democracy), *Osaka Economic Papers*, vol. 32.
3. (1982) 'Akikan jourei no keizai bunseki' (an economic analysis of the Bottle Law), *Keizai Seminar* (Economic Seminar), January.
4. (1984) 'America kara mita nihon keizai', (the Japanese economy from the American point of view), in M. Tatemoto, H. Shibata *et al.*, *Nihon Keizai no Yomikata*, (*A View on Japanese Economy*) (Kyoto: Kenkyu-jo).
5. (1984) 'Kokyo Toshi' (public investment), *Dai Hyakka Jiten* (*Heibon-sha Encyclopedia*) (Tokyo: Heibonsha).
6. (1984) 'Kokyo Keizaigaku' (public economics), *Dai Hyakka Jiten* (*Heibon-sha Encyclopedia*) (Tokyo: Heibonsha).
7. (1984) 'Kokyozai' (public goods), *Dai Hyakka Jiten* (*Heibon-sha Encyclopedia*) (Tokyo: Heibonsha).
8. (1984) 'Free-rider', *Dai Hyakka Jiten* (*Heibon-sha Encyclopedia*) (Tokyo: Heibonsha).
9. (1984) 'Seligman, Edwin Robert', *Dai Hyakka Jiten* (*Heibon-sha Encyclopedia*) (Tokyo: Heibonsha).
10. (1984) 'Shoup, Carl S.', *Dai Hyakka Jiten* (*Heibon-sha Encyclopedia*) (Tokyo: Heibonsha).
11. (1984) 'Wagner, Adolph Henrich Gotthelf', *Dai Hyakka Jiten* (*Heibon-sha Encyclopedia*) (Tokyo: Heibonsha).

12. (1984) 'Ko-gaito gaibusei no saiteki seigyo seisaku saiko: kogai no higaisha ga jikoboeishudan o katsuyo suru baai eno ippanka' (reconsideration of policies controlling environmental externalities: the cases when the offended protect themselves), *Osaka Economic Papers*, vol. 34.
13. (1985) 'Kokyo shishutsu to shotoku bunpai no ippan kinko bunseki' (a general equilibrium analysis of public expenditures and income distribution), *Osaka Economic Papers*, vol. 35.
14. (1985) 'Kansetsu minshu-sei no gorisei' (economics of indirect democracy), *Kokyo Sentaku no Kenkyu* (*Public Choice Studies*), vol. 6.
15. (1985) 'Gaibusei seigyo no tameno soho kazei' (bilateral taxation in controlling externalities), *Osaka Economic Papers*, vol. 35.
16. (1985) 'Kokusai shu-shi no kaizensaku ni yushutsu-zei ya yunyu-hojokin matawa rishi heikouzei wa genjitsuteki deha nai' (taxes, subsidies and interest adjustment taxes are unrealistic means to improve international balance of payments), *Steel Design*, No. 274, March.
17. (1986) 'Kodo-johoshakai ni okeru anzenhosho no bunseki', (international security and trade in the high technology era), *Osaka Economic Papers*, vol. 36.
18. (1986) 'America no yutakasa o sasaetekita nihonjin no chochiku o do tsukauka', (how to utilize the Japanese savings that have supported the American high standard of living), *Economics Today*, Summer.
19. (1987) 'Tanki kokusai-shushi taisaku toshiteno zeisei no (hi) yukosei ni tsuite' (on ineffectiveness of the tax systems as means to improve short-run balance of payments), *Osaka Economic Papers*, vol. 35.
20. (1989) 'Shakaijosei no henka to zeisei' (the relationship between tax systems and changes in social environment), *Zeikei Tsushin* (*Tax Notes*), June.
21. (1989) 'Log-rolling no anteisei ni tsuite' (on the stability of rolling), *Kokyo Sentaku no Kenkyu* (*Public Choice Studies*), vol. 17.
22. (1991) 'Dokusoteki kokyo sentaku kenkyu ni mukete' (toward original studies in public choice), *Kokyo Sentaku no Kenkyu* (*Public Choice Studies*), vol. 17.
23. (1991) 'Arrow no "Ippan Fukanosei Teiri" no zukeiteki shomei' (a geometric proof of Arrow's General Impossibility Theorem), *Keizai Kenkyu* (*The Economic Review*), vol. 43.
24. (1992) 'Arrow no "Ippan Fukanosei Teiri" no zukeiteki shomei-

II" (a geometric exposition of Arrow's general impossibility theorem), *Kokyo Sentaku-no Kenkyu* (Public Choice Studies), vol. 20.

25. (1992) 'Chikyu kankyo taisaku ni attate "seifu no shippai" o sakeyo', *Kokusai Kokyo Keizai Kenkyu* (Studies in International Public Economics), no. 3.

2 The Value of Freedom of Expression

Alan Peacock

PREAMBLE

It is a personal pleasure and privilege to offer this short essay on an unusual subject in honour of Hirofumi Shibata, an esteemed former colleague and friend, and an expert on public economics. He knows all too well how difficult it is to devise schemes of collective action which fulfil the requirement of maximizing the sovereignty of the individual in matters of choice.

How I came to address the problem of this contribution may be of interest. In 1985 I was appointed by the British Government as chair of a committee investigating the future financing of the British Broadcasting Corporation and we duly reported our findings the following year. The Government accepted and implemented several of our more important recommendations which were designed to make the British broadcasting system more responsive to consumer preferences. The Government were initially rather startled at the radical nature of our proposals and one in particular appears to have worried them. Our final proposal, entirely in keeping with our conclusions, was that only the normal laws of the land concerning obscenity, blasphemy, sedition and similar matters should be applied to TV and radio broadcasting and that there was no necessity for pre-broadcast vetting of programmes or instructions to broadcasting companies to avoid political controversy. To quote para. 695 of the Report, "the end of all censorhip arrangements would be a sign that broadcasting had come of age". Instead of following the spirit of our other proposals which promoted de-regulation of broadcasting the Government, to my regret, has tightened up regulations and actually appointed a Broadcasting Standards Council whose task is to draw up a 'moral code' for broadcaster.

I and others have vigorously opposed this development, without success, and have risked being regarded as supporters of licentious and violent behaviour. Of course the charge is unfounded, but, insofar as the debate is conducted in a rational manner, it is as well to examine the logic of one's own position. This is what I have tried to do in this contribution, and believe that I have demonstrated in a modest way that economic analysis offers useful guidance on how to approach the subject.

FREEDOM OF CHOICE AND FREEDOM OF EXPRESSION

My starting point embodies a value judgment, which is that people should be allowed to choose to use their resources and talents in the way which they regard as being in their best interests. This is not to say that they necessarily know where their best interests lie, but, if they do not, then equally this is not to say that others should decide for them how to act and behave. It means that individuals who are uncertain about their choices because they are not sure of the relationship between their wishes and what might satisfy them, should have an incentive to seek advice and information and to experiment in the exercise of choice. Nor does it mean that all choices have to be made in isolation. Individuals may choose to act collectively, but free choice must mean that they agree to the rules governing the making of collective choices.

This initial value judgment means that free individual choice will attach a positive value to the dissemination of information about the choices open to them, to activities which enable them to judge whether they might wish to reconsider how to spend their time and resources. However, freedom of expression implies something much more than allowing as free entry as possible into the supply of a market in information and advice. It means allowing individuals or groups of individuals to present ideas which question how society is organized and to put forward proposals which may attempt to engineer major changes in how we think and feel.

Freedom of expression, therefore, is an important component of individual freedom, but it must be recognized that sometimes the value which individuals will attach to particular forms of freedom of expression may be negative. I may be repelled by the noise of rock music which my neighbour insists on playing very loudly in the next garden, though he regards it as an adjunct to the removal of his restrictive inhibitions. Under what circumstances, if any, should he be prevented from playing rock? Are the costs of negotiating with him to turn his radio down or to restrict the noise to agreed hours worth incurring in order to obtain peace and quiet?

An even more fundamental question is whether freedom of expression extends to expressing views which support ideas about the organization of society which might entail that freedom of expression should be carefully controlled. I shall not envisage circumstances where such a view would prevail and to the extent that the community is willing to vote in a government which will restrict the right of freedom of expression to those forms of expression of which it alone approves. We must nevertheless be aware that this can happen.

These preliminary ideas point towards an agenda containing three items: (a) defining and illustrating the conditions which will ensure that freedom of expression has a positive value; (b) considering the circumstances in which conflicts may arise as a result of freedom of expression; and (c) considering how such conflicts ought to be resolved.

CONDITIONS FOR ENSURING FREEDOM OF EXPRESSION

It must be realized at the outset that all attempts at freedom of expression on offer to society entail some form of persuasion. The suppliers are concerned to persuade us to 'buy', as it were, some idea. Sometimes the acceptance of the idea brings with it the expectation that the persuaded will buy some product for which they are willing to pay. Sometimes, all that is hoped by the persuasion is that their ideas alone are accepted, but that they entail a change in the preferences of the persuaded which will increase the utility of the persuaders. Of course, the distinction is a fine one. Thus acceptance of a religious or political opinion which is novel to the persuaded may entail offering material support in the form of gifts of money to a religious order or political group and, in the latter case, to accepting the tax regime which they introduce if they become the government in power.

However, if freedom of expression is to have a positive value to a community in which it is assumed that persons have the right to accept or to reject the goods and services on offer to it, its members must have the opportunity for testing the product. The usual way in which we do this is to 'sample' the product until we are sure that the persuaders have fulfilled their promises. But the process goes further than that. A vital part of the testing process consists in being able to compare alternative products which satisfy the same 'need'. In short, the positive value of freedom of expression to the 'buyer' entails free competition in the presentation of ideas.

The importance of competition soon becomes obvious. It not only facilitates the testing process in appraising 'contingent' persuasion, i.e. where being persuaded means parting with money. It applies equally in the realm of 'ideological' persuasion, i.e. it entails competition between political parties, intellectual movements, and religions. But competition has another vital function to play in a world in which freedom of expression is to be valuable to the community. It is likely to encourage the 'seller' of ideas to provide full information on their content, for, if they fail to do so, they will be at a disadvantage compared with rivals who will be only too willing to indicate where the gaps in information are to be found. In short, competition reduces the cost to the buyer of ideas of obtaining the requisite information upon which an intelligent choice can be made.

Two examples may be helpful here. First of all, take a common form of 'contingent' persuasion – the advertising of some domestic product. It is in our interests for the car salesman to extol the virtues of a new Toyota and he must be given the same freedom to express his views as the car salesman making a pitch for a Nissan. If we already have experience in driving cars, we have some check on these views, but what we cannot expect is that he will extol the virtues of the rival product and we would be right to be suspicious if he attempts to 'knock' his rival's product. Fortunately, his rivals are only too willing to point out the differences between their products and that being 'pushed' by the Toyota salesman. However, if there were no competition for cars, there would be no incentive for the sales representative of the monopoly firm to reveal much about the product and the costs of obtaining information by the customer would be made much more difficult.

Exactly the same reasoning can be applied to the 'sale' of political or religious views. Competition with freedom of entry into the 'ideas' market must encourage the 'sellers' to be much more specific about the content of their 'product' and how it is to be differentiated. With 'freedom of expression' under conditions where different views can be expressed there is at least some prospect that 'the wool will not be pulled over our eyes'.

Let me now try to deal with two objections. The first concerns the nature of the experience of new ideas and concepts, whether contingent or not. The examples I have given emphasize rational calculation on the part of the 'buyer' of ideas and the right of those who seek information to be able to trace the connection between that information and their needs. However, often our experience of new ideas, as when we visit the theatre, the concert hall or museum, leaves us questioning our own ideas about life and work. We become confused, though perhaps elated. Sometimes we may be outraged and angry. We may not be sure whether our welfare has been increased. Does this not entail that 'freedom of expression' as found in the arts must have some separate justification than its contribution to what we perceive as being our welfare?

There are two answers to this objection. The first is that anyone who does not wish to risk the discomforture of being shocked and startled by artistic endeavours is not forced to submit themselves to the 'ordeal'. The second is that it is usually possible to obtain full information on the nature of the 'happening' which could change one's preference structure. In other words, the presuppositions for a rational calculation are there if we want to take advantage of them.

The second objection relates to circumstances where the nature of the choices we have to make cannot offer the opportunity to repeatedly sample the product as a test of the veracity of those who produce it. I may consider it desirable that everyone who is able to offer me a hip operation should have the right to inform me about the relative merits of their surgical skills. However, in the absence of technical knowledge, who am I to believe? And if I make a wrong decision, I cannot learn from my mistakes, for the mistake cannot be rectified if the operation cannot be repeated in the event of failure. Freedom of expression, in the form of freedom to give information about the nature of the service, may encourage suppliers to take advantage of the ignorance of buyers when there is no learning curve for them to move down.

Ignorance may make us vulnerable to freedom of expression which embodies a false prospectus, as with unscrupulous doctors, lawyers and, say, fortune tellers and clairvoyants, but this is not to say that a gap in our knowledge cannot be filled or if it cannot be filled very easily that we are totally at the mercy of the clever propagandist. If sufficient number of people suffer from ignorance with potentially awful consequences, then the media will have a strong incentive to investigate such situations. Professions faced with public exposure of their activities will see that it is in their interests to enforce acceptable standards, quite apart from any satisfaction which individual members will derive from behaving honestly and efficiently towards their clients. Gaps in the information system may also be filled by consumer organizations to whom the 'ignorant' can subscribe in return for guidance on the performance of those who supply them with 'one-off' purchases. In short, one important function of freedom of expression by the press is to facilitate monitoring of the performance of those providing services which cannot be adequately tested by consumers themselves.

EXTERNALITY PROBLEMS

So far the discussion has viewed freedom of expression as a service like any other available to those willing to pay for it and capable of rejection by those who are unwilling to do so. However, as with other services, the welfare effects may not be confined simply to the transactions made directly between seller and buyer. As with many other goods and services, the welfare of individuals in the community who are not parties to the transaction may have their welfare affected, either as unwilling consumers or unwilling producers.

I consider 'unwilling consumption' first of all, or what economists term 'consumption externalities'. Let us take a concrete example in the form of the famous controversy about the publication of Salman Rushdie's Satanic Verses. This is advertised as a novel by a very wellknown writer, which could be bought like any other novel, and presumably buyers expected to, and clearly did, obtain enjoyment from reading it. However, certain passages brought to the attention of the Moslem community were regarded as blasphemy, that is to say any perceived benefits by readers of a positive kind were counterbalanced by the 'disbenefits' suffered by those outraged at its blasphemous utterances. The reaction in Iran was so extreme, that Rushdie has been condemned to death and has had to hide from the world. Even in countries in which there is no theocracy, there have been requests that the book should be banned or at least removed from public display. The Satanic Verses is only one in an endless succession of 'scandals' about freedom of expression derived from public attitudes to blasphemy and obscenity.

Consider now 'unwilling production' or 'production externalities'. If freedom of expression entails public exposure to criticisms not only of doctrines held by individuals but also of their personal conduct, this usually entails access to details of their private life. The individuals concerned or their relatives and friends are frequently, if not always, unwilling 'factors of production' in the process of public exposure. The technical means now available to the 'papparazzi' – to take the more sensational purveyors of exposure – have improved enormously with 'zoom' lens TV and camera techniques, not to speak of listening-in devices, alongside more traditional means such as bribery of colleagues and servants and blackmail. Even if individuals may have property rights in privacy and in the use of private possessions such as the letters of the dead, these rights may be difficult to enforce. While our reaction is likely to be that such activities are a travesty of 'freedom of expression', even the most objective and incorruptible writer exposing personal conduct, who may himself not be interested in sensationalism for its own sake or in the pecuniary gains of their activities, imposes 'negative external benefits' on those who are the object of his enquiry. However we weigh the pros and cons of his activity, freedom of expression is not affording a positive gain to all those exposed to it, and some sort of balance has to be struck.

Thus even if one is a convinced libertarian, one has to recognize that there are conflicts between different sorts of freedom – in this case between freedom of expression and freedom of privacy. I shall look at the way a libertarian should approach such conflicts later on. What we have to note here and now is that resolution of these differences cannot be achieved by some technical means. For example, counting heads of gainers and losers would not help very much. First of all, this would entail a census – an expensive operation if every instance of conflict required one – of attitudes and it may not be always in the interests of all individuals to give their true view of how they are affected. Even if they did, what account would one want to take of the 'intensity' of feeling that individuals had for or against allowing freedom of expression or its suppression in particular instances? Even if the issue could be decided by a majority vote, this is not to say that even those who claimed to have experienced negative gains would necessarily believe that the majority decision rule was fair and reasonable. Finally, to say that a majority had decided that the gains were negative, tells us nothing about whether any action should be taken to prevent the 'offending' practice. It could even be the case that faced with this information, those using this practice might voluntarily cease to use it. In short, while technical information, such as a census, may be useful in helping a community to make a decision, the decision itself will rest on the tastes and preferences and therefore the value judgments of its members.

CONFLICT RESOLUTION AND COLLECTIVE ACTION

The resolution of a conflict of freedoms appears to call for some form of collective action. However, a libertarian would want to be very careful to conclude from this that this action should take the form of state censorship of freedom of expression backed by the force of the criminal law. It may come to that, but not before one has examined very carefully the various forms that collective action could take.

We would agree, I suppose, that freedom of expression which took the form of propagandistic activities which would actually lead to civil disturbance and dissolution of civilized behaviour must be prevented. However, it is far from easy to trace the quantitative connection between the output of such activities and the undesired result. The very assurance that entry into the ideas market was free might prevent any connection at all, for the preaching of revolution would be swamped by alternative views. Put in another way, a society committed to freedom of expression, subject to negative externalities, presupposes the existence of a populace trained in the civic virtues of tolerance and understanding of different points of view and the resolution of conflict by agreement. If these virtues are absent, then there is no way that conflict could be resolved.

Where freedom of expression imposes a substantial negative externality on a sizeable proportion of the population, it may be an overreaction to accede to state intervention to ban such activities. The extent to the externality might be minimized in some way. Thus active propaganda for pornography may have to be restricted in some way, but those who perceived benefits from watching pornographic displays can conduct their activities in private.

Where freedom of expression, as in the attack on the behaviour of a specific individual or organization, is perceived by those attacked as damaging their interests, this seems an issue best dealt with under the law of libel and slander. I agree that this tells us nothing about the scope of the law and the severity or otherwise of the damages awarded if the case is won. Communities have very different evaluations of the nature and extent of damage. A colleague of mine who wrote a book on Greek philosophy was described in a Californian newspaper reviewing his book as a wellknown homosexual. He and his British lawyers considered that this statement was libellous and warranted heavy damages, but were amazed to find that in California the statement would not be so regarded and that it might even be taken as something of a compliment!

It must be conceded, however, that some general rules need to be formulated about what forms of freedom of expression are allowable and what are not. The presence of general rules must imply some method of enforcing them, but we are not yet at the stage of arguing for criminal legislation.

One reason for proceeding with caution is that the public recognition of the detriment suffered by victims of self-expression may influence those who have attacked them and those who are tempted to follow their example to adopt a system of self-regulation. Thus professional organizations see that it is in their own interests to lay out a code of conduct for members accompanied by a disciplinary code laying down penalties for non-adherence to the code of conduct. Likewise, in the UK, advertisers submit themselves to an Advertising Standards Authority and the Press to a Press Council both of which are financed by a levy on members of the appropriate professions.

The analogy here with the detriment suffered from cigarette smoking is perhaps relevant. Smoking is not expressly forbidden but a succession of obstacles are put in the way of smokers which are designed to get them to stop or at least not to inconvenience non-smokers. Smokers are first of all warned about the possible consequences of their activities, and cigarette packets have to be marked with a government health warning. The negative externalities suffered by non-smokers are reduced by the growing number of 'no-smoking' areas in public buildings and vehicles. Finally, the smokers' pocket is hit through discriminatory taxation on tobacco.

It is reasonable to claim that my argument points to much more specific action by government than incentives offered to private organizations and warnings to 'put their house in order'. So far as I am aware, Western countries have legislation designed to control quite severely obscence and blasphemous publications and latterly to prevent the screening of comparable material by means of TV and the cinema. I do not think that there can be any hard and fast rule about the content of such legislation which has to be framed very carefully so that it does not conflict with constitutional rights to freedom of speech. What is permissible and on what terms very much depends on public opinion and how far such opinion exercises political influence. The only point I would make is that there is a case for automatic review of such legislation, rather along the lines used in voting for the annual budget, though annuality is perhaps too stringent a requirement. Every three years, say, the legislation on 'control of freedom of expression' might lapse automatically and its continuance, in whatever form, would require a new act of legislation which, if appropriate, can be an amendment of the previous enactment or simply the replication of the previous legislation.

CONCLUDING REMARKS

I have argued from rather unusual premises that 'freedom of expression' is an integral part of a free society. I have illustrated this theme with reference to economic transactions. At its simplest, freedom of expression is the provision of information which is essential in a free economy, and competition itself offers some likelihood that there is an incentive to provide accurate information. But freedom of expression is itself a necessary adjunct to the presentation of commentary and criticism of our society. Here, too, the individual has the right to accept or reject new ideas and concepts, and freedom of expression must be presented in a form where acceptance or rejection is feasible. That is to say that 'negative externalities' in the presentation of opinions must be avoided in so far as that is possible.

One would like to think that in a free society, the state of education encourages people to resolve conflicts between freedom of expression and other freedoms, e.g. privacy, so that individuals can seek redress by voluntary action within a properly prescribed set of individual property rights. If these rights are violated, one would prefer resolution of conflict through civil action rather than through the criminal code. Any such code, especially if it extends to the specification of criminal offences, should be subject to periodic automatic review.

3 Constitutional Management of Free Riders and Common Property Resources

James A. Roumasset

INTRODUCTION

The confusion surrounding the theory of public goods is revealed by the multiplicity of definitions. Many authors define public goods as those goods which are both nonrival in use and from which free riders cannot be excluded (see e.g. Musgrave 1959, Musgrave and Musgrave 1989, Starrett 1988). This definition leads to an immediate difficulty. The theory of public goods typically abstracts from transaction costs, but excludability depends on the information and enforcement costs of exclusion.

The original conception of public goods according to Samuelson (1954) avoids this difficulty by defining public goods according to the technical characteristic of nonrivalness. He later broadened the definition to apply generally to goods that generate a consumption externality:

> The possibility or impossibility to apply an 'exclusion principle' is less crucial than consumption externality, since often exclusion would be wrong where possible. (Samuelson 1969, p. 105)

Laffont (1988) follows Samuelson's lead in recognizing the preeminence of non-rivalness but adds that excludability and other characteristics can be used to construct a taxonomy of different types of public goods. Non-rivalness can also be qualified in order to incorporate the less pure cases of local public goods and club goods.

A more general approach can be based on the technical definition that public goods are characterized by economies of scale in the production of service units (number of households served times the average amount of service per household). The Samuelsonian pure public good is a polar extreme within this general definition since the maximum number of households can be included without decreasing the quantity available to others. In addition, a general theory of public goods should include explicit acknowledgement of the costs of organization. The constitutional issues discussed below are intended as a step in that direction.

NON-COOPERATIVE MODELS OF FREE RIDING

The term 'free rider' is also fraught with ambiguity but can be regarded as an umbrella for what Samuelson (1954; 1969) refers to as the game theoretic difficulties in organizing the voluntary provision of public goods. Two primary models of free riding have emerged.

The first model is the Groves-Clarke mechanism for revealing preferences for public goods (see e.g. Starrett 1988). This model is based on the assumption that the central barrier to cooperation in the provision of public goods is the imperfect information about willingness-to-pay. But surely with econometric techniques for estimating consumer expenditure systems, for reformulating preferences on the basis of underlying characteristics, and with advanced methods of market research, it is possible to obtain good estimates of willingness to pay by household characteristics.

The second model is the Nash-Cournot non-cooperative equilibrium model of voluntary provision. In this model, each consumer chooses to provide that quantity of the public good which will maximize his own utility, assuming that the amount provided by other players will remain the same as in the previous period. In equilibrium, all players equate their marginal rates of substitution to the full cost of the public good such that the sum of the marginal rates ot substitution is greater than the marginal rate of transformation (Roberts and Holdren 1972).

The Hume theorem

The 'Hume theorem' says that the degree of underprovision increases with the number of potential cooperators. This is suggested by a passage from David Hume as cited in Olson (1965):

> Two neighbours may agree to drain a meadow, which they possess

> in common: because it is easy for them to know each other's mind and each must perceive, that the immediate consequence of his failing in his part, is the abandoning of the whole project. But it is very difficult, and indeed impossible, that a thousand persons should agree in any such action it being difficult for them to concert so complicated a design, and still more difficult for them to execute it while each seeks a pretext to free himself of the trouble and expense, and would lay the whole burden on others.

This result can be derived from the condition that in the Nash non-cooperative equilibrium, each individual equates his marginal rate of substitution between the public good and the numeraire to the full cost of providing a unit of the public good. This implies that the marginal social benefits of the public good which are given by the sum of the marginal rates of substitution must be equal to the marginal rate of transformation times the number of households, *n*. That is, in the Nash non-cooperative solution, the marginal social benefits of public goods are n times the marginal social costs! This is underprovision in the extreme and clearly exaggerates the problem.

The Cobb–Douglas chicken and the folk theorem

One model that avoids the inevitability of the underprovision result is the one-period non-cooperative game known as 'Chicken'. If the consequences of all players defecting are too severe, the individual players will choose the cooperative strategy. Similarly, in 'assurance' games, the rewards of cooperation may be sufficiently high such that each player knows that the other will cooperate and still be motivated to cooperate herself (Gardner *et al.*, 1990). In general, the tendency to 'free ride' depends on the consequences of over- and under-provision.

In order to provide a general model that allows for explicit treatment of conjectures regarding the other player's strategy, preferences regarding different amounts of the public good, and full divisibility, consider the two-player game where both players' preferences are representable by Cobb-Douglas utility functions. Specifically, suppose that two individuals, Ken and Ben, maximize their utility functions:

$$U_K = X_K^{\alpha} (S_K + S_B^{a})$$

$$U_B = X_B^{\beta} (S_B + S_K^{a})$$

where: X_K is the amount of a private good purchased by Ken, S_K is the amount of the 'social good' provided by Ken, P_S is the (supply) price of the social good, $S_B{}^a$ is the amount of the social good that Ken assumes Ben will provide, and $S_K + S_B$ is the actual amount of public good provided. Now suppose that, because Ken and Ben are extremely risk-averse, or because neither player has provided the public good in the previous period, that $S_K{}^a = S_B{}^a = 0$. In this case, the sum of the quantities of the public good provided by each player will be efficient (and identical to the Lindahl equilibrium allocation). An intuitive explanation of this result rests on the presence of opposing forces in the model. To the extent that each individual's provision of the public good generates external benefits which are not taken into account in his decision calculus, there is a tendency towards underprovision. On the other hand, to the extent that individuals underestimate actual provision by the other party, e.g. $S_B{}^a = 0 < S_B$, there is a force towards overprovision. The latter force is greater the lower the value placed on unanticipated spillings, i.e. the lower the elasticity of substitution between the public and private good. Where the elasticity of substitution is one, i.e. the Cobb–Douglas case, and where $S_B{}^a = S_K{}^a = 0$, then these two forces exactly offset one another and efficient provision results – see Roumasset and Laine (1974) for a more formal proof.

Another way out of the underprovision result of the prisoner's dilemma model is through the possibility of adopting punitive strategies in repeated rounds of the game. In many cases, the threat of punishment is sufficient to induce cooperative behavior. Aumann (1981) has named this result, which is difficult to attribute to any one author, as the 'folk theorem'. One simple punitive strategy is 'tit for tat', which calls for cooperation on the first move and imitation of the other player's last move on subsequent rounds. Punitive strategies may thus provide the basis of an evolution of cooperation, even in games that are structured as non-cooperative (Axelrod 1981). Many public goods situations are likely to be such, however, that the only available punitive strategies are those that inflict self-punishment. This may render strategic behavior to induce cooperation irrational. In such situations, a higher authority may be required to administer the punishment (Jankowski, 1990).

TOWARDS A COOPERATIVE LOGIC OF COLLECTIVE ACTION

From bargaining to constitutionalism

All of the above rely on the theory of non-cooperative games to model free riding or to model remedies for free riding. The strong assumptions implicit in models of non-cooperative games are too strong, however. In practice, beneficiaries of public goods have the opportunity to bargain with one another about the quantity of the public good and the share that each beneficiary will pay and to adopt mechanisms designed to enforce the agreement. Accordingly, Shibata (1971) has modelled the provision of public goods using bargaining theory, i.e. from the perspective of cooperative games.

Shibata shows that even within the context of a cooperative framework, Pareto optimal outcomes are by no means assured. Strategic concerns in bargaining may motivate players to hold out for a higher share in the cooperators' surplus and to the same indeterminacy associated with bilateral monopoly. In Shibata's view, Wicksell and Lindahl were too sanguine about the possibility of resolving any indeterminacy either through unanimity or through some unspecified device to equalize bargaining power.

Shibata's analysis directs attention to the unsolved problems of constitutional design surrounding the efficient provision of public goods. Neither the preference revelation approach nor the prisoners' dilemma gets at the central constitutional issue involved in collective action. Certainly mechanisms exist for estimating willingness to pay and for improving on the Nash–Cournot solution through collective contracting. The problem is that group contracts may be costly to negotiate and enforce.

Common property resource management

Part 2, above, reviewed the common presumption that public goods will be underprovided due to the free rider problem. There is a related presumption in the literature on common property resources (CPRs) that CPRs will be overexploited. It is customary to cite Hardin (1968) as the source of this conventional wisdom, perhaps because of his article's dramatic title, 'The Tragedy of the Commons'. For example, the abstract of Berkes *et al.* (1989) states that "conventional wisdom holds that resources held in common will invariably be overexploited – the 'tragedy of the commons'". Similarly, Gardner *et al.* (1990) write:

> As the result of the work of scholars, such as Garrett Hardin (1968), Mancur Olson (1965), and Scott Gordon (1954), many presume that when individuals jointly use such resources, each individual is driven by an immutable logic to withdraw more of the resource units (or invest less in the resource) than is optimal from the perspective of all of the users.[1]

Curiously enough, however, Hardin did not argue that overexploitation was inevitable. Nor did he claim any originality for pointing out the possibility of overexploitation indeed he credits this idea to a pamphlet written in 1833 by William Forster Lloyd. Hardin only takes credit for paraphrasing the pamphleteer's idea, in a moment of Shakespearian inspiration. The title of the subsection in which Lloyd's idea is reviewed is 'Tragedy of Freedom in a Commons'. The subtitle concerning Hardin's proposed solution is 'Mutual Coercion, Mutually Agreed Upon'. That is, far from suggesting that the tragedy of the commons is inexorable, Hardin is in fact directing attention to the problem of constitutional design.

There are now a plethora of examples in recent literature of communities which have successfully limited overexploitation of resources held in common (Berkes *et al.* 1989, Wade 1987, Ostrom 1986). It would be misleading to view this literature as providing an empirical refutation of the theory that overexploitation of common property can only be avoided by private property or central government control. Such a proposition is theoretically unsound, notwithstanding claims to the contrary,[2] and does not logically require empirical rejection. Nonetheless, the empirical examples help to focus attention on the constitution as a possible unit of analysis for understanding collective action at the local level.

A closely related literature seeks to explain the English enclosures. The efficiency explanation is that private property will emerge when the benefits of private property exceed the costs of change (Demsetz 1967). More precisely, the efficient switch to private property occurs when the increase in benefits equals the user cost of capital required for the new arrangement.

The benefits of private relative to common property may be defined as the increase in producer surplus afforded by the switch. This difference need not be positive, as is usually supposed. Indeed, where communal grazing, cultivation and fishing are observed in economic history, there are typically economies of scale that are being exploited (e.g. villagers using one big net can catch more fish collectively than they could catch in aggregate, each using a small net). Irrigation provides something of an intermediate case. While the land itself may be privately owned, it may still be less costly to organize community waterways and community water management than each farmer providing his own water independently.

One factor that may tend to tip the balance in favor of private property is population pressure. As it becomes increasingly difficult to accommodate an increasing population due to indivisibilities in farm size, there is a tendency for Ricardian social differentiation to emerge endogenously between the landed and landless classes. As this occurs, opportunities for specialization arise between landowner/employers and hired workers. Private property facilitates such specialization to be realized through agricultural contracts, and labour markets are the result (Roumasset and Smith 1981). Other determinants of the relative efficiency of private property include the transportation infrastructure (e.g. as it affects farm-gate prices), and the available enforcement technology (e.g. barbed-wire fencing).

It efficiency is the fuel of institutional change, rent-seeking is the engine. It is the rent-seekers who undertake the political costs of realizing institutional change. Since the rent-seekers (whom Davis and North 1981, call the primary action group) are interested in enhancing their own income, not that of the economy generally, rent-seeking may result in some divergence from the efficient solution. The theory of rent-seeking behaviour, or what is sometimes called *neoclassical political economy*, does not provide unambiguous results about the nature of the departures from efficiency, however. In some cases, private property formation may lag behind the efficient switch from common to private property, due in part to the inertia imparted by peasant resistance to the change. This view leads to the hypothesis that the rental value of land will increase substantially by the time that the switch in property rights is finally actualized. This hypothesis is supported by evidence presented in Allen (1982) which shows that the English enclosures in the eighteenth and nineteenth centuries conferred rents on landlords that were two to three times as high as those which they were able to obtain under manorialism. In some instances, however, especially in the earlier enclosures, landlords were occasionally successful in overcoming political resistance and privatizing land even before it was efficient to do so (Allen 1986). In nineteenth century Hawaii, a fortuitous combination of circumstances led to revenue-seeking by the public sector which avoided the usual lag in the innovation of private property (La Croix and Roumasset 1990). In this case, the political economy forces appeared to be efficiency enhancing, thus countering the conventional presumption (see e.g. Tullock 1967) that rent-seeking is always destructive.

The growth of private property requires centralized government institutions of the type envisioned by Adam Smith to enforce those rights and to facilitate the contractual exchange that private property makes possible. Therefore, efficiency warrants the simultaneous growth of markets and central government. This 'co-evolutionary' view (Roumasset and LaCroix 1988) stands in sharp contrast to the conventional view that markets and government are alternative institutions for the allocation of resources. The dilemma is that centralized control implies centralized power (even though decision-making may be decentralized), and centralized power increases the potential for mercantilistic controls that erode competition and confer production rights on successful rent-seekers. In order to keep economic development on an efficient course, constitutional design must therefore incorporate checks and balances against the inevitable growth of rent-seeking – see e.g. Spindler, 1990, for a suggested approach.

The coevolutionary view is illustrated in Figure 3.1. The constitutional environment for economic organization is characterized according to the degrees of centralization in control and decentralization in decision-making. Three types of environments are depicted. *Res nullius* is roughly equivalent to open-access – individuals make resource use decisions independently and there is no organized attempt to limit entry. Private property, which lies at the other end of the curve, requires centralized enforcement so that decision-making can be fully decentralized. Common property management, or *res communes*, is an intermediate arrangement wherein both decision-making and control are centralized at the local level.

As an economy modernizes, the efficient constitutional environment moves from left to right along the curve. The greater the demand for specialization, the greater is the efficient degree of centralized control. The optimal degree of specialization, in turn, is a function of population pressure, technology, the level of demand and the infrastructure of exchange (especially the transportation system). The constitutional environment is therefore indirectly a function of these same determinants. This same approach can be extended, in

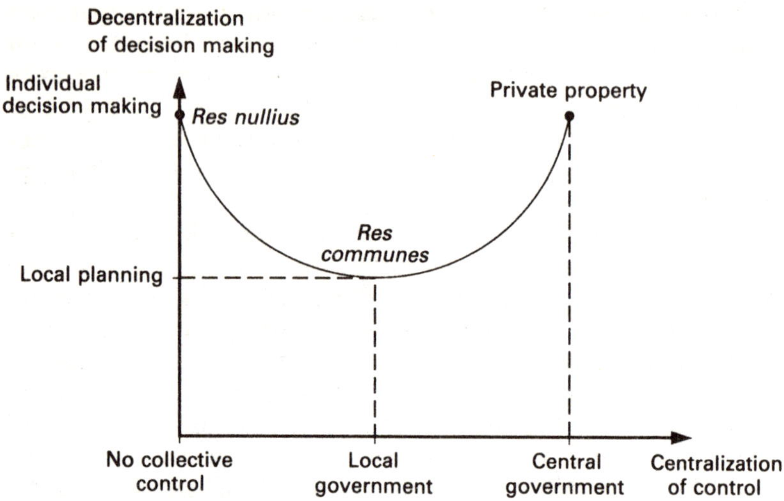

Figure 3.1 The co-evolution of markets and governance

principle, to governance structures for other aspects of the economy as well. In this way, government itself can be made endogenous instead of the current tradition of focusing on the quantity of public goods that will be provided by an exogenous government.

CONCLUDING REMARKS

Economists are trained to think of the government as an alternative to markets. It may seem natural then to conclude that common property is inefficient and that either private property or government coercion is the solution. In the coevolutionary view, however, the nature of government is endogenous. At an intermediate stage of development, the efficient governance structure for some natural resources mav be community control and decision-making. The important question then is not which activities should be shaped by pre-existing markets or by a pre-existing government but how governance structures should be designed to promote efficient resource management, whether by markets or local communities.

These desiderata provide the ingredients for an efficiency theory of the incidence of common property management. As the demand for specialization increases, the efficient governance structure moves from open access to common property management and ultimately to transferable private property. The determinants of modernization can also be used to explain the different forms of common property as well as its incidence.

The specter of endogenizing government prerequisites to market exchange also provides a vehicle for broadening the normative theory of collective action from the narrow focus on public goods. The broader theory would be based on the benefits of increasing group membership versus the constitutional costs – see e.g. Balisacan and Roumasset (1987). The benefits of increasing group membership include economies of scale in the provision of services and the gains from specialization and exchange afforded by increasing the scope of trade.

It appears that the logic of collective action has everything to do with constitutional design. A constitution is a contractual arrangement for the governance of collective action. It specifies rules of membership, rights and responsibilities, decision-making procedures for undesignated rights and duties, and a reward structure pertaining to performance. The scope of collective action extends beyond the Samuelsonian public good to economies of scale generally. Indeed, the Samuelsonian notion of consumption externality can be replaced by the notion of economies of scale in consumption services. Similarly, collective management of natural resources can be motivated by economies of scale in the use of those resources.

Since investment in the institutions of decentralized exchange is largely nonrival in nature, collective action is also warranted to define and enforce private property rights and the institutions that facilitate exchange. Given the technical parameters of an economy, there exists an ideal organization of production and consumption that maximizes the real income of the economy, or what Adam Smith referred to as the wealth of a nation that is the 'full complement' of that nation's resources. But since the organization of resources itself consumes resources, it is neither optimal nor feasible to reach that full complement of riches. Rather, the benefits of moving closer to that ideal state must be balanced against the costs of doing so. It is in this fertile ground that economists should search for a general theory of public choice.

Specifically, it is efficient for society to invest increasingly in the institutional prerequisites of specialization and exchange as economic agents become more differentiated due to the classical pressures of population and the neoclassical dividends of capital accumulation. In order for capitalism to realize the gains from decentralized decision-making and exchange, it is necessary to institute the centralized enforcement of private property. This leads to a neoclassical version of the Marxian proposition that capitalism contains the seeds of its own destruction. The centralized institutions of regulation and enforcement are vulnerable to capture by rent-seeking private interests. To avoid the spectre of a dismal decline, constitutional prophylaxis against rent-seeking is required to stay the course of Smithian abundance.

Notes

1. While Berkes *et al.* (1989) clearly associate Hardin with the conventional wisdom, their specific attribution to Hardin is more careful: "Hardin argued that such problems had no technical solutions, and emphasized the need for government controls to limit 'freedom in the commons [which] brings ruin to all'".
2. For example, Smith (1981) argues that "the only way to avoid the tragedy of the commons in natural resources and wildlife is to end the common-property system by creating a system of private property rights". (As cited by Ostrom 1986.)

References

1. Allen, R. C. (1982) 'The efficiency and distributional consequences of Eighteenth-Century enclosures', *Economic Journal*, vol. 92.
2. Allen, R. C. (1986) 'The price of freehold land and the interest rate in the Seventeenth and Eighteenth Centuries', *Discussion Paper*, No. 86–73, (University of British Columbia: Department of Economics).
3. Aumann, R. (1981) 'Survey of Repeated Games', in R. Aumann *et al.* (eds.), *Essays in Game Theory* (Manneheim: Bibliographisches Institut).
4. Axelrod, R. (1981), *The Evolution of Cooperation* (New York: Basic Books).
5. Berkes, F. D. F., McCay B. J. and Acheson, J. M. (1989) 'The benefits of the commons', *Nature*, vol. 340.
6. Davis, L. and North, D. (1971), *Institutional Change and American Economic Growth* (Cambridge: Cambridge University Press).
7. Demsetz, H. (1967) 'Toward a theory of property rights', *American Economic Review*, vol. 57.
8. Gardner, R., Ostrom, E. and Walker, J. M. (1990) 'The nature of common-pool resource problems', *Rationality and Society*, vol. 2, no. 3.

9. Gordon, H. S. (1954) 'The economic theory of a common-property resource: the fishery', *Journal of Political Economy*, vol. 62.
10. Hardin, G. (1968) 'The tragedy of the commons', *Science*, vol. 162.
11. Janokwski, R. (1990) 'Punishment in iterated chicken and prisoner's dilemma games', *Rationality and Society*, vol. 2, no. 4.
12. LaCroix, S. and Roumasset, J. (1990) 'The evolution of private property in Nineteenth Century Hawaii', *Journal of Economic History*, (forthcoming).
13. LLaffont, J-J. (1988), *Fundamentals of Public Economics* (Cambridge: MIT Press).
14. LLloyd, W. F. (1977) 'On the checks to population', in G. Hardin and J. Baden (eds.) *Managing the Commons* (San Francisco: W. H. Freeman).
15. Musgrave, R. A. (1969) 'Provision for social goods', in J. Margolis and H. Guitton (eds.), *Public Economics* (New York: St. Martin's Press).
16. Musgrave, R. and Musgrave, P. (1989), *Public Finance in Theory and Practice*, Fifth Edition (New York: McGraw-Hill).
17. Olson, M. (1965), *The Logic of Collective Action* (Cambridge, MA: Harvard University Press).
18. Ostrom, E. (1986) 'How inexorable is the "Tragedy of the Commons"? institutional arrangements for changing the structure of social dilemmas', mimeo, *Workshop in Political Theory & Policy Analysis*, Indiana University.
19. Roberts & Holdren (1972), *Theory of Social Process* (Ames, Iowa: Iowa State University Press).
20. Roumasset, J. and LaCroix, S. (1988) 'The coevolution of property rights and the state', in E. Ostrom *et al.* (eds.), *Rethinking Institutional Analysis and Development: Issues, Alternatives and Choices* (San Francisco: Institute for Contemporary Studies).
21. Roumasset, J. and Laine, C. (1974) 'Free-riders, non-cooperative games, risk aversion and the theory of government intervention', *Working Paper*, No. 38 (Davis, University of California: Department of Economics).
22. Roumasset, J. and Smith, J. (1981) 'Population, specialization, and landless workers: explaining transitions in agricultural organization', *Population and Development Review*, September.
23. Runge, C. F. (1987) 'Common property and collective action in economic development', *World Development*, vol. ?
24. Samuelson, P. A. (1954) 'The pure theory of public expenditure', *Review of Economics and Statistics*, vol. 34.
25. Samuelson, P. A. (1969) 'Pure theory of public expenditure and taxation', in J. Margolis and H. Guitton (eds.), *Public Economics* (London: Macmillan).
26. Shibata, H. (1971) 'A bargaining model of the pure theory of public expenditure', *Journal of Political Economy*, vol. 79.
27. Smith, R. J. (1981) 'Resolving the tragedy of the commons by creating private property rights in wildlife', *Cato Journal*, vol. 1, no. 2.
28. Spindler, Z. A. (1990) 'Constitutional design for a rent-seeking society: voting rule choice', *Constitutional Political Economy*, vol. 1, no. 3.

29. Starrett, D. A. (1988), *Foundations of Public Economics* (New York: Cambridge University Press).
30. Tullock, G. (1980) 'Efficient rent-seeking', in J. M. Buchanan, R. D. Tollison and G. Tullock (eds.), *Toward a Theory of the Rent-Seeking Society* (College Station: Texas A & M University Press).
31. Wade, R. (1987) 'The management of common property resources: finding a cooperative solution', *World Bank Research Observer*, vol. 2, no. 2.

4 Some Methodological Issues in the Use of Cost–Benefit Analysis in Health Care

Alan Williams

INTRODUCTION

It is a pleasure to have an opportunity both to honour Professor Hirofumi Shibata and to review some issues in welfare economics and the use of cost-benefit analysis about which I used to argue with him at the time when the Roskill Commission was providing an assessment of the rival merits of different sites for the Third London Airport (which, in the event, 20 years later has still not been built!). Since then my interests have shifted to the health care sector, where the analytical, political, and ethical problems are even more severe, but the underlying tensions are the same. This restatement of my position is thus partly designed to stimulate him (and others) to attempt once more to 're-educate' me!

VIEWS ON THE SCOPE AND METHODS OF CBA

There are two distinct views about the scope and methods of cost–benefit analysis: (a) that it is an application of Paretian Welfare Economics; and (b) that it is an attempt to systematise public decision making.

The essential difference between these two views is that in the former the analyst's role is to estimate the net efficiency gains, in money terms, following the willingness-to-pay or willingness-to-accept criteria inherent in the adoption of the *potential* Pareto improvement as the decision criterion. All other relevant considerations are to be weighed separately by the decision maker(s), the economist's contribution being restricted to consideration of Pareto efficiency. By contrast, in the second view of cost-benefit analysis, values may be elicited in a variety of ways from a variety of sources, and equity weights too may be elicited and analysed. In principle, anything that the decision maker regards as relevant may be included in the analyst's remit, and not just Paretian efficiency notions (which may not be among the decision maker's decision criteria at all).

This difference of approach clearly has a marked effect on the role of cost–benefit analysis and of the analysts who conduct it, and it is the implications of moving from the former position to the latter which is my focus of interest here.

THE PARETIAN ASSUMPTIONS

The Paretian criterion relies on the following assumptions: (a) each individual is the best judge of his/her own welfare; (b) the strength of people's preferences is properly measurable by willingness to pay; (c) the effects of the existing distribution of purchasing power upon willingness to pay are acceptable; (d) it does not matter to whom the net benefits accrue (only that there are some); and (e) in the case of the use of the potential Pareto improvement it does not matter that compensation is not actually paid.

There has been much disquiet about (c), (d) and (e), which usually leads to the notion of an 'equity/efficiency trade-off', i.e. pursuing equity goals is seen as involving 'costs' in terms of the efficiency goal. This is a somewhat misleading formulation, since Pareto 'efficiency' already contains 'equity' statements (c), (d) and (e), so 'efficiency vs. equity' should really be 'Paretian equity' versus 'some other equity'.

But one can also express disquiet about (a) and (b), for we frequently operate on the assumption that people (even adult people) *are not* the best judges of their own welfare (e.g. where a principal/agent relationship is entered into, as in the provision of health care) and there are areas of public policy where we do not (in principle at least) permit preferences expressed by willingness to pay (e.g. in the administration of justice). So every single one of the Paretian assumptions may well be challenged as inappropriate in one area of public decision-making or another.

RESPONDING TO THE CHALLENGE

There are various ways of responding to this challenge. One is to restrict the effective scope of the Paretian approach still further by specifying that it is only appropriate where all those assumptions are acceptable, which would effectively relegate economists to the sidelines. A closely related response is to set 'constraints' (of morality, legality, political feasibility, etc.) upon the range of acceptable situations, leaving the Paretian calculus to sub-optimise within those 'constraints' (e.g. second-best theorising). The weakness of the 'constraint' approach is that it implies that the 'constrained' parameter (wherever it is set) has absolute precedence over the unconstrained variables. No trade-off is permitted between (say) resource costs and the current legal constraints, though it is possible to do sensitivity analyses to see how *different* legal constraints affect overall resource costs, and thereby to 'shadow price' the constrained variable. Yet another way out of the problem is to abandon the cost–benefit approach (as strictly defined, in which all costs and benefits are evaluated in money terms) and revert to the less demanding format of the cost-effectiveness approach. In this, although *some* benefits and costs are evaluated in money terms, some are left in their 'natural units' (e.g. lives saved, reduced risk of nuclear accident, response time). Once we get to this point it is questionable whether the Paretian approach is worth sustaining any longer as the basic framework of thought.

Suppose we turn instead to the alternative 'decision-aid' approach to cost–benefit analysis. Its distinctive feature is that it starts from the assumption that 'valuations' may be derived from a variety of sources, not just from people's willingness and ability to pay. Other possible sources of value might be the direct eliciting of trade-offs from people's utility functions, or the postulated values of the responsible politicians, or 'expert' judgments from the professionals in the relevant field! Each of these alternative sources of valuation has strengths and weaknesses, and the actual valuations that emerge might not be identical, which will bring to the fore the necessity for a political/ethical decision as to whose values shall count. By implication, the Paretian approach answers this question by asserting that everyone's values count in proportion to their purchasing power. At the other extreme, it would be possible to say within a non-Paretian framework that only one person's preferences count (and that person could be the *Great Dictator* or, in a rather different political context, the median voter). But the analytical framework itself can work with whatever set of values are fed into it, irrespective of their source. It is the *relevance and acceptability of the answers* that is influenced by the nature and source of the valuations used (which is equally true of the Paretian approach). In that sense every piece of cost–benefit analysis implies a particular *political* commitment.

It is tempting to think that by adopting 'natural' units (e.g. lives saved) the valuation problems have been avoided. But this is an illusion. For instance in clinical trials in medicine it is common to use the survival rate over some arbitrarily chosen time period as the measure of effectiveness (or benefit) and by this criterion to assert that one treatment is better than another. But (say) the 2 year survival rate carries the following implicit valuation statements:

(a) to survive for less than 2 years is of no value,
(b) having survived 2 years, further survival is of no additional value,
(c) it does not matter with what quality of life people survive to 2 years, and
(d) it does not matter who you are (every survivor counts equally).

These are very strong valuation assumptions. They can be modified by adopting a different measure such as life years gained, or, better still, quality-adjusted life years gained, which might in turn be weighted according to the characteristics of the beneficiary (e.g. the parents of young children to be given more weight than solitary elderly people) so that not everyone counts equally. So although money valuations are avoided, valuation cannot be avoided altogether. And in this cost-effectiveness model, money valuations will eventually creep back in when the decision is made as to how much it is worth spending to save a life, or to keep someone alive for 2 years, or to extend life by 1 year, or to provide one extra quality-adjusted-life-year.

Health economists have tried to bridge the gap between these 'natural' units and full-scale monetary evaluation by attempting to elicit people's preferences, and even the properties of their underlying utility functions, in what has become known as the cost-utility approach (as opposed to the cost-effectiveness or cost–benefit approach).

This has generated considerable tension between the economists (and a few others) who are trying to create a single index of value of health, using psychometric methods, and those (mostly epidemiologists and sociologists) who believe this to be an impossible (and even a dangerous and/or immoral) undertaking, and who would prefer to leave the cost-effectiveness framework operating with multiple criteria of success, with no trade-offs between them. Thus life years gained might be one criterion, and qualify of life another, but it would not be considered proper to try to establish the rate at which people might be willing to sacrifice life expectancy to improve their quality-of-life, or vice versa. This 'profile' approach, in which several distinct indicators of effectiveness are displayed, is fine if the different indicators do not contradict each other, and if only the direction (rather than the size) of the differences in benefit is required in order to make a decision (e.g. if you were committed to spending a certain sum of money on an activity willy-nilly, and you simply wanted to know which course of action is more beneficial). These are very restrictive conditions however, and greatly emasculate the scope for such appraisal methods.

The tendency amongst the health economists has therefore been to take these different (Lancaster-like) attributes of health (e.g. life expectancy, physical mobility, freedom from pain/anxiety/distress, ability to engage in normal activities of daily living and/or family and social life) and try to estimate a multi-attribute utility function embracing them all.

At a technical level, one object of interest has been whether such a utility function is additive-separable or interactive, and another has been which dimensions turn out to be the most important contributors to overall satisfaction or welfare. The objective has been to attain measurements with interval properties, and to standardize them so that for each individual a set of relative values is obtained such that being healthy is rated at 1, and being dead is rated at 0 (with it being possible for some states of health to be assigned negative ratings on this scale . . . i.e. to be considered worse than being dead). These ratings of different states of (ill) health are then used as quality-adjustments to whatever length of life expectancy is under consideration. For instance, if a treatment enables people to gain 5 extra years of healthy life expectancy, it would count as 5 quality adjusted life years (QALYs). But if it offered only 5 extra years of rather unhealthy life expectancy in a state which people rated as only worth 0.4, then it would count as only 2 QALYs. The quality-adjusted life-year is then used as the unit of benefit, to replace money values (though again the money valuation of a QALY will emerge from the decision whether a QALY is worth its cost or not, when acceptance or rejection of a particular project has to be determined).

There are two other issues which both Paretian and non-Paretian approaches to cost–benefit analysis have to face: aggregation and discounting.

Most Paretian cost–benefit analysis proceeds on the (usually unthinking) acceptance of the proposition that a £ worth of benefit is a £ worth of benefit is a £ worth of benefit, no matter who gets it. There has been some desultory discussion of the use of equity weights, but on the whole this has had little practical effect on the actual studies that have been done. There has also been a tendency to concentrate on benefits which show up (or ought to show up) in GNP. Increased leisure time of the elderly or the quality of the domestic environment in which the mentally handicapped live does not figure prominently. Health economists have moved in a somewhat different direction. The commonest assumption on which aggregation proceeds is that a year of life (or a quality-adjusted year of life) is of equal value to everybody, but this has typically been offered up for discussion as an ethical postulate, to see whether people think it is an appropriate basis on which to appraise public policy with respect to health and health care. If not, some explicit discriminatory weightings need to be supplied, and the calculations reworked accordingly. Some work has been done to discover people's views on these matters, but so far, to my knowledge, no such weights have ever been used in an actual study. Most British health economists have adopted the position that improving sick people's productivity should not be counted amongst the benefits of health care (or even as cost-offsets). Two arguments have been adduced to support this apparently anomalous position (since the costs of treatment are counted). The first is that with mass unemployment the system-wide effect of sickness in the labour force is that less people are unemployed, so the adverse effect on the productivity of the sick person is offset by the favourable effect on the productivity of the otherwise unemployed person. The second is that the National Health Service was created with the express aim of ensuring that the financially better off did not get priority over the worse off when it came to access to health care. Since the 'better off' are likely to be those with the higher incomes, then if we count loss of income (or output) as an additional benefit to the actual improvement in health, then we shall be giving priority to them once more, since for the same (treatment) cost we will get greater benefits from the more productive than from the less productive.

Turning finally to discounting, in the Paretian approach two distinct arguments have been adduced in support of discounting, the social opportunity cost argument and the social time preference argument (and sometimes a mixture of both).

The former depends on the resources used in the project having alternative investment uses where the best rate of return constitutes their opportunity cost. The time preference approach simply asserts that people prefer to enjoy benefits sooner rather than later (and to bear costs later rather than sooner) and this in itself is a sufficient basis for the discount rate. The former rate could in principle be calculated, the latter has essentially to be decided (by the relevant political authority). In my view the latter is the correct position, but that does not help much in determining what the actual rate should be, especially in a Paretian framework where the social time preference rate needs to be elicited from individuals, whose private time preference rates may not coincide with the rate they think the government should use. In the alternative approach to cost–benefit analysis it is for the policy maker to choose the appropriate discount-rate, and the usual advice given is to test how sensitive the outcome might be to a reasonably realistic range of such rates. But in the health context it has been challenged whether the discounting of health benefits is appropriate to all. To the extent that this challenge rests on an opportunity cost notion (i.e. that health, unlike money, cannot be reinvested elsewhere) it is in my view mistaken, because the opportunity cost notion is not the correct justification for discounting anyway. A more subtle argument is that people's differential preference for health at various times is more closely related to the different phases of their life cycle than it is to nearness or remoteness from the present. But the same argument might be made for the marginal utility of income, and we still concede that time preference has an independent rationale. In the end we finish up in the rather pragmatic position that if we discount the time stream of costs, we must also discount the time stream of benefits, otherwise we get into quite anomalous situations.

In summary, if willingness and ability to pay, and the money values they generate, are rejected by policy makers as an acceptable basis for benefit valuation in policy analysis, economists can either retire from the scene and concentrate their energies elsewhere, in fields of public policy where such valuations are acceptable (e.g. in transport and road safety, but not in health care) or try to develop an alternative calculus which uses some other sources of valuation, and expresses them in non-monetary units (such as QALYs) which are acceptable to, and understandable by, such policy makers.

This almost invariably means that economists have to work cooperatively with other disciplines, and face the hostility that comes from trampling 'around' in their territory (plus the deep-seated suspicion that we are interested only in the sordid crude commercial aspects of life, not in its finer, more sensitive and humanitarian manifestations). But it also means that we abandon the dichotomy between efficiency and other objectives of policy, because 'efficiency' now means the least cost way of meeting all of our objectives, and since 'costs' mean 'benefits foregone', the costs are the sacrifices implied by some course of action with respect to any or all of our objectives, not just the resources which might be released for use in the private sector (or other parts of the public sector). The 'cost' of treating one patient may be that 3 others do not get treated, which brings the ethics of resource allocation firmly to the fore, and emphasises the fact that 'efficiency' is not a purely technical, value-free concept (even in its more limited Paretian sense).

But this extension of the realm of cost–benefit analysis in the field of public policy analysis threatens the policy makers too, for it claims to be able to encompass any consideration the policy maker might encompass (not just Paretian efficiency).

Since systematic analysis requires explicitness and the maximum feasible degree of quantification, it may expose assumptions (and valuations) which the policy maker would prefer to keep concealed. It is also hungry for evidence, which may be lacking, so that it also exposes those areas where facts have been replaced by expert opinion or by sheer guesswork, with the new possibility that these may subsequently be shown to be wrong and hence discredit someone or other. The analyst may therefore find himself (or herself) drawn into a power struggle, in which the analyst is usually a protagonist for openness and explicitness and the policy maker for 'discretion' and 'intuition'. In public policy analysis in a democratic setting, this raises in an acute form the issue of the analyst's accountability, which could be to the general public, to the particular public agency, to a particular person within it, to the discipline or profession, or to the analyst's own conscience. Perhaps the best general advice to budding analysts is that those who would sup with the devil should use a very long-handled spoon!

Bibliography of earlier (misguided?) publications in this same territory

1. Sugden, R. and Williams, A. (1978), *The Principles of Practical Cost-Benefit Analysis* (Oxford: Oxford University Press).
2. Williams, A. (1972) 'Cost-Benefit Analysis: bastard science? and/or insidious poison in the body politick?', *Journal of Public Economics*, vol. 1.
3. Williams, A. (1981) 'Welfare economics and health status measurement', in J. van der Gaag and M. Perlman (eds), *Health, Economics and Health Economics* (Amsterdam: North Holland).
4. Williams, A. (1985) 'The nature, meaning and measurement of health and illness: an economic viewpoint', *Social Science and Medicine*, vol. 20.
5. Williams, A. (1987) 'The importance of quality of life in policy decisions', in S. R. Walker and R. M. Rosser (eds.), *Quality of Life: Assessment and Application* (New York: Kluwer).
6. Williams, A. (1988) 'Ethics and efficiency in the provision of health care', in J. M. Bell and S. Mendus (eds.), *Philosophy and Medical Welfare* (Cambridge: Cambridge University Press).
7. Williams, A. (1988) 'Priority setting in public and private health care: a guide through the ideological jungle', *Journal of Health Economics*, vol. 7.
8. Williams, A. (1992) 'Cost-effectiveness analysis: is it ethical?', *Journal of Medical Ethics*, vol. 18.

5 Conflicts between Equity Concepts and Efficiency in Health: A Diagrammatic Approach

Anthony J. Culyer*

INTRODUCTION

The analysis of health care as a public good has previously used a device invented by Shibata (1971) in explaining why it may be efficient to develop a system of in-kind rather than in-cash subsidies (Culyer 1971). A characteristic of this approach was its emphasis on consumption of health care rather than health. In this paper a new geometrical approach to the efficient production of health in a community is developed which enables a fuller discussion than has hitherto been possible of the relationship between efficiency and various types of equity. The emphasis here is on concepts of equity (horizontal and vertical) and the possible conflicts that may occur between them. A particular intention of the paper is to identify those issues that are most urgently in need of further conceptual clarification if progress is to be made with empirical study of equity in health, especially those concepts that are in conflict, when those wishing to make jugments of equity will have therefore to decide which principle shall dominate.

CONCEPTS OF EFFICIENCY AND EQUITY

The entity whose efficient production and equitable distribution is assumed, for the purposes of this paper, to be of substantive interest is health; this paper will not deal with equity in the distribution of payments for health care nor will it consider the ways in which equity in health are best fitted into more comprehensive assessments of the distributive fairness of societies. It has often been suggested in the past that there are some entities, of which health is one, about whose distribution one is typically more concerned than others and which may give rise to what Tobin (1970) calls 'specific egalitarianism'. This is the point of departure for this paper. Whether or not health is a (mixed) public good is not of direct relevance for present purposes, though at some subsequent state it might be worth developing the conditions for health care efficiency, when health care constitutes just one bundle of inputs into the health production function.[1] It will be assumed that health can be measured (up to at least a linear transformation) by use of instruments such as the Quality Adjusted Life Year (QALY) or Healthy Year Equivalents (HYE).[2] For convenience, reference here will be to QALYs. Weighted QALY maximization will be taken as the efficiency objective and fairness in QALY distribution as the equity objective.[3]

The equity objective, following Aristotle, is described in horizontal and vertical terms. Horizontal equity requires the equal treatment of individuals who are equal in relevant aspects; vertical equity requires the unequal treatment of individuals who are unequal in relevant respects.[4] The 'respects' here considered in which equality or inequality may be assessed are: (a) the initial, or presenting, state of health; (b) the need for health; and (c) the final health state: the state of health after receiving health care.

Of these, the second and third require some elaboration. The term 'need' is employed in the specific sense of ability to benefit (Williams 1974; Culyer 1976, 1990) which embodies both supply and demand features in that the prospective benefit is in part a function of the productivity of the technologies available within health care services for the improvement of health[5] and in part a function of the social weights that are embodied in the QALY type index of health.[6]

Equity in the final health distribution will be interpreted either as equality (its horizontal version) or as some inequality which conforms with another (implicit) principle of equity (its vertical version). Such a principle may be based on the idea of desert (for example, smokers deserve to be less healthy than nonsmokers; clean livers deserve to be more healthy than loose livers) or may relate to other aspects of a person's characteristics (such as a desire to compensate for inequalities in these other characteristics, for example, inequalities in income).[7]

EFFICIENT HEALTH PRODUCTION AND ALLOCATION: A DIAGRAMMATIC APPROACH

Figure 5.1 (based on Wagstaff 1991) embodies the essential two-person framework to be used in the paper. The axes measure the prospective health (in QALYs) of two individuals *A* and *B*. These health stocks are measured over the expected future lifetimes of the individuals. I shall assume that the individuals *A* and *B* are of equal age (though not that they have an equal life expectation). Point *S* indicates the initial or endowment position in which *A* holds a stock of health Oh_A and *B* a stock of Oh_B. *S* represents the origin of what may be seen as 'investment in health' space, bounded by the dashed axes. The convex locus $f_B f_A$ is the health frontier assuming that there is production efficiency in the health care sector. Its assumed strict convexity arises either from generalized diminishing returns in the production of health for *A* and *B* or from constant returns in each but with different factor intensities. The slope of the health frontier, MC_A/MC_B, is the ratio of the marginal opportunity cost of *A*'s to *B*'s health.[8] The *W* contour is a social indifference curve indicating the rate at which QALYs for *A* and *B* are traded off implying, as drawn, that increasing QALYs for one are required to compensate for equal QALY decrements for the other and hence a degree of inequality aversion.[9]

Efficient allocation of health is at point *E*, at which *A* acquires an additional Sh'_A health and *B*, Sh'_B (flows, or additions to health stocks) with the final distribution of health h'_B and h'_A for *B* and *A* respectively.

The point *Q* on the 45° line through *S* is a reference point on the health frontier showing equal increments in health for each individual. In this paper *Q* represents 'equal treatment' defined in terms of health outcomes rather than health care inputs (which will invariably be contingent upon the diagnoses and treatments thought appropriate for particular types of patient).[10] In horizontal equity, equality of treatment for equal initial health or equal need will be defined by point *Q*, while vertical equity, involving unequal treatment corresponding to unequal initial endowments, etc. will be judged in terms of movements along the health efficiency frontier relative to *Q*.

While this construct provides the general analytical tool of the paper, its efficiency characteristics are not of primary concern. In-

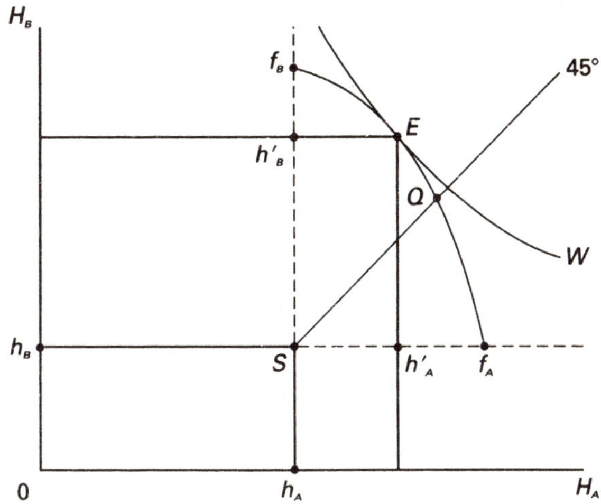

Figure 5.1

stead the focus is on equity or distributive fairness, which can now be examined in terms of the figure.

QALY EGALITARIANISM AND HORIZONTAL/VERTICAL EQUITY

QALY egalitarianism is my shorthand for a distributional value judgment popularized by Williams in a series of papers (e.g. Williams 1981): a QALY is of equal social value to whomsoever it may accrue. This social value judgment implies that the W contours are linear with slopes -1. The social value of incremental QALYs is constant and independent of the existing stock of QALYs and its distribution (there is no inequality-aversion).[11] This extremely strong value assumption is made in order to highlight its interraction with other approaches to equity.

It is perfectly possible to drop the assumption that *A* and *B* are of equal ages in efficiency analysis in order to assess the overall allocative efficiency of health care. If this is done, QALY egalitarianism implies 'ageism' in some degree since, other things equal, in most (though not all) societies the younger have a greater expectation of life. This may be modified by any discounting of future QALYs in the calculation of 'present values' of the stock of health.

In equity analysis, however, it makes little sense to do this. For example, if the objective of equal final health is equitable, it does not seem to make much sense to interpret this in terms of QALYs over future lifetimes (whether discounted or not) for the obvious reason that it is not really an issue in equity that some individuals happen to be older than others and therefore have (other things equal) fewer remaining expected lifeyears. Accordingly, the assumption that health is 'age-standardised' is retained. There may be some matters of vertical equity that this raises which cannot be considered within the restrictive assumptions of this paper, but it is not clear how they should be handled, and it seems common currency among students of health distributions that these distributions should in any case be age-standardized. Considerations of 'intergenerational' equity in health seem, *prima facie*, unlikely to affect the general conclusions to be reached in respect of age-standardized equity comparisons.

EQUALITY IN ALL THREE SENSES

Figure 5.2 assumes an initially equal distribution of health, *S*, between *A* and *B*. The health frontier is symmetrical about the 45° line indicating an equal need or ability to benefit ($Sf_A = Sf_B$). Given QALY egalitarianism, the value of a QALY per person is equal and efficiency requires the equal meeting of needs ($Sh'_A = Sh'_B$). An equal final distribution of health is feasible (the 45° line through the origin necessarily passes through the health frontier). The efficient outcome on the health frontier is indicated by point *E* and, in this special case, it can be seen that, given (a) equal initial health, (b) equal need, and (c) a desired equal final distribution, equal treatment in the sense of equal additional health is implied by maximizing (the social value of) health. There is no conflict between efficiency and the principles of equity, nor between any of the candidates for the 'respects' in which individuals are to be considered equal. A modification of QALY egalitarianism would introduce inconsistency. Suppose that two QALYs for *A* were regarded as socially equivalent to one for *B* on grounds, say, that *B* had more dependants than *A*. Then the efficiency point becomes *E'* and efficient met needs of *A* and *B* become Sh''_A and Sh''_B. Maximization of (the social value of) health is now inconsistent with equal treatment of those having an equal capacity to benefit.

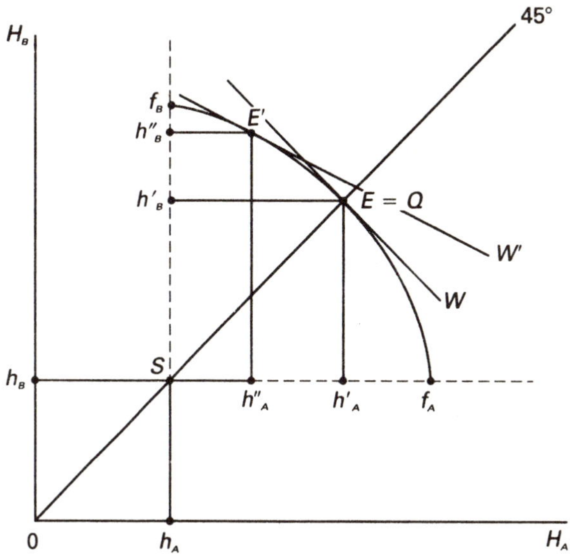

Figure 5.2

It is worth noting that this introduces a distinction not previously met in the literature on health needs: ability to benefit and met need are identical only if the health frontier is symmetrical about the 45° line and QALY egalitarianism obtains. Without the latter, for example with the social welfare contour *W′* in Figure 5.2, abilities to benefit are still equal but met needs are not.

INEQUALITY IN INITIAL HEALTH

Figure 5.3 depicts a situation in which there is inequality in the distribution of initial health. The efficiency point is *E* and this involves equal treatment for equal need (so efficiency remains consistent with this horizontal principle). The point *Q* on the efficiency frontier represents both efficient production of health (but not an efficient allocation between *A* and *B*) and equality in final health. There is thus a conflict between the goal of final health equality, equal treatment for equal need, and efficiency. Equal treatment (movement along the 45° line through *S*) is inconsistent with attaining *Q*. This arises because *S* is not on the 45° line through the origin. The

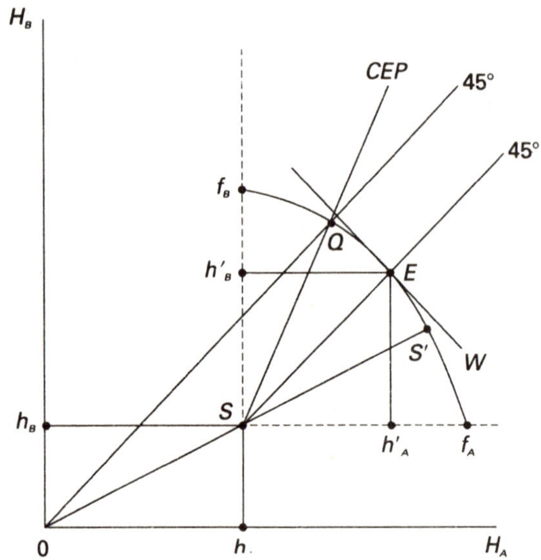

Figure 5.3

unequal treatment appropriate for the inequality represented by *S* might be thought of in terms of what is necessary to attain *Q*, viz. movement along a compensating expansion path (*CEP*) *SQ* to *Q*, which involves favouring the individual whose initial health is worse. This is consistent with productive efficiency (being on the frontier) but not with community health maximization under QALY egalitarianism. The higher the marginal cost per QALY for *A* or *B* (and retaining the symmetry of the frontier) the flatter the frontier to the left of *E* and the steeper the necessary CEP. This principle of *vertical* equity thus requires a greater relative favouring of the initially sicker (*B* over *A*) when marginal productivity falls relatively quickly.[12]

Point *S′* represents the same 'shares' in total health as exist at *S* (it is on the ray *OS* produced). This of necessity lies to the southeast of *E*, so both efficiency and equal treatment for equal need necessarily involve some compensation for the initial inequality of health, so these forms of horizontal and vertical equity are not in direct conflict (qualitatively speaking, at least).

A special difficulty arises when the 45° line lies outside the feasible set as shown in Figure 5.4. In this case, the closest it is possible to get to an equal final health distribution is at $Q = f_B$, the *CEP* becomes

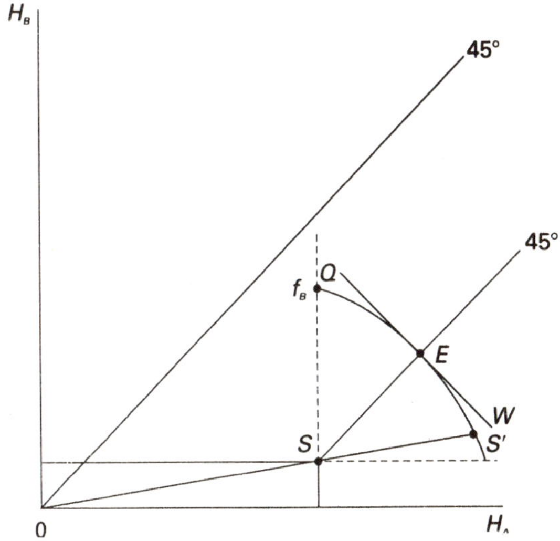

Figure 5.4

vertical and the initially sicker person receives all the additional health benefit the system can deliver. This suggests that there can be no simple proportional equity rule to apply in the case of vertical equity and that some inequalities in health are irreducible (unless one contemplates *reducing* the health of the relatively healthy!). Note, however, that *E* is still to the left of *S′* and so there is some compensation for initial inequality at the efficiency point. However, there will normally be some addition to the supply of factors to the health sector to ensure that the health frontier is intersected by the 45° line through the origin, but whether the desideratum of vertical equity is sufficiently compelling to warrant a possibly high opportunity cost to the rest of the economy is problematic. The point serves to show, however, that achieving some forms of equity is contingent upon a sufficient resource availability to the whole of the health care sector: equity cannot be considered in isolation from the overall allocation to the health care sector.

INEQUALITY OF NEED

Inequality of need arises from asymmetry in the health frontier. This case is depicted in Figure 5.5. Here *B*'s ability to benefit is greater

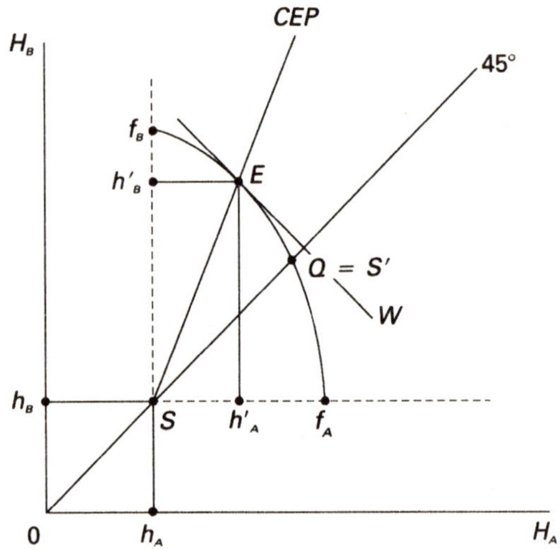

Figure 5.5

than A's ($Sf_B > Sf_A$) even though they have the same initial health. The marginal cost per QALY is equalized between A and B at E, the efficiency point, which also minimizes the (social value of) unmet need. If the appropriate vertical equity principle here is to equalize (the social value of) marginal met (or unmet) need then this is consistent with efficiency (given QALY egalitarianism). It is, however, inconsistent with the horizontal principle of equal treatment for equal initial health and with an equal final distribution, for E or any other point favouring the individual with greater need must lie to the northwest of Q.

In this case, the CEP (now compensating for inequality in need) will be the steeper (involving a wider departure from Q) the greater the divergence between the productivity of health care in promoting health between types of individual (or their capacities to benefit).

INEQUALITY OF INITIAL HEALTH AND INEQUALITY OF NEED

We may now examine a more complex case of multiple vertical inequality. This is depicted in Figure 5.6. In this figure, B's ability to

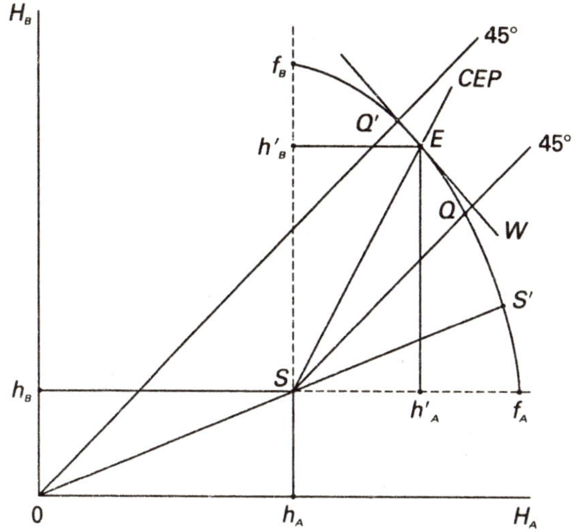

Figure 5.6

benefit is greater than *A*'s and *B* is also the initially sicker person. The efficiency point is, as before, *E*, and equal increments of health and equal final health are denoted by *Q* and *Q'* respectively. Given asymmetry in the health frontier, *E* must lie to the left of *Q* and may, depending on the relative productivity of health care in promoting *A*'s or *B*'s health, lie to the left of *Q'* as well.[13] If the appropriate vertical equity principle is to favour those with the greater need (viz. locate to the left of *Q* on the health frontier) and to favour those with the worse initial health (viz. locate to the left of *S'* on the health frontier) then any CEP with a slope > 1 is consistent with both principles. Since the CEP through *E* is such a CEP, efficiency is consistent with these two (weak[14]) vertical equity principles. So long as *E* remains in the segment *Q'S'* of the health frontier there is both a compensation for the initial inequality (*E* must lie to the left of *S'*) but *E* may also lie to the left of *Q'*, in which case there is 'overcompensation' and a reversal of inequality with the initially sicker individual having a final health state that is relatively better than the initially fitter person.

Figure 5.6 depicted the case in which the initially sicker person also had a greater capacity to benefit. Figure 5.7 depicts the other case. Here *A*, the initially fitter, also has the greater ability to benefit (Sf_A

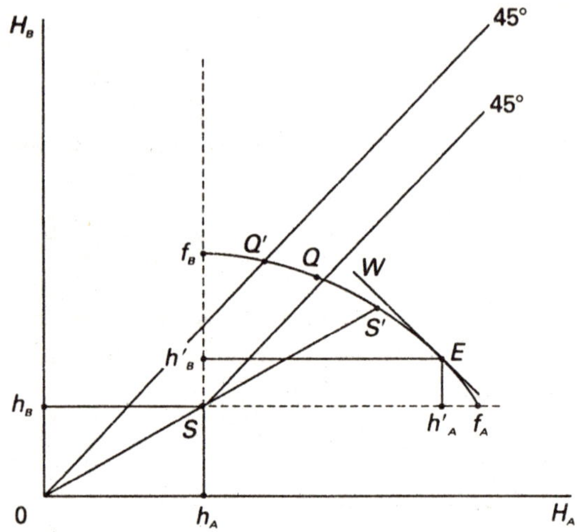

Figure 5.7

> Sf_B). The efficiency point E must lie to the right of Q and Q'. The vertical equity principle of favouring those with greater need requires a point right of Q but the vertical equity principle of favouring those with worse initial health requires one left of S'. The figure shows an E that conflicts with this principle (it is plainly possible for E to lie between Q and S'). Since E must lie to the right of Q, it is *a fortiori* to the right of Q', involving not only inequality in health but increasing inequality. The case in which the initially fitter (but still sick) individual also has the greater capacity to benefit from health care thus involves the greatest contradiction between efficiency and equity. The only consistency between efficiency and the equity principles discussed here is with the vertical principle of favouring those with the greater need (itself contingent, of course, on QALY egalitarianism). This case also raises the possibility that Q' on the 45° line through the origin may lie outside the feasible set. In this case, an equal distribution of final health is unobtainable and its closest approximation is reached by just one individual receiving all the benefits of health care.

CONCLUSIONS

In framing the principal conclusions of the paper, QALY egalitarianism will be assumed and the consistencies and inconsistencies between equity and efficiency, and between equity concepts, will be highlighted.

There are three relevant 'respects' in which individuals have been considered equal or unequal: initial health, need, and final health. The sense in which 'treatment' has been considered equal or unequal is in terms of additional health from health care consumption. In other words, 'treatment' is considered in output terms. Vertical equity has not been interpreted in any strict proportional sense but in the weak form of relatively advantageous treatment for those who are relatively deprived in one of the relevant respects. The three equalities requiring equal treatment are: equal initial health (*H*1), equal need (*H*2) and equal final health (*H*3); the three inequalities requiring unequal treatment are unequal initial health (*V*1), unequal need (*V*2) and unequal final health (*V*3). These give rise to eight possible combinations that may cause inter-equity conflict: (*H*1, *H*2, *H*3), (*H*1, *H*2, *V*3), (*H*1, *V*2, *H*3), (*H*1, *V*2, *V*3), (*V*1, *H*2, *H*3), (*V*1, *V*2, *H*3), (*V*1, *H*2, *V*3), (*V*1, *V*2, *V*3). Each is considered below.

(*H*1, *H*2, *H*3) When individuals are alike in all relevant respects, equal treatment is, of course, the appropriate response in each case so no inter-equity conflict arises. Moreover, equal treatment is also the efficient response (granted QALY egalitarianism) and there is therefore no equity-efficiency conflict.

(*H*1, *H*2, *V*3) When individuals are alike in initial health and need, equal treatment is required to meet these equity principles and also for efficiency. These imply also an equal final health distribution which is therefore inconsistent with equitable inequality in final health. In this case, therefore, it becomes important to unravel the possible justifications for final health inequality and come to a decision as to how compelling they are relative to the justifications for the other forms of equity and whether they are, if found compelling, 'worth' the efficiency loss involved.

(*H*1, *V*2, *H*3) When individuals have equal initial health but different needs and are deemed deserving of equal final health, a conflict arises between the requirements of vertical equity and efficiency on the one hand, and the horizontal equity requirements on the other. Both efficiency and vertical equity require differential treatment in favour of those with greater need; the other principles can be satisfied only by equal treatment. Again, a decision has to be made as to which equity concept is to take precedence and, should it be either horizontal principle, whether the efficiency loss is 'worth' the equity gain.

(*H*1, *V*2, *V*3) When individuals have equal initial health, but different needs, and inequality in the final health distribution is equitable, then conflict between final health inequality and the vertical equity and efficiency requirements may not arise, so long as the final inequality is an equitable inequality. There remains, however, a conflict between the equity requirement of equal treatment for equal initial health and unequal treatment for unequal need (as well as efficiency). Again, therefore, a choice between equity principles is forced.

(*V*1, *H*2, *H*3) When individuals have initially unequal health, but equal needs, and final health equality is a desideratum, equal treatment (which meets the equal needs principle and the efficiency requirement) will shift the distribution of health in favour of the initially more disadvantaged and towards greater equality in the final health distribution. However, depending on the productivity of health care, it may not be *possible* for final health equality to be attained. In either case, depending on the status accorded to final health equality as an equity objective, pursuit of efficiency and horizontal equity in treating equal needs equally may be judged insufficiently egalitarian. Again, therefore, a decision is forced as to the status to be accorded the equity principles and whether, if equality in the final health distribution is highly prized, it is 'worth' the efficiency loss.

(*V*1, *V*2, *H*3) When individuals have both different initial endowments of health and different needs, but final health equality is a desideratum, the severity of conflict depends upon the relative productivity of health care. If health care is more productive for those with the worse initial state, then both vertical principles are served, as is efficiency, by favouring the least healthy. Greater final equality of health may also result but, if the relative productivity difference is very high, pursuit of both efficiency and vertical equity in respect of the different needs may reverse the initial inequality. If health care is relatively productive for those with initially better health, then both efficiency and the pursuit of vertical equity in respect of the different needs may cause the final health distribution to be even more unequal than the initial distribution. Moreover, if available technologies of health care can offer little benefit to those who are the initially sicker, then final equality of health may not be in the feasible set.

(*V*1, *H*2, *V*3) When individuals are initially unequal in health but their needs are equal and inequality in the final health distribution is equitable, then conflict may not arise. Pursuit of both efficiency and equal treatment for equal need are served by equal increments in health, which will reduce the inequality of the final health distribution relative to the initial distribution, but still leaves those better off in the initial state better off in the final state. If this is consistent with equitable final inequality, all is well. If, however, the final distribution ought to be more unequal (or unequal in a different way) than the initial distribution, then this principle is in conflict with the others and an unambiguous choice is forced. If the final distribution is required to be one that reverses the initial distribution, then this may not lie within the feasible set.

(*V*1, *V*2, *V*3) When individuals have different initial health, different needs, and inequality in the final distribution is equitable, then there need be no conflict, as unequal treatment is implied by all three equity principles as well as efficiency. However, if the final distribution is one which should be less unequal than the initial distribution, then this is likely to obtain if health care is more productive for the relatively sicker, but there will be conflict if these individuals are, for other reasons, less 'deserving'. Conversely, if health care is more productive for the initially fitter then the final distribution is likely to be less equal than the initial distribution and conflict will arise if, for other reasons, the relatively well also happen to be less 'deserving'.

All equity principles, so long as they lie within the feasible set, are consistent with production efficiency in health care (viz. being on the health frontier), so pursuit of this form of efficiency can be uncompromisingly supported by adherents to any of the equity principles. There will, of course, always be some compromise to QALY egalitarianism that can bring allocative efficiency (and equity in the treatment of needs) into consonance with one of the other equity principles. There is, however, no guarantee that the reasons one may have for wanting to modify QALY egalitarianism would lead one to change the interpersonal weights in such a fashion as to produce such a consonance.

Efficiency, horizontal equity in respect of need, and vertical equity in respect of need are never in conflict, nor do they depend on QALY egalitarianism. They are not, however the same thing. Equal treatment for equal need is an *implication* of health maximization and has the usual utilitarian characteristic of being indifferent to distributional considerations (Sen 1973); equal treatment for equal need as an equity principle is an end in itself (and is satisfied, for example, on *any* point on a 45° line through *S* within the feasible set). Unequal treatment for unequal need is precisely specified as an efficiency condition as the increments implied by tangency between the health frontier and the highest social welfare contour. As an equity principle, it has been interpreted only qualitatively and it is plainly possible to devise quantitative vertical equity principles for the treatment of different needs (such as proportionality) which would create conflict between efficiency and the equitable treatment of individuals having different needs.

Notes

* Thanks are due to Reiner Leidl, Owen O'Donnell, Adam Wagstaff and Alan Williams for many discussions that have formed the thinking, such as it is, in this paper and to the participants at a seminar in Linköping University. I am most grateful for their insights, and especially to Adam for forcing me to consider more explicitly what has previously been dangerously implicit – and in part plain wrong.

1. In this paper the question of the social value of health vis-a-vis other sources of economic welfare arises only indirectly in terms of the resource endowments of the health care sector, which are here taken as fixed. What does arise directly is the question of the social value of health to different individuals, which is treated here as though health were the only argument of the social welfare function.
2. See for example Williams (1985), Kind and Rosser (1988), and Mehrez and Gafni (1989). For a discussion of the value content in health measures of this kind see Culyer (1978).
3. For a justification of this approach see Culyer (1990).
4. This is weaker than the principle in *Nicomachean Ethics*, book 5 and *Politics*, book 3, Ch. 9, which requires treatment *proportionate to desert*. I do not here investigate the *degrees* of unequal treatment that may be required to ensure vertical equiry.
5. Note that meeting need normally requires health services, but that this does not imply that health services are the only effective means of promoting health. Health care may not be effective at the margin either absolutely or relatively in promoting health compared to other determinants, environmental policy, changing lifestyles, and so on. A full treatment of equity (and efficiency) in health would require that these other elements be considered.
6. These typically include measures of the *characteristics* of individuals, such as absence of pain, distress and mental confusion; ability to perform social acts and activities of daily life.

7. Whether it is sensible or useful to distinguish between equity judgments about the final distribution and the social values to be attached to a unit of health for different types of individual, is a moot point. I have chosen to leave the question open in this paper and have used a value judgment later described as 'QALY egalitarianism'. This has the advantage of minimising the 'contamination' of efficiency judgments (based on QALY maximisation) by distributional judgments, and so may commend itself to economists, particularly those who might want to replace QALY egalitarianism (which accords each QALY, to whomsoever it accrues, an equal weight in the social welfare function) with, for example, a willingness-to-pay (per QALY) weight.
8. Note that it is not the ratio of the marginal costs of health care. It should also be noted, as has been pointed out to me by Owen O'Donnell, that social factors will partly determine not only the initial health distribution but also the shape of the health frontier (for example, because better educated people relate better to health professionals, are more likely to 'comply' with doctors' orders, etc.). A full treatment of equity in health ought eventually to take account of these factors.
9. Note the absence of any willingness-to-pay element in the analysis, either that of consumers directly or that of externally affected parties. It may be helpful (though it is not necessary) to imagine that health is a merit good giving rise to a derived demand for health care, with this derived demand expressed via principal-agent relationships at various decision-making tiers of the health services (of which the classic one is, of course, that of the doctor acting as agent for the patient, but others include decisions about the distribution of resource budgets within hospitals, to community practitioners, etc.).
10. Equality of treatment in the sense of equal (value of) resources (expenditure per head) is implied if there are constant returns, and equal factor intensities, in the production of *A*'s and *B*'s health, and equal factor prices. In this case, the health frontier becomes linear, with a slope -1. QALY egalitarianism implies indifference in this case as to the location of *E* on the health frontier. This version of equality of treatment is not further considered here, but see Culyer (1990) for a further discussion.
11. Inequality-aversion is discussed in a similar context in Wagstaff (1991).
12. It may be helpful to see this in terms of groups of homogeneous patients of types *A* and *B*, rather than individuals, with the proviso of equal numbers of each type.
13. The 45° line through the origin may also lie outside the feasible set, in which case *E* must be to the right of the corner solution at f_B for Q' off the 45° line.
14. 'Weak' in the sense of non-proportional.

References

1. Culyer, A. J. (1971) 'Medical care and the economics of giving', *Economica*, vol. 38.

2. Culyer, A. J. (1976), *Need and the National Health Service: Economics and Social Choice* (London: Martin Robertson).
3. Culyer, A. J. (1978) 'Need, values and health status measurement', in A. J. Culyer and K. G. Wright (eds.), *Economic Aspects of Health Services* (London: Martin Robertson).
4. Culyer, A. J. (1990) 'Health, health care expenditures, and equity', paper for the Comac-HSR conference on Equity in the Finance and Delivery of Health Care, Bellagio, Italy, September 1990. Has been published in E. van Doorslaer, A. Wagstaff and F. Rutten (eds.), *Equity in the Finance and Delivery of Health Care: An International Perspective* (Oxford: Oxford University Press).
5. Culyer, A. J. and Wagstaff, A. (1992) 'Need, equity and equality in health and health care', *Discussion Paper*, No. 95 (York: Centre for Health Economics, University of York, UK). Forthcoming in *Journal of Health Economics*.
6. Kind, P. and Rosser, R. M. (1988) 'The quantification of health', *European Journal of Social Psychology*, vol. 18.
7. Mehrez, A. and Gafni, A. (1989) 'Quality-adjusted life-years, utility theory, and healthy years equivalents', *Medical Decision Making*, vol. 9.
8. Sen, A. K. (1973), *On Economic Inequality* (Oxford: Clarendon Press).
9. Shibata, H. (1971) 'A bargaining model of the pure theory of public expenditure', *Journal of Political Economy*, vol. 79.
10. Tobin, J. (1970) 'On limiting the domain of inequality', *Journal of Law and Economics*, vol. 13.
11. Wagstaff, A. (1991) 'QALYs and the equity-efficiency tradeoff', *Journal of Health Economics*, vol. 10.
12. Williams, A. H. (1974) 'Need as a demand concept, with special reference to health', in A. J. Culyer (ed.), *Economic Problems and Social Goals* (London: Martin Robertson).
13. Williams, A. H. (1981) 'Welfare economics and health status measurement', in J. van der Gaag and M. Perlman (eds.), *Health, Economics, and Health Economics* (Amsterdam: North-Holland).
14. Williams, A. H. (1985) 'Economics of coronary artery bypass grafting', *British Medical Journal*, vol. 291.

6 Non-convexity in Shibata and Winrich

Robert E. Kohn*

INTRODUCTION

When polluters can abate emissions and victims can take measures to avoid exposure, 'a marginal increase in the preventive activities (that is, abatement) carried out by the polluters causes the marginal cost of defense (that is, avoidance) to increase'. This insight of Shibata and Winrich (1983, p. 433) is based on a chemical engineering principle that the more polluted the air or water, the lower the cost of reducing the pollutant concentration by a given percent. If the interactive effect is sufficiently strong, there is a nonconvexity such that abatement alone or avoidance alone, but not a combination of the two, is efficient. As a result of the non-convexity, programmes to efficiently control pollution by a Pigouvian scheme, such as a tax on emissions or the sale of discharge permits, may be unworkable.

The following scenario illustrates the case in which the Pigouvian approach breaks down. Suppose that the Government intends to tax emissions or sell discharge permits, observes the level of marginal pollution damage (which equals victims' voluntary marginal costs of avoidance) and, according to the standard Pigouvian prescription, sets the tax or permit price at that level of marginal damage. Prior to the Government's intercession there would be no abatement, and if the threshold marginal cost of abatement exceeds the tax or permit price, there would be no abatement after the Pigouvian intercession. If however, the nonconvexity discovered by Shibata and Winrich (1983) is present, what may be needed is an emission tax or permit price higher than the current level of marginal pollution damage and large enough to induce sufficient pollution abatement to raise the marginal cost of avoidance above the marginal cost of abatement. Then, an iterative sequence of Pigouvian prices would lead to the true global optimum at which abatement alone is efficient. The problem is that this same scenario could also result in a new equilibrium allocation that is inferior rather than superior to the initial allocation.

Unfortunately there are no marginal signals, *ex ante*, *ex post*, or even during the first stage of taxing or permitting, that would indicate whether the tax or permit price should or should not be set higher than the initial level of marginal pollution damage.

The problem that nonconvexity poses for Pigouvian taxation has long troubled economists – see, for example, Baumol (1972), Starrett (1972), Slater (1975), Kraus and Mohring (1975), and Kohn and Aucamp (1976). The issue is more pressing now that Shibata and Winrich (1983) have discovered this new and possibly pervasive cause of nonconvexity. It is appropriate that more attention be given by economists to the case in which the abating of pollution diminishes the effectiveness of avoiding exposure. In contrast to the useful, but partial equilibrium interpretation of Oates (1983), this paper is based on a general equilibrium analysis of a production possibility frontier that incorporates the potential for abatement and avoidance. When the interaction between abatement and avoidance is relatively weak, there is a region of the frontier in which an internal allocation (with both kinds of activity) is efficient. When the interaction is sufficiently strong that a second-order condition for an efficient internal allocation is violated, the frontier includes only corner solutions and there is the potential for the problem that Shibata and Winrich anticipate.

THE MODEL

Shibata and Winrich (1983, p. 432) devise a model in which the utility of consumers is maximized. Although their model is more general than the one presented here, their nonconvexity results in multiple optima, the choice of which '. . . depends upon the income distribution pattern that society deems best'. The more specific two-sector model of production-on-production externalities that is used here for examining the interaction of abatement and avoidance yields a single, unambiguous optimum. In this model, there are *m* identical firms in polluting industry *y* and *n* identical firms in receptor industry *x*. There is an inelastically supplied total quantity, L_0, of a single input, labour, which may be allocated into direct production by individual firms in quantities, L_x and L_y, into abatement, L_B, by each polluting firm and into avoidance, L_V, by each receptor firm.

The production function for good *y*, which is $Y(L_Y)$, exhibits increasing and then decreasing returns to direct labour. Each firm produces *Y* units of output and emits into the common body of water or air $E(L_B)$ units of pollution per unit of Y produced. $E(L_B)$, the emission factor, is a function of the level of abatement. The greater the quantity of labour, L_B, allocated to abatement the lower is $E(L_B)$ and therefore the partial derivative, E_L, is negative. The second derivative, E_{LL}, is assumed to be positive. The pollution flow or concentration in the body of water or air is:

$$e = m[E(L_B)]Y \tag{1}$$

The production function of good x, which is $X(L_X, Z)$, also exhibits increasing and then decreasing returns to direct labour. Production of this good is adversely affected by Z, which is pollution exposure. The derivative, X_L, is positive whereas X_Z and X_{LZ} are negative. The level of exposure inside each of the receptor firms depends upon the outside concentration, e, and upon avoidance, L_V, according to the function:

$$Z = Z(L_V, e) = [V(L_V, e)]e \tag{2}$$

where V, the avoidance factor that is multiplied times the concentration, e, is itself a function of e as well as the level of avoidance, L_V. It is assumed that the avoidance factor decreases as L_V increases (i.e. $V_L < 0$) and also as e increases (i.e. $V_e < 0$). The negative relationship between V and e, which implies that avoidance is more effective when the concentration is larger, follows from the observation of Shibata and Winrich (1983, p. 428) that 'the lower the density of pollutants in the environment, the more expensive it is to extract a given quantity of pollutants from it . . . [For example] the cost of reducing the water temperature by one degree increases as the river water's temperature approaches the normal temperature for the undisturbed river'. Although V_e is negative,

$$Z_e = eV_e + V > 0 \tag{3}$$

This follows from the chemical principle of diffusion between two mediums having different concentrations. It is also reasonable to assume that Z_L and Z_{eL} are negative and that Z_{LL} is positive. For simplicity, it is assumed that the production function for good x is decomposable in gross output and pollution damage, as in Meade (1952),

$$x = nX(L_x, Z) = n[F(L_x)][1 - Z] \tag{4}$$

so that total pollution damage equals nFZ.

The necessary conditions for a technically efficient allocation of inputs in a semi-interior solution in which the production of the polluting industry is fixed at y_0 and the variables L_X, L_Y, m and n are necessarily greater than zero whereas L_V and L_B are only non-negative, is derived from the following Lagrangian for the maximization of x:

$$\psi = nX(L_x, Z(mE(L_B)Y, L_V)) + \lambda[y_0 - mY(L_y)] + \mu[L_0 - nL_x - nL_V - mL_y - mL_B], \tag{5}$$

where parentheses indicate 'function of' and square brackets denote multiplication. The Kuhn–Tucker conditions, as prescribed by Baumol (1972, pp. 156–8), are:

$$\partial\psi/\partial L_x = nX_L - \mu n = 0 \tag{6}$$

$$\partial\psi/\partial L_V = nX_Z Z_L - \mu n \leq 0 \tag{7}$$

$$L_V[\partial\psi/\partial L_V] = 0 \tag{8}$$

$$\partial\psi/\partial L_Y = nX_Z Z_e mEY_L - \lambda mY_L - \mu m = 0 \tag{9}$$

$$\partial\psi/\partial L_B = nX_Z Z_e mE_L Y - \mu m \leq 0 \tag{10}$$

$$L_B[\partial\psi/\partial L_B] = 0 \tag{11}$$

$$\partial\psi/\partial n = X - \mu[L_x + L_V] = 0 \tag{12}$$

$$\partial\psi/\partial m = nX_Z Z_e EY - \lambda Y - \mu[L_Y + L_B] = 0 \tag{13}$$

It follows first from (6) and (12) and then from (6), (9) and (13) that:

$$X = X_L[L_X + L_V], \qquad Y = Y_L[L_Y + L_B]. \tag{14}$$

For efficiency, the number of firms, n and m, must adjust so that each firm operates at the scale at which the summed quantities of labour times the marginal product of direct labour exhausts the firm's total product. The simple form of condition (14) holds because of the Meade assumption on decomposability and also because the abate-

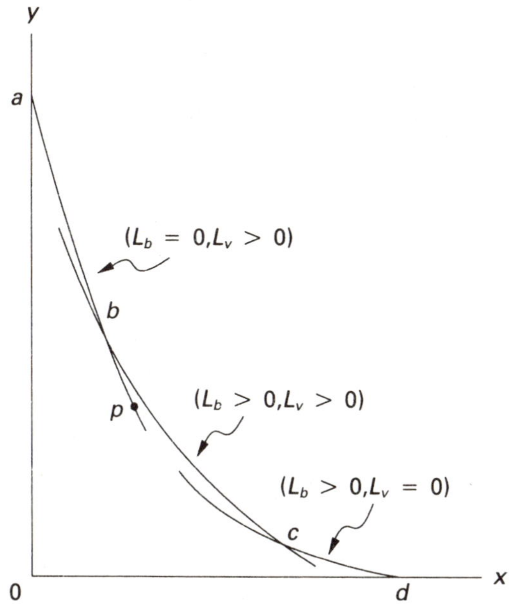

Figure 6.1 The case in which the Shibata and Winrich elasticity of interaction is less than unity or is equal to zero

ment and avoidance factors, E and V, are assumed to be independent of the levels of own output. Condition (14) also implies that when firms avoid or abate, they operate in the range of decreasing returns to direct labour, L_X and L_Y. (For more complex models in which E depends upon Y as well as L_B, see Kohn (1988a) and Harford (1989), and for models in which V depends upon X as well as upon e and L_V, see Shibata and Winrich (1983, p. 432) and Kohn (1987).

Because there is a single input in this two-sector economy and the numbers of firms are variable, the production possibility frontier is convex to the origin, as in Figure 6.1. If there were no externality, L_B and L_V would be zero and the frontier would be a perfectly straight line. In the model examined here, there are two possible shapes for the production possibility frontier. When the interactive effect between abatement and avoidance is relatively weak (or absent, as in Kohn 1988b), the frontier contains two kinks, one at b and another at c. If the community chooses to consume a combination of goods on the segment, ab, in which there are relatively many polluting firms and relatively few receptor firms, it is efficient for these few receptor firms to employ avoidance measures rather than for the many polluting firms to abate. If the community chooses a combination of goods on the segment, *cd*, in which there are relatively few polluting firms and relatively many receptor firms, then abatement alone is efficient. Conventional corner solutions such as these are considered in Coase (1960, p. 2) and in Mishan (1974, p. 1290) as well as in Shibata and Winrich (1983, p. 431). Although the inward bending of the frontier and the kinked intersections are themselves nonconvexities, these are not the focus of the present paper.

If consumers in this economy prefer a bundle of goods on the segment, *bc*, then a combination of abatement activity by polluting firms and avoidance activity by receptor firms is efficient. This is the case of multiple pollution control methods first modeled by Mishan (1974). When, however, the interactive effect of abatement and avoidance is sufficiently strong that one of the second-order conditions is violated, the middle segment, *bc*, in Figure 6.1 vanishes and points *b* and *c* coincide as in Figure 6.2. Then only the two types of corner solutions shown are efficient.

In all cases, regardless of whether the interaction between abatement and avoidance is absent, weak, or strong, the initial competitive equilibrium allocation occurs either on the curve, *aP*, in Figure 6.1, which extends to the horizontal axis and approaches point *d*, or on the curve, *aQgd*, in Figure 6.2. Along these upper segments of the two frontiers there is no abatement because, in the absence of Pigouvian intercession, polluting firms do not voluntarily spend money to abate. However, receptor firms do spend money on avoidance because, as Shibata and Winrich (1983, p. 436) explain, '. . . profit-maximizing victims will seldom remain passive but will defend themselves with the best methods available to them'.

The problem for Pigouvian policy occurs if the interactive effect is strong, but then only if, prior to government intercession, a combination of outputs on the segment, *bg*, of the inner curve, *bQgd*, in Figure 6.2 is chosen by consumers. Such a combination is characterized by point *Q*. Here, the marginal cost and damage data available to the government will misleadingly indicate that abatement is inefficient and therefore should not be induced. A marginal condition for this perverse state of affairs and a numerical example are presented in the following two sections of the paper.

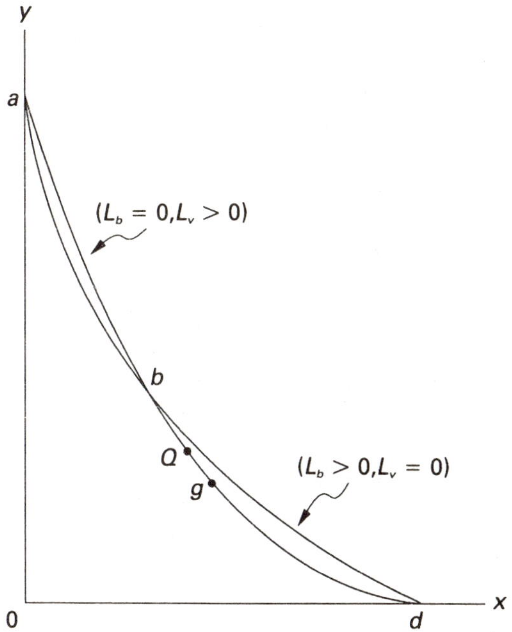

Figure 6.2 The case in which the Shibata and Winrich elasticity of interaction is greater than or equal to unity

MARGINAL CONDITIONS FOR EFFICIENCY AND A VIOLATED SECOND-ORDER CONDITION

If the strict equalities hold for Kuhn–Tucker conditions (7) and (10) above, it follows that:

$$nZ_e/Z_L = 1/(E_L Y) \qquad (15)$$

The term on the left, which is equivalent to $n[\partial L_V/\partial e]$, is the marginal cost, MCV, measured in labour units, of avoiding exposure equivalent to one whole unit of pollutant concentration, for all n receptor firms. The term on the right, equivalent to $\partial L_B/([\partial E]Y)$, is the marginal cost, MCB, measured in labour units, of abating one unit of pollutant concentration for each polluting firm. (That the marginal cost of avoidance for all receptor firms combined should equal the marginal cost of abatement of each individual polluting firm is a somewhat surprising result that Butler and Maher (1986) clarify graphically). Here, it is necessarily assumed that the threshold levels of *MCB* and *MCV* are greater than zero.

It follows from (6), (7) and (10) that:

$$MCV = MCB = nX_Z Z_e / X_L \qquad (16)$$

The term on the right, which is equivalent to $n[\partial L_X / \partial e]$, is the marginal pollution damage, *MPD*, per unit of concentration, measured in labour units and borne by the *n* receptor firms in industry *x*. It should be noted that *MCV*, *MCB* and *MPD* are mathematically negative but are interpreted as positive costs.

The second-order conditions for an internal solution on segment, *bc*, of the frontier in Figure 6.1, at which marginal condition (15) holds, require that the *MCV* curve slope upwards as L_V increases. This condition is illustrated by the upward sloping curve, MCV^1, in Figure 6.3. The *MCB* curve, which is independent of L_V, is a horizontal line.

In the strong interaction case depicted in Figure 6.2, there are only corner solutions. In the context of the numerical example developed here, there would never be an internal optimum in which L_V and L_B are simultaneously positive because the *MCV* curve would slope downwards as L_V increases. This is characterized by the dashed curve, MCV^2, in Figure 6.3. The implication of the downward-sloping curve is that a greater-than-marginal transfer of labour from abatement to avoidance would reduce the level of exposure *Z*. Therefore the intersection of a horizontal *MCB* curve and a downward-sloping *MCV* curve would never be associated with an optimum. This non-convexity is the necessary, though not sufficient, condition for the failure of Pigouvian taxation in the numerical example.

Because *MCV* is mathematically negative in this model, the *MCV* curve slopes downwards as L_V increases when:

$$\partial(MCV)/\partial L_V = n(Z_{eL} - Z_e Z_{LL}/Z_L)/Z_L > 0 \qquad (17)$$

This occurs when:

$$Z_{eL}/Z_e)/(Z_{LL}/Z_L) > 1 \qquad (18)$$

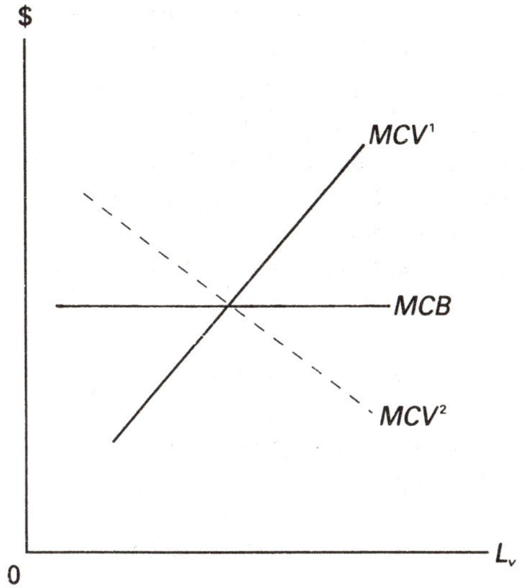

Figure 6.3 Alternative slopes of the marginal cost of avoidance curve depending upon whether the Shibata and Winrich elasticity of interaction is less than or greater than unity

This ratio of ratios may be treated as an elasticity, σ, in which:

$$\sigma = (Z_{eL}/Z_e)/(Z_{LL}/Z_L) = [(\partial Z_e/\partial L_V)/Z_e]/[\partial Z_L/\partial L_V)/Z_L] \quad (19)$$

The implication of (18) and (19) is that the term, Z_e, in the numerator of the *MCV*, falls proportionally more with an increase in L_V than the absolute value of Z_L in the denominator falls proportionately with the increase in L_V. If the interaction between abatement and avoidance, as represented by the numerator of (18) and (19), were relatively weak, then the stronger proportional decline in the marginal productivity of L_V, represented by the denominator of (18) and (19), would cause the marginal cost of avoidance to rise with L_V, as does the curve MCV^1 in Figure 6.3. When the interactive effect dominates the effect of the falling marginal productivity of L_V, a rise in L_V intensifies the Shibata and Winrich effect that a high pollution concentration has on the lowering of exposure. It follows that abatement, which would lower the concentration, and avoidance are then at cross purposes, so that one or the other, but not both together, would be efficient.

The elasticity, σ, which is useful for distinguishing weak and strong interaction, will be referred to as the Shibata and Winrich Elasticity of Interaction. All along the production possibility frontier in Figure 6.2, this elasticity is greater than 1. When the elasticity is less than 1 or equals zero, as it is along the frontier in Figure 6.1, an internal solution (in which $L_B > 0$ and $L_V > 0$) may be efficient.

The efficient corner solutions can be derived from the Kuhn–Tucker conditions by combining inequalities with equalities. In terms of absolute values they are:

$$MCV = MPD < MCB \qquad (20)$$

which holds for efficient combinations along the segment, *ab*, in Figures 6.1 and 6.2, and

$$MCB = MPD < MCV \qquad (21)$$

which hold along the segments, *cd* and *bd*.

A NUMERICAL SIMULATION

A simple example simulates, first, the case in which the Shibata and Winrich Elasticity is less than unity and an internal solution is optimal, and second, the case in which the Elasticity is greater than unity and there is the non-convexity that frustrates the application of Pigouvian correctives. The production functions in this simulation are:

$$X = [14L_x^2 - L_x^3][1 - Z] \qquad Y = 6L_Y^2 - L_y^3/3 \qquad (22)$$

The emission and avoidance factors are:

$$E = 1/(1{,}000{,}000[1 + L_B]) \qquad V = 1/(1 + e^{\alpha}L_V) \qquad (23)$$

and the resource constraint, L_0, is 30,000. The interaction between abatement and avoidance is weak when $0 \leq \alpha < 1$ and strong when $\alpha \geq 1$.

A competitive equilibrium allocation, in a weak interaction case in which $\alpha = 0.75$ and consumers purchase the combination $y = mY = 525{,}000$ and $x = nX = 312{,}082$, occurs when $L_X = 7.571140$, $L_Y =$

9.0, $L_B = 0$, $L_V = 1.635910$, $m = 2160.494$, and $n = 1146.464$, and is characterized by the point, *P*, in Figure 6.1. Assume that the government is able to measure marginal pollution costs, which (in labour units) are $MCV = MPD = 4433.74$ and $MCB = 4115.23$. It would then set the Pigouvian tax (or sell discharge permits) at 4433.74 per unit of emissions.[1]

The tax would induce polluters to abate and cause the price of good *y* to rise, whereas the reduction in pollution damage to individual firms would cause the market price of good *x* to decline. As a consequence of the change in relative prices, consumers would purchase more of good *x* and less of good *y*. In the absence of a community utility function, it can be shown that the new equilibrium allocation is superior to the old by assuming that the Pareto efficient allocation, achieved by an iterative sequence of Pigouvian prices, is one in which consumers purchase the same 525,000 units of good *y* along with 312,459 units of good *x*. This new allocation, which is characterized by a point directly to the right of *P*, on the segment, *bc*, in Figure 6.1, occurs when $L_X = 7.487426$, $L_Y = 9.076771$, $L_B = 0.1589181$, $L_V = 1.318075$, $m = 2142.376$ and $n = 1159.920$, and $MCV = MCB = MPD = 5480.77$. The respective Shibata and Winrich Elasticities for the two allocations are less than unity (0.799 and 0.817) and the observable marginal pollution costs effectively signal the path to an efficient Pigouvian solution.[2]

A competitive equilibrium allocation, in the strong interaction case in which $\alpha = 1.25$ and consumers purchase the combination $y = 525{,}000$ and $x = 294{,}396$ occurs when $L_X = 7.588392$, $L_Y = 9.0$, $L_B = 0$, $L_V = 1.705863$, $m = 2160.494$, and $n = 1135.708$. Such an allocation is characterized by point, *Q*, in Figure 6.2. Here the Shibata and Winrich Elasticity is 1.27 and the misleading marginal costs are $MCV = MPD = 3918.15$ and $MCB = 4115.23$. If the Pigouvian price is conventionally set at 3918.15, the resulting competitive equilibrium on the segment, *bgd*, in Figure 6.2, is inefficient. The Pareto efficient allocation is actually on the outer frontier segment, *bd*. However, there are no marginal signals to indicate that *Q* is any less efficient than combinations on the outer segment, *bd*. The Shibata and Winrich (1983) dilemma for Pigouvian taxation illustrates anew the problem of nonconvexity so aptly expressed by Baumol and Bradford (1972, p. 173) and so pertinent here: 'Even if we know the entire set of feasible output vectors, equilibrium prices usually tell us nothing about the Pareto-optimality of current output or even the direction in which to seek improvement'.

Nor does an emission tax set at 4115.23 or even 4200 initiate an iterative Pigouvian sequence of improvements. The allocation at Q is a local maximum and small amounts of abatement cause total outputs to decline rather than to increase. What is needed is a Pigouvian tax rate high enough to stimulate a level of abatement such that the resulting allocation of inputs is one in which the *MPD* (which equals the *MCV*) is higher, rather than lower, than the *MCB*. Then successively higher tax rates, prompted by appropriate $MCB < MPD$ signals, finally lead to the global optimum on the outer segment, *bd*, of the production possibility frontier. To demonstrate that the attained allocation is superior to the old in terms of pure output levels, it will be assumed that the new allocation is one in which $y = 525{,}000$ and $x = 307{,}531$. This combination of outputs, characterized by a point on the outer segment, *bd*, in Figure 6.2, directly to the right of Q, occurs when $L_X = 7.0$, $L_Y = 9.334833$, $L_B = 0.7818423$, $L_V = 0$, $m = 2085.886$ and $n = 1271.110$. Here (where the Shibata and Winrich Elasticity is 1.125), $MCB = MPD = 12{,}614$ and $MCV = 19{,}874$. The decline in pollution because of abatement will have raised the marginal cost of avoidance so that abatement alone is efficient. It may seem strange that the efficient level of *MPD* exceeds the initial level. This may hold regardless of whether or not there are nonconvexities (see Kohn 1988b, Table 6.1, p. 155) and is often the case if the kind of upward-iterative sequence of Pigouvian tax rates assumed by Shibata and Winrich (1983, p. 434) is to approach the efficient rate.

Although the Shibata and Winrich Elasticity of Interaction exceeds unity for competitive allocations along the outer frontier segment, *ab*, in Figure 6.2, there is no problem for a Pigouvian approach because $MCV = MPD < MCB$ in both the initial competitive and the Pareto optimal allocations. This is what Shibata and Winrich (1983, p. 435) call the laissez-faire case, in which an emissions tax or the sale of discharge permits is needed only to correct the marginal rate of substitution in consumption and, as Oates (1983, p. 372) observes, 'to provide the proper longer-run incentives for entry and exit decisions'.

At some point, *b*, on the curve *abgd*, and continuing to point *g*, the strong interaction between abatement and avoidance is a problem for Pigouvian approaches. Unfortunately, there are no marginal signals to indicate where point *b* lies or when and by how much the Pigouvian price should be set above the initial levels of *MPD*. Moving downward along the curve, *abgd*, in Figure 6.2, e and L_V decline and

n increases, and as a result, MCV rises. Eventually a point is reached, denoted by g, at which $MCV = MPD = MCB$. Below g, points along the segment, gd, characterize initial competitive allocations in which $MCV = MPD > MCB$. Along this final segment, Pigouvian approaches are again workable.

SUMMARY

When polluting firms abate, the resulting reduction in the pollution concentration may reduce the effectiveness of victims' avoidance activities. The consequence of this interaction, discovered by Shibata and Winrich (1983), is that Pigouvian prescriptions for pollution control may be unworkable. In this paper, a model is developed that incorporates this interaction between abatement and avoidance and demonstrates the failure of Pigouvian taxation.

It is shown that the interaction must be unusually strong for the Shibata and Winrich non-convexity to occur. In the context of the model presented here, the strength of the interaction is measured by the Shibata and Winrich Elasticity of Interaction. If that elasticity is less than unity, there is no non-convexity even though the interaction may be present. If the elasticity is greater than unity, the Shibata and Winrich non-convexity does exist, although the problem for Pigouvian approaches is confined to a critical subsection of the production possibility frontier. Although this critical subsection of the frontier is relatively small in the numerical example, empirical research is required to determine if it is indeed that small in reality.[3]

If consumers choose a combination of outputs on this critical segment of the production possibility frontier, and the government sets a Pigouvian tax on emissions equal to marginal pollution damage at that point, the tax will be insufficient to induce abatement. What is required in this critical region, but would be inefficient elsewhere, is a tax that is significantly larger than current marginal pollution damage. Such a tax would induce abatement and discourage avoidance, which in this region of the frontier is inefficient.

Although the model presented here is successful in replicating the interaction between abatement and avoidance and demonstrating how the Pigouvian approach breaks down, it must be emphasized that this model is much less general than that of Shibata and Winrich (1983) and lacks the broader potential they envision for the violation of second-order conditions. As a result, this model fails to replicate their case (1983, p. 426) in which, '. . . even when all the methods should be used simultaneously, equalization of their marginal costs does not necessarily optimize their utilization'. Nor does the model replicate their case (1983, p. 433) in which 'a correct efficient tax must depart from the Pigouvian dictum to take into account the externality that a marginal change in the scale of prevention imposes on the defense cost'. (In the simple model presented here the standard Pigouvian tax, set equal to conventionally measured marginal pollution damage, is still efficient. The problem is one of determining when the marginal pollution damage is at its efficient level.) It may be hoped that future research along lines begun here will succeed in capturing more of the richness of results obtained by Shibata and Winrich.

Notes

* An earlier version of this paper was presented at the annual meeting of the Illinois Economic Association on 12 October 1990. I am grateful to the discussant, Richard M. Peck, for his helpful comments.

1. The solutions, which are rounded to seven digits, are obtained with a computerized iterative algorithm in which x is maximized subject to a given value of y. The calculation of the Pareto optimal solutions is simplified by incorporating the equalities in (14). The derivatives that are needed for calculating MCV, MCB, MPD, and σ are as follows:

$$X_z = -(14L_X^2 - L_X^3), \quad X_L = (28L_X - 3L_X^2)(1 - Z)$$
$$Z_e = (1 + e^{\alpha}L_V[1 - \alpha])/(1 + e^{\alpha}L_V)^2$$
$$Z_L = -(e^{1+\alpha})/(1 + e^{\alpha}L_V)^2, \quad E_L = -1(1{,}000{,}000[1 + L_B]^2)$$
$$Z_{eL} = (-[1 + \alpha]e^{\alpha} - [1 - \alpha]e^{2\alpha}L_V)/(1 + e^{\alpha}L_V)^3$$
$$Z_{LL} = 2e^{2\alpha+1}/(1 + e^{\alpha}L_v)^3$$

2. Substituting the derivatives from footnote 1 into equation (19) yields the following expression for the elasticity:

$$\sigma = (1 + \alpha/[1 + e^{\alpha}L_V(1 - \alpha)])/2$$

Because the parameters were chosen so that e would always be less than 1 and because Z is less than 1 by definition, it can be shown that if α is less (greater) than 1, σ is less (greater) than 1.

3. The reader may wish to gauge the relative lengths of the segments in Figure 6.2 in the context of the numerical example. The coordinates of the four points of interest are approximately: $a(x = 0; y = 810{,}000)$, $b(x =$

263,070; $y = 552{,}900$), $g(x = 300{,}163; y = 520{,}000)$, and $d(x = 1{,}470{,}000; y = 0)$. It follows that the critical region of the frontier, in which the correct signals for Pigouvian taxation are absent, includes no more than 3 or 4 per cent of the maximum producible quantities of either good.

References

1. Baumol, W. J. (1972), *Economic Theory and Operations Analysis* (Englewood Cliffs: Prentice-Hall).
2. Baumol, W. J. (1972) 'On taxation and the control of externalities', *American Economic Review*, vol. 62.
3. Baumol, W. J. and Bradford, D. F. (1972) 'Detrimental externalities and non-convexity of the production set', *Economica*, vol. 39.
4. Butler, R. V. and Maher, M. D. (1986) 'The control of externalities: abatement vs. damage prevention', *Southern Economic Journal*, vol. 52.
5. Coase, R. H. (1960) 'The problem of social cost', *Journal of Law and Economics*, vol. 3.
6. Harford, J. (1989) 'Efficient scale of the pollution-abating firm: comment', *Land Economics*, vol. 65.
7. Kohn, R. E. (1987) 'The technology of pollution avoidance by firms', *Public Finance/Finances Publiques*, vol. 42.
8. Kohn, R. E. (1988a) 'Efficient scale of the pollution-abating firm', *Land Economics*, vol. 64. (Pages 58 and 59 should be interchanged.)
9. Kohn, R. E. (1988b) 'Efficiency in abatement and avoidance', *Socio-Economic Planning Sciences*, vol. 22.
10. Kohn, R. E. and Aucamp, D. C. (1976) 'Abatement, avoidance, and nonconvexity', *American Economic Review*, vol. 66.
11. Meade, J. E. (1952) 'External economies and diseconomies in a competitive situation', *Economic Journal*, vol. 62.
12. Mishan, E. J. (1974) 'What is the optimal level of pollution?', *Journal of Political Economy*, vol. 82.
13. Oates, W. E. (1983) 'The regulation of externalities: efficient behavior by sources and victims', *Public Finance/Finances Publiques*, vol. 38.
14. Shibata, H. and Winrich, J. S. (1983) 'Control of pollution when the offended defend themselves', *Economica*, vol. 50.
15. Slater, M. (1975) 'The quality of life and the shape of marginal loss curves', *Economic Journal*, vol. 85.
16. Starrett, D. A. (1972) 'Fundamental nonconvexities in the theory of externalities', *Journal of Economic Theory*, vol. 4.

7 Bertrand's Duopoly as an Edgeworth Exchange Game

Takashi Negishi

INTRODUCTION

Among the many important contributions of Professor Hirofumi Shibata to the development of economic theory, one can certainly find several seminal articles on various problems in welfare economics. According to the so-called fundamental theorem of welfare economics, a perfectly competitive allocation is Pareto optimal and any Pareto optimal allocation can be achieved through perfect competition and a proper income redistribution. Roughly speaking, this implies that perfect competition is a sufficient condition for optimal allocation. It does not mean, however, that price-taking-behaviour is necessary for optimal allocation. On this occasion, to congratulate Professor Shibata on his sixtieth birthday, I shall discuss a small problem in welfare economics, namely that of an optimal allocation achieved by non-price-taking behaviour.

Bertrand's duopoly model, which is suggested by his criticism of Cournot's duopoly model, has been traditionally considered, like Cournot's, as a non-cooperative game between duopoly firms – see Cournot (1897) and Bertrand (1883). However, the aim of this note is to consider it as an Edgeworth game of exchange (or more precisely as an Edgeworth-Farrell game) among duopoly firms and consumers.

In the following section, I shall sketch Cournot and Bertrand's duopoly models and suggest the possibility of considering Bertrand's model as an Edgeworth game of exchange. An Edgeworth box diagram is constructed in the next section with the purpose of analysing the exchange between consumers' money expenditure and the products of firms. The section after that is devoted to showing that Bertrand's duopoly equilibrium is the core of such a game, and is identical to the competitive (marginal cost pricing) equilibrium.

THE COURNOT AND BERTRAND DUOPOLY MODELS

Consider a case of a duopoly industry which is dominated by two firms. The demand function for the duopolists' product, call it the demand function for the industry, is an aggregate of the demand functions of the infinite number of individual consumers. If one assumes that the demand function for the industry slopes downwards, then:

$$q = D(p), \frac{dq}{dp} < 0 \tag{1}$$

where p is the price consumers take as given and q is the aggregate quantity demanded by them. Then, the inverse demand function

$$p = p(q), \frac{dp}{dq} < 0 \tag{2}$$

is obtained from (1). The condition for the equality of demand and supply in the industry is $q_1 + q_2 = q$, where q_1 and q_2 are the respective quantities to be supplied by the first and second firms. The profit for the first firm is:

$$p(q_1 + q_2)q_1 - cq_1 \tag{3}$$

and that for the second firm is:

$$p(q_1 + q_2)q_2 - cq_2 \tag{4}$$

where c denotes the identical marginal cost, assumed to be constant. In other words, the profit of a firm is a function not only of its own supply but also of the supply of the other firm.

As is well known, Cournot considered the Nash solution that each firm will independently maximize its profit with respect to its own supply, assuming that the supply of the other is unchanged. The conditions for this are obtained by the differentiation of (3) with respect to q_1 and (4) with respect to q_2,

$$p(q_1 + q_2) + q_1 p'(q_1 + q_2) - c = 0 \tag{5}$$

and

$$p(q_1 + q_2) + q_2p'(q_1 + q_2) - c = 0 \tag{6}$$

where p' denotes the derivative of p. By solving (5) for q_1, one gets the reaction function for the first firm, $q_1 = R_1(q_2)$. Similarly, the reaction function for the second firm is obtained from (6) as $q_2 = R_2(q_1)$. If one draws the reaction curves for the two firms corresponding respectively to reaction functions R_1 and R_2 in a $q_1 - q_2$ diagram, the Cournot–Nash solution $(\bar{q}_1, \bar{q}_2)$ is obtained at the intersection of the two reaction curves.

Suppose now, following Bertrand, that each duopolistic firm assumes that the other will keep its price (not supply) unchanged. If the price is higher than c, i.e. the identical marginal (as well as average) cost, each firm will undercut its rival by a very small margin because it will monopolize the market and obtain maximum profit by undercutting infinitesimally. This process continues until the price is equalized to the marginal cost c. The reaction function for the first firm is given for $p_2 \geq c$ as:

$$p_1 = R_1(p_2) = a(p_2 - c) + c \tag{7}$$

where p_1 and p_2 are, respectively, the prices charged by the first and second firms and a is a positive constant infinitesimally smaller than 1. Similarly, the reaction function for the second firm is given as:

$$p_2 = R_2(p_2) = a(p_1 - c) + c \tag{8}$$

for $p_1 \geq c$. Figure 7.1 shows the reaction curves for the two firms which correspond, respectively, to reaction functions R_1 and R_2 as defined in (7) and (8). The equilibrium for Bertrand's duopoly is given by the intersection of the two reaction curves, at point B, where $(p_1, p_2) = (c, c)$.

The equilibrium for Cournot's duopoly, $(q_1, q_2) = (\bar{q}_1, \bar{q}_2)$, is a Nash solution which satisfies:

$$M_1(\bar{q}_1, \bar{q}_2) \geq M_1(q_1, \bar{q}_2),\ M_2(\bar{q}_1, \bar{q}_2) \geq M_2(\bar{q}_1, q_2) \tag{9}$$

where M_1 and M_2 are, respectively, the profits of the first and second firms. Similarly, the equilibrium for Bertrand's duopoly, $(p_1, p_2) = (c, c)$, is a Nash solution which satisfies:

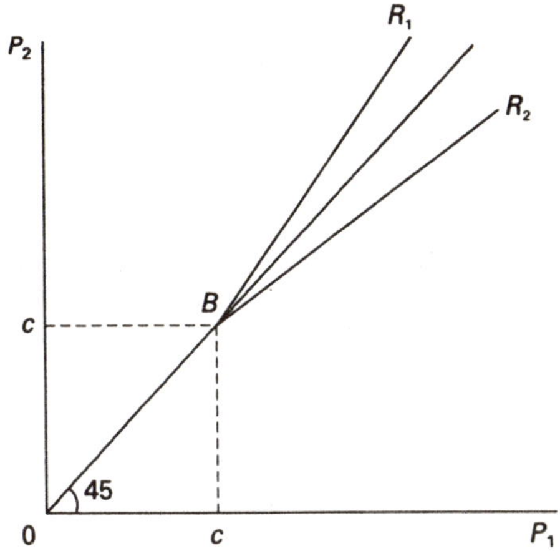

Figure 7.1

$$M_1(c, c) \geq M_1(p_1, c), M_2(c, c) \geq M_2(c, p_2) \qquad (10)$$

If Bertrand's duopoly is seen, like Cournot's, as a non-cooperative game between two firms, then, the Bertrand equilibrium is formally identical to Cournot's, both resulting in a Nash solution to this game. The only difference between them is that the quantities supplied are the strategies for firms in the Cournot case, while they are prices charged by firms in the Bertrand case. However, there is an important economic difference between the two since $p(\bar{q}_1 + \bar{q}_2) > c$ in view of (5) and/or (6).

In the traditional interpretation of both the Bertrand and Cournot duopoly models, only firms are considered as players in the game. Also, a firms' profits are assumed to depend not only on its own actions, but also on the actions of other play. Moreover, the firms may act strategically, taking their repercussions into consideration. In other words, consumers are not regarded as explicit players in such games, rather they are regarded as a part of the environment within which the games are played by the firms. It is certainly true that the role the consumers play in the Cournot model is very limited, since they merely adjust their demand to the prices given by the auctioneers who change prices so as to equate the demand with the supply as determined by the firms. However, in the Bertrand model, consumers are more active, since they not only adjust their demand continuously to prices but also drastically shift their demand from one firm to the other. In other words, consumers form a coalition with a firm so as to block the current conditions and to improve their position in the market. This suggests the possibility of perceiving the Bertrand duopoly model from the point of view of an Edgeworth game among consumers and firms.

Using box diagrams, Edgeworth considered games of exchange between two types of traders. An equilibrium in an Edgeworth game of exchange is called a core and is defined as a distribution of goods among traders, which cannot be blocked by any coalition of a subset of players which is formed with the aim of improving by themselves the position of at least some of the members without worsening that of any of them. As is well known, Edgeworth showed that the core of such a game is equivalent to the competitive (price-taking) equilibrium of exchange if the number of traders of each type is infinitely large. This equivalence theorem was then extended by Farrell to the case of duopoly in which there are only two traders of one type and infinitely many traders of another type – see Edgeworth (1881), Farrell (1970) and Negishi (1989).

BERTRAND'S MODEL FASHIONED THE EDGEWORTH WAY

Now let us consider the Bertrand duopoly model as a game between two identical firms which have the same constant unit cost, c, and infinitely many identical consumers with the same taste and same amount of money. It is convenient to use an Edgeworth box diagram of exchange between the product to be supplied by the firms and the money to be spent by a half of infinitely many consumers. In Figure 7.2, the quantity of the product is measured horizontally, and the amount of money vertically. The quantity of the product and the amount of the money to be distributed to all the customers of the firm (a half of all the consumers) are measured from the origin A, while the amount of money to be distributed to the firm and the quantity of the product to be produced by it are measured from the origin B. The vertical distance between A and B represents the quantity of money initially held by all the customers of the firm, while the horizontal distance between B and C is the quantity of the product, the cost of which is equal to AB. In other words, $AB = cBC$.

The curves in Figure 7.2 which are drawn convex to origin A are the indifference curves of the consumers. I shall assume that the identical indifference curves of the infinitely many consumers are

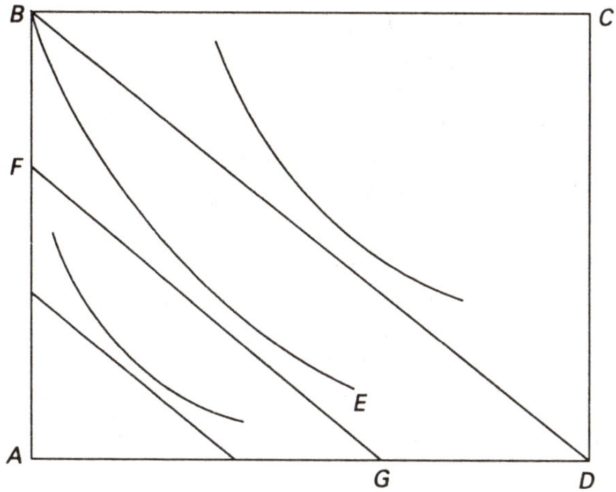

Figure 7.2

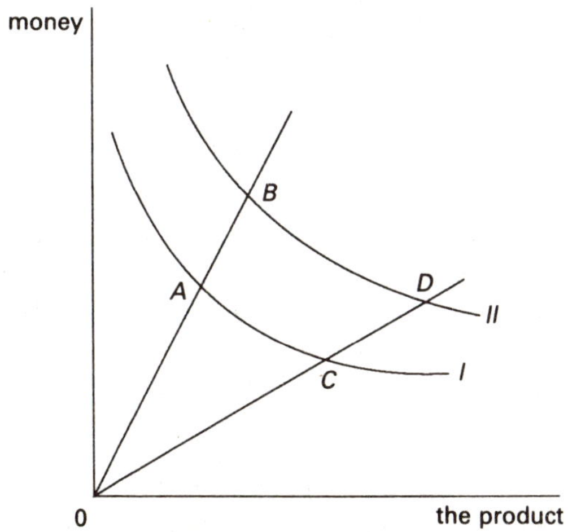

Figure 7.3

homothetic so that the marginal rate of substitution between the product and money depends only on the ratio of the quantities of the product and the amounts of money; this is depicted in Figure 7.3. Since the slopes of indifference curves in Figure 7.3 are identical at *A* and *B*, and at *C* and *D*, one can aggregate indifference curves *I* of two identical consumers into aggregate indifference curve *II* which is also an indifference curve for an individual consumer when the quantity of the product and the amount of money are doubled. In general, homothetic indifference curves of an infinitely many identical consumers can be interpreted as aggregate indifference curves as well as indifference curves of individual consumers.

In Figure 7.2, the downward-sloping parallel lines are the equi-profit lines for the firm, since the identical slopes of these lines represent the average (as well as marginal) cost *c* for the firm. The line *BD* indicates the distributions with zero profit while the profit corresponding to the line *FG* is indicated by *BF*. If there is any equilibrium in the Bertrand duopoly model, the corresponding point of distribution after the exchange cannot be located above the line *BD* in Figure 7.2, since the profit of the firm should be non-negative. In the terminology of an Edgeworth game, a distribution above the line *BD* is blocked by a coalition consisting of only one firm, since the firm can increase its profit to zero at *B*. Similarly, the equilibrium point cannot be located below the indifference curve *BE*, since a consumers' surplus must result from the exchange; otherwise, the distribution will be blocked by a coalition consisting of only the consumers.

THE BERTRAND/EDGEWORTH EQUILIBRIUM

Since there are two identical firms in the industry, we have two identical box diagrams: one for the first firm and its customers (a half of all the consumers) and the other for the second firm and its customers (the other half of all the consumers). However, the equilibrium points in the two diagrams should give the same average price for the product. Suppose this is not the case. In Figure 7.4, which is a reproduction of Figure 7.2, point *I* represents the equilibrium for the first firm and its customers, and point *II*, the equilibrium for the second firm and its customers. Note that the second firm charges the lower average price indicated by the slope of *BB*″, while the first firm charges the higher average price indicated by the slope of *BB*′. Such a distribution, however, cannot be an equilibrium one for the duopoly model, since it can be blocked by a coalition between one of the firms and some of its consumers.

Assume that both the utility and profits at point *II* are higher than that at point *I*, then consider a coalition between the first firm (i.e. the higher pricing firm) and its customers (a half of all the consumers). By lowering the price to *BB*″ and changing the distribution

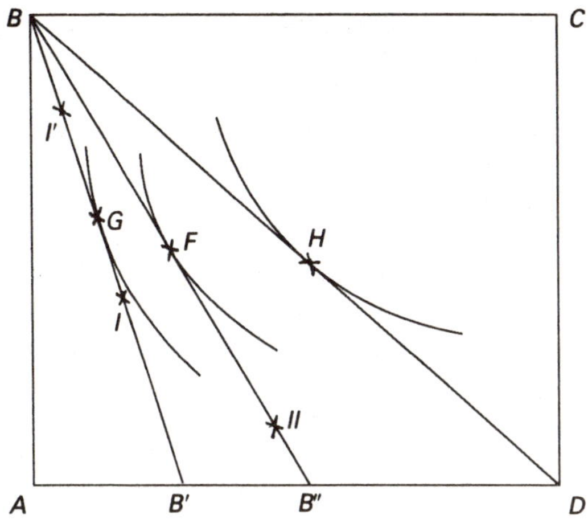

Figure 7.4

between them to point *II*, both the firm's profit and the consumers' utility will increase in the coalition, so that the distribution (*I*, *II*) will be blocked by the coalition, i.e. by the lowering of the price by the higher pricing firm and by the consumers adjusting to it. However, if the profit is higher at *I* than at *II*, then consider a coalition between the second firm (the one charging the lower price) and the customers of the first firm. By raising the price to *BB′* and choosing a point between *G* and *I*, both the firm's profit and the consumers' utility can be increased through the coalition, so that the distribution (*I*, *II*) will again be blocked by the coalition, i.e. by the raising of the price by the lower pricing firm and by the consumers adjusting to it.

Now, assume that in Figure 7.4 the utility at point *I* is higher than that at point *II*, but profit is higher at *II* than at *I*, then consider a coalition between the first firm (with the higher price) and the customers of the second firm. By lowering the price to *BB″* and choosing a point between *F* and *II*, both the profit of the firm and the utility of consumers concerned are increased in the coalition, so that the distribution (*I*, *II*) will again be blocked by the coalition, i.e. by the lowering of price by the higher pricing firm and by the consumers concerned adjusting to it.

Finally, assume that the profit is higher at *I* than at *II*, then consider a coalition between the second firm and its customers with the purpose of changing the distribution between them to point *I*.

The distribution (*I*, *II*) will be blocked by the price increase by the lower pricing firm and by its consumers adjusting to it.[1]

Since all possible cases have been entertained, it follows that it has been demonstrated that the equilibrium points, if any, for Bertrand's duopoly model must have an identical average price for the product in two box diagrams. Suppose, such a price to be that indicated by the line BB' in Figure 7.4, and I and I' are equilibrium, respective, points for the exchange between the first firm and its customers, and that between the second firm and its customers. The distribution (I, I'), however, can be blocked by a coalition between a firm and some consumers. Suppose that the utility is higher at I than at I'. The coalition between the second firm and its customers will block I' and move to I, since the profit is also higher at I than at I'. Suppose next that the utility is higher at I' than at I, and consider a coalition between the second firm and the customers of the first firm. The second firm will expand its output to a point between I' and I so that its profit should increase and so should the utility of consumers in the coalition. The equilibrium for the Bertrand model must, then, be identical in the two box diagrams.

Therefore, one needs to consider only one box diagram to find the equilibrium for a Bertrand duopoly model. Suppose that it is on the price line BB' in Figure 7.4. If it is like I', located between B and G, it will be blocked by a coalition between any one firm and its customers (i.e. half of all the consumers) since both the profit and the utility can be increased by moving to point G. In other words, such a distribution will be blocked by the expansion of any firm and the adjustments of customers to it. If it is located like I between G and B', including G, consider a coalition between any one firm, all of its customers and some of the customers of the other firm. By expanding its output (moving I downwards along BB'), the firm can increase its profit. Whereever the firm's customers may be located, at the new position of I, those of the other firm, who will join the coalition, are at B, since they will cancel their exchange with the other firm. The average position of consumers in the coalition can then be located at G, so that they are better off (or not worse off) than they were at the old position of I, provided the number of customers for the other firm who are to join the coalition is properly chosen.[2] By lowering the price slightly (by pivoting BB' to the right around B), all the consumers in the coalition can be made better off in comparison with their old situation at I. Thus, a distribution with the price higher than the marginal cost c will be blocked by the slight lowering of the price and the expansion of the output of a firm and by the consumers' adjustment to the lower price, including the selection of the firm (from which to buy) as well as the quantity. This is precisely the process of adjustments suggested by Bertrand.

Now, only points on line *BD* with slope *c* remain to be considered. If such points are between *B* and *H*, they can be blocked by the expansion of any firm and the adjustments of its customers. Points between *H* and *D* cannot be blocked by a coalition to expand output and to reduce the price. However, since the profit is zero at such points, they can be blocked by the reduction of output of a firm and adjustments of its customers to it. Then, only distribution *H* remains unblocked by coalitions. This is the core of the Bertrand duopoly model when considered as an Edgeworth game.[3] The equilibrium price in the Bertrand duopoly model has to be equal to the marginal cost *c*.

Notes

1. The limiting case, where both utility and profit are identical at *I* and *II*, can also be blocked either by the lowering of price and expansion by the lower pricing firm or by the raising of price and contraction by the higher pricing firm.
2. In the case of constant marginal cost, the number of consumers need not be infinite, since one can make the new position of *I* such that $BG = GI$, so that all the customers of the other firms join the coalition. In the case of increasing marginal cost, however, the equi-profit curves will be convex to the origin *C*, in Figure 7.4, and the output might not be increased by so much.
3. Edgeworth (1925, p. 118) came very close to this conclusion, but was prevented from reaching it, possibly because he was more interested in the case with no equilibrium due to the existence of capacity limits, and because he might not have fully realized the possibility of extending his limit theorem to the case of duopoly.

References

1. Bertrand, J. (1883) 'Review of Walras': *Théorie mathematique de la richesse sociale* and Cournot's: *Recherches sur les principes mathématiques de la théorie des richesse', Journal des Savants*.
2. Cournot, A. (1897), *Researches into the Mathematical Principles of the Theory of Wealth* (Bacon tr.; Macmillan).

3. Edgeworth, F. Y. (1881), *Mathematical Psychics* (Kegan Paul).
4. Edgeworth, F. Y. (1925), *Papers Relating to Political Economy* (London: Macmillan).
5. Farrell, M. J. (1970) 'Edgeworth bounds for oligopoly price', *Economica*, vol. 37.
6. Negishi, T. (1989), *History of Economic Theory* (Amsterdam: North-Holland).

8 Alternative Firm Objectives and the Welfare Effects of Entry

Kotaro Suzumura*

INTRODUCTION

In an industry characterized by economies of scale, entry of new firms leads to undesirable duplication of fixed costs, so that it is technologically more efficient to have a smaller number of larger firms than to have a larger number of smaller firms. From the viewpoint of allocative efficiency, however, oligopolistic market distortion is greater when there are fewer and larger firms than when there are more and smaller firms. Recently it was shown by Mankiw and Whinston (1986) and Suzumura and Kiyono (1987) that the merit of securing higher technological efficiency outweighs the demerit of incurring lower allocative efficiency in a wide class of oligopolistic industries with a result that the socially second-best number of firms is smaller than the equilibrium number of firms.

The implication of this simple result is rather serious, as it goes squarely counter to the widespread presumption that free entry is always desirable for the enhancement of economic welfare. So important is the message of this simple result that careful scrutiny of the robustness thereof seems to be called for. Several existing works along this line include Konishi, Okuno-Fujiwara and Suzumura (1990) and Vickers (1989) – see also Vickers and Yarrow (1988, Ch. 3). The former shows, among others, that the so-called 'excess entry theorem', which was originally established in the framework of partial equilibrium analysis, can essentially be preserved in the presence of general equilibrium interactions, whereas the latter exemplifies the message that the theorem is in need for substantial qualification if one were to discard the assumption of symmetric equilibrium.

Throughout the preceding analyses, however, it is commonly assumed that the oligopolistic firms are profit maximizers pure and simple.[1] In view of many alternative hypotheses on the firm objectives which are put forward in the literature, it is worthwhile to investigate if the message of the excess entry theorem is kept intact even when firms are not simply maximizing profits. In the spirit of a case study, I shall analyse this problem when firms are profit-constrained sales-maximizers in the sense of Baumol (1958) and Portes (1968).[2] In the next section, I shall introduce my model of oligopolistic competition among profit-constrained sales-maximizers. It will be shown that the excess entry theorem indeed needs several qualifications if firms are not pure and simple profit maximizers. In the following section, it is exemplified that this need is for real and cannot be thrown out as pathological. The note concludes with a section on some observations.

A MODEL OF COMPETITION AMONG PROFIT-CONSTRAINED SALES-MAXIMIZERS

Consider a single homogeneous product market. The inverse demand function for the product is denoted by $p = f(Q)$, where p is price and Q is aggregate output in the market. I assume that $f(\cdot)$ is twice continuously differentiable and $f'(Q) < 0$ for all $Q \geq 0$ with $f(Q) \geq 0$. When there are n firms, the profit of firm i is denoted by

$$\pi_i(\mathbf{q}) = f(Q)q_i - c(q_i) \quad i = 1, 2, \ldots, n \tag{1}$$

where $\mathbf{q} = (q_1, q_2, \ldots, q_n)$, $Q = \Sigma_{i=1}^{n} q_i$, and $c(\cdot)$ is the cost function which is common for all firms. It is assumed that $c(\cdot)$ is twice continuously differentiable with $c'(q) > 0$ for all $q \geq 0$.

I assume that each firm i tries to maximize its sales revenue $f(Q)q_i$ subject to the minimum profit constraint $\pi_i(\mathbf{q}) \geq \pi_0$, where π_0 is the minimum permissible level of profit. Assuming Cournot conjecture, and letting λ_i denote the Lagrange multiplier for firm i, the Kuhn–Tucker first order conditions are given by:

$$(1 + \lambda_i)\{f'(Q)q_i + f(Q)\} - \lambda_i c'(q_i) \leq 0 \quad i = 1, 2, \ldots, n \tag{2}$$

$$\sum_{i=1}^{n} q_i[(1 + \lambda_i)\{f'(Q)q_i + f(Q)\} - \lambda_i c'(q_i)] = 0 \tag{3}$$

$$f(Q)q_i - c(q_i) \geq \pi_0; \quad i = 1, 2, \ldots, n \tag{4}$$

$$\sum_{i=1}^{n} \lambda_i\{f(Q)q_i - c(q_i) - \pi_0\} = 0 \tag{5}$$

where $q_i \geq 0$ and $\lambda_i \geq 0$ for $i = 1, 2, \ldots, n$.

Throughout this note, I shall concentrate on the symmetric equilibrium where the equilibrium firm output $q_*(n)$ and the Lagrange multiplier value at equilibrium $\lambda_*(n)$ are both positive. Note that the positivity of $\lambda_*(n)$ requires that the minimum profit constraint is binding at equilibrium, which is guaranteed if marginal revenue is positive at equilibrium – see Baumol (1958, pp. 61–2) and Portes (1968, p. 237).

It follows from (2), (3), (4) and (5) that, at equilibrium, one has:

$$f(nq_*(n)) + q_*(n)f'(nq_*(n)) = \Lambda_*(n)c'(q_*(n)) \tag{6}$$

$$f(nq_*(n))q_*(n) - c(q_*(n)) = \pi_0 \tag{7}$$

where $\Lambda_*(n) = \lambda_*(n)/\{1 + \lambda_*(n)\}$. It is clear that $0 < \Lambda_*(n) < 1$.

Let $N(\pi_0)$ denote a set of positive numbers such that the system (6) and (7) have an economically meaningful solution $\{q_*(n), \lambda_*(n)\}$ if and only if $n \in N(\pi_0)$. The succeeding analysis applies only to the case where the incumbent number of firms lies in $N(\pi_0)$.

To gauge the welfare performance of this industry, define the net market surplus function $W(q, n)$ by:

$$W(q, n) = \int_0^{nq} f(Q)dQ - nc(q) \tag{8}$$

which is nothing other than the sum of consumers' and producers' surpluses. Along the lines of Mankiw and Whinston (1986) and Suzumura and Kiyono (1987), I shall consider the second-best problem faced by a government which can control the number of firms in the industry but not their competitive behaviour once they enter. Analytically speaking, the focus of attention is on the second-best net market surplus $W_*(n)$, which is defined by

$$W_*(n) = W(q_*(n), n) \tag{9}$$

Suppose that there are $n \in N(\pi_0)$ firms in the industry. Should the government increase the number of firms beyond n so as to make this industry more competitive? Or should the government restrict the number of firms less than n in the name of keeping 'excessive competition' under control? To answer this question, differentiate (9) with respect to n and invoke (7) to obtain:

$$W'_*(n) = \pi_0 + nq'_*(n)\{f(nq_*(n)) - c'(q_*(n))\} \tag{10}$$

It is clear from (10) that the verdict will hinge squarely on the sign of $q'_*(n)$ and that of $\Delta_*(n) = f(nq_*(n)) - c'(q_*(n))$.

To make progress, differentiate (7) with respect to n and invoke (6) to obtain:

$$q'_*(n)[(n-1)q_*(n)f'(nq_*(n)) - c'(q_*(n))/\{1 + \lambda_*(n)\}] \quad (11)$$
$$= -\{q_*(n)\}^2 f'(nq_*(n))$$

Since $f'(Q) < 0$ and $c'(q) > 0$ by assumption, one obtains from (11) that $q'_*(n) < 0$. Differentiating $Q_*(n) = nq_*(n)$ and invoking (11), one also obtains:

$$Q'_*(n)[(n-1)q_*(n)f'(nq_*(n)) - c'(q_*(n))/\{1 + \lambda_*(n)\}] \quad (12)$$
$$= q_*(n)\{f(nq_*(n)) - c'(q_*(n))\}$$

Given the assumptions made, (12) implies that

$$Q'_*(n) < (\textit{resp.} >) 0 \leftrightarrow f(nq_*(n)) > (\textit{resp.} <) c'(q_*(n)) \quad (13)$$

Then, back to (10), one is now ready to conclude as follows:

Proposition (a) If $\Delta_*(n) < 0$, so that price is less than marginal cost at equilibrium, then $W'_*(n)$ is unambiguously positive. Therefore, it is welfare-improving to increase the number of firms marginally.

Proposition (b) If $\Delta_*(n) > 0$, so that price exceeds marginal cost at equilibrium, then the marginal welfare verdict remains ambiguous. However, if the minimum permissible level of profit is very small, say 0, then it is welfare-improving to decrease the number of firms marginally.

Once formally derived, this proposition is quite easy to understand. If price is less than (respectively, exceeds) marginal cost, an addition of new firm increases (respectively, decreases) aggregate output by virtue of (13). Since the inverse demand function is downward sloping, price goes down (respectively, goes up), so that consumers' surplus increases (respectively, decreases). The minimal profit constraint being binding before and after the entry of a new firm, each firm earns π_0, so that the increase of one firm increases producers' surplus just by π_0. Hence an unambiguous increase of the net market surplus obtains. If price exceeds marginal cost and $\pi_0 = 0$, a deletion of one incumbent firm increases consumers' surplus, keeping producers' surplus at the previous level of zero. Once again, an unambiguous increase of the net market surplus obtains.

AN EXAMPLE

Since the verdict is quite sharply dependent on whether price exceeds or falls short of marginal cost at equilibrium, it may not be out of place to construct an example which shows that both cases are indeed possible when firms are profit-constrained sales-maximizers.

Let $f(Q) = a - bQ$, $c(q) = K + cq + dq^2$ and $\pi_0 = 0$, where $a > c > 0$, $b > 0$, $K > 0$ and $d > 0$. Equations (6) and (7) then become:

$$a - b(n + 1)q_*(n) = \Delta_*(n)\{c + 2dq_*(n)\} \quad (14)$$

$$q_*(n)\{a - c - (bn + d)q_*(n)\} = K \quad (15)$$

whereas the difference between price and marginal cost, $\Delta_*(n)$, becomes

$$\Delta_*(n) = \{a - c - (bn + d)q_*(n)\} - dq_*(n) \quad (16)$$

where the expression within curly brackets is positive by virtue of (15). It is clear from (16) that $d = 0$ (constant marginal cost) implies $\Delta_*(n) > 0$. However, if the slope of the marginal cost, d, is large enough, it is quite possible that $\Delta_*(n) < 0$. Indeed, if $a = b = 1$, $c = 1/4$, $d = 5$ and $K = 1/100$, one gets:

$$\Delta_*(n) = 3/4 - (n + 10)\{3/4 + \sqrt{9/16 - (n + 5)/25}\}/(n + 5) \quad (17)$$

which enables one to verify that $\Delta_*(5) < 0$.

CONCLUDING REMARKS

Recollect that the excess entry theorem was originally proved with the purpose of casting serious doubts on the universal validity of the widespread belief in the role of competition as an efficient allocator of resources. That being the case, the mere fact that the theorem fails to hold in some situations does not necessarily lessen the thrust thereof. Nevertheless, the fact that the theorem does not in general apply to oligopolistic competition among profit-constrained sales-maximizers deserves attention in view of the frequent invocation of this alternative hypothesis on the firm objective in the literature. At the very least, it certainly calls for more systematic exploration on the relation between the alternative firm objectives and the welfare effect of competition. The purpose of this note is served if it succeeds in driving this simple point home.

Notes

* In preparing this note, I have benefited from several discussions I have had with Professors Huw Dixon and Sajal Lahiri of the University of Essex. Needless to add, they should not be held responsible for any verdicts of and/or remaining defects in this note.

1. This is quite explicit in the analyses of Konishi, Okuno-Fujiwara and Suzumura (1990), Suzumura and Kiyono (1987) and Vickers (1989). In contrast, Mankiw and Whinston (1986) made an assumption to the effect that, for any number of firms, the resulting equilibrium price exceeds marginal cost, which is guaranteed if firms are profit maximizers and the inverse demand function is downward sloping, but not necessarily otherwise.
2. According to Baumol (1958, p. 187), 'the typical large corporation in the United States seeks to maximise not its profits but its total revenues which the businessman calls his sales. That is, *once his profits exceed some vaguely defined minimum level*, he is prepared to sacrifice further increases in profits if he can thereby obtain larger revenues'. Even when this profit-constrained sales-maximization hypothesis is not accepted *in toto* as a full-fledged alternative to the profit-maximization hypothesis, it is quite commonly invoked whenever some deviations from the pure and simple profit maximization are analysed in the literature. See, among many others, Fershtman and Judd (1987) and Vickers (1985).

References

1. Baumol, W. J. (1958) 'On the theory of oligopoly', *Economica*, vol. 25.
2. Fershtman, C. and Judd, K. L. (1987) 'Equilibrium incentives in oligopoly', *American Economic Review*, vol. 77.
3. Konishi, H., Okuno-Fujiwara, M. and Suzumura, K. (1990) 'Oligopolistic competition and economic welfare: a general equilibrium analysis of entry regulation and tax-subsidy schemes', *Journal of Public Economics*, vol. 42.

4. Mankiw, N. G. and Whinston, M. D. (1986) 'Free entry and social inefficiency', *Rand Journal of Economics*, vol. 17.
5. Portes, R. D. (1968) 'Input demand functions for the profit-constrained sales-maximizer: income effects in the theory of the firm', *Economica*, vol. 35.
6. Suzumura, K. and Kiyono, K. (1987) 'Entry barriers and economic welfare', *Review of Economic Studies*, vol. 54.
7. Vickers, J. (1985) 'Delegation and the theory of the firm', *Economic Journal*, vol. 95, *Conference Supplement*.
8. Vickers, J. (1989) 'The nature of costs and the number of firms at Cournot equilibrium', *International Journal of Industrial Organization*, vol. 7.
9. Vickers, J. and Yarrow, G. (1988), *Privatization: An Economic Analysis* (Cambridge: MIT Press).

9 Collective Choice on a Set of Games

Rubin Saposnik*

INTRODUCTION

In this paper, I consider a situation in which players have a choice of which game among a set of available games to play. Hence, the problem is one of collective choice, where the set of alternatives is a set of games, played, specifically, in coalitional form. The fact that organizations from society as a whole, including the family, not only function in accordance with certain rules and procedures, but must also determine what these are, provides motivation for studying this problem.

Implicitly, I assume that all games under consideration are on equal footing as potential candidates: there is no bias in favour of what might be the *status quo* game. Explicitly, I assume that players rank games according to Shapley (1953) values: one way of viewing which for a game to a player is as the contributions of the player to all possible coalitions; where coalitions form randomly, one player at a time, around the player, with the complement coalition also forming in random order, all coalitions being equally likely – see, for example, Kuhn and Tucker (1953). I also assume throughout that all players know, or at least believe, that they will be awarded the Shapley value of each game. A consensus in the organization that efficiency (in the usual sense that imputations exhaust the worth of the grand coalition) is paramount, supports this knowledge or belief. Moreover, Roth (1977; 1988) has shown that under an extended notion of risk neutrality, the Shapley value is the utility function of a player over the class of finite coalitional games.

Moreover, I assume that in comparing games, a player will exert some effort on behalf of the preferred game, and that this effort is in proportion to the difference in the Shapley value between the games. Individual efforts are aggregated to social effort, thereby providing a social ranking over the set of games. It follows quite easily that there exists an optimal game in terms of this ranking. Furthermore, an optimal game in this 'positive' effort-maximal sense will, under appropriate conditions, be optimal in a 'normative' utilitarian social welfare sense, and coversely. Finally, although it is possible for one game to dominate another in terms of the social effort ranking, it may not be Pareto superior in terms of the worth of the grand coalition. In fact, a very strong condition on individual effort functions is both necessary and sufficient for the social effort ranking to rank games so as to agree with the ranking according to the worth of the grand coalition.

In the four sections of the paper, I, respectively: define the set of games; develop individual preferences and effort functions, and the associated social ranking games; establish the existence of an effort-maximal game showing, incidentally, that such a game maximises an appropriately defined social welfare function, and derive a necessary and sufficient condition on individual effort functions for ranking games according to social effort to agree with ranking games to the worth of the grand coalition; and provide a summary and conclusion.

THE SPACE OF GAMES

A game in coalitional form (v, N), $N = \{1, \ldots, n\}$ is a mapping v: $2^N \to R$, where 2^N is the power set of N and v is superadditive, i.e. for all $S, T \subset N$, $S \cap T = \Phi$ implies $v(S \cup T) \geq v(S) + v(T)$. For all $S \subset N$, $v(S)$ is the worth of the coalition S, $v(N)$ is the worth of the grand coalition and $v(\Phi) = 0$.

Let G be a collection of games (v, N) such that for all $S \subset N$, $0 \leq v(S) \leq B$ for some $B > 0$. The following result (stated as lemma) follows immediately.

Lemma 1 G is a compact set in $R_+^{2^N}$.

Proof Identify each game (v, N) with its range. To illustrate, the game

$$(v, \{1, 2, 3\})$$

may be represented as:

$$\{v(\Phi) = 0, v(\{1\}), v(\{2\}), v(\{3\}), v(\{1, 2\}), v(\{1, 3\}), v(\{2, 3\}), v(\{1, 2, 3\})\}$$

a point in R^8_+.

In general, represent the game $(v, N)\varepsilon G$ by:

$$\{0, v(\{1\}) \ldots v(\{n\}), v(\{1, 2\}) \ldots v(\{1, n\}) \ldots$$
$$v(\{n = 1, n\}) \ldots v(\{1, \ldots, n - 1, n\}), v(N)\}$$

Given the standard topology, the lemma is a standard result.

INDIVIDUAL PREFERENCES AND EFFORT FUNCTIONS

The Shapley value for player $i\varepsilon N$, s_i, is given by $s_i = \frac{1}{n!} \Sigma[v(P_iU\{i\}) - v(P_i)]$, where P_i is the set of players proceeding i in permutation P_i and where P_i ranges over all permutations of N.

Players compare games by preference relations $\underset{i}{\gtrsim}$, where, for (v, N), $(v', N)\varepsilon G$:

$$(D.1)\ (v, N) \underset{i}{\gtrsim} (v', N) \leftrightarrow s_i(v, N) \geq s_i(v', N)$$

Indifference i and strict preference $\underset{i}{>}$ are defined in the usual way.

The effort function e_i: $GxG \rightarrow R$ of player i is given by:[1]

$$(D.2)\ e_i[(v, N), (v', N)] = \max k_i[s_i(v, N) - s_i(v', N), 0]$$
$$\text{for some } 0 \leq k_i \leq$$

k_i is the part of the gain player i would realize in game (v, N) over game (v', N) that player i is willing to contribute to the support of (v, N) and may be viewed as indicating the extent to which player i is seeking rent. Were G to consist of only two genuinely plausible elements (v, N) and (v', N) where – suppressing subscripts – $(v, N) > (v', N)$, a player might have a subjective probability function $P(e)$ then (v, N) would prevail: the optimum value of k would then be the solution to the problem:

$$\max P(k[s(v, N) - s(v', N)])s(v, N) + \{1 - P(k[s(v, N)$$
$$- s(v', N)])\} - k[s(v, N) - s(v', N)]$$

where $0 \leq k \leq 1$. Moreover, to the extent that players deemed the number of plausible candidates to be large so that a number of head-to-head comparisons would be required, players are confronted with a kind of 'budget constraint'.

SOCIAL PREFERENCES

Social preference is determined by effort as follows: For (v, N) and $(v', N)\varepsilon G$:

$$(D.3)\ (v, N) \underset{*}{\geq} (v', N) \leftrightarrow \sum_{i=1}^{n} e_i[(v, N)$$

$$(v', N)] \geq \sum_{i=1}^{n} e_i[(v', N), (v, N)]$$

where $ni = 1$. Again, indifference $*$ and strict preference $\underset{*}{>}$ are defined in the usual fashion.

By lemma 1 and the continuity of s_i, there exists $(v^*, N)\varepsilon G$ such that:

$$\sum_{i=1}^{n} k[s_i(v^*, N) - s_i(v, N)] \geq 0 \text{ for all } (v, N)\varepsilon G$$

$$\text{and } 0 \leq k_i \leq 1 \tag{1}$$

Let $N_v^* = \{i\varepsilon N | s_i(v^*, N) \geq s_i(v, N)\}$. Then rewriting (1), one has:

$$\sum_{i\varepsilon N_v^*} k_i s_i(v^*, N) + \sum_{i\varepsilon N - N_v^*} k_i s_i(v^*, N) \geq$$

$$\sum_{i\varepsilon N_v^*} k_i s_i(v, N) + \sum_{i\varepsilon N - N_v} k_i s_i(v, N) \tag{2}$$

or

$$\sum_{i\varepsilon N_v^*} k_i[s_i(v^*, N) - s_i(v, N)] \geq \sum_{i\varepsilon N - N_v^*} k_i[s_i(v, N) - s_i(v^*, N)]$$

$$\text{for all } (v, N)\varepsilon G \tag{3}$$

By $(D.2)$, $\Sigma_{i=1}^{n} e_i[(v^*, N), (v, N)]$ is equal to the LHS sum in (3) and

$$\sum_{i=1}^{n} e_i[(v, N), (v^*, N)]$$

is equal to the RHS sum in (3). Consequently, $(v^*, N) \underset{*}{\geq} (v, N)$ for all $(v, N)\ \varepsilon G$.

Reversing the order of the argument, one can see that $(v^*, N) \underset{*}{\geq} (v, N)$ for all $(v, N) \varepsilon G$ implies that:

$$(v^*, N) = \arg\max \geq k_i s_i(v, N), \ (v, N)\varepsilon G$$

Summarizing, one has:

Proposition 1 Given $0 \leq k_i \leq 1$, there exists $(v^*, N)\varepsilon G$ such that $(v^*, N) \underset{*}{\geq} (v, N)$ for all $(v, N)\varepsilon G$ and $\Sigma_{i=1}^{n} k_i[s_i(v^*, N) - s_i(v, N)] \geq 0$.

Roth (1988) has shown that if players are risk-neutral in the usual sense of equating lotteries with their expected value as well as risk neutral in the sense he refers to as 'strategic risk neutrality,'[2] then the Shapley value is the player's utility function U_i. Applying Roth's theorem to Proposition 1 yields the following:

Corollary If players are risk-neutral in the sense of Roth, (v^*, N) is $\underset{*}{\geq}$ optimal if, and only if, (v^*, N) maximizes the utilitarian social welfare function $\Sigma\, k_i U_i(v, N)$ for some $0 \leq k_i \leq 1$.

Finally, given $(v, N), (v', N)\varepsilon G$ with $(v, N) \geq (v', N)$, the Pareto criterion would suggest that (v, N) should be socially at least preferred as (v', N). This is the case since for any imputation $x' = (x'_1, \ldots, x'_n)$ of $v'(N)$ there exists an imputation $x = (x_1, \ldots, x_n)$ of $v(N)$ such that $x_i > x'_i$ for all i. Formally, define the relation $\underset{\cap}{\geq}$, with associated $\underset{\cap}{\sim}$ and $\underset{\cap}{>}$, by:

(*D*.4) For $(v, N), (v', N)\varepsilon G, (v, N) \underset{\cap}{\geq} (v', N) \leftrightarrow v(N) \geq v'(N)$.

That $\underset{\cap}{\geq}$ and $\underset{*}{\geq}$ do not agree, in general, is illustrated by the following example. Let $N = \{1, 2, 3\}$. Consider the games (v, N) and (v', N) where:

$$v(\{i\}) = 0 \ i = 1, 2, 3; \ v(\{ij\}) = 2ij = 1, 2, 3 \ i \neq j; \ v(\{1, 2, 3\}) = 4$$

and

$$v'(\{1\}) = 2; \quad v'(\{i\}) = 0 \quad i = 2, 3;$$
$$v'(\{1, j\}) = 2j = 2, 3 \quad v'(\{2, 3\}) = 1; \quad v'(\{1, 2, 3\}) = 3$$

Comparing the Shapley values, one gets:

$$s_1[(v', N)] - s_1[(v, N)] = \frac{2}{3} s_i[(v, N)] - s_i[(v', N)] = \frac{5}{6} i = 2, 3$$

Setting $k_1 = \frac{1}{2}$, $k_2 = k_3 = \frac{1}{6}$ gives $(v', N) \underset{*}{>} (v, N)$ while $v(N) > v'(N)$. Thus $(v', N) \underset{*}{>} (v, N)$ and $(v', N) \underset{\cap}{>} (v', N)$.

The following proposition derives a necessary and sufficient condition for the ranking $\underset{\cap}{\geq}$ to agree with the ranking $\underset{*}{\geq}$:

Proposition 2 For $(v, N), (v', N) \varepsilon G$, $(v\ N) \geq (v', N) \underset{\cap}{\geq} (v', N) \leftrightarrows (v, N) \underset{*}{\geq} (v', N)$, if, and only if, $k_i = k_j$ for all $i, j = 1, \ldots, n$.

Proof Suppose $k_i = k_j$ for all $i\ j = 1, \ldots, n$. Then reversing the argument in the proof of Proposition 1, and by the efficiency property of the Shapley value:

$$\textstyle\sum_{i=1}^{n} e_i[(v, N), (v', N)] \geq \sum_{i=1}^{n} e_i[(v', N), (v, N)] \rightleftarrows \sum_{i=1}^{n}[s_i(v, N) - s_i(v', N)] = v(N) - v'(N) \geq 0$$

To prove the necessity, suppose without loss of generality that $k_i > k_n$, $k_i = k_j ij \neq 1, n$ and $s_n(v', N) = s_1(v, N) > s_n(v, N) = s_1(v', N)$, $s_j(v, N) = s_j(v', N)$. Then

$$\textstyle\sum_{i=1}^{n} e_i[(v, N), (v', N)] = k_1[s_1(v, N) - s_1(v', N)] > k_n[s_n(v', N) - s_n(v, N)] = \sum_{i=1}^{n} e_i[(v', N), (v, N)]$$

Thus $(v, N) \underset{*}{\gneqq} (v', N)$ while, by the efficiency property of s_i, $v(N) = v'(N)$ so that $(v, N) \underset{\cap}{\sim} (v', N)$, completing the proof.

Proposition 2 shows that it is possible for a game (v^*, N) to be effort optimal but not Pareto optimal. However, if players are risk-neutral in the Roth sense (1977;1988), linear combinations of Shapley values are utilitarian social welfare functions; hence Pareto optimality must be satisfied. The example presented above 'works' because strategic neutrality is violated.[3]

SUMMARY AND CONCLUSIONS

When members of an organization must decide on the rules and procedures governing the organization, collective choice in a set of coalitional games becomes an appropriate paradigm. To the extent that players in this type of game evaluate games in terms of the expected value of their marginal contributions or that the organization places a high priority on efficiency (Pareto optimality) in imputations of the games, the Shapley value takes on plausibility as a criterion for players to evaluate these games.

To influence the choice process, each player exerts some effort on behalf of his or her preferred game in pairwise comparisons; the game having the greatest total effort eliminates the other. One sees that if players are risk neutral in the Roth sense, effort-maximal games coincide with games that maximize a utilitarian social welfare function.

Finally, effort-maximal games coincide with Pareto-optimal games if, and only if, all players are equally 'hedging' or 'rent seeking'. Given Roth risk neutrality, effort maximality, Pareto optimality and strict (i.e. all weights equal) utilitarian social welfare function maximization yield identical choice sets.

Notes

* I am indebted to seminar participants at West Virginia University, and particularly to Roger Tutterow for his comments.

1. While effort is expressed in utility units, it naturally takes the form of cash and time.
2. 'Strategic risk neutrality' is defined in terms of games of the form:

$$v_R(S) = 1 \quad \text{if} \quad R \subset S; \qquad \text{otherwise } 0$$

for each subset $R \subset N$. If the neutrality of R is r, $f(r)$ is the player's estimate of his/her bargaining power in the v_R game. A player is *strategically risk-neutral* if $f(r) = \frac{1}{r}$ for $r = 1, \ldots, n$. The result applies to all coalitional games (v, N) since the v_R games constitute a basis.
3. Strategic neutrality implies that the bargaining power of players in the v_R games depend only on the cardinality of R. Consequently, the Shapley values in the example violate strategic neutrality.

References

1. Kuhn, H. W. and Tucker, A. W. (1953) *Contributions to the Theory of Games: Vol. II* (Princeton: Princeton University Press).
2. Roth, A. E. (1977) 'The Shapley value as a von Neumann-Morgenstern utility', *Econometrica*, vol. 45.
3. Roth, A. E. (1988) 'The expected utility of playing a game', in his (ed.), *The Shapley Value* (New York: Cambridge University Press).
4. Shapley, L. S. (1953) 'A value for *n*-person games', *Contributions to the Theory of Games: Vol. II* (Princeton: Princeton University Press).

10 International Harmonization of Taxes

Carl S. Shoup*

INTRODUCTION

Harmonization of tax systems across countries, a subject to which Hirofumi Shibata has made such important contributions, is becoming a topic of ever widening interest as the European Community approaches border-free trade in 1992 and as other areas of the world consider forming free trade groupings or common markets. This suggests a question: have the tax systems of the world become substantially harmonized already, so that formation of those unions may prove somewhat easier than commonly anticipated?

This paper attempts a partial answer to this question, by noting the extent to which certain major taxes have spread across the world, and the degree to which some of the operative details of those taxes are similar, country to country.

For the individual income tax, we inquire (1) how many countries are now using it? (2) are there notable differences in the top rates of tax? (3) are capital gains and losses treated more or less uniformly across countries? (4) how many countries allow deduction of medical expenses? (5) deduction of life insurance premiums?

As to the corporate income tax, (6) how many countries impose it? (7) are the rates, at least the top rates, fairly uniform? (8) how similar are the details for carry-over of operating losses?

What about the value-added tax – (9) its extent, and (10) standard rates?

And finally, (11) are taxes on labour income (payroll taxes), to finance old-age benefits, found in many countries, and (12) at what rates?

A country, in this study, is a political jurisdiction that has complete freedom to levy any kind of tax, at any rate or rates, without approval from any other jurisdiction.

The mere counting of countries, as in asking how many impose a corporate income tax, might seem unproductive because of great differences in size and degree of economic development. The counting does reveal, however, the extent to which the tax in question has proved adaptable to differing cultures and economic circumstances.

Extremely small countries have been omitted from the present survey, which does not cover the thirteen countries with populations less than 100 000. This leaves about 170 countries to be compared.

A distinction is drawn here between the architectural features of a tax system and the engineering features of a particular tax. Tax architecture is the pattern of taxes used, and, for each tax, the definition, in general terms, of the tax base and the level of tax rate or rates. Tax engineering formulates the operative details of a particular tax: for example, if a carryover of operating loss is allowed, under a corporate income tax, is it a carry-back or a carry-forward, or both, and for how many years (Shoup 1990)? A third aspect of a tax system, tax administration, is not covered in the present paper.

The tax rates cited are statutory rates, not effective rates.

INDIVIDUAL INCOME TAX

Architectural aspects

Geographical extent of the individual income tax

The extent of the spread of the individual income tax around the world is somewhat surprising. This is a tax that requires appreciable record keeping and computational effort by individuals and families, even where most of it is collected by withholding at the source. Yet, from the data at hand, it appears that some two-thirds of the countries in the world levy an individual income tax. The basis for this estimate is as follows.

The accounting firm of Price Waterhouse, surveying 104 of the 109 countries in which it operates, found that 92 of the 104 impose an individual income tax (1990 data).[1] This 88 per cent is impressive, even allowing for the fact that an accounting firm will tend to locate in those countries with the greatest accounting needs; total accounting needs are of course generated by a great variety of factors other than the individual income tax.

With respect to the roughly eighty other countries, if only twenty of them employ the individual income tax, then about two-thirds of all the countries in the world use this tax.

Top rate of the individual income tax

When we turn to the levels of rates of this tax that obtain in the 92 countries in the Price-Waterhouse survey, harmonization is far less evident, as might be expected. To compare the 92 rate structures in any comprehensive manner is not possible here, but a comparison of the highest bracket rate across countries gives some hint of the total disparity.

The range of the highest bracket rate is from 10 per cent in Bolivia to 90 per cent in the Soviet Union, but a better sense of the degree of disparity is achieved by considering only those top rates that are found in at least four countries each. At one extreme, the lowest top rate levied by four or more countries is 25 per cent (by exactly four); the highest is 60 per cent (by five countries). The other top rates that are found in four or more countries are: 30 per cent (five countries), 35 per cent (six countries), 40 per cent (four countries), 45 per cent (nine countries), 50 per cent (twelve countries), 55 per cent (four countries), and 56 per cent (four countries). The range, from a 25 per cent rate to a 60 per cent rate, is quite wide, and the distribution of the 53 countries within this range is fairly even, with some concentration at the 50 per cent level.

Capital gains and losses

Another architectural feature of the individual income tax is the inclusion, or exclusion, of capital gains and losses in computing taxable income.

Unfortunately, very little information is readily available on whether capital losses are deductible. Presumably, a country that includes capital gains in taxable individual income allows some, if not complete, deduction of capital losses, but this is uncertain. The following findings are restricted to capital gains in the 92 countries covered by Price Waterhouse.

The question posed is: does the country tax capital gains at all? A 'yes' answer therefore includes even those jurisdictions that tax such gains very lightly, or that tax only a few types of capital gain. A 'no' answer means that all capital gains go completely tax-free. A legally separate capital gains tax is treated here as if it were a part of the individual income tax.

Sixty of the 92 countries tax some or all capital gains, and 30 do not (for 2, the information is not adequate). This two-thirds proportion is probably higher than most observers would have conjectured, given the number of developing countries in the group. Still, it is far from being substantial harmonization, even under the loose test of do they tax gains at all? In some countries the rate applied to gains is so low or the coverage of gains is so restricted that the regime is close to that of zero taxation of all capital gains.

Engineering aspects

Among the many detailed provisions defining the individual income tax, the following two were selected for tabulation and comparison of countries: the taxpayer is allowed, or denied, deduction of (a) at least some medical expenses, (b) at least some part of premiums paid for life insurance.

Medical expense deduction

Deduction for medical expenses is harmonized to about the same moderate degree as is the treatment of capital gains, and is tilted in the same direction, unfavorable to the taxpayer. Only 32 of the 92 countries allow the individual to deduct part or all of the family's medical expenses; 58 permit no deduction at all (again, for 2 the information is inadequate).

Life insurance premium deduction

On deduction for life insurance premiums paid, the 92 countries split almost evenly: 44 allow some or complete deduction, 45 permit no deduction at all (for 3 the information is incomplete).

It seems odd, at first sight, that 12 more countries allow deduction for life insurance premiums than for medical expenses. The hardship element seems more evident in the latter. Do the data reflect a more persuasive power of the insurance industry than of the medical profession? Or do more taxpayers take out insurance than pay medical bills? More likely explanations are: (1) some countries offer free, or subsidized, medical care, to some degree, whereas no country offers free or subsidized life insurance (Eden 1990; Shaw 1990); (2) 'the primary reason for the (premium) deduction is not "hardship", but the belief that it will increase savings' (Due 1990).

A subsidiary question is this: do the 32 countries that allow deduction of medical expenses also allow deduction of life insurance premiums? If so, there is at least some consistency here. If not, the picture is even less 'harmonious'. And that is what it turns out to be. Only 21 of the 32 medical-deduction countries also allow deduction of life insurance premiums. We might have expected almost all of them to do so, given the much greater number of countries that allow premium deduction than allow medical deductions.

High top rate and deductibility

Are the countries with high top rates the ones that allow deduction for medical expenses and life insurance premiums? The US federal tax reform in the 1980s featured a decrease in the top rate coupled with a repeal or limitation of certain personal-expense deductions, a restriction that was the less protested as the deduction was now to be worth somewhat less.

In the countries with low top rates this logic tends to hold, though not strongly. A 'low' top rate is taken here as 30 per cent or less, which obtains in fourteen countries. In this group, there are twenty instances of no deduction being allowed for either medical expenses or life insurance premiums, and only eight instances of deductibility of one or the other.

At the high end of the top rates, here taken as 60 per cent or higher, where we might expect a majority for deductibility, yes and no are almost evenly matched among the fifteen countries in this group: 16 instances of deductibility of either one of the outlays, 14 instances of no deductibility.

CORPORATE INCOME TAX

Architectural aspects

Geographic extent of the corporate income tax

Although the corporate income tax requires fairly sophisticated accounting, it is in force in 98 countries of the 104 covered by the Price Waterhouse survey. Four of the 104 levy no corporate income tax;[2] in another (Bolivia) the tax is in fact based on net worth, not income, and in another (Bahrain) it applies only to oil companies. Saudi Arabia is included here, although it taxes only foreign corporations.

Of the remaining seventy or so countries, if only about fifteen impose the tax, then, as with the individual income tax, two-thirds of all countries use the general-scope corporation income tax.

Top corporate tax rates

Most of the corporate income taxes throughout the world do not carry a rate scale that is progressive with profit, but there are enough of them that do to make useful the concept of a top rate. Some corporate income taxes are levied at rates that vary somewhat with type of activity, but in these instances the rate used here is the rate applicable to corporations in general.

At first view there seems to be very little harmonization of the top rates of this tax. The nearly one hundred countries scatter over forty three different top rates. But these rates are fairly well concentrated in the range 30 per cent to 50 per cent inclusive (81 countries). The only notable bunching greater than three countries occurs at tax rates of 20 per cent (five countries), 30 per cent (seven countries), 35 per cent (fourteen countries), 40 per cent (twelve countries) and 50 per cent (eleven countries). There are, to be sure, instances of near bunching. For example, a group of rates of 42, 42.5, 43, 43.5, 43.725, 44, 44.5 and 45 contains fourteen countries.[3] The fractional rates are sometimes the result of adding two taxes, both of them national corporate income taxes with differing names, one of them being expressed as a per cent, not of profits, but of the other tax.

Engineering aspects

Carry-over of operating losses

A corporation is assessed under the income tax on one year's income. If a year of loss occurs, should the corporation be allowed to carry that loss over to a year of profit, reducing that profit for tax purposes? Not to do so would penalize such a corporation relative to others with the same total profit over a span of years but with no loss years.

The carry-over of a loss can be either, or both, a carry-back to a previous year of profit or a carry-forward to a later year of profit. The carry-back gives rise to a tax refund, since tax will already have been paid on the full profit of that earlier year.

The carry-over, being a somewhat sophisticated tax feature, might not be expected on a broad scale in developing countries. In fact, however, almost all countries in the Price Waterhouse survey, developed or developing, provide a carry-over of some sort. Carry-over is denied by only 8 of the 98 countries. Four of them are small Latin American countries, two are Persian Gulf oil producing states, and the other two are the Philippines and the Soviet Union.[4]

The type of carry-over allowed is overwhelmingly the carry-forward. Only 11 countries permit a carry-back, and all 11 allow a carry-forward of whatever remains unabsorbed by the carry-back. The need to make a tax refund for a carry-back is presumably the chief reason for this pattern.

A carry-forward alone is seriously incomplete for most corporations that incur occasional losses if it is limited to the year or two immediately following the year of loss. The length of the carry-forward period must therefore be considered. Here there is a clustering of countries at three periods: three years, five years, and open-ended.

Interestingly enough, the most widely used of these three is the open-ended period. Twenty-nine countries allow a corporation to carry forward a given year's loss as long as need be to absorb that loss fully in the profits of later years. Many of these countries halt the carry-forward if control of the corporation changes substantially, or if the line or lines of business change; in effect, it is no longer the same corporation.

The majority of those countries that allow an unlimited length of carry-forward are developing countries. The only European country in this group is Belgium. The USA almost belongs in this group, with its 15-year carry-forward, and a 3-year carry-back.

A five-year limit to a carry-forward of any given year's loss is almost as popular as the indefinite carry-forward: twenty-two countries. Eight European countries are in this group; one, France, allows a three-year carry-back also.

The cluster of the three-year group consists almost entirely of small developing countries.

We may consider a five-year limit for a carry-forward as being adequate, on the whole. Seventy countries allow this, or a longer period. Therefore, on this point, substantial harmonization already exists.

VALUE ADDED TAX (VAT)

Architectural aspects

The value added tax is a tax on the value that a firm adds to the goods and services it buys from other firms, by using its own labor force and capital equipment. The sum of all the values added, from the extractive stage through manufacturing, wholesaling and retailing, is the final retail price. The value added tax is therefore essentially the same as a retail sales tax, but collected in installments at the various stages of production and distribution. In Europe, especially, it has replaced the old turnover tax on gross sales, which made no allowance for tax paid at earlier stages.

Only architectural aspects of the VAT will be considered here, and only two of these: geographical extent, and standard rate. Attention is centered on the comprehensive type of VAT, which extends all the way down through the retail stage. Some countries use the VAT technique but do not include the retail stage. Some others exempt many retail firms by a small-size test.

Geographical extent of the VAT

The value added tax is notably widespread, considering how recently it has developed. Of 101 countries on which Price Waterhouse supplies information as to the VAT, 42 now use this tax in its comprehensive form, or will do so by 1991. Almost all of the European countries and most of those in Latin America are in this group, but only 4 in Africa.

As to the countries not covered by Price Waterhouse, apparently only a few have adopted the VAT. A recent World Bank study of the value added tax in developing countries lists eight that Price Waterhouse does not put in this class, and the 42 noted above include 10 countries not included in the World Bank study. Some of these VATs were enacted after the World Bank study was made, and some do not fit the definition of a comprehensive VAT, to which the World Bank listing was restricted. On the whole, probably about fifty countries now impose, or are scheduled shortly to impose, a comprehensive VAT.[5] A few more, perhaps five or ten, apply the tax only to one or more stages above the retail stage.

The value-added tax, which started long after the two income taxes, has as yet spread far less widely, but in at least two broad areas where common markets may be formed before long – North America and Latin America – this tax is already used widely (the US has no VAT, but most of the states levy its economic equivalent, the retail sales tax).

Standard rates of the VAT

Many of the VAT countries use more than one tax rate, but here we refer only to the standard rate, applicable to most of the taxable goods and services. The rate given is the tax-exclusive rate, not the tax-inclusive one (see below).

A 10 per cent rate is used by ten countries, and six use a 15 per cent rate. Otherwise there is no notable clustering of countries at a particular rate.

The range of standard rates is from 3 per cent (one country) to 25 per cent (three countries), but the latter rate is not very important, since the countries that use it also exempt a large part of the economy from the tax. The significant range, therefore, is from 3 per cent to 23.46 per cent.

The 23.46 per cent rate (Sweden) is in fact stated in the law as 19 per cent, but that is the rate applied to the sales price including the VAT itself (tax-inclusive rate). It is the equivalent of a 23.46 rate on the sales price exclusive of this tax. (In either case, from the gross tax thus computed there is subtracted the VATs paid at earlier stages, as shown on the invoices of vendors to the firm).

For example, if a VAT of 10 per cent is imposed on the price of a good as that price is stated before adding the tax, and if this price is $10, then the price including tax is $11, and one dollar tax is only 9.0909 . . . per cent of the $11 tax-inclusive price. In the present survey, this tax-inclusive rate is not used; all VATs are stated as a percentage of the price before tax (tax-exclusive rate) (see Shoup 1990, pp. 12–13). It is not always clear from the sources whether the rates quoted there are tax-inclusive or tax-exclusive, but since the great majority of VAT jurisdictions are known to use tax-exclusive rates, it is here assumed that the rate stated is tax-exclusive, barring a statement to the contrary.

The great scattering of the standard VAT rates among countries is further shown by the fact that nine rates are used by only one country apiece. Another six rates are to be found, each, in only two countries.

On the whole, the standard rates are surprisingly high, at least compared with the retail sales tax rates in the states of the US. Those state tax rates cluster in the range of 3 per cent to 6 per cent (Universal Almanac, p. 170). In contrast, only five of the VAT countries impose a standard rate of 6 per cent or less, while twenty-three of them use rates between 12 per cent and 20 per cent inclusive – two at 19 per cent and three at 20 per cent. To be sure, those VAT countries probably exempt or low-rate a larger part of the goods and services than do the retail sales taxes in the US. Moreover, the only non-European countries with a standard VAT rate above 16 per cent are Brazil, Ivory Coast, Niger, Senegal and Uruguay. Still, the height of the VAT rates is impressive.

Harmonization of the VAT rates will evidently require considerable changes in some countries. A few changes may be necessary within the European Community, where the standard rates range from 12 per cent in Luxembourg and Spain to 19 per cent in Belgium and Italy – see El-Agraa (1990, pp. 280–3).

PAYROLL TAXES FOR OLD AGE PENSIONERS, INVALIDITY PENSIONS AND DEATH BENEFITS

Architectural aspects

A biennial publication of the Unites States Social Security Administration, Social Security Programs Throughout the World, gives a country-by-country summary for each of five programmes: old age, invalidity and death; sickness and maternity; work injury; unemployment; and family allowance. In each instance, for each country, the sources of funds for the programme are noted. We concentrate here on the first of these five programmes, and compare the tax measures employed to finance the benefits paid on account of old age, invalidity, and death.

Since these taxes are tied closely to the benefits, one might expect the tax rates to vary among countries as the benefit levels vary. Harmonization does not require near uniformity, internationally, of tax rates, given unequal benefit levels. Still, wide differentials in tax rates might prove troublesome in an attempt to form an economic union.

Here, we consider only the architectural aspects, and only three of these: geographical extent of the programme; type of tax used to finance it; and level of tax rate.

Geographical extent of the programme

The programme for old-age, invalidity and death benefits is very widespread. The source noted above covers 145 countries, including a few geographical entities, e.g. Hong Kong. Only 9 of these 145 have no such programme.

Tvpe of tax used to finance the programme

Of the 136 countries that do have this programme, only 4 finance it entirely from general-fund revenues (Australia, Hong Kong, New Zealand, and South Africa). The other 132 countries, levying a tax earmarked for the benefits, all use a tax on labour income, in one or more of its three forms: tax on the employee, tax on the employer, tax on the self-employed. We refer to these collectively as 'payroll taxes'.

In 34 of these 132 countries the programme draws partly on general funds to supplement the earmarked tax revenues. The 98 other countries finance this programme wholly through the payroll tax. With only a few exceptions, no other kind of tax is earmarked for this benefits program in any country.[6] There is indeed a remarkable degree of harmonization on this one architectural aspect.

Rates of tax

The rates of payroll taxes that finance part or all of this programme are spread over a wide range from country to country; there is virtually no harmonization of payroll tax rates. This can be inferred from taking a sample consisting of the first one-third of the 132 countries listed alphabetically, from Algeria to Greece, i.e., 44 countries. From these 44 countries, eight are omitted[7] because comparisons are difficult: multiple rates, etc. We have then a net sample of 36 countries.

In a country that taxes both the employer and the employee on the same wage, the two taxes are added to give a single combined rate.

The tax rate ranges among the 36 countries from 3 per cent in El Salvador to 26 per cent in Argentina, a wide range indeed. Moreover there is even less clustering about a few rates than exists for the value added tax. In fact, the largest size of cluster is only two, and this occurs only eight times (16 countries). But many of the differing rates are very close to each other.

One might think that the lower payroll tax rates would be found in those countries where general fund revenues are called upon to help finance this programme. As it turns out, the opposite is nearer the truth. Of the eighteen 'low-rate' countries, i.e., those with a payroll tax rate of less than 10 per cent, only one-third call on general funds to supplement the revenue from that tax (Bolivia, Cape Verde, Colombia, Costa Rica, Dominican Republic and El Salvador), while, of the eleven 'high-rate' countries (payroll tax rate, 15 per cent or more), nearly three-quarters do call on general funds to help finance the programme (Argentina, Austria, Belgium, Brazil, China, Egypt, German Federal Republic and German Democratic Republic).

Accordingly, the payroll tax rates appear to be positively related to the level of total financing of the programme rather than varying inversely with the general-fund segment of that total.

CONCLUSION

As more countries consider grouping themselves in economic unions of one type or another, they will find a mixed picture as to the need for measures of tax harmonization.

On the one hand, the major forms of tax are already fairly widespread. On the other hand, the rates of any particular tax vary considerably over countries. Precise equality of tax rates is not necessary, but some partial alignment over the countries of a union may well prove desirable.

The tax engineering features, in contrast, must probably remain disparate, to accommodate the tax in question to differing cultures and economic circumstances.

In any event, the movement toward economic unions of various types seems likely to continue. As an example, a recent issue of Tax News Service (22 August, 1990) reports that:

> On 6 July 1990 the Presidents of Argentina and Brazil signed the 'Act of Buenos Aires', which will create a common market between the countries within 5 years (instead of 10 years as previously established). The Act will reduce many tariffs to zero and eliminate non-tariff barriers for all products by 31 December 1994. (p. 246).

Moreover, 'U.S. President Bush proposed the establishment of a free trade zone covering both American continents (dubbed "Initiative of the Americas"). In general, the proposal was received positively by many Latin American countries. Brazil and Argentina agreed to negotiate regarding the proposed free trade zone'.

APPENDIX: NUMBER OF COUNTRIES COVERED

The number of independent taxing jurisdictions in the world to be covered by the present study has been arrived at by

(1) consulting four lists of countries: (a) the 159 member States of the United Nations; (b) the 172 countries, as opposed to territories, described in the Universal Almanac; (c) the 145 jurisdictions covered

by Social Security Programs Throughout the World – 1989, which includes, as countries, 'not only independent states but also certain geographical entities such as Bermuda, Hong Kong, and Taiwan' (p. v), and (d) the 104 countries and territories in the Price Waterhouse Information Guides on Individual Taxes and Corporate Taxes,

(2) then excluding the eleven jurisdictions with less than 100,000 population (Andorra, Isle of Man, Liechtenstein, Marshall Islands, Micronesia, Monaco, Nauru, San Marino, Tonga, Tuvalu, and Vatican City). None of these excluded entities are member states of the United Nations. The Price Waterhouse compilation includes the Isle of Man and Liechtenstein, and these two are included in the findings drawn from this source.

Included, because of their economic importance and relative freedom of tax policy, although some or all of them may not have complete tax autonomy, are: Bopthuthatswana (South Africa), Byelorussia, Channel Islands (Guernsey, Jersey), Hong Kong, Macau, Netherlands Antilles and Puerto Rico. None of these are member states of the United Nations except Byelorussia.

Altogether, the present study covers 170 jurisdictions ('countries').

Notes

* I am indebted to John F. Due, Lorraine Eden, and G. K. Shaw for comments on an earlier draft of this paper.

1. The twelve that do not levy the individual income tax are: Bahamas, Bahrain, Bermuda, Brunei, Cayman Islands, Kuwait, Oman, Qatar, Saudi Arabia, United Arab Emirates, Uruguay and Vanuatu.
2. They are: Bahamas, Bermuda, Cayman Islands, and Vanuatu.
3. Including the Soviet Union (45 per cent) in its 1990 tax reform legislation (Turro 1990, p. 794).
4. A five-year carry-forward was introduced in the Soviet Union in 1990 for ventures with foreign participation in excess of 30 per cent – see Turro, 1990, p. 793.
5. Including the Soviet Union in its 1990 tax reform – see Turro, 1990, p. 795.
6. In two countries a flat amount per week is required of the employer and/or employee, without regard to the level of wage (Bermuda, and, employment-related pensions, Denmark). In a few countries a universal pension is financed by a specified rate on one's taxable income (Denmark, Finland, Sweden). The Netherlands and Norway employ a tax on the insured person's income. Paraguay taxes pensioners on their pensions.

The exact base for taxing the self-employed varies somewhat among countries.

7. Belize, Bermuda, Bulgaria, Canada, Cuba, Czechoslovakia, Denmark and Finland.

References

1. Due, J. F. (1990), letter to Shoup, October 8.
2. El-Agraa, A. M. (ed.) (1990), *The Economics of the European Community* (Oxford: Philip Allan; New York: Prentice Hall International and Simon & Schuster). Third edition. First edition, 1980.
3. Gillis, M., Shoup, C. S. and Geraldo, P. S. (eds.) (1990), *Value Added Taxation in Developing Countries: A World Bank Symposium* (Washington, DC: The World Bank).
4. International Bureau of Fiscal Documentation (various issues), *Tax News Service: A Bi-Weekly Report* (Amsterdam: IBFD).
5. *New York Times*, 14 October 1990, Travel Section.
6. Price Waterhouse (1990) 'Corporate taxes: a Worldwide summary', in Information Guide (New York and London; Price Waterhouse).
7. Shaw, G. K. (1990), letter to Shoup, 5 October.
8. Shibata, H. (1967) 'The theory of economic unions: a comparative analysis of customs unions, free trade areas, and tax unions', in Carl S. Shoup (ed.), *Fiscal Harmonization in Common Markets, Vol. I: Theory* (New York: Columbia University Press).
9. Shoup, C. S. (1990) 'Melding architecture and engineering: a personal retrospective on designing tax systems', in Lorraine Eden (ed.), *Retrospectives on Public Finance* (Durham, NC: Duke University Press).
10. Turro, J. (1990) 'Soviet Union adopts new tax system', *Tax Notes International*, vol. 2, No. 8, pp. 793–796.
11. United States Department of Health and Human Services (1989), *Social Security Programs Throughout the World -989*, Research Report #62, publication No. 13–11805, May (Washington, DC: Social Security Administration).
12. Wright, J. W. (ed.) (1989; 1990), *The Universal Almanac 1989* (New York: Andrews and McMeel).

11 Time, Space and the Income Tax

Richard M. Bird

INTRODUCTION

It is now widely accepted that inflation, when combined with a progressive rate structure, distorts the real structure of the income tax. Inflation results in income being shifted into higher tax brackets even though taxpayers experience no increase in their real (before tax) incomes: this process has been given the evocative name of 'bracket creep'. Moreover, since exemptions, deductions, and rates in an unindexed system do not increase at the same rate as inflation, the result of the rise in nominal income is that taxable income rises even more quickly. Tax liabilities may thus increase when real incomes are constant, or even falling, and the effective rate of unindexed income taxes tends to rise over time. Even in countries with very moderate rates of price increase such as Japan, these effects may be quite marked over time, as Ishi (1989) has demonstrated.

To get around some of the inequalities created by inflation, the indexing of personal exemptions and tax brackets has been adopted, at varying times and to varying degrees, in a number of countries in recent years, especially during and after the sharp bout of inflation ensuing on the oil crises of the 1970s (OECD 1986).[1] In 1985, for example, the USA introduced indexing in this sense – a development recently characterized as 'perhaps the most powerful symbol of the revolt against the postwar tax system' because 'indexing shifted power back from the government to taxpayers and voters' (Lindsay 1990, p. 49). In contrast, in Canada, where indexing was introduced much earlier in 1974, federal officials made the case for this measure on less apocalyptic equity grounds (Allan, Dodge, and Poddar 1974) – and when inflation subsided a decade later, the extent of indexing was reduced. Both the equity and the political economy cases for indexing may be outweighed in practice in many countries by the relative ease of securing incremental revenue from an unindexed rate structure, but this does not lessen their intellectual appeal.

The pros and cons of indexing rate brackets and exemptions for inflation may be disputed (OECD 1986). Not only are the intellectual arguments in favour of such indexing appealing, however, but they have also clearly influenced policy in a number of important countries. Indeed, most authors who accept the traditional Schanz–Haig–Simons comprehensive income tax as an appropriate policy goal are now invariably careful to specify that the relevant tax base must be defined in real rather than nominal terms. Moreover, even some who instead favour the currently fashionable base among academics (if not governments), namely, consumption, often do so in part at least because of the problems to which inflation gives rise under the income tax (McLure *et al.* 1989).

The principal objective of the present note is simply to point out that exactly analogous problems arise for income taxes when there are spatial differences in the cost of living. Just as a dollar in 1990 is not the same in terms of purchasing power as a dollar in 1989, so a dollar in Canada's northern regions is not the same in terms of purchasing power as a dollar in the south. If there is an equity case for adjusting the tax system to take into account the first sort of differential, precisely the same case can be applied with respect to the second. Logically, therefore, those who accept the need for temporal indexing should accept the need for spatial indexing. The present paper attempts, in a very preliminary fashion, to develop a few of the implications of this line of reasoning.[2]

The next section sets out in a little more detail the equity case for regional differentials in income taxes and demonstrates on the basis of Canadian data that the problem – if it is considered to be one – may well be significant, at least in large and regionally diverse countries. The third section then reviews briefly experience in two countries (Canada and Australia) with regional income tax differentials. Finally, the last section of the paper briefly sketches two possible extensions of the analysis of the spatial dimensions of the income tax: the efficiency implications of regional tax differentials (and their relation to some traditional arguments in the federal finance literature), and the appropriate taxation of citizens residing in other countries. In no case is the analysis offered in the present brief paper either very complete or fully satisfactory. The objective of this paper, however, is less to supply convincing answers than to raise some troublesome questions that appear to deserve considerably more careful consideration than they have so far received.

THE EQUITY CASE FOR SPATIAL INDEXING

It was asserted above that 'real' income is generally considered a more appropriate criterion for taxation than nominal income.[3] In particular, it is difficult to think of any convincing equity argument for imposing a progressive rate schedule on differentials in nominal income. As noted above, however, if tax burdens should in principle be compared in real terms over time, they should, for exactly the same reasons, be compared in real terms over space. Where there are geographical variations in the cost of living, applying a uniform tax schedule to equal amounts of nominal income which in fact represent different amounts of real income must therefore be inherently inequitable.

The point may be illustrated with Canadian data. A 1982 study, for example, found that the regional cost of living varied by 7 per cent, with Newfoundland (the poorest province) having the highest costs (Denny and Fuss 1982). A more recent study, using a different data base, by Dean (1988) found even more significant spatial differences in living costs between different areas in Canada. The order of magnitude of these differences is not too different from the temporal variations in purchasing power that led to the introduction of inflation indexing in Canada in 1974.

Nonetheless, the fact that these regional differences have not been taken into account for income tax purposes may perhaps be understandable, not so much in equity terms as simply because this issue has not really come into the political arena. If one extends the comparison to Canada's sparsely inhabited northern territories, however, matters are quite different. Not only are the cost-of-living differentials much greater, but there has in fact been considerable political discussion of the inequity of applying the unmodified federal income tax in the north.

The dimensions of the potential inequity are great. The cost of living in the largest community in the north (Yellowknife) is, for example, about one-third greater than that in the nearest southern city (Edmonton). Elsewhere in the north, the differentials are even greater. Drawing on a variety of sources for the early 1980s, for instance, Bird and Slack (1983) reported that the cost of living throughout the Northwest Territories ranged between 25 and 90 per cent higher than the Canadian average. Such cost-of-living differentials between north and south in Canada are so large that it seems impossible to justify the application of the same tax rates to the same nominal incomes. As Dean (1981) demonstrated, the result of doing so is to impose effective rates on the same real income that are from one-third to two-thirds higher in the north than in the south. Inequities of this magnitude seem unlikely to be tolerated for long and indeed, some measures have been taken to alleviate them in Canada.

While, as noted above, the differentials between regions in the south were much smaller, they still approach in magnitude the temporal differentials whose perceived inequity led to the introduction of indexing in Canada in 1974. Similar and perhaps even larger differentials might also be expected in other large countries, especially with respect to their more far-flung components: for example, the USA (Alaska and the various territories) and Australia (the Northern Territory). The next section reviews briefly the limited recognition that has been accorded this fact of life in the income taxes of two of these countries.

As yet, however, no country seems to have taken what would seem to be the logical step of introducing formal spatial indexing. The reasons for this reluctance, while beyond the scope of the present note, perhaps lie in the obvious political risks of doing so. Once the spectre of regional differentiation is introduced, where will it end? If a good case can be made for treating the north separately from the south, what about the obvious differences between rural and urban areas, between large metropolitan areas and other urban areas, between city *A* and city *B*, and so and on. Perhaps most importantly, unlike temporal indexing, which may (as the earlier quotation from Lindsay suggests) unite almost all citizens against the state, spatial indexing sets region against region, city against city, and citizen against citizen. Issues with clearly marked geographical effects are inevitably politically controversial, certainly in democratic states with geographically-based political constituencies. From a political economy perspective, spatial indexing thus looks totally different from temporal indexing, regardless of how similar they may appear from an equity perspective.

EXPERIENCE WITH SPATIAL INDEXING

The title of this section is somewhat misleading since no country actually indexes for spatial differentials in real income, perhaps for the reasons just adumbrated. Nonetheless, there is some recognition of the gross inequity of ignoring very large cost-of-living differentials in both Canada and Australia. In Canada, such recognition is currently limited to a 'northern deduction' in Australia; there is a rather similar 'zone allowance'.

Since 1987, Canada has provided a special northern deduction for taxpayers residing for six months or more north of 60 degrees latitude (as well as for some isolated communities further south). In 1989, the deduction was $225 per month plus an additional $225 per month for taxpayers who were sole claimants maintaining a self-contained domestic establishment – what nonlawyers might loosely call a 'home'. This deduction was introduced to replace a previous system of exempting certain employer-provided fringe benefits (mainly housing and travel) which had been subjected to severe criticism both for its limited nature and its arbitrariness. A special task force set up in 1989 to examine this system accepted the basic equity case for spatial indexing: 'A tax system applied uniformly on the basis of income alone imposes a greater burden in real terms on individuals living in regions with higher costs of living' (Canada 1989, p. 12). But it rejected such indexing in practice on the grounds that there was no reliable basis for comparing different regional incomes and instead recommended a continuation of the special deduction within a redefined 'northern zone'

Somewhat similar 'zone allowances' have existed in Australia since 1945. These allowances now take the form of tax credits, with the size of the credit varying with the remoteness of the region and the number of dependents. Most inhabitants of the sparsely inhabited interior and northern regions of Australia are eligible for these allowances. The original rationale for introducing zone allowances was again clearly horizontal equity (Taxation Review Committee 1975) and subsequent investigations (e.g. *Report 1981*) have generally reaffirmed the argument that, rough as it may be, the degree of equity in the income tax system is desirably strengthened as a result of the existence of the zone allowances.

Canada thus allows a special regional tax deduction, particularly for housing, and Australia provides a special regional tax credit, with the amount varying with the number of dependents. Neither provides any formal system of spatial indexing. The choice of the deduction or credit approach obviously depends in part upon the rationale for recognizing regional differentials in the first place. If the purpose is to alleviate the hardship of living in remote regions – what one Australian study called 'uncongenial climatic conditions, isolation, loss of social amenities and higher cost of living' (Treasury 1974, p. 25) – the credit approach may seem more logical since there is no reason to think the poor suffer less than the rich from such hardships. For this reason, Australia changed from a deduction to a credit in 1975. Such a change was also considered in Canada (1989).

Such a change seems misconceived, however, What is at issue is the appropriate definition of net income. If a dollar of income received in a particular region really provides its recipient less in terms of discretionary economic power than does a dollar in the rest of the country, then it does so regardless of how many dollars the recipient has. The basic equity case for a regional differential requires an adjustment in the tax base (or, equivalently, in the rates applied to that base): it cannot be satisfied by the tax credit approach.

If the deduction approach is to be applied equitably, however, it is essential to include all forms of compensation, whether received in kind or in money, in the tax base. Since many taxpayers in remote regions receive extensive in-kind benefits (especially housing) from their employers, the question of how such 'fringe benefits' are to be valued must also be addressed. As the OECD (1988) has recently shown, this is a controversial and difficult issue which is resolved differently in different contexts by different countries. In the present context, it is especially relevant that a number of countries (e.g. the US, Australia, the United Kingdom) specifically exclude from income, or value at very favourable rates, accomodation provided by employers to further their business activities, especially in remote areas where alternative accomodation is not available.[4] In a case like the Canadian north, where the fuel costs alone of heating a small two bedroom house can easily exceed the full rental value of a much more luxurious dwelling (utilities included) in, say, Toronto, it clearly makes no sense to include either the market value or the cost of providing such accomodation in taxable income.

An alternative approach might be to value the benefits from employer-provided housing at comparable prices for similar accommodation elsewhere. For example, if a similar house rented for $500 a month in Edmonton (or some composite southern city), then $500 a month would be set as the maximum taxable benefit, even if the market rent in the north is actually $1500 and the cost to the employer of providing the accommodation is also $1500. While this scheme is obviously rough, it would result in taxing fringe benefits only to the extent they exceed the amount needed to reflect the higher cost of living in remote areas. If, for example, employees were charged rents less than the 'comparable' rent established, they are not simply being compensated for higher living costs but are being subsidized: any such noncompensating incentive should of course be included in taxable income.

SOME POSSIBLE EXTENSIONS

The preceding discussion has been entirely in equity terms. The argument was basically that there is a strong a priori case in equity for a regionally-differentiated central income tax in countries in which there are significant regional cost-of-living differences. In addition, where differential levels of public services are provided in different regions, there may also be a case for geographically differentiated central taxes (as well as differential local taxes) on efficiency grounds. What is required for the efficient allocation of resources is not uniform tax rates but a uniform 'fiscal residual', or differential between taxes paid and benefits received (at the margin) by taxpayers at the same income level residing in different regions (Buchanan 1950). If the costs of providing a given level of services are higher in one area than in another, taxpayers in the high-cost area receive less services for their tax dollars even if those taxes are levied on 'real' (private) incomes.

In Canada's north, for example, services which most Canadians take for granted (e.g. roads) are virtually nonexistent and other services (e.g. education) cost twice as much per student and appear to be of inferior quality (Dean 1989). Such evidence suggests that, to avoid uneconomic interregional migration, taxes on northern residents should be lower than those levied elsewhere, not simply equal, as they would be if the tax system were adequately indexed as suggested above – and certainly not higher, as they are in fact. Of course, there is much more to the connections between equity, efficiency, and tax differentiation than can be mentioned here.[5] But this brief reference may suffice to suggest that there is indeed much more to be discussed.

Finally, consider the implications of the above discussion with respect to the appropriate design of income taxes in an open economy. In modern societies, governments provide substantial services (e.g. health, education) to workers. At the same time, workers are taxed to pay for these expenditure programmes. The simple analysis of international trade suggests strongly that there is often a case in both equity and efficiency terms for explicitly favourable tax treatment of workers who do not reside full time in their home country. To make the case most strongly, suppose that labour mobility (for the relevant subset of citizens) is high, that the home country in question is a relatively small supplier to the world market (a 'price taker') and that workers abroad are neither taxed by, nor receive services from, the country in which they work. These assumptions, while extreme, are by no means completely unrealistic with respect to highly skilled artisans and professionals working in many developing countries. Since such workers also clearly receive fewer benefits from the services provided by their home governments, they should pay lower taxes than workers who remain at home. Unless such an adjustment is made, the supply of persons willing to work abroad will be less than optimal, and those who, for whatever reason, choose to do so will be inequitably treated.

It would clearly be going too far to assert on the basis of this simple and incomplete argument that all labour income earned abroad should therefore in principle be exempt from personal income taxes. To mention only a few relevant factors: many workers abroad work in countries which provide significant services to residents (including those who may not pay local taxes); even residents abroad receive some (at least potential) services from their home country; and some labour income is earned abroad by persons (e.g. consultants) who do not in fact reside outside their home country for significant periods of time. On the other hand, it seems clearly both inequitable and inefficient to subject all citizens, wherever they reside, to the same tax schedule as the US does in principle. Even if the rationale for doing so is constructed entirely in 'ability to pay' terms – as is customary (Musgrave 1969) – nonresidents who do not share in the benefits (increases in real income) presumably resulting from the public expenditure to which they are being asked to contribute are clearly not in an 'equal position' with residents. (Incidentally, note that the cost-of-living argument set out earlier in this paper may work in either direction.)

The conclusion suggested by this very brief and preliminary discussion of a rather complex issue is obviously that persons who reside abroad for significant periods of time and who receive labour income from foreign sources should either be taxed at lower rates or have a significant portion of their income excluded from the tax base which their home country subjects to tax. Many countries, of course, have provisions along these lines, including the US. As a rule, however, such exclusions are viewed as 'concessions' or 'incentives', that is, as some form of 'tax expenditure' that requires special justification as a superior alternative to an outright government subsidy (Surrey and McDaniel 1985). As the above suggests, however, differential tax treatment of labour income earned by residing abroad for significant periods of time may be fully justified in both equity and efficiency terms.

Notes

1. The more complex question of indexing the tax base of business and capital income (McLure *et al.*, 1989) is not discussed here: no industrial country has yet taken any significant steps in this direction in any case.
2. An earlier, and even less developed, consideration of this question may be found in Bird and Slack (1983).
3. This case is argued particularly eloquently in Allan, Dodge, and Poddar (1974).
4. For references, see Bird and Slack (1983).
5. For some relevant discussions, see Buchanan (1950; 1952), Scott (1950; 1952; 1964), Graham (1964), Boadway and Flatters (1982), and Bird (1984).

References

1. Allan, J. R., Dodge, D. A. and Poddar, S. N. (1974) 'Indexing the personal income tax: a federal perspective', *Canadian Tax Journal*, vol. 22.
2. Bird, R. M. (1984) 'Tax harmonization and federal finance: a perspective on recent Canadian discussion', *Canadian Public Policy*, vol. 10.
3. Bird, R. M. and Slack, N. E. (1983) *Report on the Taxation of Northern Allowances* (Yellowknife: Northwest Territories Information).
4. Boadway, R. and Flatters, F. (1982) *Equalization in a Federal State: An Economic Analysis* (Ottawa: Ministry of Supply and Services).
5. Buchanan, J. M. (1950) 'Federalism and fiscal equity', *American Economic Review*, vol. 40.
6. Buchanan, J. M. (1952) 'Federal grants and resource allocation', *Journal of Political Economy*, vol. 60.
7. Canada (1989), *Report of the Task Force on Tax Benefits for Northern and Isolated Areas* (Ottawa: Ministry of Supply and Services).
8. Denny, M. and Fuss, M. (1982) 'Regional price indexes: the Canadian practice and some potential extensions' (Paper for Statistics Canada Conference on Price Measurement, Ottawa).
9. Dean, J. M. (1981) 'The interaction of federal and territorial income tax rates: the case of the Northwest Territories' (Paper for Canadian Regional Science Association, Halifax).

10. Dean, J. M. (1988) 'The effect of cost-of-living differentials on tax liabilities in Canada', *Canadian Tax Journal*, vol. 36.
11. Dean, J. M. (1989) 'Estimating the cost of providing certain health and education services in the N.W.T. as compared to the rest of Canada' (Paper for Department of Finance, Government of the Northwest Territories).
12. Graham, J. F. (1964) *Fiscal Adjustment and Economic Development* (Toronto: University of Toronto Press).
13. Ishi, H. (1989), *The Japanese Tax System* (Oxford: Clarendon Press).
14. Lindsay, L. B. (1990) *The Growth Experiment* (New York: Basic Books).
15. McLure, C. E. *et al.* (1989) *The Taxation of Income from Business and Capital in Colombia* (Durham: Duke University Press).
16. Musgrave, P. B. (1969) *United States Taxation of Foreign Investment Income: Issues and Arguments* (Cambridge, Mass.: International Tax Program, Harvard Law School).
17. Organisation for Economic Co-operation and Development (1986), *Personal Income Tax Systems under Changing Economic Conditions* (Paris: OECD).
18. Organisation for Economic Co-operation and Development (1988), *The Taxation of Fringe Benefits* (Paris: OECD).
19. *Report of the Public Inquiry into Income Tax Zone Allowances* (1981) (Canberra: Australian Government Publishing Service).
20. Scott, A. D. (1950) 'The evaluation of federal grants', *Economica*, vol. 19.
21. Scott, A. D. (1952) 'Federal grants and resource allocation', *Journal of Political Economy*, vol. 60.
22. Scott, A. D. (1964) 'The economic goals of federal finance', *Public Finance*, vol. 19.
23. Surrey, S. S. and McDaniel, R. P. (1985), *Tax Expenditures* (Cambridge, Mass.: Harvard University Press).
24. Taxation Review Committee (1975), *Full Report* (Canberra: Australian Government Publishing Service).
25. Treasury (1974) 'Personal income tax – personal allowances', *Treasury Taxation Paper*, No. 7 (Canberra: Australian Government Publishing Service).

12 Four Basic Rules of Optimal Commodity Taxation

Tatsuo Hatta*

INTRODUCTION

Since the celebrated article by Diamond and Mirrlees (1971) was published, the field of optimal commodity taxation has grown impressively. Although a large portion of this literature has been devoted to the study of the distributional implications of optimal taxation, various new results have also been obtained regarding the efficiency aspects of optimal commodity taxation by extending the seminal works by Ramsey (1927) and Samuelson (1951). In this paper, I survey in detail the results in the latter group.

I will derive these results either as equivalents or as corollaries of the following four basic rules of optimal taxation: (a) the Marginal Deadweight Burden rule, (b) the Samuelson rule, (c) the Diamond–Mirrlees rule, and (d) the Ramsey rule. These logically equivalent rules have distinctly different economic interpretations. Their symmetric nature makes them particularly useful bases for classification of other tax rules. To emphasize the strategic importance of these four basic rules, I will identify them as *Rules*, while calling all other tax rules *Propositions*.

Many excellent surveys are already available on this topic.[1] However, they fail to fully exploit the symmetric nature of the four basic rules. It is hoped that my classification will create some order in the currently unwieldly accumulation of optimal tax rules.

The paper begins by defining the issue, goes on to present the model and explain its implications for proportional and uniform tax structures, continues by setting out the four rules and their corollaries, and finishes with concluding remarks.

THE ISSUE

In the Arrow–Debreu general equilibrium model, imposing an equal *ad valorem* tax rate on all goods leaves the economy Pareto optimal. In this model, therefore, a proportional taxation of all goods including leisure attains an efficient resource allocation for a given government revenue.

In reality, however, the tax office cannot obtain precise data on the hours of leisure consumption by a taxpayer, even though it can obtain data on his wage income from the employer. If the tax payer were asked to spontaneously report the hours of his leisure consumption, there would be a strong incentive for him to understate it and this would simultaneously enable him to underscore his hourly wage rate, thus enabling him to reduce his claimed tax base for the leisure tax in a multiple way. For this reason the leisure tax is seldom installed in reality.

In the real economy, tax is imposed on wage income, rather than on leisure consumption. A wage tax encourages leisure consumption, just as uniform taxes on all commodities – throughout this paper, I will call a non-leisure good a 'commodity'; hence 'all goods' will consist of 'all commodities' plus leisure. Thus a simultaneous imposition of taxes on all commodities and wages at the same rate would reinforce the encouragement of leisure consumption, distorting the leisure-consumption choice unequivocally.

Since distortions are inevitable under any combination of the wage tax and taxes on commodities, it becomes necessary to design the least cost combination of distortionary commodity taxes and the wage tax that raises a given revenue. The optimal tax theory characterizes the structure of such taxes.

In general, the optimal tax structure is non-uniform in order to counteract the distortions created by the non-availability of the leisure tax. Imposing a high tax rate on complements of leisure (e.g. yacht and concerts) and subsidizing substitutes of leisure (e.g. dish washer and microwave oven) would discourage leisure consumption, serving to counteract such distortions.

In making commodity tax rates non-uniform, however, a policy maker faces a trade off since the non-uniformity of the commodity tax rates creates new distortions in the choice among the commodities, even though it may reduce the distortion in the leisure-consumption choice. The optimal tax structure is the one that strikes the balance in this trade off.

THE MODEL

I make the following assumptions:[2]

1. There is only one consumer in the economy, who consumes leisure and n commodities. Producers produce these n commodities and a public good by applying leisure (labour).

The variables indexed by 0 are associated with leisure, and those indexed by $1, \ldots, n$ with the commodities. The quantity of the public good is designated by r.

2. The consumer is a perfect competitor and maximizes his utility level under the given budget.

The prices he faces are called consumer's prices and are denoted by the vector $q' = (q^0, q^1, \ldots, q^n)$. Denote the consumer's net demand vector by $x' = (x^0, x^1, \ldots, x^n)$. Then his budget equation requires that

$$q'x = 0 \tag{1}$$

This equation is easier to understand if it is rewritten as

$$q^1x^1 + \ldots + q^nx^n = q^0(-x^0)$$

Note that the RHS represents the wage income since q^0 is the wage rate and $-x^0$ (> 0) is the leisure endowments minus leisure consumption, which is labour supply. I denote his compensated demand function for leisure and commodities by

$$x = x(q, u) \tag{2}$$

where u represents his utility level.

3. The consumer's net demand for leisure is negative, and his net demand for all other goods is positive on the relevant domain of the prices.

Thus,

$$x^0 < 0, x^1 > 0 \ldots \quad \text{and} \quad x^n > 0 \tag{3}$$

The first inequality simply states that the consumer's leisure endowment is greater than the amount he consumes. Strict inequalities are assumed so that we can freely use interior maximization conditions.

4. The production possibility frontier is of the constant cost type.
The frontier is represented by

$$p'x + r = 0 \tag{4}$$

where $p = (1, p^1, \ldots, p^n)$ are constants. The units of r are so chosen that its coefficient in this equation is one. This equation may be easier to understand if it is rewritten as

$$p^1x^1 + \ldots + p^nx^n + r = -x^0 \tag{5}$$

The term $-x^0(> 0)$ on the RHS is the amount of labour available to producers. Coefficient $p^i(i = 1, \ldots, n)$ is the marginal cost of the ith commodity in terms of labour input.

5. Producers maximize their profit, taking producers' prices as given.
Hence, the economy is always on the production frontier. Also this assumption implies that if one good is less profitable than another, resources will be reallocated from the former industry to the latter through the market mechanism. This, together with assumptions 3 and 4, implies that the producers' price vector for leisure, commodities and the public good is proportional to $(p', 1)$.

6. The producers' price of leisure is the numeraire.
Thus, the producers' prices of leisure and commodities are equal to p.

7. Specific excise taxes and a wage tax are imposed. Taxes are the only reason why producers' prices diverge from consumer's prices. There are no other taxes; in particular, there is no lump-sum tax.
Thus,

$$q^i = t^i + p^i \qquad i = 0, \ldots, n \tag{6}$$

where $p^0 = 1$, and t^i is the specific tax rate on the ith good. For commodity i, positive and negative values of t^i correspond to taxes and subsidies, respectively. When a positive income (wage) tax is imposed on labour rather than on leisure, the consumer's take-home pay is less than what his employer pays. This implies that $q^0 < p^0$; hence $t^0 < 0$. Thus an increase in t^0 implies a *decrease* in the income tax rate.

I assume that

$$t^i + p^i > 0 \qquad i = 0, \ldots, n \tag{7}$$

In view of (6), this is equivalent to assuming that $q^i > 0$ for all i.

8. The tax revenue collected is spent on the public good. Hence,

$$t'x = r \tag{8}$$

Equation (8), however, is also implied by (1), (4) and (6). So I will not explicitly consider this equation below.

Substituting (2) into (1) and (4), one gets

$$q'x(q, u) = 0 \tag{9}$$

$$p'x(q, u) + r = 0 \tag{10}$$

These two equations contain $n + 3$ variables, q, u and r. When $n + 1$ elements of (q, u, r) are exogenously given, the two equations determine the remaining variables. If a combination (q, u, r) satisfies both equations (9) and (10), then q is a *solution* or *equilibrium price vector* of the model for the corresponding (u, r). The t vector associated with the solution vector q for the given (u, r) will also be called a *solution* or *equilibrium tax vector* for the model.

Given q, the model of (9) and (10) will yield solutions for u and r. In view of (6),[3] the solution functions for these variables can be written as functions of t:

$$r = \rho(t) \tag{11}$$

$$u = \mu(t)$$

Finally, note that equation (9) can be equivalently stated in terms of the expenditure function as:

$$m(q, u) = 0 \tag{9'}$$

where

$$m(q, u) \equiv q'x(q, u)$$

PROPORTIONAL AND UNIFORM TAX STRUCTURES

We will first discuss three properties of the equilibrium vectors of our model for q and t, before studying the optimal tax structure itself. The first two properties were emphasized by Mirrlees (1976). The third property, which is concerned with a special case of the second property, will be used in the proofs of the propositions in this paper.

Property I A proportional tax structure yields zero revenue

Here, a tax structure is called *proportional* if all goods share an identical *ad valorem* tax rate, i.e., if

$$\frac{t^i}{q^i} = \lambda \qquad i = 0, \ldots, n \tag{12}$$

or

$$t = \lambda q$$

for some scalar λ. Under a proportional tax structure, therefore, tax rates on all goods including t^0 have the same sign. Note that a positive wage tax is represented by a negative t^0 in the model. If a positive wage tax is imposed in a proportional tax structure, therefore, the tax rates on all goods must be negative. Then all the revenue from the positive wage tax is spent on subsidies on commodities, yielding a zero net revenue. If, however, the proportional tax rates are positive, all the revenue from commodity taxes is spent on wage subsidies, again yielding a zero net revenue.

To see this formally, observe that under a proportional tax structure,

$$q = \theta p \tag{13}$$

holds for some scalar θ from (6) and (12). Hence (1) reduces to

$$p'x = 0$$

A comparison of this and (4) yields $r = 0$.[4]

This implies that in this model a proportional tax is infeasible for a positive r. *A fortiori*, it cannot be optimal. This is in contrast to classical models, where a proportional tax is not only feasible but also optimal. Note that classical models make the unrealistic postulate that the value of leisure rather than that of labour is taxable.

Property II The solution vector for t in the model of (9) and (10) for a given r and u is not unique; Moreover, two different solution vectors for t are not proportional

Suppose that q_* is an equilibrium price vector for the model of (9) and (10). Since $x(q, u)$ is homogeneous of degree zero with respect to q, substituting $q = \kappa q_*$ for q also satisfies both equations (9) and (10), if κ is a positive constant. Thus a proportional increase in q_* does not affect the real equilibrium.

In other words, if

$$t_* = q_* - p \tag{14}$$

is an equilibrium tax vector, so is

$$t = \kappa q_* - p \tag{15}$$

This tax vector is *equivalent* to the original tax vector t_* for any positive constant κ. Under equivalent tax vectors, the real equilibrium, hence the government revenue, remain the same. Thus one can normalize the tax vector by choosing one element to be of a specified value. But note that, in general, equivalent tax vectors are not proportional to each other, as can be seen by comparing (14) and (15). Incidentally, this also implies that an optimal tax structure is not unique, and that two optimal tax structures are not in general proportional to each other.

Normalization of a tax vector often yields a simple explanation of the properties of the tax vector. For example, suppose that an equilibrium tax vector t_* represents a proportional tax structure, and that the corresponding consumer price is given by $q_* = t_* + p$. Then since $q_* = \theta p$ for some scalar θ from (13), we find from (15) that

$$t = \kappa\theta p - p$$

is also an equivalent tax vector to the proportional tax structure. By choosing κ so that $\kappa\theta = 1$, we have $t = 0$. Thus the zero vector is equivalent to any proportional tax structure. Since $t = 0$ obviously gives a zero revenue, this gives an alternative proof of Property I above.

Property III Any uniform tax structure is equivalent to wage taxation

A tax structure is called uniform if all *commodities* share an identical *ad valorem* tax rate, i.e. if

$$\frac{t^i}{q^i} = \lambda \qquad i = 1, \ldots, n$$

for some λ. Thus a proportional tax structure is a special form of the uniform tax structure in that t^0/q^0 is also equal to the *ad valorem* commodity tax rate.

Wage taxation is imposed if

$$t^0 \neq 0 \qquad \text{and} \qquad t^i = 0 \qquad \text{for} \qquad i = 1, \ldots, n \tag{16}$$

It is readily seen that wage taxation, too, is a special form of the uniform tax structure. In fact, one can show that any given uniform tax structure is equivalent to a wage taxation. Suppose that t_* is a uniform tax vector and q_* the corresponding consumer price vector. Then one observes

$$q^i_* = \theta p^i \qquad i = 1, \ldots, n \tag{17}$$

for some scalar θ from (6). However, from (15) one notes that t^* as defined above is equivalent to

$$t = \frac{1}{\theta}\, q_* - p \tag{18}$$

Substituting (17) for q_* in (18), one obtains (16). Therefore any uniform commodity tax is equivalent to wage taxation.

THE MARGINAL DEADWEIGHT BURDEN RULE

Let me now turn to optimal tax rules.

I assume that the government chooses q to maximize the utility level in the model of (9′) and (10) for a fixed level of r:

$$\max_{q,\,u} u \qquad \text{ST} \qquad x'(q, u)p + r = 0 \qquad m(q, u) = 0 \tag{19}$$

Definition Let q_* be an optimal solution of (19). A tax vector t is called an optimal tax structure if it satisfies $t = q^* - p$.

Definition[5] The social marginal cost of a unit increase in the tax rate of good i is defined by $x_i'p(\equiv x_i^0p^0 + \ldots + x_i^np^n)$.

Since this is the partial derivative of the LHS of (10) with respect to t^i, it represents an additional resource cost needed to produce the compensated consumption bundle caused by a unit increase in t^i.[6]

Proposition 1 Under an optimal tax structure, the social marginal cost of a unit increase in each tax rate is proportional to the private marginal cost of a unit increase in that tax rate:

$$x_i^0p^0 + \ldots + x_i^np^n = \alpha m_i \qquad i = 0, \ldots, n \tag{20}$$

i.e.

$$x_q'p = \alpha m_q \tag{21}$$

holds for some scalar α.

Proof[7] From the Lagrangean

$$V = u - \lambda(x'(q, u)p + r) - \psi m(q, u) \tag{22}$$

Its first-order conditions are:

$$\begin{aligned} \lambda x_u'p + \psi m_u &= 1 \\ \lambda x_q'p + \psi m_q &= 0 \end{aligned} \tag{23}$$

The last equation yields

$$x_q'p = \alpha m_q \tag{24}$$

where $\alpha = -\psi/\lambda$. Q.E.D.

In terms of the interpretation of (21), given in the statement of the proposition, α has to be positive. Indeed, this natural conjecture follows from (23) when the normality condition $x_u'p > 0$ holds.[8]

Diamond and McFadden expressed the *deadweight burden* of taxation as "the difference between income needed at consumer prices q

and tax revenue collected", i.e. $m(q, u) - t'x(q, u)$. The partial derivative of this with respect to t^i yields:

Definition The *marginal deadweight burden* of the tax rate of the *i*-th good is defined by

$$(x_i^0 t^0 + \ldots + x_i^n t^n)$$

It turns out that the marginal deadweight burden of the tax rate of the i-th good is equal to the social marginal cost of the tax rate. Indeed, the Hicksian demand rule, $x_i'q = 0$ and (6) give:

$$x_i'p = -x_i't \tag{25}$$

This and Proposition 1 immediately yield our first rule:

Rule I (Marginal Deadweight Burden) Under an optimal tax structure, the marginal deadweight burden of a unit increase in each tax rate is proportional to the demand for that good:

$$-(x_i^0 t^0 + \ldots + x_i^n t^n) = \alpha x^i \qquad i = 0, \ldots, n \tag{26}$$

i.e.

$$-x_q't = \alpha x \tag{27}$$

holds for some scalar α.

Since

$$\frac{\partial}{\partial t}\,[x'(p + t, u)t] = x_q'(p + t, u)t + x(p + t, u) \tag{28}$$

Rule I immediately implies the following:

Proposition 2 (Diamond and McFadden) If an optimum is attained under a tax structure, the marginal deadweight burden of a unit increase in each tax rate is proportional to the increase in the government revenue caused by the same tax increase:

$$\frac{\partial}{\partial t}\,[x'(p + t, u)t] = \nu x_q't \tag{29}$$

holds for some scalar ν.

THE SAMUELSON RULE

The inverse compensated elasticity rule

Applying the symmetry property of the substitution matrix x_q to Rule I, one immediately obtains:

Rule II (Samuelson 1951) If an optimal tax structure is attained, a proportional increase in all tax rates proportionally reduces the compensated demand vector:

$$x_0^i t^0 + \ldots + x_n^i t^n = -\alpha x^i \qquad i = 0, \ldots, n \tag{30}$$

i.e.

$$x_q t = -\alpha x \tag{31}$$

holds for some α.

Note that the LHS of (31) represents the compensated change in the demand bundle induced by a proportional change in the t vector because

$$x_q t = \frac{\partial x(p + \theta t, u)}{\partial \theta}\Big|_{\theta = 1}$$

Suppose that an optimal tax structure is attained in an economy where cross demand elasticities among the commodities are negligible. Since one percentage increase in all the tax rates decreases the compensated demand for all goods proportionally, a commodity with a low demand elasticity must have a high tax rate. To state this interpretation precisely, one needs a few definitions.

Definition The q^j elasticity of compensated demand for good i is defined by:

$$\eta_j^i \equiv \frac{x_j^i}{x^i} q^j$$

In particular, η_i^i is defined as the *demand elasticity* for good i, and η_0^i as the *wage elasticity of demand* for good i. It is claimed that the demand elasticity for good i is higher than that for good j if $-\eta_i^i > -\eta_j^j$.

Definition The difference between the *ad valorem* tax rate of good i and that on leisure shall be called the intrinsic tax rate of good i, and will be denoted by

$$\tau^i \equiv \frac{t^i}{q^i} - \frac{t^0}{q^0}$$

Proposition 3 (Inverse Compensated Elasticity Rule) Assume that the cross-substitution terms among the commodities are all zeros, i.e.

$$x_q = \begin{pmatrix} x_0^0 & x_1^0 & \cdots & x_n^0 \\ x_0^1 & x_1^1 & & 0 \\ \vdots & 0 & \ddots & \\ x_0^n & & & x_n^n \end{pmatrix}$$

Under an optimal taxation, the intrinsic tax rate of a commodity is inversely related to its demand elasticity, i.e.

$$\tau^i = \frac{\alpha}{-\eta_i^i} \qquad i = 1, \ldots, n$$

for some scalar α.

Proof Under the assumptions of the proposition, Rule II implies that

$$x_0^i t^0 + x_i^i t^i = -\alpha x^i \qquad i = 1, \ldots, n$$

In the elasticity notation,

$$\eta_0^i \frac{t^0}{q^0} + \eta_i^i \frac{t^i}{q^i} = -\alpha \qquad i = 1, \ldots, n$$

However, the Hicksian homogeneity rule gives

$$\eta_0^i + \eta_i^i = 0 \qquad i = 1, \ldots, n \tag{32}$$

By eliminating η_0^i from these two equations, one gets the proposition. Q.E.D.

Note that if t^0 is zero, the *ad valorem* tax rate for each good is inversely related to its demand elasticity. This proposition implies that a low tax rate should be imposed on a good with a high demand elasticity. However, this proposition is not as useful as it first looks; a good with a high demand elasticity usually has a strong substitute, but the proposition rules out the existence of any substitute other than leisure.

In view of (32), Propositions 3 may be restated as follows.

Proposition 4 Assume that the cross-substitution terms among the commodities are all zeros. Then under an optimal tax structure, the intrinsic tax rate of a commodity is inversely related to the wage elasticity of demand for that commodity, i.e.

$$\tau^i = \frac{\alpha}{\eta_0^i} \qquad i = 1, \ldots, n$$

for some scalar α.

As was pointed out in the first section, a uniform tax would encourage leisure consumption. Thus reducing the tax rates on strong substitutes of leisure accompanied by a revenue-offsetting increases in other tax rates would help offset the excessive leisure consumption. Proposition 4 implies that a low tax rate should be imposed on a strong substitute of leisure when the cross-substitution terms among the commodities are all zeros. The reason is simple. Since the cross substitution effects among the commodities are zero, nonuniform commodity taxes do not create distortions among commodities. That is why the commodity tax structure can be widely differentiated to have large effects on discouraging leisure consumption under the assumption of the proposition.

An extension of this interpretation would suggest that a high tax rate should be imposed on a complement of leisure in order to discourage leisure consumption. But this is a vacuous statement since equation (32) implies that no commodity can be a çompliment for leisure when cross substitution effects among the commodities are zero.

Uniform tax structure

Suppose that the optimum is attained by a wage taxation with zero tax rates for all commodities. A proportional increase in all the tax rates in this case is an increase in t^0. Rule II indicates that then an increase in t^0 should increase the compensated demand for all goods proportionately. If a wage taxation is optimal, therefore, wage elasticities of compensated demand for all goods must be equal. The following proposition states this formally:

Proposition 5 (Corlett and Hague, Sadka) A uniform tax structure is optimal if and only if wage elasticities of demand are equal for all commodities, i.e.

$$\eta_0^1 = \ldots = \eta_0^n \tag{33}$$

Proof It suffices to prove that $(t^0, 0, \ldots, 0)$ attains optimal if and only if (33) is satisfied. Rule II implies that $(t^0, 0, \ldots, 0)$ is optimal if and only if

$$x_i^0 t^0 = -\alpha x^i \qquad i = 0, \ldots, n$$

Thus,

$$\eta_0^i \frac{t^0}{q^0} = -\alpha \qquad i = 0, \ldots, n$$

Since

$$\eta_0^0 = \ldots = \eta_0^n$$

holds if and only if (33) is satisfied,[9] one gets the proposition. Q.E.D.

Proposition 4 implies that a uniform tax is optimal if (33) holds and if cross-elasticities among commodities are zero. Proposition 5 shows, however, that the last proviso is unnecessary. The reason for this is obvious from our interpretation of Proposition 4. A nonuniform commodity taxation is optimal to the extent that it can moderate the excessive consumption created by the non-availability of leisure taxation. When wage elasticities of demand for all commodities are equal, a nonuniform commodity taxation can not perform this function. Thus the reason for the commodity tax structure to be nonuniform disappears regardless of the cross elasticities among commodities.[10]

THE DIAMOND–MIRRLEES RULE

So far I have characterized the optimal tax rules in terms of compensated demand functions. These rules can be restated in terms of ordinary (or uncompensated) demand functions.

Let $\tilde{x}(q, m)$ be the ordinary demand function. Then

$$x(q, u) \equiv \tilde{x}(q, m(q, u)) \tag{34}$$

and one has the Slutsky decomposition

$$x_q = \tilde{x}_q + \tilde{x}_m \tilde{x}' \tag{35}$$

Rule III (Diamond–Mirrlees) Under an optimal tax structure,

$$\tilde{x}_i^0 t^0 + \ldots + \tilde{x}_i^n t^n = -\beta \tilde{x}^i \qquad i = 0, \ldots, n \tag{36}$$

i.e.

$$\tilde{x}_q' t = -\beta \tilde{x}$$

holds for some β.

Proof[11] Substituting (35) for x_q in Rule I, one has $\tilde{x}_q' t + \tilde{x}\tilde{x}_m' t = -\alpha x$, which proves Rule III, where $\beta = \alpha + \tilde{x}_m' t$. Q.E.D.

Unlike Rule I, one cannot interpret this rule in terms of deadweight burden; the LHS of (36) is not a marginal deadweight burden. But the following extension of the rule, which is similar to Proposition 2, in view of (27), holds.

Proposition 6 If an optimum is attained under a tax structure, a unit increase in the tax rate of each good will increase the government revenue proportionally to the demand of each good:

$$\frac{\partial}{\partial t}\left[\tilde{x}'(p + t, 0)t\right] = \gamma \tilde{x}(p + t, 0)$$

holds for some scalar γ.

Proof Since

$$\frac{\partial}{\partial t}\,[\tilde{x}'(p + t, 0)t] = \tilde{x}_q'(p + t, 0)t + \tilde{x}(p + t, 0)$$

Rule III immediately implies the proposition. Q.E.D.

While Rule II was derived from Rule I by taking advantage of the symmetry of x_q, an ordinary demand function version of Rule II cannot be easily derived from Rule III, since the matrix $\tilde{x}_q$ is not always symmetric, unlike x_q. Thus Rule III does not in general imply $\tilde{x}_q t = -\beta\tilde{x}$. Moreover, if the entire matrix of $\tilde{x}_q$ is symmetric, then either leisure or all the commodities must be inferior,[12] which is obviously unrealistic.

Nevertheless, all the cross-substitution terms between *commodities* can be symmetric without the presence of inferiority. Then a counterpart of Rule II can be derived for the uncompensated substitution matrix.

Define $\hat{t}$, $\hat{x}$, $\hat{x}_m$, and $\hat{x}_q$ *by*

$$\hat{t} = \begin{pmatrix} t_1 \\ \vdots \\ t^n \end{pmatrix}, \hat{x} = \begin{pmatrix} \tilde{x}^1 \\ \vdots \\ \tilde{x}^n \end{pmatrix}, \hat{x}_m = \begin{pmatrix} \tilde{x}_m^1 \\ \vdots \\ \tilde{x}_m^n \end{pmatrix}, \hat{x}_0 = \begin{pmatrix} \tilde{x}_0^1 \\ \vdots \\ \tilde{x}_0^n \end{pmatrix}$$

and

$$\hat{x}_q = \begin{pmatrix} \tilde{x}_1^1 & \cdots & \tilde{x}_n^1 \\ & & \cdots \\ \tilde{x}_1^n & \cdots & \tilde{x}_n^n \end{pmatrix}$$

Then one gets the following:

Proposition 7 (The Symmetry Rule) Suppose that $\hat{x}_q = \hat{x}_q'$. If an optimal tax structure satisfies $t^0 = 0$, a proportional increase in all tax rates proportionally reduces the uncompensated demand vector for commodities:

$$\tilde{x}_1^i t^1 + \ldots + \tilde{x}_n^i t^n = -\beta x^i \qquad i = 1, \ldots, n \tag{37}$$

i.e.

$$\hat{x}_q \hat{t} = -\beta \hat{x} \tag{38}$$

for some β.

Proof The assumptions of the proposition and Rule III yield

$$\hat{x}_q \hat{t} = \hat{x}_q' \hat{t} = -\beta \hat{x}. \text{ Q.E.D.}$$

The proposition implies that under its provisos an optimal tax structure does not affect the proportions of consumption among different commodities.

When uncompensated cross-elasticities among commodities are zero, x_q is of course symmetric. Thus Proposition 7 implies that a one percentage increase in all the tax rates reduces the uncompensated demand for all commodities proportionally. Therefore, the tax rate must be high for a commodity with a low uncompensated demand elasticity. This interpretation will be precisely stated in Proposition 8.

Definition The q^j elasticity of uncompensated demand for good i, $\tilde{\eta}^i_j$ is defined by:

$$\tilde{\eta}^i_j \equiv \frac{\tilde{x}^i_j}{x^i} q^j$$

In particular, $\tilde{\eta}^i_i$ is called the uncompensated demand elasticity for good i, and $\tilde{\eta}^i_0$ the wage elasticity of demand for good i. It is claimed that the demand elasticity for good i is higher than that for good j if $-\eta^i_i > -\eta^j_j$.

Proposition 8 (Inverse Uncompensated Elasticity Rule) Assume that the uncompensated cross-substitution terms among the commodities are all zeros, i.e.

$$\tilde{x}_q = \begin{pmatrix} \tilde{x}^0_0 & \tilde{x}^0_1 & \cdots & \tilde{x}^0_n \\ \tilde{x}^1_0 & \tilde{x}^1_1 & & \\ \vdots & 0 & \ddots & 0 \\ \tilde{x}^n_0 & & & \tilde{x}^n_n \end{pmatrix}$$

Then the intrinsic tax rate of a good is inversely related to its uncompensated demand elasticity, i.e.

$$\tau^i = \frac{\lambda}{-\tilde{\eta}^i_i} \qquad i = 1, \ldots, n$$

for some scalar λ.

Proof Under the assumptions of the proposition, Rule III implies that

$$\tilde{x}^0_i t^0 + \tilde{x}^i_i t^i = -\beta \tilde{x}^i \qquad i = 0, \ldots, n \tag{39}$$

However, the demand rule,

$$\tilde{x}_i' q + \tilde{x}^i = 0 \qquad i = 0, \ldots, n \tag{40}$$

and the assumptions of the proposition imply

$$\tilde{x}^0_i q^0 + \tilde{x}^i_i q^i + \tilde{x}^i = 0 \qquad i = 0, \ldots, n$$

Substituting this equation for $\tilde{x}^0_i$ in (39), one gets

$$\tilde{x}^i_i (t^i q^0 - q^i t^0) = -(\beta q^0 - t^0)\tilde{x}^i \qquad i = 1, \ldots, n \tag{41}$$

This immediately yields the proposition. Q.E.D.

Note that the *ad valorem* tax rate of each good is inversely related to its uncompensated demand elasticity when t^0 is zero.

Proposition 8 is an uncompensated elasticity version of Proposition 3, but Proposition 4 does not have a counterpart in terms of uncompensated wage elasticities.

THE RAMSEY RULE

One can now derive an ordinary demand function version of Rule II without making a specific assumption on demand parameters.

Substituting (35) for x_q in Rule II, and then applying (8), one gets:

Rule IV (Ramsey) Under an optimal tax structure,

$$\tilde{x}_q t = -\alpha \tilde{x} - r \tilde{x}_m \tag{42}$$

holds for some α.

Since $\tilde{x}_q t = \dfrac{\partial \tilde{x}(p + \theta t, 0)}{\partial \theta}\Big|_{\theta = 1}$, Rule IV states that the actual percentage fall in demand induced by a proportional tax-rate increase is larger for goods with a large income elasticity. This rule implies, however, that when r is sufficiently small, a proportional tax-rate increase should reduce demand for every good proportionally. This is the celebrated Ramsey Rule. See Samuelson (1982) for an historical note on Rules II and IV.

A glance at the RHS of (42) suggests that, if $\tilde{x}$ and $\tilde{x}_m$ are proportional, this equation is simplified.

Proportion 9 (The Homotheticity Rule) Suppose that the utility function underlying the demand function x is homothetic with respect to commodities. Suppose also that an optimal tax structure satisfies $t^0 = 0$. Then a proportional increase in all tax rates proportionally reduces the uncompensated demand vector for commodities:

$$\hat{x}_q \hat{t} = \gamma \hat{x} \tag{43}$$

holds for some γ.

Proof Note that, in view of (44), in note 10, the definition of the homotheticity of the underlying utility function implies that $x_m = \theta x$ locally holds for some θ. Rule IV and the assumptions of the proposition therefore yield that

$$\hat{x}_q \hat{t} = [\hat{x}_0 | \hat{x}_q] t = -\alpha \hat{x} - r \hat{x}_m = -(\alpha + r\theta)\hat{x}. \text{ Q.E.D.}$$

Note that (38) and (43) are identical. In fact, one can show that the provisos of Proportion 9 imply those of Proposition 7.[13]

Finally, one notes that the four basic rules of optimal taxation are mutually equivalent. So far, I have proved Rule IV from Rule II, and Rules II and III from Rule I. However, one can further derive Rule I from Rule III by noting the symmetry of expression (35), and then Rule III from Rule IV by substituting equation (35) for x_q. Thus the equivalence of the four basic rules is established.

CONCLUDING REMARKS

If all goods were taxable, an equal tax rate on all goods would attain an optimum, which is what Musgrave would recommend. However, in an economy where leisure is not taxable, a uniform tax structure would stimulate leisure consumption excessively. A divergent tax structure can moderate the excessive leisure consumption by imposing relatively high tax rates on relatively complementary leisure commodities, which is what Corlett and Hague would recommend. But the divergence among commodity tax rates creates new distortions among commodities, posing a trade-off in utility improvement. A tax structure is optimal when it strikes a balance in this trade-off between the Corlett and Hague type force for divergence and the Musgravian force for uniformity.

In this paper, optimal tax rules have been classified under the four basic rules, which are mutually equivalent. Rules I and II are stated in terms of compensated demand functions, while Rules III and IV in terms of ordinary demand functions. Rules III and IV are derived by applying the Slutsky decomposition to Rules I and II, respectively.

In terms of economic interpretation, the four rules can be paired differently. Rules I and III imply the revenue effect of a unit increase in the tax rate of each good is proportional to the quantity demanded of the respective good. On the other hand, Rules II and IV imply that when all taxes are proportionally increased from the optimal levels, the equilibrium consumption vector shrinks proportionally under appropriate assumptions.

Notes

* Various versions of this paper were used as lecture notes for my courses at Johns Hopkins, Columbia, and Osaka Universities. I have benefited from many helpful comments by those who took these courses, especially Toshihiro Ihori, Mike Ormiston, Ailsa Roel, and Rajiv Vohra. I would like to thank Maureen Germani for her editorial assistance. Financial assistance by Inamori Foundation is gratefully acknowledged.

1. See, for example, Sandmo (1976), Mirrlees (1976), Mirrlees (1981; 1987), Samuelson (1982), Homma (1985), and Auerbach (1985).
2. The following assumptions are the same as those Hatta (1986) employed for his model of tax reform, except that here I specify the taxes in *specific* form rather than *ad valorem* form, following the tradition of the literature on optimal taxation.

3. For the properties of the function ρ, see section 5 of Hatta and Haltiwanger (1986).
4. This also follows from (8). Substituting (12) directly for q in (1), one obtains $t'x = 0$. A comparison of this and (8) also yields $r = 0$.
5. A functional symbol with a subscript will indicate the derivative, the gradient, or the Jacobian matrix of the original function with respect to the variable or the vector denoted by the subscript. For example,

$$x^i_j \equiv \frac{\partial x^i}{\partial q_j},\ x_j \equiv \frac{\partial x}{\partial q_j},\ x_q \equiv \frac{\partial x}{\partial q},\ x^i_u \equiv \frac{\partial x^i}{\partial u},\ \text{and } x_u \equiv \frac{\partial x}{\partial u}$$

6. The expression $x^0_i p^0 + \ldots + x^n_i p^n$ is the aggregate of all the substitution terms of good i weighted by the marginal costs, and was called *ASM*(i) in Hatta (1977).
7. The present proof follows that of Mirrlees (1976). The maximization problem of (19) can be formulated in alternative ways. Let u^* be the maximized value of the utility level in the maximization problem of (19). Then a vector q^* is a solution of (19) if and only if it is a solution of the following minimization problem:

$$\min_q \quad x'(q, u^*)p; \quad \text{ST} \quad m(q, u^*) = 0$$

The solution of this problem minimizes the total amount of resources needed to produce a bundle that sustains u^*. This immediately makes it clear that an optimal tax vector minimizes excess burden given the household budget constraint.

It is readily seen that the solution vectors of problem (19) and the following problem are also equivalent:

$$\min_q \quad m(q, u^*); \quad \text{ST} \quad x'(q, u^*)p + r = 0$$

Indeed, Diamond and McFadden derived Rule I essentially through this minimization problem.
8. When the RHS of the production constraint is increased, the total amount of resources available in this economy is exogenously increased. Hence the new value of u must be increased. In view of (22), λ is therefore positive. The positivity of λ and the normality condition are equivalent. However, when the RHS of the constraint of the expenditure function is increased in problem (19), it is the same as a lumpsum subsidy given to the consumer. This means that now the revenue has to be raised not only for the public good but also to finance the lumpsum subsidy. Since the distortionary taxes have to be raised in the economy with the same amount of total resources, the welfare level is reduced. In view of (22) therefore ψ must be negative; thus α is negative.
9. The proof may be given as follows: from the Hicksian homogeneity and symmetry rules, one has

$$\begin{aligned} 0 &= q^0x^0_0 + q^1x^1_0 + \ldots + q^nx^n_0 \\ &= q^0x^0\eta^0_0 + q^1x^1\eta^1_0 + \ldots + q^nx^n\eta^n_0 \end{aligned}$$

Thus (1) and (33) imply.

$$\begin{aligned} 0 &= (q^0x^0)\eta_0^0 + (q^1x^1 + \ldots + q^nx^n)\eta_0^1. \\ &= (q^0x^0)(\eta_0^0 - \eta_0^1). \end{aligned}$$

Q.E.D.

10. Note that there is a type of utility function under which the optimal tax structure is always uniform.

Definition The utility function underlying the demand function x is said to be homothetic with respect to commodities, if

$$x_u^i(q, u) = \varepsilon(q, u)x^i(q, u) \qquad i = 1, \ldots, n \tag{44}$$

for some function $\varepsilon(q, u)$.

Definition The utility function u is separable with respect to commodities, if there exist functions v and h satisfying:

$$u(x) = v[x^0, h(x^1, \ldots, x^n)]$$

Lemma 1 If a utility function is both separable and homothetic with respect to commodities, then $\eta_0^1 = \ldots = \eta_0^n$ at any consumption bundle.

Proof A theorem on separability by Gorman states that a utility function is separable with respect to commodities if and only if

$$x_0^i(q, u) = \psi(q, u)x_u^i(q, u) \qquad i = 1, \ldots, n$$

for some function ψ, which is independent of i. Applying (44) to this one gets

$$x_0^i(q, u) = \psi(q, u)\varepsilon(q, u)x^i(q, u) \qquad i = 1, \ldots, n$$

for some function $\varepsilon(q, u)$. One therefore has the lemma. Q.E.D.

Proposition (Deaton) If the utility function is both homothetic and separable with respect to commodities, then a uniform tax structure is optimal.

Proof This follows from Proposition 4 and Lemma 1. Q.E.D.

11. Define the indirect utility function v by $v(q, m) \equiv \mu(\tilde{x}(q, m))$. The problem (19) may be alternatively formulated as

$$\max_{q} \; v(q, 0) \quad \text{ST} \quad \tilde{x}'(q, 0)p + r = 0$$

The Lagrangean form is

$$V = v(q, 0) - \lambda(\tilde{x}'(q, 0)p + r)$$

A first order condition is

$$V_q = -v_m \tilde{x} - \lambda \tilde{x}_q' p = 0$$

This and (40) immediately yield Rule III. Q.E.D.

Diamond–Mirrlees and Sandmo proved Rule III first and then went on to prove Rule II by using the Slutsky equation. This is the reason why they formulate the model in terms of the uncompensated demand function.

12. The symmetry of all the cross-substitution terms including leisure means that $\tilde{x}_i^0 = \tilde{x}_0^i$ for all i. This and (35) imply that $\tilde{x}^i \tilde{x}_m^0 = \tilde{x}^0 \tilde{x}_m^i$ for all i. Since x^0 is negative, this leads one to the conclusion that either leisure or all the commodities must be inferior.
13. In fact, one can prove the following: (i) $\hat{x}_q = \hat{x}_q$, holds if (ii) $\hat{x}_m = \theta \hat{x}$ holds for some θ.

Proof Since

$$\tilde{x}\tilde{x}_m' = \left[\frac{x^0 x_m^0 \; x^0 \hat{x}_m'}{\hat{x} x_m^0 \; \hat{x} x_m'}\right]$$

(35) implies that

$$\begin{aligned} & \hat{x}_q - \hat{x}_q' \\ = \; & (x_q - \hat{x}_m \hat{x}') - (x_q' - \hat{x}\hat{x}_m') \\ = \; & \hat{x}\hat{x}_m' - \hat{x}_m \hat{x}' \end{aligned}$$

Thus (ii) yields (i). Q.E.D.

References

1. Auerbach, A. J. (1985) 'The theory of excess burden and optimal taxation', in A. J. Auerbach and M. Feldstein (eds.), *Handbook of Public Economics* (Amsterdam: North Holland).
2. Corlett, W. J. and Hague, D. C. (1953–54) 'Complementarity and the excess of burden of taxation', *Review of Economic Studies*, vol. 21.
3. Deaton, A. (1979) 'Optimally uniform commodity taxes', *Economics Letters*, vol. 2.
4. Diamond, P. A. Mirrlees, J. (1971) 'Optimal taxation and public production: I', *American Economic Review*, vol. 8.
5. Diamond, P. A. and McFadden, D. L. (1974) 'Some uses of the expenditure function in public finance', *Journal of Public Economics*, vol. 3.
6. Gorman, W. M. (1971), *L.S.E. Lecture Notes*, mimeo (London: LSE).

7. Hatta, T. (1977) 'A theory of piecemeal policy recommendations', *Review of Economic Studies*, vol. 44.
8. Hatta, T. (1986) 'Welfare effects of changing commodity tax rates toward uniformity', *Journal of Public Economics*, vol. 29.
9. Hatta, T. and Haltiwanger, J. (1986) 'Tax reform and strong substitutes', *International Economic Review*, vol. 27.
10. Mirrlees, J. (1976) 'Optimal tax theory: a synthesis', *Journal of Public Economics*, vol. 6.
11. Mirrlees, J. (1987) 'Optimal taxation', in *Handbook of Mathematical Economics: Vol. 2* (Amsterdam: North Holland).
12. Ramsey, F. (1927) 'A contribution to the theory of taxation', *Economic Journal*, vol. 37.
13. Sadka, E. (1977) 'A theorem of uniform taxation', *Journal of Public Economics*, vol. 7.
14. Samuelson, P. A. (1951) *Memorandum for U.S. Treasury*, later published as 'A theory of optimal taxation', *Journal of Public Economics*, vol. 30, 1986.
15. Samuelson, P. A. (1982) 'A chapter in the history of Ramsey's Optimal Feasible Taxation and Optimal Public Utility prices', in Svend Andersen *et. al* (eds.), *Economic Essays in Honour of Jorgen H. Gelting* (Copenhagen: Danish Economic Association).
16. Sandmo, A. (1976) 'Optimal taxation – an introduction to the literature', *Journal of Public Economics*, vol. 6.

13 The Political Economy of Earmarked Taxes

Jack Wiseman* and John Posnett

INTRODUCTION

If all public expenditures are financed from a general fund, spending for particular purposes will be influenced by the size but not the composition of tax revenues. Earmarking exists when this condition is breached, because spending for some purposes is determined by the revenue raised from a particular tax source.

Earmarking is not unusual, and is indeed an important policy instrument in some contexts. For example, more than two-fifths of state and around one-fifth of federal government revenues are commonly earmarked in the US. The empirical importance of the practice is not reflected in the economics literature devoted to earmarking, which is not extensive. This may owe something to the fact that the definition embraces a diversity of situations which could be argued to have different policy characteristics. But it may also be related to the shortcomings of the analytical constructs used for the evaluation of earmarking. It is this analytical framework which is our concern.

THE ANALYTICAL BACKGROUND

Before 1963, earmarking was fairly generally condemned by economists, essentially on the ground that it prevented a budgetary decision-maker from making efficient allocational decisions. This was changed, effectively by the publication of a paper by Buchanan (1963), which offered a very different approach leading to markedly different insights. It might have been expected that the Buchanan approach would displace the earlier formulation, or at least that the nature of the differences between the two would be subjected to further examination. Instead, and despite the apparent conflict between the two approaches, the subsequent literature appears to have reintegrated them; evolving models of voter-behaviour in a context which is essentially that of latter-day welfare economics. An elucidation of these developments provides a useful background for a reappraisal of earmarking. A typical conclusion of the 'traditional orthodoxy' would be:

> 'Probably the worst danger to good budget practice in state governments is the dedication of particular revenues to particular funds, from which particular activities are financed . . . The segregation and earmarking of special receipts for special purposes has the effect of removing from budget practice its real reason for being the intelligent control of expenditure.' (Taylor 1953, p. 26)

McMahon and Sprenkle (1970; 1972) provide a typical exposition. They specify a model in which the demand for public expenditure is given exogenously by the budgetary authority. Desired expenditure on a particular service is determined by demand and supply (expenditure cost) conditions. Earmarking can be evaluated by its effects upon the relationship between actual expenditure (determined primarily by current-period earmarked receipts), and desired expenditure, divergence of the two being evidence of 'inefficiency'. The crucial inference is that earmarked taxes will produce an efficient outcome only if the income elasticities of tax receipts and service expenditures are equal. If the elasticity of tax receipts with respect to income is greater than the income-elasticity of desired expenditures, then actual expenditures will exceed desired expenditures. (This will be the case if the earmarked tax is sufficiently progressive or if the income-elasticity of the tax base is sufficiently high). If on the other hand the income elasticity of tax receipts is less than the income elasticity of desired expenditures, actual expenditures will be less than desired expenditures. This requires that the tax base be regressive or the income elasticity of the tax base relatively low.

From the point of view of the budgetary decision-maker, then, it must be concluded that if a tax on a good or service cannot be justified for other reasons, it cannot be justified by the logic of earmarking.

Buchanan's innovation is to replace the preferences of the 'budgetary decision-maker' by those of the individual voter. Earmarking thus becomes an instrument for the implementation of individual choices given expression through the political rather than the market process. Consider the position of a representative individual voter whose preferences correspond with median preferences over all dimensions of budgetary choice. Earmarking permits such an individual to vote separately about the quantity of each service to be supplied at a fixed 'tax price', while with general fund financing he will be able to vote only to accept or reject a predetermined bundle of services to be supplied in a given ratio. The two choice-situations will be identical only in the chance situation that the bundle ratio is identical with the 'mix' of services that would have been chosen with independent voting. In all other situations, the services favoured in the general funding 'mix' will be oversupplied, and others underprovided, relative to the consumption set desired by the median voter.

In the Buchanan model, earmarking thus has the potential value of improving the efficiency of collective choice (the responsiveness of the political process to individual preferences), by removing one impediment to the revelation of preferences. General fund financing permits voters to choose only between predetermined bundles of services. With earmarking, they can vote independently on specific budget allocations, such as spending on fire or police services. In comparison with markets, the analogue of general funding would be the tie-in sale, and of earmarking a set of independent markets. The latter provides a superior choice-outcome unless there are technical differences between the two situations (such as economies of scale in delivery).

The two approaches invite contrasting policy conclusions. The traditional orthodoxy rejects earmarking as an impediment to efficient behaviour by the budgetary decision-maker, while the Buchanan model justifies earmarking as a useful means of ensuring that the budget properly reflects voter-preferences.

CONFLICT OR COMPLEMENTARITY?

The manifest difference between the two formulations lies in the initial specification of the problem. The orthodox model identifies efficiency with the ability of the budget-holder to allocate expenditure 'optimally' (from the point of view of the budget-holder), between alternative forms of public provision. For Buchanan, the purpose is to satisfy the demand of the voter for publicly-provided goods and services, efficiency being identified with the ability of the voter to direct public expenditures to the desired end-uses. This would seem to be a fairly fundamental difference. Nevertheless, it is fair to say that it has not been reflected in the more recent literature. Rather, the two approaches have come to be treated as complementary, or, more precisely, integrated in a model of consumer-and-voter behaviour which is essentially an extension of neoclassical welfare economics. Within this general context, the literature explores the implications of detailed variations in grant-forms, consumer- and voter-behaviour, etc., in order to evaluate the policy characteristics (and paradoxes) of earmarking – see, for example, Goetz (1968), Goetz and McKnew (1972), Browning (1975), Shepsle (1975), Athanassakos (1990).

To understand and evaluate this development, it is necessary to examine more closely the underlying assumptions of the original models. What we have called the 'traditional model' is concerned with an exogenously-determined demand for public expenditures by a 'budgetary authority' (that is, a government). Taken at face value, this would appear to imply an autonomous government taking decisions without direct reference to the wishes of voters or consumers. This would seem to be the interpretation of government which Buchanan wished to reject, both in his alternative treatment of earmarked taxes and in his other more general criticisms of the treatment of government in neo-classical economics. It implies either a government which is entirely passive, or is an omnicompetent dictator whose behavioural characteristics (demand for public expenditures) are not seen to require explanation. (The only traditional behavioural model of the role of the budget-holder would be Pigou's 'unitary being', balancing tax receipts and public expenditures at the margin in the same fashion as a private consumer. The earmarking literature does not make explicit use of this device; it is nevertheless of interest in the light of the form taken by subsequent contributions).

Conceptually, the Buchanan approach is in striking contrast. Far from being exogenously determined, public spending is to be guided by the preferences of voters, and the efficiency of earmarking as a policy instrument is to be appraised by the extent to which it facilitates or obstructs the emergence of a budget which reflects those preferences. However, Buchanan's exposition makes use of the concept of the representative voter. This carries important implications for the role of government, an appreciation of which will facilitate understanding of subsequent developments. The central thrust of the representative (median) voter literature is that, to be elected, governments must offer the menu of policies which accords with the preferences of the median voter. It is implied that, once elected, these are the policies which the government is obliged to implement. This has the paradoxical consequence that a model purporting to explain government behaviour produces a situation in which, at least between elections, the government is the passive instrument of the wishes of the median voter.

It is the passive role assigned to government which provides the key to subsequent developments. Since there is no need for an 'independent' theory of government behaviour in either the traditional or the Buchanan construct, orthodox Paretian welfare economics can be extended in ways which permit comparison of general fund financing and earmarking simply by introducing a new character – the 'voter-consumer'. As the cited literature demonstrates, this opens some interesting analytical doors. It remains to be considered whether the result provides a satisfactory guide to public policy.

GOVERNMENT AS LEVIATHAN

Although the fact is not generally recognized, we do not think it fanciful to describe much of the recent earmarking literature as a clone of optimal tax theory. The passive role assigned to government facilitates the incorporation of voter-consumers into a standard welfare economics model. This is straightforward in the case of the Buchanan construct, and requires only a Pigovian interpretation of the role of the budget-holder in the orthodox model (since the unitary being is the intellectual progenitor of optimal tax models). It is not our intention to suggest that this literature should be treated as irrelevant. To varying degrees, it will need to be adapted in response to the criticisms which follow. But it has produced insights of ongoing interest, for example in identifying a much richer variety of possible outcomes (and hence of policy options) than did the earlier constructs. In some cases (e.g. Kimenyi, Lee and Tollison 1990), the policy insight would appear to be little affected by the proposed new perspective. Nevertheless, it has to be recognised that the integrated model has serious shortcomings as a guide to earmarking policy.

Most fundamentally, the 'integrated' literature is prescriptive in the sense that the objectives of policy are defined by the model (the Pareto-optimality conditions) rather than emerging from the preferences of the citizen-voters; the citizen is simply the 'demander' of objectively-identified public goods. Effectively, the earmarking literature is part of the now-considerable body of writing which treats public choice as an extension of the domain of welfare economics.

In so far as this literature can ascribe only a passive role to government (fulfilment of the Pareto-optimality conditions incorporating the demands of the median voters), it emasculates the fundamental insight which gives substance to the study of public choice; that an understanding of choice-through-government is an integral part of understanding choice in general, including market choice (Buchanan and Tullock 1962). More specifically, it obscures the importance of Buchanan's reinterpretation of the implications of earmarking. There is however another line of development which treats public choice as part of an evolving theory of political economy. This facilitates escape from the deficiencies of the welfare model, provides a role for government as a quasi-independent actor, and in the process throws up different insights concerning the nature and potential of earmarking.

For our present purpose, the most interesting political economy model is that of government-as-Leviathan. Summarily, this treats the government as a grouping of individuals to whom members of the relevant society delegate the right to take decisions on their behalf, subject to the constraints imposed by extant (constitutional) etc. rules and procedures. This general approach to the role of government is becoming formalized in the emergent discipline of constitutional economics. In the present context, the significant insight it provides is that the rules and institutions of society cannot be interpreted simply as means of translating the wishes of citizens into acts of policy. They are needed also because individuals in their capacity as members of a government must be expected to pursue their own goals, which cannot be assumed to be identical with the goals of the citizens who elected them. Unless constrained, that is, governments will behave in improperly coercive fashions, and an important purpose of constitutional etc. rules and devices is to limit the freedom of government in this regard; to curb 'Leviathan'.

The Leviathan model of public choice provides much richer insights into the realities of government behaviour than does the median voter model. It is also much more consonant with Buchanan's general position, and with the spirit of his 1963 paper; this is adequately demonstrated by his role in the development of the Leviathan concept – see Buchanan (1975) and Brennan and Buchanan (1980).[1]

A NEW PERSPECTIVE

Acceptance of government-as-Leviathan leads to a quite different interpretation of the role and possibilities of earmarking. The fundamental new insight is that the opportunity-cost situation facing the individual voter can no longer be confined to a choice between bundles of goods or services in exchange for (earmarked) tax contributions. The voter may also be concerned, for example, about the extent to which earmarking implies undue coercion, by requiring him to contribute disproportionately to the provision of goods which he does not wish to consume. This might lead citizens to prefer general fund financing, or to prefer earmarking to be restricted to lower levels of government even though centralised delivery might use less resources (this might help explain, e.g. the greater significance of earmarking at the state than at the federal level in the USA). On the other hand, earmarking may be believed to impose more satisfactory constraints on government behaviour than would general fund financing.

The range of these new possibilities is rich in diversity, and not easily incorporated into the orthodox welfare models. In the illustration just provided, for example, voters might also think it appropriate to change rules (laws, constitutions) which appeared conducive to the emergence of improperly coercive earmarking behaviour. Such possibilities are outside the scope of the usual optimal-taxation type models, but are central to a political economy/public choice interpretation.

Further, it is of fundamental importance that, early-Buchanan notwithstanding, the extant models are *prescriptive* in character, in that in their normative mode they purport to identify 'efficient' public policy (effectively by compatibility with the Pareto-optimality conditions). In contrast, freedom from unacceptable coercion, which the Leviathan construct identifies as the benchmark of 'efficiency', is by its very nature a subjective judgment of individual voter-citizen-consumers. Information about their personal preferences can be inferred only (and imperfectly) from their behaviour in the variety of relevant choice-situations (markets, elections, participation in political parties and other groups; or whatever). The practical concern of political economy in this situation cannot be the prescription of what citizens *should* want, but must rather be the identification of, and provision of information about, the options available to them in specific policy situations. It is illegitimate for the political economist to claim to be able to prescribe 'best' policy in respect of earmarking (or indeed in any other context). At most, he/she can provide a menu which identifies the nature and relevant characteristics of the policies between which voters may wish to choose; and the practical value of this agenda will be determined by the extent to which its contents incorporate the values to which individuals attach importance, including their perceptions of tolerable coercion.

In the case of earmarking, it follows that it is more likely to be fruitful to set out the implications of a concrete proposal (such as, for example, the recent US proposal to earmark the tax on tobacco for the provision of health care) in ways that better inform voter-choice (which may embrace but will not be confined to the kinds of choice-issue dealt with in the welfare economics literature), than to continue to pretend that there exists some external rule by reference to which all such issues might be decided. The only relevant general principle of the libertarian society (with which, conceptually at least, the Paretian model is itself concerned) is that the preferences of citizens should prevail. The advisory role of the political economist is thus not to prescribe choice but to better inform it, and the most satisfactory intellectual construct for the purpose is the one most likely to embrace the totality of concerns of the citizen-voter. It is in this context that the Leviathan model emerges as clearly superior to the available alternatives. While this argument undoubtedly gives the political economist a less authoritative policy role, what is lost in breadth of prescription may be more than recouped in practical relevance, and consequently in the influence of advice on actual policy outcomes.

The proof of the pudding is in the eating; it would be gratifying to support the argument by illustrative examples. But this is clearly not within the scope of the present article. A useful current case study would be the recent change in local authority finance in the United Kingdom. This replaces a local property tax (the local rate) by something close to a pure poll tax (the community charge). The major justification for the change is the argued need to make local authorities more directly accountable to the local electorate, by relating what is argued to be a fairly uniform level of consumption of a bundle of services to the size of the per capita levy used to finance them. The situation differs from the normal earmarking situation in that the tax charge is on the individual citizen rather than on a good or service. But the essential characteristics of the problem are present. The policy has provoked enormous controversy, and there is little doubt that much of this has been a *dialogue des sourds*, encouraged by the lack of any satisfactory conceptual context for policy debate. We have no doubt that an elucidation of the issues in a Leviathan–public-choice framework would be an illuminating and practically helpful exercise.

But what must be reiterated, in conclusion, is the importance of this evaluation of earmarking for our general understanding of the contribution of economics to policy making. The earlier models, though ostensibly concerned with the implications of freedom of individual choice, lead to essentially prescriptive propositions about earmarking policy. The model which we suggest escapes this unjustifiable paternalism. The economist can set out the relevant possibilities, including those for government-as-Leviathan. But the decision as to how he/she chooses to be coerced (and hence the choice of 'best' policy) must rest with the individual citizen. The economist can strive to offer a comprehensive menu, but not to choose the meal.

The importance of this observation transcends the specific policy context which has concerned us here.

Notes

* Professor Jack Wiseman sadly passed away on 20 January 1991. This joint article is one of his last contributions in the long list of publications he has written during his distinguished career.

1. Confirmation of this view became available at the time of writing, in the form of a forthcoming contribution from Buchanan (1991) to the earmarking literature. Buchanan's paper differs from the present one in approach and coverage, but evaluates earmarking in a fashion essentially sympathetic to the one proposed here. The same is true of some other essays in this book. This perhaps encourages the view that the desirable shift in perspective which failed to occur after Buchanan's earlier contribution has now begun to happen.

References

1. Athanassakos, A. (1990) 'General fund financing versus earmarked taxes: an alternative model of budgetary choice in a democracy', *Public Choice*, vol. 66.
2. Browning, E. K. (1975) 'Collective choice and general fund financing', *Journal of Political Economy*, vol. 83.
3. Brennan, G. and Buchanan, J. M. (1980) *The Power to Tax* (Cambridge: Cambridge University Press).
4. Buchanan, J. M. (1963) 'The economics of earmarked taxes', *Journal of Political Economy*, vol. 71.

5. Buchanan, J. M. (1975) *The Limits of Liberty: Between Anarchy and Leviathan* (Chicago: Chicago University Press).
6. Buchanan, J. M. (1991) 'The constitutional economics of earmarking', in R. E. Wagner (ed.), *Charging Beneficiaries for Public Services: User Charges and Earmarked Taxes in Principle and Practice* (London: Routledge).
7. Buchanan, J. M. and Tullock, G. (1962) *The Calculus of Consent: Logical Foundations of Constitutional Democracy* (Ann Arbor: University of Michigan Press).
8. Goetz, C. J. (1968) 'Earmarked taxes and majority rule budgetary processes', *American Economic Review*, vol. 58.
9. Goetz, C. J. and McKnew, C. R. (1972) 'Paradoxical results in a public choice model of alternative government grant forms', in J. M. Buchanan and R. D. Tollison (eds.), *Theory of Public Choice* (Ann Arbor: University of Michigan Press).
10. Kimenyi, M. S., Lee, D. W. and Tollison, R. D. (1990) 'Efficient lobbying and earmarked taxes', *Public Finance Quarterly*, vol. 18.
11. McMahon, W. W. and Sprenkle, C. M. (1970) 'A theory of earmarking', *National Tax Journal*, vol. 23.
12. Shepsle, K. (1979) 'Institutional arrangements and equilibrium in multidimensional voting models', *The American Journal of Political Science*, vol. 23.
13. Taylor, P. E. (1953) *The Economics of Public Finance* (New York: Macmillan).
14. Wagner, R. E. (ed.) (1991) *Charging Beneficiaries for Public Services: User Charges and Earmarked Taxes in Principle and Practice* (London: Routledge).

14 Equivalence of the Destination and Restricted Origin Principles in the Case of Non-general Taxes*

Theodore A. Georgakopoulos and Theodore Hitiris

INTRODUCTION

A well known proposition in tax union and tax harmonization theory is that, under certain conditions and provided one deals with truly general commodity taxes, the destination and the restricted origin principles[1] of taxation are equivalent – see Whalley (1979), Berglas (1981), Cnossen and Shoup (1987), and Bos and Nelson (1988). In this note, we show that equivalence of the two principles holds also in the case of non-general taxes, but under a different set of conditions. Namely, in the case of truly general taxes equivalence obtains when tax rates in the member countries are equal and trade balances are in bilateral equilibrium, whereas in the case of non-general taxes member countries must levy equal rates on the same product in inverse relation to the bilateral trade balance of the initial equilibrium. A notable exception from this rule is the case of VAT, when the tax liability is calculated according to the credit method, as in the European Community (EC), and trade is conducted by VAT-registered traders. Then, equivalence obtains even if the member countries's tax rates on the same product are unequal, but they are set in inverse relation to the bilateral trade balance of the initial equilibrium.

ANALYSIS

Assume that there are three countries (1, 2, 3) and three commodities (X_1, X_2, X_3), all produced and consumed in each country. Comparative advantage considerations suggest that, under free trade, country 1 exports X_1, country 2 exports X_2, and country 3 exports X_3, but they are all deficient in and import the other two commodities. To simplify the analysis, assume free trade conditions[2] and fixed exchange rates, initially equal to unity.[3] Next, countries 1 and 2 form an economic union and agree to apply a non-general commodity tax at common rates t_1, t_2 and t_3. For comparability with the relevant literature on general taxes, assume that the commodity prices (P_1, P_2, P_3) are given internationally and are not affected by the union members' tax changes.[4] Therefore, the relative consumer prices in the member countries are:

$$P_1(1 + t_1)/P_2(1 + t_2),\ P_1(1 + t_1)/P_3(1 + t_3)$$
$$P_2(1 + t_2)/P_3(1 + t_3) \qquad (1)$$

and the relative producer prices, which under the destination principle equal the international terms of trade, are:

$$P_1/P_2,\ P_1/P_3,\ P_2/P_3 \qquad (2)$$

The balance of trade equilibrium conditions, under the destination principle, are given as:

$$\begin{aligned} P_1(X^2_{11} + X^3_{11}) &= P_2X^1_{22} + P_3X^1_{33} \\ P_2(X^1_{22} + X^3_{22}) &= P_1X^2_{11} + P_3X^2_{33} \\ P_3(X^1_{33} + X^2_{33}) &= P_1X^3_{11} + P_2X^3_{22} \end{aligned} \qquad (3)$$

where X^j_{ik} gives country k's exports of product i to country j (for i, j, k = 1, 2, 3).

Assume now the member countries decide to change over to the restricted origin principle. Since the same rate applies on each commodity in the members of the union, the change in the tax regime leaves their consumer and producer prices unaffected. However, the terms of trade between the member countries change because each one of them charges its tax on exports to the partner country and commodity tax rates differ by definition. These terms of trade are now given as $P_1(1 + t_1)/P_2(1 + t_2)$. The new balance of trade equilibrium conditions become:

$$P_1[X^2_{11}(1 + t_1) + X^3_{11}] = P_2X^1_{22}(1 + t_2) + P_3X^1_{33}$$
$$P_2[X^1_{22}(1 + t_2) + X^3_{22}] = P_1X^2_{11}(1 + t_1) + P_3X^2_{33} \quad (4)$$
$$P_3[X^1_{33} + X^2_{33}] = P_1X^3_{11} + P_2X^3_{22}$$

The conditions for unchanged relative consumer and producer prices are given by:

$$P_1/P_2 = \bar{P}_1/\bar{P}_2,\ P_2/P_3 = \bar{P}_2/\bar{P}_3,\ P_1/P_3 = \bar{P}_1/\bar{P}_3 \quad (5)$$

where barred variables stand for prices under the destination principle and unbarred for prices under the restricted origin principle.

Substituting (5) in (4) yields:

$$\bar{P}_1[X^2_{11}(1 + t_1) + X^3_{11}] = \bar{P}_2X^1_{22}(1 + t_2) + \bar{P}_3X^1_{33}$$
$$\bar{P}_2[X^1_{22}(1 + t_2) + X^3_{22}] = \bar{P}_1X^2_{11}(1 + t_1) + \bar{P}_3X^2_{33} \quad (6)$$
$$\bar{P}_3X^1_{33} + \bar{P}_3X^2_{33} = \bar{P}_1X^3_{11} + \bar{P}_2X^3_{22}$$

where X^j_{ik} stands for quantities traded under the destination principle. Given that (3) holds under the destination principle, the first equation in (6) can only be satisfied if $t_1\bar{P}_1X^2_{11} = t_2\bar{P}_2X^1_{22}$, from which it follows that $t_1/t_2 = \bar{P}_2X^1_{22}/\bar{P}_1X^2_{11}$. Therefore, the two principles are equivalent (production, consumption and trade remain unaffected) when tax rates are equal in the member countries, and are set in inverse relation to the bilateral trade balance of the initial equilibrium.[5]

RELEVANCE TO EC DISCUSSIONS ON TAX HARMONIZATION

The authors of previous papers on truly general taxes have related their theoretical findings to the problem of VAT harmonization in the EC and have made various recommendations – see Whalley (1979), Berglas (1981), Cnossen and Shoup (1987), and Bos and Nelson (1988). However, with regard to the EC's VAT, two problems emerge: (a) in contrast to the requirements of the theory, most members of the EC apply more than one VAT rate and all of them exempt certain commodities and services; hence, in the EC the VAT is not a truly general tax and, therefore, the findings of previous studies cannot apply to the case of the EC; and (b) in the EC the VAT is calculated on the basis of the invoice method, whereby the tax liability is the difference between output tax and input tax (EC Commission 1985); this calls for a modification of our findings.

Suppose all intra-EC trade is conducted by VAT-registered traders. Under the invoice method and provided the tax levied on exports is set by the importer against his tax liability in his own country (EC Commission 1985), the tax burden of imported commodities is the same in each member country, irrespective of whether tax rates differ between them. When the restricted origin principle is applied, relative commodity prices to producers and consumers in the member countries are given by equations (1) and (2) respectively and remain unaffected. However, the terms of trade between the union partners change, since each member country charges its own tax on the other members and tax rates differ both between countries and among the products in each country. Under the restricted origin principle, the new balance of trade equilibrium conditions become:

$$\begin{aligned} P_1[X^2_{11}(1 + t^1_1) + X^3_{11}] &= P_2X^1_{22}(1 + t^2_2) + P_3X^1_{33} \\ P_2[X^1_{22}(1 + t^2_2) + X^3_{22}] &= P_1X^2_{11}(1 + t^1_1) + P_3X^2_{33} \\ P_3(X^1_{33} + X^2_{33}) &= P_1X^3_{11} + P_2X^3_{22} \end{aligned} \tag{7}$$

where t^1_1 is the tax rate levied on commodity X_1 by country 1, and t^2_2 is the rate levied on commodity X_2 by country 2.

The conditions for unchanged relative consumer and producer prices are again given by (5). Substituting (5) in (7) yields:

$$\begin{aligned} \bar{P}_1[X^2_{11}(1 + t^1_1) + X^3_{11}] &= \bar{P}_2X^1_{22}(1 + t^2_2) + \bar{P}_3X^1_{33} \\ \bar{P}_2[X^1_{22}(1 + t^2_2) + X^3_{22}] &= \bar{P}_1X^2_{11}(1 + t^1_1) + \bar{P}_3X^2_{33} \\ \bar{P}_3X^1_{33} + \bar{P}_3X^2_{33} &= \bar{P}_1X^3_{11} + \bar{P}_2X^3_{22} \end{aligned} \tag{8}$$

Given that (3) holds under the destination principle, the first equation of (8) can only be satisfied if $t^1_1\bar{P}_1X^2_{11} = t^2_2\bar{P}_2X^1_{22}$, from which it follows that $t^1_1/t^2_2 = \bar{P}_2X^1_{22}/\bar{P}_1X^2_{11}$. Therefore, when intra-EC trade is conducted by VAT-registered traders and the tax liability is calculated on the invoice method, the only condition for equivalence of the destination and the restricted origin principles is that tax rates levied on intra-EC traded commodities must be set in inverse relation to the bilateral trade balance of the initial equilibrium, but tax rates can now differ in the member countries.

However, not all intra-EC trade is conducted exclusively by VAT-registered traders. Some trade is conducted by non-registered traders and some by border-crossing final consumers for personal purchases. Sales by post to final consumers also cannot be compensated for tax differentials between the member countries. Under such conditions rates must be equalized in the member countries, if relative producer and consumer prices are to remain unaffected and Pareto inefficiencies to be avoided. If rates differ among the member countries, neither flexibility of prices and wages nor of exchange rates can correct for Pareto inefficiencies. To avoid excessive inefficiencies, the EC Commission has suggested the approximation of VAT rates in the member countries (EC Commission 1985).

CONCLUSIONS

The preceding analysis shows that the restricted origin and the destination principles of taxation can be equivalent even in the case of non-general taxes, but the relevant conditions are different from those necessary for equivalence in the case of truly general taxes: tax rates on the same product must now be equal in the member countries and inverse to the bilateral trade balance of the initial equilibrium. Equalization of rates is however not necessary in the case of VAT, when the tax liability is calculated on the basis of the invoice method, as in the EC, and all trade is conducted by VAT-registered traders.

Notes

* Financial support received by T. Georgakopoulos from the EC (*Jean Monnet Project*) and research facilities provided by the Research Center of the Athens University of Economics and Business are gratefully acknowledged.

1. The Shibatian term 'restricted origin principle' refers to a mixed destination-cum-origin principle of taxation (Shibata 1966). Under the restricted origin principle, trade between the economic union and third countries is taxed according to the destination principle, while intra-union trade is subject to the origin principle. This principle, which facilitates the

abolition of internal frontiers, is favoured by the EC Commission and has recently been declared by the European Council to be the medium term objective of the EC in the field of tax harmonization (EC Commission 1989).

2. Since tax rates levied on the various commodities are the same in the member countries, the presence of trade impediments, such as tariffs, does not change the arguments.
3. The assumption of fixed exchange rates does not affect the results because exchange rate flexibility cannot correct for area discriminatory price changes, due to the interdependence of exchange rates – see Berglas (1981, p. 382, footnote 4).
4. This model is more general than those used by Whalley (1979) and Berglas (1981), since it does not require complete specialization in the member countries and places no restrictions on trade flows, so that trade deflection can take place.
5. If tax rates were unequal, trade deflection would follow, consumers in the high-tax country 1 importing all products via the low-tax country 2, while producers exporting all products to country 3, where they realize higher prices. In this case equivalence does not hold.

References

1. Berglas, E. (1981) 'Harmonization of commodity taxes', *Journal of Public Economics*, vol. 16.
2. Bos, M. and Nelson H. (1988) 'Indirect taxation and the completion of the internal market of the EC', *Journal of Common Market Studies*, vol. 27.
3. Cnossen, S. and Shoup, C. S. (1987) 'Coordination of value-added taxes', in S. Cnossen (ed.), *Tax Coordination in the European Community* (Deventer, Holland: Kluwer).
4. EC Commission (1985) *Completing the Internal Market*, White Paper (Brussels: EC Commission).
5. EC Commission (1989) 'Indirect taxation', *Bulletin of the European Communities*, vol. 22, no. 11.
6. Shibata, H. (1966) 'The theory of economic unions: a comparative analysis of customs unions, free trade areas, and tax unions', in C. S. Shoup (ed.), *Fiscal Harmonization in Common Markets, Vol. I* (New York: Columbia University Press).
7. Whalley, J. (1979) 'Uniform domestic tax rates, trade distortions and economic integration', *Journal of Public Economics*, vol. 11.

15 Indexation and Macrodynamics

Toshihiro Ihori*

INTRODUCTION

The recent surge of price movement since the 1970s has interested economists in automatic or discretionary adjustments to fiscal drag or fiscal dividends – see, for example, Musgrave and Musgrave (1977). There has been increased interest in alternative ways of living with inflation rather than ridding the system of it. A general system of indexation of nominal economic variables to actual inflation rates would diminish the pains of inflation associated with imprecise estimates incorporated in adjustments in nominal economic variables.

It seems that there are three important economic variables to be indexed in an inflationary economy: wages, taxes and government expenditures. The macroeconomic implications of indexing wages are sufficiently developed in the literature – see Gray (1976), Gultekin and Santomero (1979), and Fischer (1986). I shall analyze the implications of indexing government expenditures and/or taxes. If the government does not introduce the indexing process in an inflationary economy, real government expenditure may keep decreasing, hence crowding in capital accumulation, while real tax revenue may keep increasing, hence crowding out capital accumulation.

Little analytical investigation of the general property of the adjustment process for tax indexation or government-expenditure indexation has been attempted in the current literature.[1] This is partially because most analyses examine the effect of exogenous supply and demand disturbances on the level of real income and prices in the presence of indexation. Gultekin and Santomero (1979) and Fischer (1983) analyze the impact of indexation on overall economic stability.[2] I shall analyse the impact of the adjustment process on stability as well. However, my main concern is with comparative statics of the adjustment process towards indexation in an inflationary economy.

The questions examined in this paper are: Does the speed of adjustments matter for steady state properties? How does it affect the long run equilibrium values of capital accumulation and government deficits? I shall consider these issues using a variation of the conventional monetary growth model.

In the next section, I formulate the indexation process of taxes and government expenditures. I follow this by developing the conventional monetary growth model to investigate the relationship between the speed of indexation and capital accumulation. In the section after that, I examine the dynamic properties using a phase diagram. This is followed by a section in which I investigate comparative statics before proceeding to make concluding remarks.

INDEXATION PROCESS

Adjustments towards tax indexation

The term indexation has generally been referred to as the automatic adjustment of nominal economic variables for movements in an overall price index. First, I formulate indexation of taxes. Given a passive policy which holds tax rates unchanged, a built-in increase in revenues from the progressive tax structure leads to a rising surplus at a full-employment level of income, thereby exerting a fiscal drag on the growing economy. In the progressive tax system, nominal tax revenue will increase at a higher rate than the price level.[3] As long as the growth rate of nominal tax revenue is greater than the actual rate of inflation, real tax revenue will increase. Unless it is offset by fiscal dividends, this automatic rise in revenues will become a fiscal drag siphoning too much of the economic substance out of the private economy and thereby choking expansion. This situation is not consistent with the long-run equilibrium. Sooner or later, the tax system has to be adjusted so that all the real per capita variables will remain constant in a system of indexation.

By definition, one has

$$Dt = (b - \pi)t \qquad (1)$$

where b is the growth rate of per capita taxes and t is the real per capita tax revenue. $D = d/dt.b$ is given by

$$b = \eta_p \pi + \eta_y G$$

where η_p is the elasticity of nominal per capita tax revenue with respect to prices, η_y is the elasticity of nominal per capita tax revenue with respect to real per capita income, and G is the growth rate of real per capita income. A progressive tax structure means that $\eta_y > 1$. Without any indexation, $\eta_p = \eta_y$. Full indexation means that $\eta_p = 1$.

Under the progressive structure at the initial state $\eta_p = \eta_y > 1$. Keeping η_y at its initial value (> 1), adjustments towards indexing taxes might well be described by changes in η_p. However, for simplicity, I formulate the adjustment process as follows:

$$Db = \alpha_t(\pi - b) \tag{2}$$

where α_t represents the speed of adjustment towards indexation. Immediate full indexation corresponds to $\alpha_t = \infty$, no adjustments towards indexation to $\alpha_t = 0$, and gradual adjustments to $0 < \alpha_t < \infty$. In the short run real per capita income $f(k)$ may fluctuate ($G \neq 0$), but in the long run equilibrium $f(k)$ remains constant ($G = 0$). The difference between b and π may be regarded as the degree of progression. Therefore, for simplicity, it is formulated that as long as $b > \pi$, the government changes the tax structure so as to reduce the growth rate of nominal per capita tax revenue.[4]

In the progressive tax structure one would normally expect $b > \pi$. However, one cannot exclude the case of $\pi > b$. Suppose land holding taxes are imposed and the official price of land rises much less than the actual price of land during inflation. Then, the growth rate of nominal tax revenues from land holding taxes will be less than the rate of inflation.

Adjustments towards government expenditure indexation

By definition, one has

$$Dg = (a - \pi)g \tag{3}$$

where a is the growth rate of nominal government spending and π is the rate of inflation.

Indexing government expenditures may take many forms. One possible way to formulate the degree of indexation, the conventional one, is

$$a = \alpha_g\pi + (1 - \alpha_g)e \quad (0 \leq \alpha \leq 1) \tag{4'}$$

where α_g represents the degree of indexation and e the expected rate of inflation. Full indexation corresponds to $0 < \alpha_g < 1$. As in the tax-indexation case, I adopt an alternative formulation:[5]

$$Da = \alpha_g(\pi - a) \tag{4}$$

Indexation and hysteresis

From (1) and (2) one gets

$$Db = \alpha_t Dt/t$$

or

$$b = -\alpha_t \log t + \gamma \tag{5–1}$$

where $\gamma = b_0 + \alpha_t \log t_0$. γ is determined by the initial values of b_0 and t_0.

Similarly, one gets

$$a = -\alpha_g \log g + w \tag{5–2}$$

where $w = a_0 + \alpha_g \log g_0$.

In the long run, $\pi = a = t$. The long run equilibrium is dependent on the initial state and the degree of indexation. The steady state equations do not suffice to uniquely determine the equilibrium value. The dependence of an equilibrium on the initial state and the path the economy experiences towards the equilibrium is called hysteresis – see Buiter and Gersovityz (1981).

In the long-run equilibrium one gets

$$t^* = T(\pi^*, \alpha_t, b_0, t_0) \tag{6–1}$$

$$g^* = G(\pi^*, \alpha_g, a_0, g_0) \tag{6–2}$$

where

$$T_{\pi^*} = -t^*/\alpha_t < 0$$

$$T_{\alpha_i} = -(\log t^* - \log t_0)t^*/\alpha_t$$

$$G_{\pi^*} = -g^*/\alpha_g < 0$$

$$G_{\alpha_g} = -(\log g^* - \log g_0)g^*/\alpha_g$$

$$T_{\pi^*\alpha_i} = t^*/\alpha_t^2 > 0$$

$$G_{\pi^*\alpha_g} = g^*/\alpha_g^2 > 0$$

Therefore, if $b_0 \geq$ (*resp.* $<$)π^*, then $t^* \geq$ (*resp.* $<$)t_0 and $T_{\alpha_i} = \frac{dt^*}{d\alpha_i} \geq$ (*resp.* $<$) 0. In the tax-indexation one has the following proposition:

Proposition 1 Suppose that the growth rate of nominal tax revenue is initially higher (lower) than the long-run equilibrium rate of inflation. Then, the higher the adjustment speed of indexing taxes, the less (more) is the long-run real tax revenue.

As we have seen before, $b_0 > \pi*$ may be called the normal case. In this case, when the adjustment speed is high, one can attain the fully indexed tax structure soon, hence a built-in increase in tax revenues is not very large. If $b_0 < \pi*$, b will eventually be increasing to attain the long-run equilibrium. Hence, when the adjustment speed is high, a built-in decrease in tax revenues is not very large.

In the government-expenditure-indexation case as a_0 is less than π_0, one normally has $a_0 < \pi*$. Hence, $g^* < g_0$ and $G_{\alpha_g} = \frac{dg^*}{d\alpha_g} > 0$. g^* is increasing with α_g. One has:

Proposition 2 The higher the adjustment speed of indexing government expenditures, the more is the long-run real government expenditure.

When the adjustment speed is high, one can attain the indexed government-expenditure structure soon, hence a built-in decrease in real government expenditures is not so large.

A MONETARY GROWTH MODEL

Government budgetary constraint

From now on, I shall investigate the relationship between the adjustment speed of indexing and capital accumulation. The model developed here is basically the traditional monetary growth model – see, for example, Feldstein (1980). First of all, the government budget constraint may be written as

$$\delta = g - t = \mu m \tag{7}$$

where δ is the size of the real per capita deficit, μ is the rate of monetary expansion, and m is the real per capita holdings. The government budget deficit is financed through the printing of money.

As stressed in Christ (1979), the government budget constraint implies that one of the policy variables is endogenously determined. In this paper the rate of monetary expansion is given by the monetary authority. Thus, in the government-expenditure-indexation case, g is determined by the adjustment process towards government-expenditure indexation, and t is endogenously determined. However, in the tax-indexation case t is determined by the adjustment process towards tax indexation, and g is endogenously determined.

The money market

The demand for money L varies positively with the level of income and inversely with the rate of interest, i. i is equal to the expected rate of inflation e plus the marginal product of capital $f'(k)$. $i = e + f'(k)$. k is the capital–labour ratio. Following Hadjimichalakis (1972) and others, for simplicity, I shall permit the market for the capital stock and the money market to be out of equilibrium, and the actual rate of inflation to be different from the expected one.[6] With regard to the dynamic behaviour, I shall adopt the Walrasian view that when there is excess demand (supply) the price rises (falls). Thus,

$$\pi = \varepsilon[m - L(i)f(k)] + e \tag{8'}$$

where π is the actual rate of inflation and ε is a positive constant for the speed of adjustment in the money market.

From (8′), one gets

$$\pi = \pi(m, k, e) \tag{8}$$

where

$$\pi_m = \varepsilon$$

$$\pi_k = -\varepsilon(Lf' + L'f''f)$$

$$\pi_e = -\varepsilon L'f + 1$$

Saving and capital accumulation

The supply of saving is proportional to the household's real disposable income:

$$s = \sigma[f(k) - t - em] \tag{9}$$

The saving propensity δ will be assumed to be constant;[7] thus, one assumes away the analysis of the redistributive effect of the progressive tax system on savings. Disposable income is equal to national income minus both the government's tax receipts and the fall in the (expected) real value of the money holdings.

All saving must be absorbed in either real capital accumulation or additional real money:

$$s = Dk + nk + Dm + nm \tag{10}$$

where n is the population growth rate.

Furthermore, by definition:

$$Dm = (\mu - n - \pi)m \tag{11}$$

Substituting (9) and (11) into (10), one gets:

$$Dk = \sigma[f(k) - g] - (1 - \sigma)(\mu - e)m - nk \tag{12}$$

MACRODYNAMICS IN A PHASE DIAGRAM

Tax indexation

First of all for simplicity the expected rate of inflation is assumed to be fixed. The adjustment system towards tax indexation may be summarized by the following three equations:

$$Dk = \sigma[f(k) - t] - [\sigma e + \mu - \pi(k, m; e)]m - nk \tag{13}$$

$$Dm = [\mu - n - \pi(k, m; e)]m \tag{14}$$

$$Dt = [-\alpha_t \log t + \gamma - \pi(k, m; e)]t \tag{15}$$

It will be useful to draw a phase diagram in the $(m - k)$ plane. Suppose for a while t is given by its initial value t_0. Differentiating (13) implicitly, one derives the formula for the slope of the $Dk = 0$ curve:

$$\left.\frac{dm}{dk}\right|_{Dk=0} = \frac{\sigma f' - n + \pi_k m}{\sigma e + \mu - \pi - \pi_m m} \tag{16}$$

At $m = 0$ along the $Dk = 0$ curve, $\delta[f(k) - t] = nk$. Define the k for which $\delta[f(k) - t] = nk$ as k_A and k_B $(0 < k_A < k_B)$. k_B is the maximum sustainable k, i.e. the 'Solow k'. One can easily show that for $k_A < k < k_B$ and $m > 0$, $\delta e + \mu - \pi > 0$ along the $Dk = 0$ curve. This is because $\delta[f(k) - t] - nk > 0$ for $k_A < k < k_B$. From (13) one gets:

$$[\sigma(\mu - n) + n - \mu]m = \sigma[f(k) - t] - nk > 0$$

It follows that $\delta(\mu - n) + e > 0$ for $k_A < k < k_B$ and $m > 0$. At k_A, $k_A \left.\frac{dm}{dk}\right|_{Dk=0} > 0$ and at k_B, $k_B \left.\frac{dm}{dk}\right|_{Dk=0} < 0$. Hence, the $Dk = 0$ curve has roughly the shape of Figure 15.1. Note that it does not have to be uniformly concave. It achieves a maximum for $\bar{k}$ such that $\delta f'(k) - n + \pi_k m = 0$. Above the $Dk = 0$ curve $Dk < 0$ and below is $Dk > 0$.

The $Dm = 0$ curve is upward sloping, as can be seen from

$$\left.\frac{dm}{dk}\right|_{D_m=0} = -\frac{\pi_k}{\pi_m} > 0 \tag{17}$$

Above the $Dm = 0$ curve, $Dm < 0$ and below it, $Dm > 0$.

An increase in t will shift the $Dk = 0$ curve downwards:

$$\frac{dk_A}{dt} = \frac{\sigma}{\sigma f' - n} > 0$$

and

$$\frac{dk_B}{dt} = \frac{\sigma}{\sigma f' - n} < 0$$

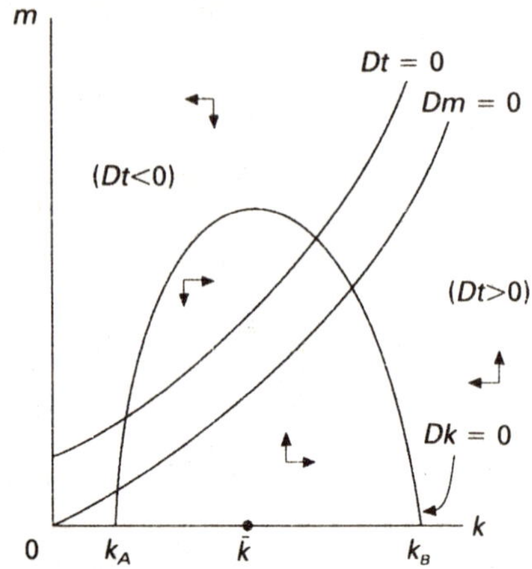

Figure 15.1

Note that the $Dm = 0$ curve is independent of t.

One can also draw the $Dt = 0$ curve in Figure 15.1. From (15):

$$\left.\frac{dm}{dk}\right|_{Dt=0} = -\frac{\pi_k}{\pi_m} > 0 \tag{18}$$

The $Dt = 0$ curve is upward sloping and its slope is the same as that of the $Dm = 0$ curve. Above the $Dt = 0$ curve $Dt < 0$ and below is $Dt > 0$. An increase in t will shift the $Dt = 0$ curve downwards. As can easily be shown, if b_0 is higher (lower) than π^*, the $Dt = 0$ curve at $t = t_0$ is above (below) the $Dm = 0$.

Suppose the economy is out of an old equilibrium point I_0 and $\pi_0 < \pi^*$. At I_0, $b_0 > \pi_0$ because of the progressive tax structure. Then the adjustment process (2) will begin to work. There are two possibilities: $b_0 > \pi^* > \pi_0$ or $\pi^* > b_0 > \pi_0$.

Figure 15.2 corresponds to the $b_0 > \pi^* > \pi_0$ case. Point I_0 must be below the $Dt = 0$ curve. In this case, as t increases, both the $Dt = 0$ curve and the $Dk = 0$ curve will shift downwards. The economy will move to the long run equilibrium point E. If α_t is high, the $Dk = 0$ curve shifts to small extent since the equilibrium value of k is relatively high.

Figure 15.3 illustrates the $\pi^* > b_0 > \pi_0$ case. At first, t increases, hence the $Dt = 0$ curve shifts downwards. However, in this case,

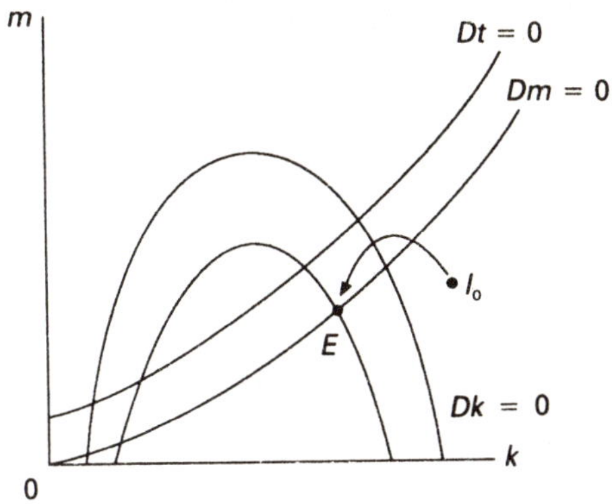

Figure 15.2

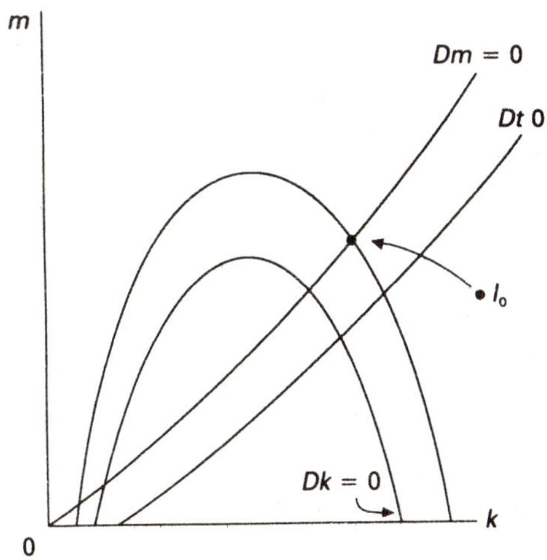

Figure 15.3

sooner or later, the economy will move into the region of $Dt < 0$. Then t will turn downwards, and both the $Dt = 0$ and the $Dk = 0$ curves will shift upwards. The economy will move to the long-run equilibrium point E. If α_t is then low, the $Dk = 0$ curve will shift to a great extent since the equilibrium value of k is relatively high. The lower α_t, the more is the upward shift of the $Dk = 0$ curve and the more the equilibrium values of k^*, m^* and δ^*. In other words, fiscal drag is more likely to occur when the speed of adjustment is higher.

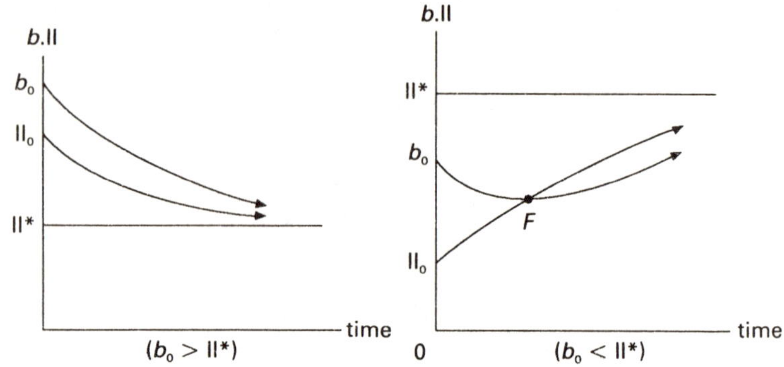

Figure 15.4

This seemingly paradoxical result suggests that the sign of $b_0 - \pi^*$ is important for long-run properties. There is an intuitive explanation for this. Figure 15.4 illustrates the b time path. In the long-run equilibrium b will converge to π^*. One knows that if $\pi^* > b_0$ then $t^* < t_0$. Hence, if $b_0 < \pi^*$, there must be a turning point like F. After F, b is smaller than π, hence $Dt < 0$. When the adjustment speed is small, a decrease in t during the adjustment process will be large, hence, to a large extent, one can avoid fiscal drag.

Thus, one has the following corollary of Proposition 1.

Corollary 1 Suppose $b_0 > (<)\pi^*$. Then, the higher α_t, the higher (lower) are k^*, m^* and δ^*.

Government expenditure indexation

The adjustment process towards government expenditure indexation may also be described in a similar phase diagram. In this case, one always has $\pi^* > \pi_0 > \alpha_0$. The $Dg = 0$ curve is below the $Dm = 0$ curve at $g = g_0$. As g decreases, the $Dg = 0$ curve shifts upwards and also the $Dk = 0$ curve shift upwards. If the speed of adjustment α_g is low, the $Dk = 0$ curve will shift to a great extent since the equilibrium value of k is relatively high. Then, one has:

Corollary 2 The lower α_g, the higher are k^*, m^* and δ^*.

Note that a decrease in α_g means an increase δ^* and a decrease in g^*.

This is because an increase in m^* at a given level of μ is associated with a decrease in t^*.

COMPARATIVE STATICS

For simplicity, consider the government-expenditure-indexation case; the tax-indexation case may be analysed in a similar way. In the long-run equilibrium one has:

$$\sigma[f(k^*) - g^*] = (1 - \sigma)nm^* + nk^* \tag{19}$$

$$m^* = L[\pi^* + f(k^*)]f(k^*) \tag{20}$$

$$\mu = n + \pi^* \tag{21}$$

$$\pi^* = -\alpha_g \log g^* + w \tag{22}$$

Now consider the comparative statics of an increase in π^* (or μ) on k^*. One has

$$\frac{\partial k^*}{\partial_{\pi^*}} = \frac{(1 - \sigma)nL'k + \sigma G_{\pi^*}}{\sigma f' - n - (1 - \sigma)n(Lf' + L'f''f)} > 0$$

The numerator is negative. The denominator is also negative under the stability condition. Hence, an increase in π will stimulate capital accumulation. This is the well-known Tobin effect.

Furthermore, one has

$$\frac{\partial^2 k^*}{\partial\pi\partial\alpha_g} = \frac{\sigma G_{\pi^*\alpha}}{\sigma f' - n - (1 - \sigma)n(Lf' + L'f''f)} < 0$$

An increase in the degree of indexation will reduce the Tobin effect.

Proposition 3 An increase in the indexation adjustment speed will reduce the Tobin effect.

Finally, consider the long-run effect on the real per capita deficit, δ^*. One has

$$\frac{\partial \delta^*}{\partial \pi^*} = m^* + \mu \left(\frac{\partial m^*}{\partial \pi^*} + \frac{\partial m^*}{\partial k^*} \frac{\partial k^*}{\partial \pi^*} \right)$$

One knows that $\frac{\partial m^*}{\partial \pi^*} < 0$ and $\frac{\partial m^*}{\partial k^*} \frac{\partial k^*}{\partial \pi^*} > 0$. Thus, unless the (absolute value of) interest elasticity of money demand is not very large, an increase in π is likely to raise δ^*.

CONCLUDING REMARKS

In this paper, I have analysed the impact of adjustments towards indexing the tax system or government-expenditure structure on overall economic stability and long-run comparative statics. If the government does not introduce the adjustment process in an inflationary economy, real government expenditure will keep on decreasing, hence crowding in capital accumulation (as fiscal dividends), while real tax revenue will keep on increasing, thus crowding out capital accumulation (as fiscal drag).

It has been shown that the indexing system is hysteresis, hence the long-run equilibrium is dependent on the initial state and the adjustment speed. An increase in the adjustment speed of indexation will reduce the Tobin effect. In the government-expenditure-indexation case, the growth rate of the initial nominal expenditure is always less than the equilibrium rate of inflation. Hence, the higher the degree of indexation, the higher the equilibrium value of real expenditure. In the tax-indexation case, it is possible that the growth rate of nominal tax revenues is initially higher than the long-run equilibrium rate of inflation. In such a case, the higher the speed of adjustment, the more is the long-run equilibrium capital intensity. If the growth rate of nominal tax revenues is initially smaller than the equilibrium rate of inflation, the higher the degree of indexation, the less is the long-run equilibrium capital intensity.

The analysis in this paper suggests two factors which are relevant to the macro-dynamic implications of the adjustment process of indexing taxes: whether the growth rate of nominal tax revenues is initially greater than the long-run rate of inflation, and how fast is the speed of adjustment. The government can choose the appropriate speed of adjustment so as to minimize fiscal drag.

Notes

* This paper was prepared for the IIPF conference in Buenos Aires, 28–31 August 1989.

1. Dornbusch and Simonsen (1983) cover problems in the area of inflation, debt, and indexation. However, they do not discuss the problem of tax and/or government indexation. Bruce (1981) examines the effects of supply and demand disturbances in the presence of income tax indexation. Peston (1982) considers the implications of the government's response in terms of expenditure to exogenous wage push.
2. They do not incorporate the adjustment process towards indexation.
3. It is true that even in the indexed system the growth rate of nominal per capita tax revenue may be higher than the rate of inflation when real per capita income is growing. For simplicity, however, in this paper I investigate indexation in terms of the relationship between the growth rate of nominal per capita tax revenue and the rate of inflation. This approach may be justified in terms of the framework of the standard monetary growth model in that real per capita income remains constant in the long run equilibrium.
4. (2) may be rewritten in terms of η_p:

$$D\eta_p = \frac{1}{\pi}[\alpha_t((1-\eta_p)\pi - \eta_y G) - (\eta_p D\pi + \eta_y DG)]$$

   One could consider other formulations of η_p, but the qualitative conclusions would be almost the same.
5. Suppose the expected rate of inflation is based on adaptive expectations. Then

$$De = \beta(\pi - e)$$

where β is the speed of adjustment. Then, substituting the above equation into (4′), (4′) may be rewritten as:

$$Da = \beta(\pi - a) + \alpha_g D\pi$$

   which is very close to (4), in the sense that the system will still be hysteresis.
6. If π is always equal to e, there is no reason to introduce indexation because people can fully adjust to inflation.
7. As is well known, the conditions for the full rationality are quite restrictive – no corner solutions, no liquidity constraints, no childless families, and so on – and may not be fully met. In this case, there is no reason to assume that the capital stock will be driven to the optimal level. My assumption of a fixed, not necessarily optimal, savings rate captures this phenomenon. Furthermore, if people are fully rational, there is no reason to introduce indexation.

References

1. Bruce, N. (1981) 'Some macroeconomic effects on income tax indexation', *Journal of Monetary Economics*, vol. 8.
2. Buiter, W. H. and Gersovityz, M. (1981) 'Issues in controllability and the theory of economic policy', *Journal of Public Economics*, vol. 15.
3. Christ, C. F. (1979) 'On fiscal and monetary policies and the government budget restraint', *American Economic Review*, vol. 69.
4. Dornbusch, R. and Simonsen, M. H. (1983) *Inflation, Debt and Indexation* (Cambridge: MIT Press).
5. Feldstein, M. (1980) 'Fiscal policies, inflation, and capital formation', *American Economic Review*, vol. 70.
6. Fischer, S. (1983) 'Indexing and inflation', *Journal of Monetary Economics*, vol. 12.
7. Gray, J. A. (1976) 'Wage indexation: a macroeconomic approach', *Journal of Monetary Economics*, vol. 2.
8. Gultekin, B. and Santomero, A. M. (1979) 'Indexation, expectations, and stability', *Journal of Money, Credit, and Banking*, vol. 11.
9. Hadjimichalakis, M. G. (1972) 'Equilibrium and disequilibrium growth with money – the Tobin models', *Review of Economic Studies*, vol. 39.
10. Musgrave, R. A. and Musgrave, P. B. (1977) *Public Finance in Theory and Practice* (New York: McGraw-Hill).
11. Peston, M. (1982) 'A note on the validation of cost push', *Journal of Public Economics*, vol. 16.

16 Bank Capital Regulation

Larry Benveniste, John Boyd and
Stuart I. Greenbaum*

INTRODUCTION

This is an essay on the public regulation of bank capital, an economically scarce resource used in the production of financial intermediation services. We view capital requirements as one among a variety of regulatory intrusions into banking aimed at controlling moral hazard problems stemming from the public provision of a 'safety net'. The term safety net is taken to subsume the lender of last resort (LLR) facility, deposit insurance and the various implicit guarantees provided to banks. Hence, discussion of bank capital requirements makes sense only in the broader context of the extant set of regulatory interventions and the corresponding safety net provisions.

We begin by fleshing out this all-important context by relating bank regulations to particular moral hazards arising from the public provision of LLR facilities and deposit insurance, and go on to discuss the history of bank capital and capital regulation. In the third section, we show why we attribute the stability of banking in the post-Second World War era to hidden capital, in the form of the earlier subsidies provided banks via deposit rents, tax advantages, and entry restrictions, before proceeding to explore a variety of reform proposals, and presenting a summary and conclusions.

BANK CAPITAL AND MORAL HAZARD

Fractional reserve banking almost inevitably supports liquid bank liabilities with assets exhibiting credit risk. This seems to be a natural outgrowth of the substitution of intermediary liabilities (warehouse receipts) for corresponding collateral (precious metals, for example) as a means of payment or medium of exchange. But fractional reserve banking is vulnerable to periodic trauma in the form of bank runs with attendant social costs. This acknowledged flaw, however, is amenable to correction with a thoroughly credible LLR. This discovery gave rise to the central bank, and since coinage is historically reserved as a sovereign privilege, the central bank has tended to be a governmental institution. This is the original and most basic explanation for governmental intrusion in banking, and the LLR facility is likewise the primal element in what has come to be known as the public safety net. Through time, the safety net has been expanded to include deposit insurance along, with a variety of implicit supports and guarantees of the banking and payments system.

Note that the LLR provides banks with a loan commitment free of explicit cost; a bank can 'put' illiquid assets to the central bank in exchange for high-powered money on pre-specified terms. (Since the discount rate can vary, the contract resembles a floating-rate loan commitment.) Therefore, the introduction of an LLR should lead banks to hold fewer liquid assets (reserves) than they would otherwise.

This bank adaptation to the introduction of an LLR represents a moral hazard problem for the central bank. The reduction in voluntarily held bank reserves shifts deposit seigniorage from the public sector to privately-owned banks, and this diversion represents an extraordinary cost to the government and a subversion of the intended purpose of the LLR. The most direct way to address this moral hazard problem is to institute legal reserve requirements. Hence, reserve requirements emerge as a response to a moral hazard problem associated with the LLR facility, which in turn was a response to the vulnerability of fractional reserve banking.

The reason for belaboring this story (and we surely have) is that it generalizes to virtually all major facets of public regulation and supervision of banking. These facets, including capital requirements in particular, can be viewed as responses of the public guarantor to moral hazard problems arising from the safety net. In the case of capital requirements, the moral hazard derives principally from deposit insurance, without which bank capital is held, among other reasons, to control the cost of bank borrowing. (This is sometimes referred to as the 'indirect source of funds' function of bank capital.) A bank with little capital can expect to pay a higher rate for its borrowed funds (deposits) because of credit risk. But the introduction of deposit insurance eliminates this risk premium and thereby decreases banks' incentives to hold capital. The consequent reduction in bank capital represents an added cost to the deposit insurer, since bank capital serves as a deductible on the deposit insurance policy.

The regulatory capital requirement can then be viewed as a device to mitigate a moral hazard problem arising from the public provision of deposit insurance.[1]

THE HISTORY OF BANK CAPITAL REGULATION

Until about a decade ago, bank capital adequacy may have exercised the intellectual periphery of the banking community, but it did not seem to be a high priority in public policy circles.[2] Apart from the past decade, bank asset quality has not been a problem since the 1930s. Even earlier, the Real Bills Doctrine circumscribed the appropriate scope of commercial banking in a way that minimized credit risk. The central problem of commercial banking almost always has been liquidity, and the traditional focus of regulation has been cash assets, or reserves. Credit risk and capital were afterthoughts, in neat contrast to the thrift industry where the priorities were reversed.

Ironically, capital standards became an issue in the 1980s, a decade in which most capital measures have been flat to slightly rising, as indicated in Table 16.1. The broader sweep of history, captured in Figure 16.1, indicates that capital ratios have been declining with near secular monotony. For example, before 1850 almost 50 per cent of bank assets were financed with capital, but by the turn of the century, capital had shrunk to less than 20 per cent. In 1929, about 14 per cent of bank assets were financed with capital, and by the end of the Second World War, just over 6 per cent of bank assets were capital funded.

Since that time, the pattern is more subtle. Total bank capital rose a bit from the mid-1940s through the mid-1960s, then declined through the mid-1970s, and rose thereafter. In 1986, total capital stood at 6.8 per cent of bank assets, the same as in 1950. Equity capital, the narrower measure, traces a similar cyclical pattern, but ends the period at 6.2 per cent of bank assets compared with the 6.8 per cent shown in 1950.

Equity capital as a proportion of risk assets traces a somewhat different pattern in the post-Second World War era. Reaching a peak of 11.8 per cent in 1960, it sank to a nadir of 6.8 per cent in the mid-1970s. It then rose somewhat erratically to just under 8 per cent in 1986. Thus the emergence of bank capital as a public policy issue comes in a period when capital is no longer declining, in contrast to

Table 16.1 Commercial bank capital ratios since Second World War

Year	*Risk*[1] *assets 1*	*Risk assets 2*	*Total capital*	*Debt*[2] *capital*	*Equity capital*	*TC/ TA*[3]	*EC/ TA*[3]	*EC/ RA1*	*EC/ RA2*
1945[4]	85.7	–	8.7	0	8.6	5.5	5.5	10.1	–
1950	104.1	–	11.3	0	11.3	6.8	6.8	10.8	–
1955	14.2	–	15.0	0	24.0	7.2	7.2	10.5	–
1960	174.7	–	20.7	0	20.6	8.1	8.1	11.8	–
1965	255.7	–	29.9	1.7	28.3	8.0	7.5	11.0	–
1970[5]	448.7	–	42.6	2.1	40.5	6.9	6.6	9.0	–
1971	512.7	–	47.0	3.0	44.0	6.8	6.3	8.6	–
1972	602.5	–	52.4	4.0	48.4	6.4	6.0	8.0	–
1973	720.6	–	59.9	4.2	53.7	6.1	5.7	7.5	–
1974	868.0	–	63.3	4.3	59.1	6.1	5.6	6.8	–
1975	815.0	–	68.7	4.4	64.3	6.3	5.9	7.3	–
1976[6]	955.3	–	77.5	5.2	72.3	6.6	6.1	7.6	–
1977	1 083.1	–	85.1	5.8	79.3	6.4	5.9	7.3	–
1978	1 244.4	–	93.3	5.9	87.4	6.2	5.8	7.0	–
1979	1 295.4	1 248.0	103.4	6.3	97.1	6.1	5.7	7.5	7.8
1980	1 419.3	1 361.0	114.1	6.5	107.6	6.2	5.8	7.6	7.9
1981	1 598.0	1 530.0	124.8	6.5	118.3	6.1	5.8	7.4	7.7
1982	1 741.0	1 665.0	136.2	7.3	128.9	6.2	5.9	7.4	7.7
1983	1 832.0	1 755.0	147.7	7.1	140.6	6.3	6.0	7.7	8.0
1984	–	1 949.0	164.6	10.2	154.4	6.6	6.2	–	7.9
1985	–	2 146.0	183.9	14.7	169.2	6.7	6.2	–	7.9
1986	–	2 307.0	199.2	16.9	182.3	6.8	6.2	–	7.9

Notes:
1. Risk assets 1 = foreign assets + domestic assets – (cash + due from) – US Treasury obligations.
2. Risk assets 2 = foreign assets + domestic assets – (cash + due from) – US Government obligations.
3. Sanctioned for capital adequacy purposes by the Comptroller of the Currency in 1962.
4. Total assets include foreign and domestic assets.
5. Before 1969, total assets included loans net of reserves for loan losses. Starting in 1969, these reserves were moved to the liability side, and loans included in total assets were reported gross.
6. Beginning in 1976, loan valuation reserves became a contra-asset and total assets were reported using loans net of reserve.

Source: Federal Reserve.

earlier experience. Despite a pronounced weakening of bank capital ratios in the 1960s and into the 1970s, we had no explicit capital requirements until the International Banking Act of 1978. To the extent that we had capital standards at all, they were informal parts of the examination process, or bargaining chips in connection with

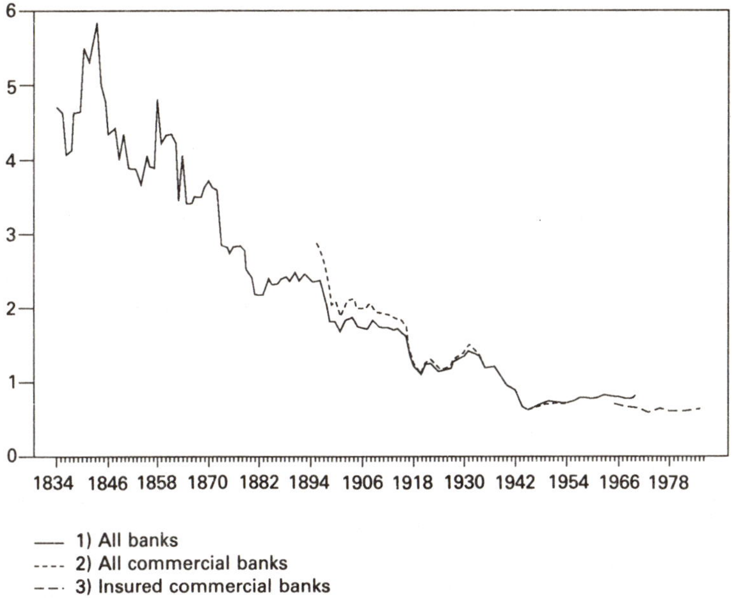

Figure 16.1

bank holding company applications. In contrast, explicit capital (net worth) requirements have been central to the regulation of the thrift industry since the deposit insurance legislation of the 1930s.

Recent concern for bank capital is obviously motivated by the rising loan losses and bank failures of the past decade, and these symptoms are not reflected in the gross capital ratios that serve as macro measures of leverage and exposure. Bank failures have risen from an average of less than 10 per year in the mid-1970s to over 200 per year more recently. The average size of failed institutions has risen as well. Even these striking figures belie the gravity attached to the demise of leading financial institutions like Continental Illinois, Seafirst, and virtually all of the major banks in Texas.

The growth of bank asset quality problems is further indicated by charge-offs in the past decade. These have risen from $3.5 billion in 1976 to $16 billion in 1986. Provisions for commercial bank loan losses grew from well under $5 billion in the mid-1970s to $40 billion in 1987. Expressed as a per cent of loans, charge-offs grew from 30 basis points in the late 1970s to 100 basis points in 1987 – see Pierce and Chase (1988).

HIDDEN CAPITAL IN BANKING

Whereas formal bank capital requirements are but a decade old, deposit insurance has been around for half a century. Why has a 50-year-old potential problem come to the fore only in the last ten years?

For most of the period in question, banks' accounting capital was augmented by hidden capital based on monopoly rents earned on deposits in those years when entry restrictions were more effective and interest rate ceilings on deposits were binding. Even apart from the interest rate ceilings (introduced as recently as the 1960s in the thrift industry), deposit insurance and tax concessions elevated bank profits, and those profits were not totally dissipated by competition. Otherwise, explaining the bank failure experience in the half century following the Great Depression would be difficult indeed.

In the 1930s the solution to more than a decade of increasingly debilitating bank failures was an essentially voluntary three-party contract among the government, depositors, and bank owners. Depositors accepted a submarket (probably below risk-free) return on deposits in exchange for a less-than-full-faith-and-credit, but still credible, government guarantee of deposits. In exchange for suppressed deposit costs, elevated barriers to entry, and a variety of tax concessions, bankers accepted governmental intrusion in the forms of monitoring (examinations) and restriction of investment opportunities (regulation).

The consequent rents were undoubtedly dissipated in part by subsidizing borrowers and by non-price competition for deposits. But the dramatic change in the frequency of bank failures strongly suggests that a portion of these rents were retained by bank owners. These became the basis for the hidden capital that restrained bank risk-taking proclivities by functioning as a kind of bankruptcy cost.

Because of the accounting convention of carrying deposits at their terminal rather than present value, the deposit rents led to an overstatement of liabilities and an understatement of capital. Bankers understood this well; the idea was memorialized in the concept of 'core deposits'. This disparity between economic and accounting capital served the ends of regulation in two distinct ways. First, since the bank's charter is jeopardized by the exhaustion of accounting capital, the wedge between economic and accounting capital serves as a bankruptcy cost. Second, the hidden capital provided regulators with a cushion so that banks could be closed while still having a positive economic value. The ability to intervene before economic capital was exhausted explains why losses sustained on failed institutions tended to be so small. It also explains why failed institutions were so rarely liquidated: the franchise value was preserved precisely because accounting conventions ignored it.

So long as economic capital exceeds accounting capital, we have a regulatory argument against current value accounting. If the inequality is reversed, however, the regulator can be victimized by terminal value accounting, since intervention is sanctioned only after economic capital is exhausted. Erosion of banks' hidden capital is injurious to the regulator since it reduces the risk abatement incentives as well as the regulator's cushion of protection.

Note that carrying assets as inflated values (as in the case of lesser developed country debt) has the opposite effect, offsetting benefits that accrue as a result of deposit rents. LDC debt and other asset quality problems that emerged in the early 1980s therefore compounded the problems associated with the earlier loss of deposit rents.

Thus, dissipation of monopoly rents tracing back to the inflation of the 1970s altered the structural equilibrium of the post-Depression period. One more nominal contract subverted by inflation! Entry barriers crumbled, interest rate ceilings were dismantled, deposit costs rose and became more volatile. Banks' hidden capital was dissipated. Weakened risk-abatement incentives altered bank investment decisions. Consequent losses were hidden by accounting conventions that resulted in a widening divergence between the book and economic values of assets. By permitting banks to carry assets as inflated values, the wedge between economic and accounting capital was further narrowed, compounding the incentive problem.

This explains the emergence of the potential moral hazard problem that was always embedded in the deposit insurance contract. Policymakers recognized this moral hazard, but bribed bankers to behave. Inflation withdrew the bribe, and the consequences are history.

PROPOSALS FOR REGULATORY REFORM

In light of the preceding discussion, an ever-increasing chorus of calls for regulatory reform in banking comes as no surprise. Most proposals fall into two categories: those that would attenuate the safety net, and those that would introduce more compelling risk-mitigating incentives. The former proposals include reducing deposit insurance coverage, instituting co-insurance, and even eliminating deposit insurance.[3] One hundred per cent reserve, or so-called 'narrow' banking, belongs in this category as well.

Proposals in the second category include risk-based deposit insurance, risk-related capital requirements, and increased capital requirements.[4] The Basle Agreements and the forthcoming FHLBB capital requirement reforms fall into the second category, since they raise capital requirements and make them (crudely) risk progressive. Proposals to implement current value accounting, continuous monitoring, and expeditious closure of failing institutions belong in this category too. To this list of frequently discussed reforms we shall add (and then dismiss) another: restoring banks' hidden capital.

Attenuating the safety net

A number of reform proposals call for a diminished governmental role in banking. Elimination of deposit insurance is one such proposal. Reducing coverage but retaining some deposit insurance is a less radical variant. This could be achieved through co-insurance, for example, with a fixed percentage of deposits being covered. Alternatively, as recently proposed in Association of Reserve City Bankers (1988), the current $100 000 insurance limit could be made per individual or organization rather than per account. There are innumerable variations on this theme.

'100 per cent' reserve banking is a related, if seemingly different, reform. This idea, discussed by Simons (1936) and later by Friedman (1960), was recently rediscovered and repackaged under the label of 'narrow banking.' The basic idea is to sever the payments (medium-of-exchange) function of banks from their lending function. Public policymakers would define some class of bank liabilities that must be made default risk free for example, all liabilities that serve as means of payment. These would be secured with highly liquid, duration matched, credit-risk-free assets, such as deposits at the Federal Reserve or US Treasury securities. Since this special class of deposits would be secured by risk-free claims, the government's only exposure would be to loss by fraud, and presumably this could be readily controlled by auditing. Hence, deposit insurance could be provided with minimal governmental exposure. All risky assets would then be financed with uninsured liabilities. These could be deposits, but there would be no government guarantee against their default. Banks could continue to intermediate risky claims, as long as risk-free assets remained adequate to secure insured deposits, and co-mingling were avoided.

Under 100 per cent reserve banking, a substantial fraction of currently risk-free bank liabilities would become risky, i.e., all of those used to finance bank loans and investments other than cash assets and US government and agency issues. It is in this sense that 100 per cent reserve banking attenuates the safety net, and is similar to co-insurance, or doing away with deposit insurance. Any of these changes would put more bank creditors at risk, some bank creditors at more risk, or both, and would impose more market discipline on banks through monitoring by creditors. A concomitant effect of all these changes, however, would be to increase the risk of bank runs (or some modern mutation thereof) and the potential for systemic instability.

However, some increase in the risk of bank runs may be inevitable, perhaps even desirable, in reducing moral hazard. Examining of periods when banking regulation was less intrusive, several studies conclude that although bank runs and failures were indeed more common than they are today, the attendant social costs were minimal – see Rolnick and Weber (1984).[5] We confess to a vague discomfort when contemporary scholars review traumas of the past and conclude conditions were not really so bad (but this could be a symptom of our own advancing age).

History notwithstanding, there remains a major difficulty with any proposal that seeks to increase market discipline in banking. That problem is one of 'time inconsistency'. Any government policy is said to be 'time consistent' if it remains optimal after it has been followed for any length of time – see Kydland and Prescott (1977). Time consistency is a property that any sound government policy must exhibit. But it is not clear that policies which result in increased likelihood of bank runs and systemic failures can be time consistent. If the regulatory authorities promulgate strict policies when the banking system is functioning normally, they may have little incentive to adhere to such policies in times of turmoil. The benefits of the policy are long-run, defined in terms of incentives and the signals sent to banks and the markets. The costs, however, are short-run, defined in terms of systemic instability and political and economic dislocation. Who would want to risk the stigma of precipitating the 'Panic of 19??'? Like corporate decision-making, public policy may tend to be myopic, with the public regulators announcing that they will bail out failing institutions this 'one time only'. Such inconsistency is eventually internalized by market participants who then (correctly) predict future bailouts. That is why such policies are not credible and are therefore ineffective.[6]

Time consistency suggests that it will be difficult to implement any policy calling for a substantial increase in the market discipline of banks. Nevertheless, because of time inconsistency, some reinforcement of market discipline seems desirable. Recall that deposit insurance was introduced for two ostensible reasons: to provide risk-free investment opportunities for 'widows and orphans' and to provide a backup against a failure to administer the LLR facility properly. Clearly, widows and orphans have a far more expansive set of investment alternatives today than in the 1930s. Also, arguably, at least, our understanding of monetary policy is somewhat improved. Thus, the need for deposit insurance is diminished.

Providing disincentives to risk taking

A second category of reform proposals leaves the safety net intact but provides more compelling risk-abatement incentives. These include risk-progressive regulatory taxes, current value accounting, continuous monitoring, expeditious closure of failing institutions, and increasing regulatory capital ratios.

Risk-progressive regulatory taxes

Risk-based deposit insurance premia and risk-based capital requirements are comparable. They are even formally equivalent, since capital can be viewed as an insurance deductible paid by bank owners. Thus, in many models, the same results can be obtained with risk-adjusted premia, given a capital requirement, or with risk-adjusted capital requirements, given a deposit insurance premium schedule.

A number of studies have suggested how variable deposit insurance premia might achieve economic efficiency. Most treat the deposit insurance contract as a put option, following Merton (1977). This approach is intuitively attractive, since the derived premia are those which would be charged by competitive private market insurers including an appropriate market risk premium.[7] A major drawback, however, is that such estimates take the distribution of bank asset values as given and ignore moral hazard – which is what gave rise to the problem in the first place.

As Diamond (1986) explains in a discussion of unresolved issues in finance:[8]

> Private information about the ex-ante risk and value of assets can give rise to moral hazard problems with deposit insurance. Most studies of these problems assume complete markets where intermediaries provide no services. This implies that any distortion caused by deposit insurance is a net social loss. It would be interesting to investigate the second-best optimum with useful intermediaries and the moral hazard constraint on deposit insurance pricing.

The point is that we simply do not know how to structure risk-progressive deposit insurance premia, even theoretically. The same is true with risk-adjusted capital requirements. One possibility is to acknowledge our ignorance and employ approximations without pretence. This could be thought of as an exercise in learning-by-doing whereby we iterate towards a desired result. However, such a learning exercise could be costly. The risk-progressive capital requirements of the Basle Agreements display an agnostic, rough-and-ready-quality. Five risk classes are established for assets and off-balance sheet items. Each class is weighted from 0 to 1.0 with cash and short-term US Treasury bills receiving the lowest weight and most bank loans receiving the highest. All other assets are assigned weights of 0.1, 0.2, or 0.5, based on some seemingly arbitrary assessment of their risk.[9]

It's difficult to believe that classifying assets into five categories can capture the subtleties of bank asset risks. Even if this approach constitutes a move in the right direction, there are serious difficulties with this sort of crudity. First, we can easily delude ourselves with hollow and specious gestures. Second, by creating categorical interstices, we invite banks to game the system. Finally, errors in defining risk categories can be expected to result in the misallocation of economic resources.

In response to Basle, banks will seek to minimize the cost of capital requirements. Asset holdings in those categories for which the capital requirements are perceived as low will be expanded. Mortgages seem to belong in this category. Likewise, those categories with a high weight will receive smaller allocations. Interest rates on the various asset classes will presumably adjust accordingly. Within categories, there will be a tendency to allocate funds to those investments with the highest expected rates of return, which generally means the highest risk.[10]

This industry has long experience with inventing creative responses to regulatory restrictions. Note, for example, the panoply of 'non-deposit deposits' arrayed to circumvent reserve requirements, deposit insurance premia, and (earlier) Regulation Q ceilings. Banks will undoubtedly circumvent the risk-progressive capital standards as well. The regulators' zeal in finding and plugging loopholes will limit the circumvention. This 'regulatory dialectic' is apt to be costly in several ways. It consumes resources directly and results in misallocations. However, bank regulation is not unique in this regard; most government interventions display similar attributes. Although a total neutralization of the risk-progressive capital requirements seems unlikely, the usual dialectic waste is predictable.

Current value accounting, continuous monitoring and expeditious closure of failing banks

Numerous reform proposals incorporate the same alluringly simple idea: get rid of accounting deceptions, monitor closely, and close banks expeditiously as their net worth approaches zero – see White (1988). Effective implementation of such a programme would obviate insurer losses and the need for an insurance fund. According to the advocates, candour, vigilance and will (against time inconsistency) are the sole requirements. Such a policy would intervene shortly prior to the exhaustion of banks' net worth. The consequent expropriation would constitute yet another cost of regulation. If such a policy were followed consistently, the deposit-insuring agency need never sustain a loss, and without losses there can be no moral hazard.

Current value accounting is an integral part of this proposal. Rather than carrying most assets at acquisition costs or terminal values as banks do now, loans and securities and liabilities would also be market-to-market. If continuous monitoring is to preclude insurer losses, improved accounting is essential.

The problems with this class of proposals revolve around the cost, quality, and timeliness of the required information. For such plans to succeed, the deposit insurers would need a great deal of information not now readily available moreover, they would need the information on a timely basis. In fact, the information requirements might well exceed what is now available to the management of most banks. Regulatory monitoring would need to be done on a real-time basis, because the value of financial assets can change abruptly. Also, the value of many financial claims are correlated, and therefore diversification is of limited value in hedging large jumps. The October 1987 crash illustrates the point. Monitoring once per year or quarter is inadequate if the objective is to protect the deposit insurer. This is one clear lesson of volatile capital markets: 'continuous monitoring' would have to be continuous, or nearly so.

The deposit insurer's problem closely resembles a class of intensively studied economic problems – those with 'costly state verification.' In this context, banks which have relatively complete information regarding their financial condition (or 'state') are 'informed agents.' The deposit insurer, on the other hand, is 'uninformed', since it does not know the financial state of the banks. Of course, if it did know the banks' state, it would make sense to condition the insurance premium on the banks' exposure. But the deposit insurer is not directly involved, and cannot simply accept the banks' avowal either since the banks have an incentive to claim minimal risk, whether true or not.

One possible response to this information asymmetry is to ignore the risk state and treat all banks identically. That is what we do now, but with moral hazard as a result. Another possible approach is to inform the uniformed agent, i.e. to have it learn the true financial condition of each insured bank. Hence, continuous monitoring.

Since costly state verification problems are not new, we have some idea about what is required. Economic efficiency may be achieved by clever contracting (Townsend 1979, Gale and Hellwig 1985) through the choice of an appropriate institutional arrangement (Diamond 1984, Williamson 1986, Boyd and Prescott 1986) or by the appropriate choice of a monitoring technology (Mookerjee and P'ng 1987, Townsend 1987). What is not efficient in any of the contexts examined is the full-information solution implied by continuous monitoring. That's because the production of this information by the deposit insurer is costly and redundant, given that the banks know their condition. Indeed, economic efficiency is achieved by minimizing the amount of such redundant information that is produced.[11]

Current value accounting, continuous monitoring, and expeditious closure of banks are a snare. This collection of reforms has extraordinary appeal in its elegance and simplicity, much like the narrow bank. However, closer examination of informational problems elicits a generous measure of skepticism. Even if this programme lacks the promise of a cure-all, however, we need to note that current accounting practices are egregiously anachronistic at best, and improvements are easily within grasp. For example, more bank assets (liabilities, too) are tradeable (and traded), and many off-balance-sheet items can now be usefully priced with option valuation techniques. Thus, current value accounting is more feasible than ever before. Narrowing the scope of obfuscation is an unimpeachable goal, and on one level the call for current value accounting is little more than a plea for disclosure. If one believes, as we do, that more market discipline is desirable, then calls for the wider application of current value accounting are to be applauded. Our skepticism is based on the strongly held view that banking involves proprietary and not readily disclosed information, and this feature of banking limits the extension of current value accounting. This is more than a nice point!

Increasing regulatory capital ratios

Elevated capital requirements is another reform intended to influence bank risk-taking incentives. This intervention is of particular interest, since the Basle Agreements call for minimum capital of 7.25 per cent of assets by the end of 1990 (of which at least half must be 'core capital') and at least 8.0 per cent of assets by the end of 1992 (again at least half of which must be core capital). Core capital includes common equity and minority interests in consolidated subsidiaries, but it excludes loan loss reserves, both allocated and general.[12]

These changes clearly constitute an elevation of regulatory capital requirements. An important question is: will such changes have the intended mitigating effect on moral hazard, risk of bank failure, and expected losses of the FDIC? The answer is probably yes, but we will argue there are likely to be unintended and undesirable side effects, too.

Since the ratio of bank equity to total assets will increase, the fraction of total claims against bank assets that are not insured will rise, and the fraction that are insured will fall. *Ceteris paribus*, this means that in bankruptcy states, private losses will be higher and insurer losses will be lower. Here, *ceteris paribus* means that banks do not take risk-increasing actions to offset the effect of the increased capital requirement. It is doubtful that the authorities would knowingly permit banks to circumvent increased capital requirements, for example, by accepting greater credit risk.[13]

In a sense, increasing capital requirements is the natural replacement for the lost deposit rents, since the risk-abatement incentives are the same. Increased capital imposed a higher bankruptcy cost on banks, and before deposit rents were dissipated, the possibility of losing future deposit subsidies served that role. The higher the regulatory or hidden capital, the more bank shareholders had to lose in bankruptcy, and the more cautious they were likely to be. Thus, the risk effects of higher regulatory capital are straightforward. Increased capital requirements will most likely have the intended effect on banks' risk-taking and on the future expected losses of the insurer.[14]

However, if increased capital requirements reduce the insurer's expected losses, they also reduce any remaining subsidy to the banking system. The insurer's gain must come at someone's expense and the current shareholders of banks are the someone. This can be demonstrated assuming complete markets. Define V as the market value of a bank's assets and A as the next-period realization of its assets. Further, suppose there are three classes of claims against that realization, and the total value of all claims always equals the value of the underlying assets. Hence, changes in the composition of claims cannot affect V.[15]

The first class of claims is risk free and pays R_f in all future states; the present value of such debt is D_f. The second class of claims is equity, which returns $A - B_f - P$, provided $A > R_f + P$, and zero otherwise. The present value of equity is E. The insurer can be viewed as the third claimant. It receives an insurance premium P in all (non-bankrupt) states in which $A \geq R_f + P$. In bankrupt states, $A < R_f + P$ and the insurer receives $A - D_f$. The present value of the insurer's claim is F, and by construction,

$$V = D_f + E + F$$

Now suppose, as above, that capital regulation is tightened in such a way that the insurer is made better off, i.e. F increases. Then, since V cannot change, either E, D_f, or both, must decline. But D_f is the value of the risk-free claim, hence it cannot change, either. All that can change is E; it follows that any increase in F must be exactly offset by a fall in E.[16]

The complete markets assumption constitutes reaching, and we would not want to interpret the implications too literally, especially not the one-for-one match between FDIC gains and shareholder losses. Nevertheless, if increased capital standards force banks to a privately sub-optimal scale or financial structure, a transfer takes place that impoverishes the bank. The details of the transfer will depend, of course, on the exact provisions of the increased capital requirement. For example, an increase in the insurance premium – which represents a particular kind of capital requirement increase – will transfer wealth directly from shareholders to the government. A sale of new equity that either replaces subsidized deposits or results in asset holding assets that cannot support the required return on the new equity, will again transfer wealth, but from old shareholders to the insurer. It also will permanently increase the cost of obtaining future equity, since the new shareholders will anticipate future abuse. If the bank chooses to adapt to a higher capital standard by reducing its leverage rather than selling equity, it will again sustain losses by foregoing subsidized deposits. An increase in capital may actually reduce profits!

No matter how one proceeds, there is a law of conservation at work, assuming the bank is of optimal scale and structure at the outset. Moreover, the improvement experienced by the insurer must be weighed against possible future costs in the face of higher capital costs to banks and, perhaps even more importantly, in terms of the altered incentives to risk-taking that bankers experience as their private property is compromised.

Markets have memories, and future investors can be expected to demand a higher risk premium in response to any transfer from shareholders to the insurer. Moreover, any impoverishment of shareholders can be expected to weaken bank owners' aversion to risk. Thus, whereas increased capital requirements may provide the insurer with gains that are not ill-gotten (after all, they are largely subsidy reversals), neither are they unalloyed.

Putting the hidden capital back in banking

This leads us quite naturally to another possible solution to the moral hazard problem in banking. That is, to restore the hidden capital or to provide banks with some unique value inextricably tied to their charters. For example, suppose that regulatory capital ratios were raised substantially, but that at the same time, the Federal Reserve began paying interest on legally required reserves. Clearly, interest-bearing reserves could offset the cost of increased capital requirements. This would maintain or restore the value of a bank charter while reducing the moral hazard problem due to deposit insurance.[17]

Congress has never shown much sympathy for this idea, but their enthusiasm is inevitably tempered by the needs of the day. Anyway, there is another problem with this proposal, or any other along these lines. For hidden capital to play its intended role, banks must earn monopoly rents, and this necessitates that entry into banking be effectively restricted. Not only would such a system be politically unpopular, it also would result in a variety of inefficiencies. The cure could be worse than the ailment!

SUMMARY AND CONCLUSIONS

Bank capital requirements serve to control a moral hazard arising from deposit insurance. However, until recently the need for capital requirements was suppressed by a pool of hidden capital in banking arising from deposit rents, tax abatements, and entry restrictions. The hidden capital diffused banks' risk-taking proclivities by serving as a kind of bankruptcy cost.

The deposit rents were dissipated substantially by the inflation of the 1970s, and the hidden capital was further eroded by subsequent asset quality problems related to LDC, energy, and agricultural lending. Tax advantages were gradually lost, and barriers to entry crumbled as well. The loss of hidden capital diminished the bankruptcy cost and reduced banks' aversion to risk. The value of the deposit insurance option could be inflated by increasing leverage. Hence, the need for a capital requirement has increased.

Unfortunately, increasing the capital requirement is not without attendant costs. If capital is substituted for insured deposits (which are presumably still cheaper than capital), bank profits may actually fall. But even if not, capital will not increase dollar-for-dollar with the equity commitment of new shareholders. The insurer's gain comes at the expense of existing shareholders, and this loss of shareholders has precisely the same impact on risk-taking proclivities as the loss of hidden capital. New shareholders cannot be expropriated, i.e. not until they are committed. But, the new shareholders can be expected to learn from the experience of the old, and therefore require an appropriate risk premium to allow for the possibility of future regulatory expropriations. As a consequence, the initial increase in the capital requirement increases the future cost of accessing equity markets. This cost will tend to be underestimated by relatively short-lived regulatory and government officials because the cost is remote in time and oblique in effect. However, it is nonetheless real, and it should give us pause in our zeal to raise capital requirements.

Yet another source of pause is the clearly less compelling need for deposit insurance in a world with enhanced access to risk-free claims, and with a presumably better mastery than we had in the 1930s of macroeconomic policy, particularly as it relates to the LLR facility. Some scaling bank of deposit insurance should be possible. In addition, while continuous monitoring may be something of a 'will-of-the-wisp', accounting practices are amenable to improvement, provided that our Big Eight brethren can be cajoled. Moreover, many off-balance-sheet items are amenable to valuation using option pricing technologies. Thus, current value accounting is more feasible than earlier, notwithstanding the sizable fraction of bank claims that are not readily valued. Meaningful partial steps along the path to current value accounting are possible, but we should not underestimate the accountants' reluctance to become appraisers, especially in this litigous age. The academic's zeal for current value accounting often ignores the cost or availability of professional liability insurance, which is just as much a cost of state verification as the junior auditor's hourly pay for counting herring in a barrel.

Just as surely, the lure of risk-based capital requirements may prove to be a snare. This simple idea may prove simplistic, in which case bankers merely shuffle their assets, at real social cost, to placate the regulator by playing at the interstices of the prescribed risk categories. There is already extensive discussion about substituting mortgages and mortgage-backed securities for other assets to permit greater leverage. The junior pieces of senior-subordinated structures and residual claims to mortgage pools could become the hottest game in town.

If our message seems pessimistic, perhaps it should. For most of the post-Depression era we have enjoyed extraordinarily good fortune in regulating our financial institutions. For forty years, we essentially eliminated bank failures and achieved a high degree of system stability. This achievement was not without a cost, but the cost was well hidden. So well hidden, indeed, that few understood the basis for the stability. How else can we explain the dramatically altered performance of the last decade, one in which failures and losses have escalated monotonously and ominously. We see no panacea. A return to the good old days of generous subsidies seems both unlikely and undesirable. Yet the need for reform is compelling. The combination of a scaled back safety net, somewhat elevated and crudely risk-based capital requirements, and improved financial reporting may be our only recourse.

We have no illusions about the difficulty of reforming public policy in a setting of structural disequilibrium. We will undoubtedly stumble through the present morass, perhaps with the naive good luck enjoyed for the past forty years. However, it would be far better, it seems to us, to restore a measure of equilibrium by closing the thousands of redundant financial institutions currently dotting the horizons before redesigning the safety net and concomitant regulatory practices.

Notes

* The usual disclaimer applies with regard to institutional endorsements of the views expressed herein.

1. This story can be reformulated and presented somewhat less transparently in an option pricing framework, where the reduction in capital increases the variance of returns and thereby increases the value of the option presented to the bank in deposit insurance form – see Merton (1977).
2. See the Commission on Money and Credit studies, particularly Guthman, Jacobs, and Lerner (1960), for a discussion of the bank capital problem.
3. This is not to be confused with eliminating the FDIC and FSLIC insurance funds only to substitute full-faith-and-credit government guarantees. The latter proposal reduces the ambiguity of a depositor's claim against the government but does not reduce the government's exposure. Whether reducing such ambiguity would serve a constructive purpose in terms of incentives is an interesting question in its own right.
4. Bernheim's (1988) interesting proposal to heavily tax extraordinary profits – the presumptive fruits of excessive speculation – would likewise fall into this category.
5. A related argument is that deposit insurance is simply redundant. That is, bank runs, if not failures, can be contained effectively with appropriate administration of the LLR facility. This would require providing prompt and unstinting credit to individual banks and to all banks when there is the threat of a systemic breakdown. To be sure, aggressive LLR policy can contain any bank run or systemic instability, and could do so without deposit insurance. However, LLR lending results in moral hazard, too. Emergency lending is a substitute source of funding necessitated when private lenders (depositors) withdraw. In this situation, private creditors are leaving a bank because of suspicions. In some cases

their suspicions will be correct. When they are, creditors avoid financial losses at the expense of the LLR. The more forthcoming the LLR, the more losses are shifted from the private to the public sector.

6. One solution to time inconsistency is to find a way in which policymakers can precommit to follow an announced rule. Unfortunately, this proves to be difficult. Regulations can be changed, laws can be rewritten, and even governments come and go. The time inconsistency problem in bank regulation is illustrated by the extreme difficulty we encounter in allowing large banks to fail.
7. To the extent that bank failures result in negative externalities, the competitive private market insurance premium would not be optimal.
8. Chan, Greenbaum and Thakor (1988) follow up on Diamond's suggestion of studying deposit insurance in an imperfect information environment. This work suggests that 'fairly priced' deposit insurance is not feasible and that efficiency requires cross-subsidization from low- to high-risk banks.
9. The 0.1 category includes US governments with maturity greater than 91 days, all US agency issues, and Federal Reserve Bank stock. The 0.2 category includes all claims on domestic depository institutions, claims on foreign banks with an original maturity of one year or less, and full-faith-and-credit municipal securities. The 0.5 category includes municipal revenue bonds and similar obligations. Also, as a result of a late revision (August 1988), this category includes most conventional mortgages which had been in the 1.0 category. For a discussion of *Basle Agreement* risk classifications, see Federal Reserve System (1988).
10. For a discussion of likely bank responses to the new regulations, see Goldman Sachs (1988).
11. Loosely, the idea is for the uninformed agent to produce just enough information so that in equilibrium it is in the interest of the informed to honestly reveal their information. The continuous monitoring proposals also ignore an important entailment of recent research on financial intermediation. Diamond (1984), Ramakrishnan and Thakor (1984), Williamson (1986), and Boyd and Prescott (1986) show that financial intermediaries produce information about would-be borrowers and appropriate the value of the information by originating loans and holding them. Once made, loans are worth more to the intermediary than to the open market because the intermediary has produced costly and proprietary information about the loans. The value of the information is embedded in the loans, and the market can obtain it only by incurring redundant information costs (since representations of the informed intermediary are hardly credible). Thus, even if market values for bank loans could somehow be obtained, these would understate economic value by some unknown amount. In fact, according to the theory, this is one reason that the loans are made by financial intermediaries in the first place. Of course, if all bank loans could be securitized and actively traded, this theory would be irrelevant. But that seems (to us) a good bit in the future.
12. Unallocated loan loss reserves are included in supplementary capital. However, in view of the difficulty in distinguishing loan loss reserves that

are freely available from those that may in reality reflect existing problems in loan portfolios, the requirements include a phase-down of the extent to which loan loss reserves may be included in the capital base. There is initially no limit, but by 1990, loan loss reserves may constitute no more than 1.5 per cent of weighted risk assets and, by 1992, no more than 1.25 per cent (see Federal Reserve System 1988).

13. This is precisely what happened in the thrift industry with the rapid growth of securitization, see Chan, Greenbaum and Thakor (1988), and Greenbaum and Thakor (1987).
14. It is not difficult to construct examples in which requiring banks to hold more capital has no effect on their risk of failure, see Kareken (1987). These examples are fragile, however, depending critically on the assumption of complete markets and finite states of nature. In such a world it is always possible for an insured bank to choose its asset portfolio so that it will be bankrupt in all states but one. Moreover, it is always optimal for it to do so, regardless of how much capital it is required to hold. If, however, poststate asset values are represented by a continuous probability distribution, this result will not obtain.
15. This is the Modigliani-Miller Theorem in another guise.
16. If we were to allow for the existence of uninsured creditors of the bank (if such still exist), they might share in losses along with shareholders.
17. There may be another reason for paying interest on reserves. A good case can be made that paying interest on reserves, in conjunction with permitting banks to pay interest on demand deposits, would contribute to the efficiency of the payments system. However, such arguments are beyond the scope of this study.

References

1. Association of Reserve City Bankers (1988) *Beyond Capital Regulation: Strengthening the FDIC Insurance Fund and Systemic Liquidity*, March.
2. Bernheim, B. D. (1988) 'The crisis in deposit insurance', *ARCB–BRC Working Paper*.
3. Boyd, J. H. and Prescott, E. C. (1986) 'Financial intermediary-coalitions', *Journal of Economic Theory*, vol. 38.
4. Chan, Y.-S., Greenbaum, S. I. and Thakor, A. V. (1988) 'Is fairly priced deposit insurance possible?', *BRC Working Paper*, No. 152 (Evanston, Illinois: Northwestern University).
5. Chan, Y.-S., Greenbaum, S. I. and Thakor, A. V. (1986) 'Information reusability, competition and bank asset quality', *Journal of Banking and Finance*, vol. 10.
6. Diamond, D. W. (1984) 'Financial intermediation and delegated monitoring', *Review of Economic Studies*, vol. 51.
7. Diamond, D. W. (1986) 'Asset services and financial intermediation', *Working Paper*, No. 182 (Chicago: Center for Research in Security Prices, Graduate School of Business, University of Chicago), July.

8. Diamond, D. W. and Dybvig, P. H. (1983) 'Bank runs, deposit insurance, and liquidity', *Journal of Political Economy*, vol. 91.
9. Federal Reserve System (1988) 'Capital risk-based capital guidelines', *12CFR Part 225, Appendix B* (Regulation Y docket #R-0628).
10. Friedman, M. (1960) *A Program for Monetary Stability* (New York: Fordham University Press).
11. Gale, D. and Hellwig, M. (1985) 'Incentive-compatible contracts: the one period problem', *Review of Economic Studies*, vol. 52.
12. Goldman Sachs (1988) *Risk-Based Capital Adequacy Standard: Impact on Bank Portfolios and Fixed Income Markets* (Goldman Sachs and Co).
13. Greenbaum, S. I. and Thakor, A. V. (1987) 'Bank funding modes: securitization versus deposits', *Journal of Banking and Finance*, vol. 11.
14. Guthmann, H. G., Jacobs, D. P. and Lerner, E. M. (1960) *Risk Capital in Financial Institutions* (Washington DC: Commission on Money and Credit).
15. Kareken, J. H. (1987) 'The emergence and regulation of contingent commitment banking', *Journal of Banking and Finance*, vol. 11.
16. Kydland, F. E. and Prescott, E. C. (1977) 'Rules rather than discretion: the inconsistency of optimal plans', *Journal of Political Economy*, vol. 85.
17. Merton, R. C. (1977) 'An analytic derivation of the cost of deposit insurance and loan guarantees: an application of modern option pricing theory', *Journal of Banking and Finance*, vol. 1.
18. Moohkerjee, D., and P'ng, I. (1987) 'Optimal auditing, insurance, and redistribution', *Graduate School of Business Research Paper*, No. 887 (Stanford University).
19. Pierce, J. L. and Chase, S. B. (1988) *The Management of Risk in Banking* (The Association of Reserve City Bankers).
20. Ramakrishnan, R. T. S. and Thakor, A. V. (1984) 'Information reliability and a theory of financial intermediation', *Review of Economic Studies*, vol. 51.
21. Rolnick, A. J. and Weber, W. E. (1984) 'The causes of free bank failures: a detailed examination', *Journal of Monetary Economics*, vol. 14.
22. Simons, H. (1936) 'Rules versus authorities in monetary policy', *Journal of Political Economy*, vol. 46.
23. Townsend, R. M. (1979) 'Optimal contracts and competitive markets with costly state verification', *Journal of Economic Theory*, vol. 21.
24. Townsend, R. M. (1988) 'Information constrained insurance: the revelation principle extended', *Journal of Monetary Economics*, vol. 21.
25. White, L. J. (1988) 'Market value accounting: an important part of the reform of the deposit insurance system', *ARCB-BRC Working Paper*.
26. Williamson, S. (1986) 'Costly monitoring, financial intermediation, and equilibrium credit rationing', *Journal of Monetary Economics*, vol. 18.

17 A Collective-choice and Microeconomic Approach to Macroeconomics: From Sticky Prices and Lags to Incentives

Mancur Olson*

INTRODUCTION

As Don Patinkin (1982) has persuasively agrued, the most distinctive and fundamental innovation in Keynes's *General Theory* is the idea that the quantity of *real* output of the economy as a whole can change when aggregate demand changes, and in changing move the economy toward an aggregative equilibrium. The argument, explained in even the most elementary textbooks, that the economy as a whole will be in equilibrium when the intention to spend out of income is just equal to income, had not, Patinkin argues, been anticipated by any work published before the *General Theory*. Though some economists before Keynes's *General Theory* had analyzed fluctuations in aggregate demand, they had taken it for granted that these changes in aggregate spending mainly changed the price level rather than aggregate real output and did not argue that movements in the latter could establish a new equilibrium.

In the half-century since the *General Theory* was published, there has come to be a virtual consensus among both Keynesian and anti-Keynesian economists that the Keynesian result of widespread involuntary unemployment due to insufficient aggregate demand requires the assumption that at least some prices or wages are 'fixed' or at least 'sticky'. Though the very strong assumption of permanently fixed wages or prices that would be needed for a long-run equilibrium with continuing underutilization of resources is widely regarded as unrealistic, the assumption that there are some sticky or slow-to-change wages or prices that can generate involuntary unemployment and fluctuations in real output remains a staple feature of Keynesian analyses. The centrality and ubiquity of this assumption is best seen from the macroeconomic theory textbooks, almost all of which assume, in the chapters that explain depressions and unemployment, that prices remain stuck at disequilibrium levels even as the level of aggregate output changes. Even the most sophisticated work in the Keynesian tradition, such as the new 'disequilibrium macroeconomics' associated with early Barro-Grossman and with Edmond Malinvaud, assumes that some prices are stuck at disequilibrium levels, and then goes on to show (in analyses that are in all other respects meticulously grounded in microeconomic general equilibrium theory) how this can generate macroeconomic difficulties for the economy as a whole.

The notion that there is *some* stickness of at least some prices or wages that can cause temporary fluctuations in employment and real output is also part of monetarism, when monetarism is defined in a strict or narrow sense and thus distinguished from the 'new classical' or 'new equilibrium' macroeconomics built around the assumptions of rational expectations and continuous market-clearing. Some of the 'lags' in monetarism are sticky prices or wages under another name. Monetarists frequently emphasize that an unexpected increase in the quantity of money leads initially to an increase in aggregate real output and later, with variable and unpredictable lags, to an increase in prices. As Milton Friedman (1982 p. 64) puts it, 'faster monetary growth tends to be followed after some three to nine months by economic expansion, slower monetary growth by economic contraction . . . Because prices are sticky, monetary growth initially affects output and employment. But these effects wear off. After about two years, the main effect is on inflation'.[1] Though the foregoing quotation is from a column Friedman wrote for a lay audience, the same view is clearly embodied in several of his professional writings. Consider, for example, his classic 1968 article setting out the concept of the 'natural rate of unemployment'. There (Friedman 1968, pp. 9 and 10) he argues that, while no amount of money creation could permanently reduce the rate of unemployment below its natural rate, an initial increase in the price level or an acceleration of the rate of inflation would temporarily reduce unemployment, because 'prices and wages have been set for some time' on the basis of the previous policy and it 'takes time for people to adjust to a new state of demand'. At the same time, it must be said that Friedman and most other monetarists view a market economy as more resilient in responding to fluctuations in demand than most Keynesians do, and to this extent those lags attributable to price and wage stickiness are quantitatively less important in their thinking than in Keynesian macroeconomics.

Here, I will argue that the belief that sticky prices or wages are a fundamental part of the explanation of unemployment and idle capacity is in large part flatly false, and that even where this belief is not totally incorrect it misconceives the role and inspiration of price stickiness. When the incentives that give rise to involuntary unemployment and excess capacity are understood, it becomes clear that sticky prices or wages are not in any way necessary for involuntary unemployment and idle capacity. Neither is such stickiness sufficient, even in combination with severe monetary or other demand shocks, to explain involuntary unemployment and idle capacity. Most types of price and wage stickiness have little or nothing to do with unemployment or macroeconomic fluctuations; it is only a subset of a subset of the types of price and wage stickiness that are significantly related to unemployment, idle capacity, or recession. Even this subset of a subset of the set of sticky prices and wages has little or no significance for the average level of unemployment and idle capacity in a society, and is important only for the extent of the deviations of the actual level of utilization of resources from the mean level of resource utilization in the society. Finally, both the Keynesian and the monetarist theories are also unsatisfactory because price or wage stickiness appears in these theories as an ad hoc assumption or implicitly as a lag.

This paper will also argue that the stickiness of the very special subset of sticky prices and wages that is relevant for macroeconomics is a result of certain features of the socio-economic process. Accordingly, its origins should be traced to the incentives faced by the actors in the economy. If the relevant price or wage stickiness had been due to physical, biological, or random factors it could safely be regarded as exogenous. But it is, I shall argue here, due to economic and political considerations that influence and are influenced by the state of the macroeconomy, and therefore should be endogenous to our conceptions of macroeconomics.

PRICES

Prices stuck too low

If it is a coincidence that prices or wages are in some sense at the 'wrong' levels and will (let us say, because they are costly to change) achieve the 'right' level for macroeconomic performance only with a lag, then they should, on average, be 'too low' as often as they are 'too high', a variable that fluctuates randomly will tend to be below its mean level as often as it is above this level. Similarly, if the lags in prices and wage changes that are significant for macroeconomics are due to physical, technological, or biological causes, it would be reasonable, at least initially, to assume the symmetry that is usually found in nature. We know that our automobiles need bigger engines to give us quick acceleration to overcome inertia when we are going 'too slow' than would be needed to maintain a constant speed, but they also need brakes because it takes extra resistance to overcome momentum if we suddenly find we are going 'too fast'. Similarly, it would seem natural to suppose that prices could be stuck either 'too low' or 'too high', and that lags in adjustment to monetary or other aggregate demand shocks would tend to be symmetrical upward and downward.

But Keynesians and monetarists alike agree about one feature of the business cycle that, I shall argue, is inconsistent with such symmetry. There tend to be co-movements of prices and quantities, with increases in the price level and in real output going together. As one text tersely puts it, 'Prices are generally procylical' (Parkin 1984, p. 90). This is, of course, a feature of the business cycle that is also emphasized by the 'new classical' or new equilibrium macroeconomists, such as Robert Lucas (1977, pp. 7–29; 1981, p. 217), who do not, in general, use the concepts of sticky prices and wages, but assume continuous market-clearing instead.

To see the inadequacy of the assumption that the business cycle is due partly to prices that are temporarily stuck at inappropriate levels because of natural inertia or coincidence, consider a situation in which certain prices are initially 'too low', or become so because they were set in nominal terms and there is an unanticipated increase in demand. Let us consider this situation first in partial equilibrium terms, because that will offer an immediate intuitive insight into the matter, and later consider it in a general equilibrium context. Consider first a perfectly competitive industry in equilibrium, so that all

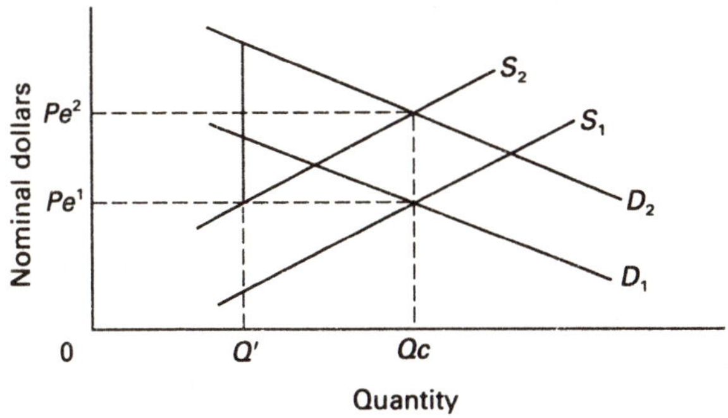

Figure 17.1

mutually advantageous transactions are consummated and there is full employment of the resources in the industry. Suppose further that this industry is so small in relation to the economy as a whole that the impact of this industry on the economy as a whole and on the price level can be ignored. Suppose now that there is then an increase in the money supply and the price level and that, in the economy as a whole, money is neutral. Then the nominal supply and demand curves will tend to change as in Figure 17.1. If prices in this industry were perfectly flexible and money is neutral, the new nominal price would be Pe^2 and the real or relative price of this product would be unchanged. Since we are considering lags in the form of price stickiness, let us assume that the price is stuck for a time at its old level Pe^1. Of course, as long as the price is stuck at the old level, the quantity that is supplied and traded is only OQ', and there are real losses of income in the triangle given by the new nominal demand and supply curves to the right of OQ', and employment in the industry will tend to diminish. Obviously, these losses taken by themselves would lead us to expect that unanticipated increases in the money supply and the price level would lead to a reduction in the gains from trade and to recession. But this is the opposite of the procyclical movement of prices that macroeconomists of all schools of thought observe.

The foregoing example may be troubling because it both involves the assumption of perfect competition and is partial equilibrium in character. So before turning to the general equilibrium context, let us consider an industry that is monopsonized, or which because of government intervention (say, in the form of price, wage, or rent controls) has a price that is too low to maximize the gains from trade

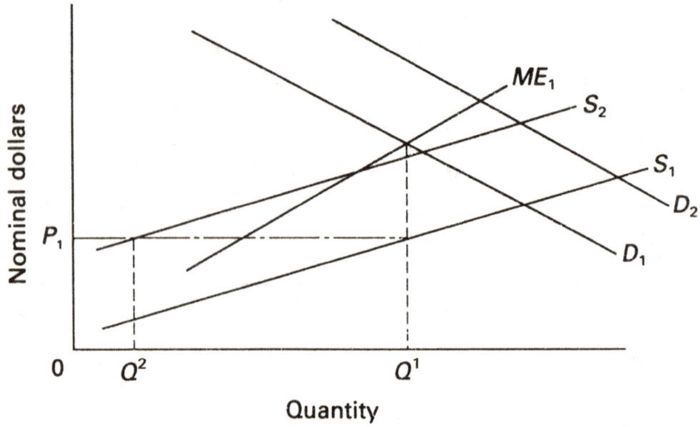

Figure 17.2

in the industry. Retaining the assumptions that this industry is too small significantly to influence the economy as a whole or the price level, and that there is an unanticipated increase in the money supply and price level with money being neutral in the economy as a whole, we get the situation in Figure 17.2. A sticky or lagged price will make the trade and employment in this industry go down (to OQ^2) as the price level goes up and we again get a contradiction with the consensus observation that prices are procyclical.

To be sure, when only one industry that is small in relation to the economy as a whole has a price that is stuck too low to maximize the trading and employment in the industry, the resources that would have been employed in this industry had there been Pareto-efficient prices at all times would seek employment in other industries. So there need be no involuntary unemployment because of sticky prices in a single industry. But what would happen if prices were for a time stuck too low in a large part of the economy?

There is no need to offer an original answer to this question, for it has been already answered in a most interesting and compelling fashion by the early Barro and Grossman, by Malinvaud, and by other contributors to the new disequilibrium economics. The answer, just as the intuition prompted by the previous examples suggests, is that when a great many prices and wages are stuck too low an increase in the price level will reduce real income and employment. When prices are stuck too low, an increase in demand, such as would result from an increase in the government deficit financed by the printing of new money, would *reduce* real income. There is even a 'supply multiplier' that is the obverse of the familiar Keynesian multiplier (Barro and Grossman 1976, especially pp. 78–87; Malinvaud 1977), and this supply multiplier can be used to show that a *reduction* in the government deficit and the money supply could lead to an *increase* in real income and employment by a *multiple* of the reduction in the deficit.

So prices and wages that are fixed too low, or which rise to the appropriate levels only with a lag, are clearly inconsistent with the virtually universal observation of procyclical movements of prices. The sticky price or wage or monetarist lag approach, when prices are for a time stuck too low, should lead us to expect the opposite of what is normally observed in the upturn of the business cycle. It should lead us to expect that unanticipated increases in aggregate demand due to increases in the money supply or to any other causes, and increases in the price level, would directly bring about recessions or depressions.

It may be objected that the believers in sticky prices and the equivalent monetarist lags always meant that prices or wages were stuck too high and simply took it for granted that they were not stuck too low. Perhaps, but if so, they should have explained this remarkable asymmetry. Prices could hardly always be stuck too high rather than too low because of coincidence or random factors. If inertia or some physical, technological, or biological factors are responsible, it should be surprising if they should always generate this remarkable asymmetry, which should surely then be explained. Similarly, if prices are costly to change, it must surely be costly either to increase or reduce them, so the assumption that prices are costly or slow to change, taken by itself, is also inconsistent with the procyclical movements of prices. If sticky prices of an unsymmetrical kind are responsible for macroeconomic problems, there is even less excuse than there would otherwise be for dealing with them merely through ad hoc assumptions or through mere references to lags.

Prices stuck too high

Let us now consider monopoly prices. For reasons that will soon be evident, we must deal separately later with monopolies that result from collective action of firms or workers, such as in a cartel, and first consider only the power that some individual firms have to vary price without losing all sales. For the present purposes, a firm may face a downward sloping demand curve either because one firm controls what might, loosely speaking, be termed an entire 'industry', or alternatively because there is Chamberlinian monopolistic competition in the large group. Monopoly power of either of these kinds will be described here as 'monolithic' monopoly to distinguish it from monopoly due to collective action to collude, or to lobby the government to establish arrangements that are functionally similar to cartels.

Since monopoly prices will (unless there is 'perfect' price discrimination) be too high for a Pareto-efficient allocation of resources, it is obvious that if monopolies set prices in nominal terms, and then face unexpected increases in demand and in the general price level, any lag or stickiness in their prices will tend to increase economic efficiency. If monopolistic firms should lag behind the rest of the economy in adjusting their prices to an increase in the general price level, their prices will not, when there is unexpected inflation, be so much above the marginal cost or competitive price as they normally are, and (if any possible 'second best' problems may be set aside) we may then be sure that economic efficiency will increase. Indeed, if the demand curves of firms with monopoly power unexpectedly shift to the right for any reason, and the monopoly firms are slow in adjusting their prices to these shifts, there will, in general, be a period during which the monopoly firms are nearer to marginal-cost pricing and economic efficiency will increase. Of course, an unexpected deflation or disinflation will have the converse effect on any monopolies that are relatively slow in adjusting their nominal prices, and monopoly power will then tend temporarily to increase when there is an unexpected drop in demand.

Accordingly, if only monopoly prices are sticky, or if they are stickier than other prices, this stickiness would be consistent with the observed procyclical pattern of price movements. Though I could dismiss sticky competitive or monopsonistic prices as inconsistent with the observed co-movements of prices and quantities, I cannot on this ground exclude the possibility that sticky monopolistic prices are significantly implicated in the macroeconomic problems. Thus we should explore the possibility that monolithic monopolies might be a source of involuntary unemployment, idle capacity, and recessions.

Disequilibrium prices

One difficulty with monolithic monopoly as an explanation of an economy-wide underutilization of resources is evident from the words that are used in everyday language to describe conditions in depressions and recessions. There are complaints especially at such times that firms 'cannot sell' their outputs or 'move' their inventories. There are, particularly during recessions and depressions, complaints about 'surpluses', 'gluts', 'buyers' markets', and, of course, 'involuntary unemployment', and not simply about 'low prices' and 'low wages'. This terminology and its widespread usage hint that disequilibria, or markets that do not clear, exist or are at least widely thought to exist. Recessions and depressions are, of course, not only or even mainly periods of deflation, but also periods of reduced output and employment, and this too is consistent with the language suggesting that some firms or individuals are unable to trade at going prices. These perceptions appear to be embodied in many monetarist writings as well as in Keynesian macroeconomics (though not, of course, in the new equilibrium macroeconomics); monetarist writers such as Friedman and Schwartz attribute the widespread unemployment during the great depression of the 1930s mainly to unexpected reductions in the money supply, and unemployment on such a scale as this would suggest that perhaps there are disequilibria. In Keynesian models of involuntary unemployment and depression there are certainly disequilibria. The standard textbook formulations of Keynesian theory for an economy with underutilized resources explicitly assume that firms and workers stand ready to supply additional output at the going prices. In Keynes's own theory it is the workers who stand ready, at any time there is involuntary unemployment, to supply additional labour at the existing wage.

What is needed, if the sticky prices approach is to be consistent with the procyclical movements of prices over the cycle and at the same time to rationalize Keynesian models and the foregoing observations, is prices that are not only monopoly prices, but also disequilibrium prices. Thus it is only the subset of sticky prices and wages that are monopoly prices that can be significantly implicated in the macroeconomic problem, and of this subset of prices only the further subset that are also disequilibrium prices or wages that are of concern.

Even brief reflection is sufficient to make clear that monolithic monopoly cannot explain the disequilibria that are required for a Keynesian model or rationalize the language and observations that have just been mentioned. A disequilibrium with gluts, surpluses, or involuntary unemployment entails that there should be mutually advantageous transactions that are not consummated. A monolithic monopolist will of course maximize profits when marginal cost equals marginal revenue and, when it has this level of output, it is in equilibrium and does not find any further trades advantageous. At the monopoly price that is in the interest of the firm with monopoly power the consumer is welcome to buy as much as the consumer wishes at that high price, so the consumer is not in disequilibrium either. The situation is not Pareto-efficient, but the market clears. If the monolithic monopolist is slow to adjust its price to changing demand it obviously foregoes profits it might otherwise have obtained. But these foregone profits give the monolithic monopolist an incentive to change its prices promptly: there is no reason to suppose that the prices of monolithic monopolists are slower to adjust to changing conditions than other prices. If the monolithic monopolist's 'menu' is so complicated that it is difficult for it to change its prices, it would have every reason to complain about the costs of changing prices rather than about 'gluts' or 'surpluses', but it is complaints about gluts and surpluses and the difficulty of selling output or moving inventories that are recounted rather than complaints about the costs of changing prices.

It is particularly difficult to see how monolithic monopoly could explain the involuntary unemployment of labour; the inefficiency arising from monolithic monopoly will tend to reduce welfare or real income in the economy as a whole and will tend somewhat to reduce the real wage of labour, but it is difficult to see how it could cause a disequilibrium in the labour market that could give rise in involuntary unemployment. Some individual workers could have a differentiated type of labour to sell and face a downward sloping demand curve for their labour and obtain a monopoly wage for this differentiated labour, but at this monopoly wage such a worker would not wish to sell any further hours of labour and would not be involuntarily unemployed.

The most fundamental difficulty with any approach to unemployment, recession, and depression that relies on the assumption of sticky prices and lags is that it does not begin with the incentives and constraints faced by the actors in the economy. We shall see that, if we reconceptualize the macroeconomic problem of underutilization of resources completely, and analyse the problem in terms of the motives of the actors in the economy, the macroeconomic problems arising from price and wage stickiness will also be explained. Thus we turn now to an entirely different, incentive-oriented approach to the underutilization of resources that, it is claimed, will also clear up the problem of price and wage stickness and the equivalent monetarist lags.

THE INCENTIVES

Keynesian and anti-Keynesian economists agree that Keynesian economics does not have an adequate microeconomic foundation. Interesting as it is in other ways, in this respect Keynesian (and disequilibrium) macroeconomics is as unsatisfying as a murder mystery in which the victim is killed for no reason at all. The main anti-Keynesian macroeconomic and monetary theories are not usually criticized as inconsistent with microeconomics, but I will argue here that these theories also ignore some microeconomic motives that are a source of some fundamental microeconomic problems. Even the 'new classical' or 'new equilibrium' macroeconomics associated with Lucas, Sargent, Wallace, and Barro's more recent writings suffers from the neglect of a ubiquitous incentive that has been widely understood in microeconomics since at least the time of Adam Smith. This neglected incentive does not have any significant relation to the new equilibrium macroeconomics seminal assumption of rational expectations, and the present paper will assume that all expectations are rational. But the neglected incentive at issue is, I shall argue, fatal to the other pillar of the new classical macroeconomics, the contention that all markets continuously clear.

Most of the narrowly monetarist (as opposed to new classical) writing leaves the impression that if only the quantity of money supply grew at a steady and predictable rate under a non-discretionary monetary rule, there would be no serious macroeconomic problems. This policy preoccupation with the money supply is not well explained in terms of incentives. Who in the government or the central bank has an incentive, when there is a discretionary monetary policy, to bring about a depression or recession? Experience suggests that incumbent politicians, at least, often lose their jobs in such situations. The appeal at this point to mistakes, ignorance, and repeatedly erroneous predictions is not only inconsistent with rational expectations, but also lacking in microeconomic foundations.

The inadequate explanation of adverse outcomes in Keynesian and even monetarist thinking is best illustrated by comparison with the theory of externalities, public goods, and (more generally) of collective action. Undesirable outcomes, such as excessive pollution or the non-provision of necessary public goods under laissez-faire, are properly explained in microeconomic theory in terms of the incentives individual decision-makers face. In a sufficiently large group, it will not be rational for an individual to curtail his pollution, or to make voluntary contributions to finance the cleaning up of the environment, however much he values a pollution-free environment. The individual in a sufficiently large group will get only a minuscule share of the benefits of whatever sacrifice he makes in the interest of a cleaner environment, but will bear the whole costs of that sacrifice, and accordingly has an incentive to cease making any contribution to the public good of a clean environment long before a Pareto-efficient level of environmental quality has been achieved.

The Keynesian and monetarist explanations of undesirable social outcomes such as depressions and involuntary unemployment do not explain how anyone gained from behaving in ways which caused depressions and involuntary unemployment in the way the theory of externalities, public goods, and collective action explains why an individual will often gain from ignoring the losses brought about by his pollution. This paper argues that any really satisfactory macroeconomic theory must explain who gains from behaving in ways that generate involuntary unemployment and underutilization of other resources, and then offers an approach to macroeconomics that explains such evils as the result of incentives confronting participants in economies with certain types of institutions.

Variations in the natural rate of unemployment

There are obviously different patterns of incentives across societies and historical periods. The economic institutions and policies, and therefore the pattern of incentives, that prevailed in Great Britain or the USA, for example, in the 1840s, are different in many obvious ways from those that prevail in these countries today. The character of economic institutions and economic policies in Germany just after national unification was completed in 1871, or in the early 1950s, are different in some conspicuous ways from those in Germany today. The pattern of economic institutions, policies, and incentives in Taiwan or Korea today is greatly different from those that exist in most of Western Europe or North America. There are even substantial differences in economic institutions across the different states of the USA (Olson 1983). The differences in economic institutions and policies, and thus of patterns of incentives, that have just been referred to are, as I claim to have shown elsewhere (Olson 1982), associated with significant differences in the success different economies have in taking advantage of the opportunities for economic growth, and also differences in social structure and political life. If, as this paper argues, macroeconomic performance is also explained in large part by the pattern of incentives, then it should not be surprising if macroeconomic problems and performance were also different in different countries, regions, and historical periods.

The approach to macroeconomics outlined in this paper entails that there should be such differences in macroeconomic problems and performance over time and space. It turns out that, if my theory is correct, the extent to which there are actors in the economic system with the capability and the incentive to generate idle capacity and a depressed economy can vary considerably across societies and historical periods. In particular, the number of actors who have the capability and incentive to generate *disequilibrium* situations where markets will not clear, such as involuntary unemployment, can vary considerably from one time and place to another. This implication of the theory offered here suggests tests that discriminate between the approach to macroeconomics that I propose and the established macroeconomic and monetary theories, for the established theories say little or nothing about how macroeconomic problems should differ across states, countries, or historical periods. In the *General Theory*, Keynes had no hesitation in applying his theory to the greatly different societies of Europe in mercantilistic times. Milton Friedman emphasizes that inflation is 'always and everywhere' a monetary phenomenon, and the whole tenor of his writings suggests that monetarism as a whole is applicable to every society that uses money.

The incentive to trade in any disequilibrium

It is instructive to begin the search for the incentive to generate macroeconomic problems with the new equilibrium economics and its conclusion that markets always clear. Though many economists find the notion that markets are always in equilibrium and that all unemployment is voluntary implausible if not bizarre, this idea does have one very powerful argument in its favour. This is the argument made earlier that, if a market is not in equilibrium, parties on both the selling and buying sides of the market must be able to make themselves better off by making transactions with one another. If the parties are aware of the gains they could achieve by making a transaction, they will be motivated by these gains to make a deal. If they should happen for a time to be unaware of these potential gains, then they know of no transactions that they would like to make that they have not made, and they are accordingly in equilibrium until they obtain information about the unexploited opportunities for mutual gain. This is a most fundamental and powerful argument and any adequate approach to macroeconomics must accommodate it. The Keynesian and disequilibrium theories, and some of the early monetarist writings, do not address this argument and are to that extent fundamentally unsatisfactory.

I have claimed to show elsewhere that this argument makes it possible to define 'involuntary unemployment' in a strict and precise way that is also broadly consistent with common language (Olson 1982, chapter 7). The essence of this definition is evident when we note that a worker could not be involuntarily unemployed if the worker placed a higher value on his or her time, when it is used for leisure or production at home, than that time would be worth to any employer. Such a worker would not agree to take a job at a wage any employer could advantageously pay. Similarly, if a worker will accept work only if he is given a wage in excess of his marginal revenue product to any employer, then the worker is asking for a gift rather than a job and is not involuntarily unemployed. There can be involuntary unemployment only if a worker without a job values his own time at less than that time would be worth to some employer – only in the area above the supply curve of labour, given by the marginal opportunity cost of labour, and below the demand curve for labour given by points on the marginal revenue product of labour curves for firms.[2]

Whenever there is really involuntary unemployment, then, *both* involuntarily unemployed workers and employers will gain from making a deal that puts the unemployed workers to work. It is possible, of course, that it could take some time for the workers and the employers to find each other, and that they would have to invest some time or other resources in search. But note that workers will have an incentive to devote full time to job search only if the discounted present value of the job they expect to find exceeds the opportunity cost of the time spent searching. In the absence of externalities or institutional arrangements that will be dealt with later, workers will tend to use their time searching only if this is also the use of their time that also maximizes social welfare. In these special conditions, investments in search are the most productive use of the worker's time, and thus should not be defined as involuntary unemployment any more than investments in education should.

Though it does not offer any careful definition of involuntary unemployment, or even concede the possibility of involuntary unemployment, the new equilibrium macroeconomics has been built in large part upon the idea that, if there were a disequilibrium in a market, that would imply unrealized gains from trade. This, in combination with the assumption that expectations and investments in information through search are rational, is taken to imply that there can be no markets that are out of equilibrium and no involuntary unemployment. Though I have not seen others put the matter in this way, I find it instructive to think of the new equilibrium macroeconomics as inspired by this question: 'How can there be involuntary unemployment or disequilibrium in any market when this implies that all the parties concerned have an incentive to make deals that would end the disequilibrium?'

Reversing the question

I propose that we should begin to reconstruct macroeconomics by reversing this question.[3] Macroeconomic theory should, I submit, begin with the question: 'Are there any actors who have the incentive and the capability to block mutually advantageous transactions among potential buyers and sellers, and thus to prevent markets from achieving equilibrium and eliminating involuntary unemployment?' At some times and places there have obviously been recessions, and sometimes even such deep depressions as the great depression in the US starting in 1929. At this time real income fell very substantially, and there was also virtually a consensus that involuntary unemployment was widespread. There was also, in the US at this time, obvious dissatisfaction with the incumbent political leadership or political and economic system. The widespread beliefs that involuntary unemployment occurs, at least at some times and places, along with the severity of some depressions and the frequency of recessions, suggests that it would be worthwhile to ask whether there are ever any actors with an incentive to block the mutually advantageous transactions that would eliminate any disequilibria and involuntary unemployment.

There is a growing literature in economics on 'the growth of government'. Much of this literature, and important political movements as well, claim that the growth of government is perhaps the most serious economic problem of our time. In view of this, it is natural to ask whether politicians and government officials have an incentive to block mutually advantageous transactions. Are incentives to generate unemployment, or poor economic performance generally, inherent in democratic electoral competition? Or in the incentives facing leaders of government in other types of political systems?

There are certainly circumstances in which governmental leaders could have an incentive to pursue inflationary policies. An incumbent politician might find the political costs of financing governmental spending through budget deficits and printing money lower, at least in a short run that might be decisive for the politician, than would explicit taxation. Thus a search for political incentives that would give rise to inflation might well be fruitful.

By contrast, electoral competition *by itself* does not give a politician an incentive to generate a recession or depression. If a politician were to block a mutually advantageous transaction between an involuntarily unemployed worker and a potential employer, he could well lose the votes of both. Even casual observation, moreover, reveals that incumbent political parties and presidents like to run for re-election on 'peace and prosperity' records. It is hard to imagine how, if other things were equal, an incumbent party's chances of re-election would not be helped by better economic performance. Even in dictatorial systems, the dictator has an incentive to make the economy of the country he controls work better, since this will generate more tax receipts he can use as he pleases and usually also reduce dissent.

If incumbent political parties do not have an inherent incentive to block the mutually advantageous transactions that would insure full employment and equilibrium in all markets, then who does? I argued earlier that, though sticky monopoly prices, unlike other sticky prices, were consistent with the procyclical movement of prices over the business cycle, monolithic monopoly was not consistent with the disequilibria that appear to exist in certain situations and that are certainly needed to rationalize a Keynesian underemployment equilibrium.

Collective action

Let us now examine monopoly power attained through collective action. It will simplify the exposition if we suppose that the collective action takes the form of collusion or cartelization, though the argument also applies to the results of lobbying for those types of government intervention that are functionally equivalent to collusion or cartelization. The conditions that make collective action possible in cases where there are 'selective incentives' or small numbers, but not

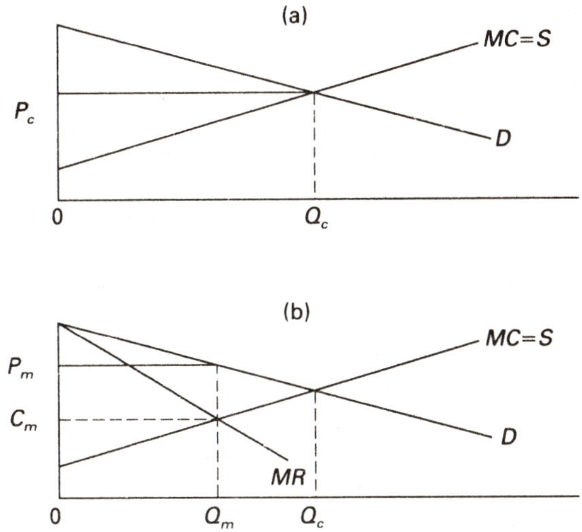

Figure 17.3

possible in other cases, will not be explained here because they are set out in *The Logic of Collective Action* (Olson 1965). The argument here builds upon the finding that collective action is possible for some groups and not for others. In the example that will be offered, it is assumed that the sellers in the market can organize for collective action but that the buyers cannot.

Though collective action is much more likely if there is a small or oligopolistic number of sellers, let us for ease of exposition suppose that we begin with a perfectly competitive market as shown in Figure 17.3a. The supply curve is as always derived from the marginal cost curves of the firms or (if a labour market is at issue) from the opportunity cost at the margin of the workers' time, and indicates, of course, the amount that the firms or workers wish to sell at each price. If the suppliers are able to obtain the monopoly price or wage that maximizes their joint gains, they will obviously sell the amount given by the intersection of the industry marginal revenue curve (shown in Figure 17.3b) with the marginal cost or supply curve, and charge price P_m.

Note that this supracompetitive price, unlike those that result from monolithic monopoly or monopolistic competition, does not clear the market: it leaves each member of the group that engaged in collective action in disequilibrium. Each separate seller would obtain P_m from selling another unit, and could provide this unit at a cost of only C_m.[4] The groups that engaged in collective action can protect the supra-competitive price and their above-normal returns only by preventing others from entering the market to undercut the price or replace them as sellers, so potential entrants are also put in a disequilibrium position. We now have found the incentive that brings about the absence of market clearing that is a universal and widely observed attribute of situations where there are involuntarily idle resources. It is the search for supra-competitive returns through collective action.

I believe that this simple and straightforward explanation of the disequilibrium character of depressions has heretofore been overlooked because the study of collective action has never been considered part of macroeconomics. (The foregoing argument requires that collective action be possible for some groups with common interests, but not for others. If all groups with common interests could organize for collective action, bilateral monopoly solutions and 'core' allocations with efficient levels of trade and employment could readily occur. But it has been demonstrated logically elsewhere that some groups should be able to organize collective action and that others should not, and a large empirical and experimental literature supports this theoretical presumption.)

The incentive to generate unemployment of resources

Note also how this argument relates to the new equilibrium economics and my reversal of the question it posed. The new equilibrium economics asked how involuntary unemployment or disequilibrium could possibly occur when this implied that both buyers and sellers could gain by engaging in transactions that ended the involuntary unemployment or disequilibrium. We observed that involuntary unemployment and disequilibrium appeared to be commonplace in some societies and historical periods, and accordingly asked who had an incentive to block the mutually advantageous transactions that would insure equilibrium and full employment.

The incentive that generates the macroeconomic problems of unutilized resources is also now clear. *It is the gains from non-competitive prices and wages obtained by collective action*: it is the gains in the rectangular areas such as $P_m - C_m$ times OQ_m in Figure 17.3b. All of those firms and workers that obtain a supracompetitive price or wage through collective action can obtain their gains if and only if they can block mutually advantageous transactions between buyers and those firms or workers that would profit from offering what they have to sell at prices below P_m. There is an exactly analogous gain in the less common cases where collective action obtains monopsony power, and this gain is also obtainable if and only if mutually advantageous transactions that would have increased output or employment are blocked. There is also an incentive to seek gains through individual or monolithic monopoly, and the achievement of such gains also violates the necessary conditions for Pareto-efficiency. But individual monopoly or monopsony does not generate involuntary unemployment or disequilibrium and thus has no salience for the macroeconomic problems that are under consideration here.

When, as here, we follow the traditional microeconomic approach of finding the incentives that give rise to a problem, we resolve the paradox of simultaneous inflation and unemployment, or stagflation. In a Keynesian model, unemployment is due to too little aggregate demand and inflation is due to too much aggregate demand. The widespread occurrence in recent times of simultaneous inflation and unemployment therefore contradicts a Keynesian model in the most fundamental way. But the incentive to seek noncompetitive prices and wages is obviously not eliminated by inflation, so simultaneous inflation and unemployment is in no way inconsistent with the argument offered here.

Unemployment and idle capacity without any lags or stickiness

It is now possible to deal with the claim, made earlier in this paper, that sticky prices or wages are not necessary for, and are sometimes not in any way implicated in, involuntary unemployment and disequilibrium. This is most obviously evident if we suppose that the collusion or cartel shown in Figure 17.3b sets quantity rather than price. It will still have to block mutually advantageous transactions that would bring equilibrium and full employment. The gains from collective action to obtain monopoly gains are still there even if there is no price or wage rigidity, and these gains can still be obtained only by blocking mutually advantageous transactions. If the cartel, collusion or lobby stipulated that it would sell quantity OQ_m and the demand curve shifted randomly up or down, there would be changing and perfectly flexible prices, but there could still be disequilibrium and involuntary unemployment. Thus sticky prices and wages are definitely not necessary for the macroeconomic problem of involuntary unemployment and underutilized capacity.

HOW OPTIMIZATION CAN GENERATE STICKINESS

It was argued at the outset of this paper that those sticky prices and wages that are significantly implicated in macroeconomic problems are not due to random, coincidental, or physical factors, but are the results of the socio-economic process and should accordingly be analyzed as endogenous parts of the macroeconomic problem. I claim to have shown elsewhere (Olson 1982) that organizations and collusions for collective action will make decisions more slowly than individual firms, workers, or consumers. If the collective action in question is oligopolistic collusion or lobbying by small groups of firms, the group may be able to act collectively by a consensual agreement. The firms in an oligopolistic collusion may be able to bargain until they get unanimous agreement about how much each firm restricts output. But each firm will have an incentive to hold out for a larger share of the sales at the collusive price, which price will tend to assure supra-normal profits. If, say, a small number of large firms in some industry are informally cooperating to lobby the government to get some special-interest legislation, they will again have to agree on exactly what to lobby for and how the costs of this lobbying are to be apportioned, and there will again be conflicts of interest. Thus in general all groups small enough to act collectively by voluntary agreement (the 'privileged' and 'intermediate' groups analyzed in *The Logic of Collective Action*) will need to bargain until consensus is achieved. This can take a considerable amount of time and delay decisions.

These problems of consensual bargaining can be avoided if by-laws providing for elections that allow decision-making without unanimous consent are adopted. Sufficiently large groups have no alternative to such constitutional procedures. But these by-laws will in turn introduce delays of their own. There may need to be a vote of the whole membership, or of the governing council or all of the local leaders, before a strike can be called or a new collective bargaining agreement made. Sufficiently important changes may require waiting for annual meetings or even drawn out political struggles, or possibly even changes of leadership. Thus decision-making according to by-laws is also normally slower than decision-making by unorganized individuals and firms.

The hardest problem for organization or collusion for collective action to deal with is the conflict of interest among members over the costs of the collective action. There are not only the direct costs of organizational dues, lobbying costs, and so on, but often also the burdens and rewards of the noncompetitive prices that collusion, cartelization, or lobbying seek to obtain. There is a serious conflict of interest over who has to restrict output how much and about who gets how much of the sales at the supracompetitive price. In a labour cartel there is normally a conflict of interest about who gets laid off if the supra-competitive wage leads to lay-offs. Though there are reasons that have been explained elsewhere (Olson 1982) why some organizations for collective action will set quantities rather than prices, the conflicts of interest that have just been mentioned will prompt most organizations to set prices rather than quantities. Though a monopoly price may, of course, be obtained by restricting quantities, this will normally require agreeing on a quota for each seller, and disputes over this threaten the cohesion of organizations for collective action. So in most cases a noncompetitive price will be set, and impersonal rules or impartial buyers will determine how the benefits of this noncompetitive price are shared. A seniority rule will normally determine who gets laid off if there is a cutback in demand, and the customers in industries with differentiated products may determine which firm sells how much at the cartel or collusive price.

In societies where there has been little or no inflation, organizations for collective action will have had no reason to set prices in indexed or real terms. Even in societies that have had significant amounts of inflation but no hyperinflation, it will often be in the interest of such organizations to set at least part of their price or wage in nominal terms. This is partly because indexed contracts can make the participants worse off than nominal contracts when there are real shocks (as Stanley Fischer and others have shown) and partly because of the tardiness and other imperfections of cost-of-living indexes. Thus, except in hyperinflationary societies, organizations for collective action will normally set prices, and set them partly or wholly in nominal terms.

Thus we now have the subset of the subset of the set of sticky prices that are significantly involved in the macroeconomic problem of underutilized resources. It is only the subset of sticky prices that are also monopoly prices that can be significant for macroeconomics, for only these are, as an earlier section of this paper showed, consistent with the observed pattern over the business cycle. Of these, only the further subset that are also disequilibrium prices are significant for involuntary unemployment and the underutilization of other resources, and these prices and wages in turn are only those that result from collective action. When, as is most often the case, the organizations set prices rather than quantities and set prices at least partly in nominal terms, we get the sticky prices or wages that are significant for macroeconomics.

The fact that most sticky prices are stuck too high rather than too low is not a coincidence, but a reflection of the far greater prevalence of collective action to achieve monopoly than monopsony. This greater prevalence of collective action to monopolize than to monopsonize is in turn explained by the wider availability of 'selective incentives' to sellers than to buyers and by the greater frequency of concentration and small numbers among sellers than buyers. Since these asymmetries have been analyzed elsewhere, they will not be discussed again here.

Yet price and wage stickiness or monetarist lags, it must be emphasized, are by no means necessary for the macroeconomic problem of underutilization of resources. The incentive to seek noncompetitive prices and wages is the real source of the problem, and it will lead to blocked transactions even when quantities rather than prices are set, and when there is monopsony no less than when there is monopoly. And when collective action does take the form of generating sticky prices and wages that give rise to the familiar business cycle pattern, this stickiness is essentially an incidental side effect of the incentive that gave rise to the problem. Theories of macroeconomics should accordingly begin with the motive or incentive that is the heart of the problem rather than with one of the side effects it has in certain commonplace cases.

THE GENERAL EQUILIBRIUM CONTEXT

When the foregoing argument is put in a general equilibrium framework, it becomes clear that the macroeconomic problems of involuntary unemployment and underutilized resources can vary greatly from one society and historical period to another. If only a tiny part of the society is subject to coalitions that engage in collective action, the resources that are blocked from making transactions in the few sectors under the control of coalitions can move to the larger unorganized sector and obtain returns that are only slightly lower than they would have earned had there been no distributional coalitions. But when, as is true now in some societies such as Great Britain and the older and long-stable north-eastern and older middle-western parts of the USA, the diversity of organizations and coalitions for collective action is so great that large proportions of the economy are covered by them, then such a large quantity of resources are blocked from making transactions in the organized sectors that they greatly depress rates of return in the unorganized sectors. This leads to what I have elsewhere called the 'selling apples on street corners syndrome'; that is, to serious involuntary underemployment and to extra unemployment in queuing and searching for positions in the organized sector. This searching and queuing is not a socially optimal investment in information, as job search is in an economy free of organizations from collective action would be, but a competition for monopoly rents and governmental subsidies.

In the interest of brevity, I shall not here set out the additional material needed to make the argument logically complete. I shall instead simply apologize to those readers who have not read my books on *The Rise and Decline of Nations* and *The Logic of Collective Action*, and are therefore confronted here with a paper that cannot be fully comprehensible to them.

When natural rates of unemployment are unnaturally high

It may already be intuitively evident, though, why the theory in question predicts that, in societies like the USA and Great Britain in the middle of the nineteenth century, or Germany at about the time of national unification, or in Taiwan and Korea since the 1960s, very little involuntary unemployment or idle capacity has been evident, even in periods of deflationary or disinflationary shocks. In countries like Britain and the USA today, by contrast, the density of organizations for collective action and the microeconomic policies they have lobbied from government is so great that there are serious problems of unemployment and underutilized capacity even when these economies are in aggregative equilibrium, and very serious problems when there are even modest disinflationary shocks.

One moral of the present argument, then, is that if the coalitional structure and microeconomic policies are bad enough, there is no macroeconomic or monetary policy than can put things right. Another moral is that macroeconomics, like microeconomics, must go beyond Keynesian and monetarist formulas and analyze the structure of the incentives. Macroeconomic evils, like other social and economic phenomena, would not persist unless they brought gains to some.

Notes

* I am thankful to the National Science Foundation, Resources for the Future, and the Thyssen Stiftung for support of my research.

1. I am thankful to Herb Stein for his help in finding this quotation.
2. When there is more than one variable factor of production or other complications, the demand for labour is not given by the marginal revenue product of labour curve, but it will always consist of points on marginal revenue product curves.
3. I am thankful to Jean-Christian Lambelet of the University of Lausanne for making it clear to me that my argument (in Chapter 7 of Olson 1982) really 'reverses the question' posed by the new equilibrium macroeconomists – see Lambelet (1983).
4. Some individual members of the coalition could be in equilibrium because their marginal costs rose so rapidly, and their 'share' of aggregate coalition output was so large that they would not wish to offer more, even at the supracompetitive price.

References

1. Patinkin, D. (1982) *Anticipations of the General Theory* (Chicago: University of Chicago Press).
2. Friedman, M. (1982) 'Defining Monetarism', *Newsweek*, 12 July 12.
3. Friedman, M. (1968) 'The role of monetary policy', *American Economic Review*, vol. 58.
4. Parkin, M. (1984) *Macroeconomics* (Englewood Cliffs, N.J.: Prentice Hall).
5. Lambelet, J. C. (1983) 'More on Mancur Olson's recent book: some comments on his theory of stagflation', ????
6. Lucas, R. E. (1981) 'Understanding business cycles', in R. E. Lucas, *Studies in Business Cycle Theory* (Cambridge: MIT Press). Also, in Karl Brunner and Allan Metzler (eds.), *Stabilization of the Domestic and International Economy* (Amsterdam: North-Holland).
7. Lucas, R. E. (1981) *Studies in Business Cycle Theory* (Cambridge: MIT Press).
8. Brunner, K. and Metzler, A. H. (eds.) (1977) *Stabilization of the Domestic and International Economy* (Amsterdam: North Holland).
9. Barro, R. and Grossman, H. (1976) *Money, Employment, and Inflation* (Cambridge and New York: Cambridge University Press).
10. Malinvaud, E. (1977) *The Theory of Unemployment Reconsidered* (Oxford: Basil Blackwell).
11. Olson, M. (1983) 'The South will fall again: The South as leader and laggard in Economic Growth', *Southern Economic Journal*, vol. 49.
12. Olson, M. (1982) *The Rise and Decline of Nations* (New Haven and London: Yale University Press).
13. Olson, M. (1965) *The Logic of Collective Action* (Cambridge, Mass.: The Harvard Economic Series, Harvard University Press).

18 The Fisher Effect and the Term Structure of Interest Rates

Vito Tanzi*

INTRODUCTION

While many studies have analysed the relationship between the nominal interest rate, R, and the expected rate of inflation, π, a truly satisfactory empirical test of the Fisher effect is still not available. As a consequence, it is still an open question whether that effect is an accurate description of reality. The reasons are several.

First, many of these studies have used actual rates of inflation to generate proxies for expected rates. Thus, regardless of the expectation hypothesis used to derive the expected rate of inflation, they have tested the Fisher hypothesis jointly with the hypothesis that expectations, however formed, are unbiased.

Second, the studies that have used survey data on inflationary expectations may have avoided the problem described above. However, they have not avoided a second and perhaps more serious problem, namely, the change over time of the real rate of interest.[1] Typically covered many years, it could not be assumed that the real rate would have remained constant. Changes in this rate may bias the coefficient of the variable representing inflationary expectations. For example, if, over the period considered in the analysis, the productivity of capital falls, economic activity becomes more depressed and the rate of inflation accelerates, the reduction in the real rate that is likely to accompany these changes will result in a coefficient of π significantly below one. This may be interpreted as a rejection of Fisher's hypothesis.

Several studies have tried to get around this problem by introducing some of the factors that influence the real rate into the estimated equations. But, so far, none has introduced all these factors. Therefore, it is difficult to interpret the estimated coefficient of the inflationary expectations variable or to reconcile the results obtained in different studies. For example, while two of these studies (Tanzi 1980; Wilcox 1983) found that introducing some of these factors in the regression equation raises the value of the coefficient of π to a level not significantly different from one, two other studies (Melvin 1982; Makin and Tanzi 1984) found coefficients on π as low as 0.55 and 0.70, respectively, or significantly lower than one.

Finally, and somewhat related to the previous point, even in the absence of supply and demand shocks and of real balance or portfolio effects, the relationship between R and π may be distorted by tax effects especially when there is no monetary or fiscal illusion.[2]

This paper proposes a simple and relatively clean empirical test of the Fisher effect that, it is hoped, avoids to a large extent the shortcomings mentioned above. Quite apart from its relevance to the Fisher effect, the paper can also be seen as a contribution to the literature on the term structure of interest rates. The next section is a theoretical discussion of the Fisher effect and of the difficulties encountered in testing it. The remaining sections deal, respectively, with providing outlines of a new test of that effect, presenting the empirical results, and drawing some conclusions.

A NOTE ON THE FISHER EFFECT

From Fisher's theory one can write the theoretical relationship between R and π in at least four different ways:

$$R_t = r + \pi_t \tag{1}$$

$$R_t = r + b\pi_t \tag{2}$$

$$R_t = r_t + \pi_t \tag{3}$$

or

$$R_t = r_t + b\pi_t \tag{4}$$

(1) is the most rigid version. It states that the nominal rate is equal to a constant, r, plus the expected rate of inflation. (2) gives the theoretical version behind the tests conducted in the early 1970s.[3] It assumes that the nominal rate is equal to a constant plus a factor equal to the expected rate of inflation times a coefficient b that may

no longer be one. In this version of the Fisher hypothesis the implication is that the 'real rate' is constant but that somehow, perhaps because of money illusion or some other factor, inflation may not have a one for one effect on interest rates. (3) implies still another hypothesis: namely that inflationary expectations are fully incorporated, one for one, in the nominal rates but that there are fundamental real changes going on in the economy that may bring about changes in r_t, the 'real rate'.[4] Thus in empirical tests one has to account for these changes. (4) theorizes that the 'real rate' may change independently of the rate of inflation while, at the same time, nominal rates may not incorporate fully (or may incorporate more than fully) the effect of inflation.

The difficult *empirical* problem in testing the Fisher hypothesis (apart from the measurement of π) has always been how to separate the effects on R associated with a Fisher effect that may not lead to a one for one adjustment of R for changes in π,[5] from the effects on R associated with changes in the value of r_t, which do not result directly from changes in the rate of inflation. When one correlates R against π in isolation, or when one leaves out factors that may influence r_t, this separation is not possible so that the results cannot be properly interpreted. In these cases biases created by omitted variables may lead to wrong conclusions.

Although this has not been recognized in the relevant literature, there are at least two ways to define the 'real rate'. One is simply $R - \pi_t$, that is the 'real rate' that individuals expect to receive over a given period, *given their inflationary expectations* and given all the other changes going on in the economy.[6] The other is the (counterfactual) rate of interest that, *ceteris paribus*, would exist *if there were no inflation*. Strictly speaking, this is r_t in (4). Given π, the first definition of the 'real rate' is observable while the second, which represents a counterfactual situation, is not. These two concepts may be widely different although this distinction does not seem to have been fully appreciated in the literature. In fact the literature on the Fisher effect has not been explicit as to which concept of the 'real rate' was being used in particular discussions.

As indicated in the previous paragraph, $R - \pi_t$ can change because of direct changes in r_t or because of values of b different from one. Thus while some changes in $R - \pi_t$ are associated with inflation, others are not. Is it possible to identify the factors that bring about these two different kinds of changes? Factors that tend to change $R - \pi_t$ by directly changing the value of r_t are the productivity of capital, the price of energy, the level of economic activity, and some others. Presumably these changes can occur and often occur independently of the rate of inflation. However, in a general equilibrium setting they may also be influenced by, or may in turn influence, the rate of inflation. These indirect relations are ignored in this article. Factors that tend to change $R - \pi_t$ by making b in (4) diverge from one are the tax effect, on the one hand, and fiscal illusion on the other. To become operational these effects *require the existence of inflation*. They operate in different direction with the tax effect tending to make b greater than one while the fiscal illusion effect tends to reduce the value of b.

Of the various factors that have been mentioned in the literature as affecting $R - \pi_t$, the one that creates the greatest analytical difficulty for our classification is the Mundell–Tobin effect. This factor becomes operational when there is inflation, but since it operates at least in part through changes in real variables (such as the saving rate), one could conclude that it also affects r_t. It is the only factor that would imply that $r_t = f(\pi)$. Many writers have maintained that it is the Mundell–Tobin effect that brings about a value of b smaller than one (see, *inter alia*, Melvin 1982). But it is not clear whether this interpretation is correct if the Mundell–Tobin effect operates through r_t.

Several recent studies have provided convincing evidence that the 'real rate' changes when factors such as the productivity of capital, the price of energy, the level of economic activity, and the tax legislation in effect, vary.[7] These factors change over time so that the 'real rate' cannot be assumed to be constant in studies that correlate R_t with π over many years or even decades. However, reducing the number of observations to the point where these factors could be assumed to remain unchanged would reduce the degrees of freedom to such an extent as to make regression analysis impossible; and introducing variables that take into account all these factors may not be feasible. Thus in most tests one faces the possibility that the results may be biased by omitted variables. It would be desirable if one could test the Fisher hypothesis by keeping the period of analysis relatively long and still somehow neutralize the changes in the 'real rate'. A simple way that we hope achieves this objective is described below.

DESCRIPTION OF THE NEW TEST

Assume that at a given moment t individuals can buy bonds of maturity l or s and that l exceeds s by a period equal to k. Let the (annualized) nominal rate of interest be R^l for bond of maturity l and R^s for bonds of maturity s. Let the rates of inflation, expected over the relevant periods, be respectively π^l and π^s. Then (4) can be rewritten specifically for the two periods as:

$$R_t^l = r_t^l + b\pi_t^l + \mu_t^l \tag{5}$$

and

$$R_t^s = r_t^s + b\pi_t^s + \mu_t^s \tag{6}$$

Here μ refers to the error term. If the individual buys the longer-maturity bond, he has only one decision to make over the l period. If he buys the shorter maturity bond, he will have to decide what to do with his financial capital, first for the s period and then for the k period. Whether at the beginning of the period he buys the long- or the short-maturity bond depends to a large extent on the conditions that he expects to prevail over the s and the k periods and on his liquidity needs.[8] If the market is efficient, it will adjust the rates of return on the two bonds so that there will be no scope at time t for systematic gains by shifting from one type of financial asset to the other. Individual lenders may, however, still feel that they can beat the market by shifting from one type of bond to the other. Also changing liquidity needs may induce some of these shifts.

(5) and (6) state that the interest rates that individuals expect to receive, over the two periods considered, depend on the inflationary expectations and on the expected 'real rates'. In a changing inflationary environment, as for example the one that prevailed from the 1960s to the early 1980s, the inflationary expectation for the longer period is likely to be different from that for the shorter period. In fact there is evidence from survey data that this is the case. Thus these differences should play some role in the determination of the term structure of interest rates.

But what about the expected 'real rate' r_t? Should r_t also play a role in the determination of the term structure of interest rates? The answer to this question depends to a considerable extent on how different the two maturities are. If one were considering a 6-month

Treasury bill and a 10-year Treasury bond, one would have to assume that the 'real rates' could be substantially different over those maturities. During a 10-year period the productivity of capital, the price of energy, the level of economic activity, the relevant tax laws, and all the other factors that may cause 'real rates' to change would probably change. Furthermore, individuals might have systematic expectations about these changes. But what if one is considering, say, 6-month and 12-month Treasury bills? Can one seriously argue that the expectations for the factors mentioned above would be different (and systematically different) for the period s as compared to the period l? It would seem reasonable, in such case, to assume that at time t the 'real rate' of interest expected over period l is not different from that expected over period s except for a possible preference based on maturity.[9] Thus the maintained hypothesis is that:

$$r_t^l - r_t^s = \alpha_0 + \mu_t^d \tag{7}$$

That is, 'real rates' can differ by an amount equal to a constant, α, plus a random error, μ_t^d. The average value of μ_t^d is expected to be zero. Thus, if Fisher was right, and the hypothesis implicit in (7) holds, the difference between π^l and π^s must tend to be fuly reflected in the difference between R^l and R^s and this would provide a test of the Fisher effect.

Define $R_t^l = R_t^s = \Delta R_t$ and $\pi_t^l - \pi_t^s = \Delta\pi_t$. Subtracting (6) from (5) and inserting (7) gives the basic equation to be estimated, namely:

$$\Delta R_t = r_t^l - r_t^s + b\Delta\pi_t + \Delta\mu_t \tag{8}$$

where $\Delta\mu_t = \mu_t^l - \mu_t^s$. Since $r_t^l - r_t^s = a_0 + \mu_t^d$, (8) becomes:

$$\Delta R_t = \alpha_0 + b\Delta\pi_t + \mu_t^f \tag{9}$$

where $\mu_t^f = \mu_t^d + \Delta\mu_t$.

In the empirical tests R^l and R^s will refer respectively to nominal interest rates on 12- and 6-month US Treasury bills, while π^l and π^s will refer to Livingston's biannual survey data on inflationary expectations for similar periods.[10] These expectations have been used often in the literature. It has also been argued that they are consistent with the rational expectations hypothesis (Mullineaux 1978; 1980).[11]

Before proceeding with the presentation of the empirical estimations there are three issues that need to be addressed.

First, as indicated above, (9) will provide a valid test of Fisher's hypothesis only if the assumption implied in (7) holds. In other words, there must not be any systematic difference between the 'real rate' for 6-month Treasury bills and that for 12-month Treasury bills. In view of the closeness of the two maturities considered, one could perhaps simply assume that this is so and leave it at that. However, it would be preferable to be able to provide at least some support for the assumption made. One supporting piece of evidence is provided by the correlation coefficient between the 6-month and the 12-month expected 'real rates'.[12] That coefficient is 0.99. Another piece of evidence is provided by the fact that the coefficients for the level of economic activity, perhaps the most important among the factors that, over the short run, may induce systematic changes in the expected 'real rates' for the two maturities considered, were found to be almost the same for 6 and 12 months in earlier work by the author.[13] However, as economic activity does change over the cycle, and cycles have been a common feature of the American economy, an attempt will be made below to take this factor into account.

The second issue relates to the effect that the existence of income taxes may have on the coefficients of the inflationary expectation variable. The author was among those who, more than a decade ago, theorized that when taxes are present, nominal rates should increase by more than the rate of inflation, *ceteris paribus* (see Tanzi 1976). This Darby–Feldstein–Tanzi hypothesis has been subjected to a few empirical tests with results that are somewhat ambiguous. Some authors have found 'some' tax effect but none seems to have found an effect as large as would be expected from the original hypothesis.[14] The reasons may be several and may range from the possibility of the existence of fiscal illusion, whereby individuals (just as the tax laws) do not distinguish, at least for some periods, between nominal and 'real' interest rates, to the explicit recognition that alternative uses of funds (i.e. other than buying taxable financial assets) may also be taxed on their nominal, rather than just real, gains so that lenders may not have the option of escaping the taxes by investing in other assets. In this case the effect of expected inflation on nominal interest rates is no longer equal to $\frac{\pi}{1 - T}$, as one would conclude from the Darby–Feldstein–Tanzi hypothesis, but equal to $\frac{\pi(1 - \theta)}{1 - T}$, where π is the expected inflation, T is the tax rate on interest income received from (taxable) financial instruments, and θ is the tax rate on other (alternative) investments. Obviously, the closer is θ to T, the lower is the tax effect and the closer to one would be the value of b in a test of the Fisher effect. In any case a value of θ greater than zero implies a reduction of the tax effect.[15] The tax effect may also be reduced by: (a) the possibility that *borrowers* may be taxed on inflationary gains, as when they use FIFO accounting or depreciate their assets on the basis of historical costs, so that their willingness to pay higher rates is reduced; or (b) by the existence of tax-exempt lenders and borrowers; or (c) by tax evasion; or finally (d) by capital inflows that may accompany higher interest rates induced by some tax effect.[16]

As a consequence of this tax-related discussion, we can conclude that nominal rates should respond *at least* one-for-one with anticipated inflation rates. A finding of b (in (9)) close to one may mean that there is no tax effect. However, it could also mean that a tax effect may have been masked by a measurement error-induced downward bias in b.

The third issue related to the 'liquidity premium' that one would expect to find when comparing two securities of different maturity. Although earlier thinking, mainly associated with the writings of Keynes and Hicks, had argued that longer-maturity securities should carry a higher rate of interest to compensate individuals for their loss of liquidity and, therefore, for the higher capital-value risk, several writers have recently raised doubts about the size and even the sign of this 'liquidity premium'. For example, Pesando (1975, p. 1317) has expressed a preference for the expression 'term premium' as 'there is no presumption that *ceteris paribus* term premiums should increase monotonically with the maturity of the debt instrument'. Woodward (1983, p. 348) has concluded that 'nothing of a high order of generality could be said about the sign of the liquidity premium'. The reason for this is that the income risk, which is greater for shorter-maturity securities than for longer-maturity securities, may be more important than the capital risk for individuals who wish to have a guaranteed income over a given period of time. Empirically, however, there has been some evidence that 'there is a liquidity premium, significantly greater than zero' (McCulloch 1975, p. 116).[17]

As a consequence of these various writings it can be concluded that it is not clear what to expect for the constant term α_0 in (7). As one is dealing with 6- and 12-month maturities for securities for which the default risk is zero, we should expect that the risk premia would be fairly similar. Thus, on balance we might expect either a zero or a (small) positive constant term.

Table 18.1 Regression results for equation (9)

Period	α_0	$\hat{b}$	$\bar{R}^2$	*D-W*	*SEE*
1956 II–1981 I	−0.0700	+0.8391	0.522	1.416	0.177
	(0.029)*	(0.121)**			
1966 II–1981 I	−0.0987	+0.8628	0.555	1.495	0.197
	(0.038)*	(0.142)**			
1969 II–1981 I	−0.0804	+0.9144	0.595	1.597	0.209
	(0.044)	(0.155)**			
1971 II–1981 I	−0.0718	+0.9359	0.605	1.642	0.227
	(0.052)	(0.170)**			

Notes:
1. Parentheses enclose standard errors.
2. * indicates significance at the 5 per cent level.
3. ** indicates significance at the 1 per cent level.

EMPIRICAL RESULTS

The empirical results for various periods for (9) are shown in Table 18.1. They indicate three things. First the term structure of interest rates, ΔR, and the term structure of inflationary expectations, $\Delta\pi$, are clearly correlated, with $\bar{R}^2$ generally close to 0.60. The Durbin–Watson statistic is low for some of the periods but generally at acceptable levels. Second, the coefficients of the inflationary expectations variable, b, are not significantly different from one. This is what one would expect from the traditional Fisher hypothesis. There is thus no obvious evidence of a tax effect. In fact, all the coefficients fall below one. Third, the constant term, α_0, is insignificantly different from zero in the regression covering more recent periods. However, though very small, it is significantly different from zero and negative for longer periods. This implies that, *ceteris paribus*, individuals prefer 12-month Treasury bills over 6-month ones.

As indicated earlier, of the many factors that may lead to a change in the 'real rate' of interest the one that plausibly could have a differential and important impact on the rates for two periods that are as close as 6 and 12 months is the level of economic activity. Economic activity follows a cyclical pattern and cycles have been far from rare in the periods covered. Furthermore, economic activity can easily change between the first and the second half of a year. Therefore, it would seem wise to take it into account in our estimations. I shall try to do it in two different ways. First, I shall add in (9) an independent variable that measures the level of economic activity. This variable will be described by the letter G_t and will be called the gap. It is defined as:

$$G_t = \left(\frac{\text{actual } GNP_t - \text{potential } GNP_t}{\text{potential } GNP_t}\right) 100$$

Thus, during periods of high economic activity G_t will tend to be positive. During recessions or periods of slow economic activity G_t will be negative. Over the whole period considered by our analysis, G_t varied from a positive value of more than 6 per cent for some semesters to a negative value of more than 8 per cent. This is the same variable used in Tanzi (1980). In that work, it proved to be very important in explaining significant changes in the 'real rate' of interest.[18] The equation to be estimated becomes:

$$\Delta R_t = \alpha_0 + b\Delta\pi_t + cG_t + \mu_t^f \tag{10}$$

In (10), G_t will measure the gap for a one-year period centred at time t. This implies that individuals have already observed the behaviour of the economy during the past two quarters and have some expectations of how the economy will perform during the next two. However, G_t is the actual gap rather than the expected gap. A more careful test would have to use *expected*, rather than actual, economic activity.

An alternative way of entering economic activity in our estimation involves the use of the difference between the gap over the maturity period of the 12-month securities and the gap over the maturity period of the 6-month securities. Here again, actual data will be used although it would have been preferable to use variables related to the expectations that individuals have at time t about those activities. In this case, the equation to be estimated becomes:

$$\Delta R_t = \alpha_0 + b\Delta\pi_t + c\Delta G_t + \mu_t^f \tag{11}$$

This equation says that if G is higher in the second half of the year than in the first, one would expect as a consequence that rates for maturities covering this second half would be higher, *ceteris paribus*, than rates for maturities covering only the first half. Thus, there would be a positive effect on ΔR.

Table 18.2 Regression results with economic activity for equation (10)

Period	α_0	*b*	*c*	$\bar{R}^2$	*D-W*	*SEE*
1959 II–1981 I	−0.118 (0.037)**	+0.8998 (0.121)**	+0.0206 (0.010)	0.555	1.64	0.172
1966 II–1981 I	−0.1391 (0.039)**	+0.9361 (0.151)**	+0.0188 (0.014)	0.566	1.67	0.195
1969 II–1981 I	−0.1229 (0.075)	+0.9552 (0.167)**	+0.0147 (0.021)	0.586	1.67	0.212
1971 II–1981 I	−0.1188 (0.088)	+0.9812 (0.185)**	+0.0159 (0.024)	0.593	1.72	0.230

Notes:
1. Parentheses enclose standard errors.
2. ** indicates significance at the 1 per cent level.

Tables 18.2 and 18.3 show, respectively, the results when (10) and (11) are estimated. Table 18.2 reconfirms the results obtained in Table 18.1: the adjusted R^2 are similar to those in Table 18.1. However, there is a considerable improvement in the Durbin–Watson statistic: now there are no borderline values. The coefficients of $\Delta\pi$ are highly significant (at the 1 per cent level) and not significantly different from one as expected from the Fisher effect. Furthermore, they have increased in value coming very close to one. This again confirms the importance of $\Delta\pi$ in determining the term structure of interest rates. There is again no obvious evidence of a tax effect in the sense that the coefficients of $\Delta\pi$ are not higher than one. The gap, however, is not significant for any of the periods. Finally, the constant term remains negative as in Table 18.1 and for the two longer periods it is significantly different from zero. This again would seem to indicate that, *ceteris paribus*, individuals have some preference for one-year securities as compared with 6-month ones.

The results in Table 18.3 are perhaps more interesting. From a statistical point of view those results are better than either those in Table 18.1 or in Table 18.2. The $\bar{R}^2$ are significantly higher, reaching almost 0.70 for the most recent period. Furthermore, the values of the Durbin–Watson statistic are even higher than in Table 18.2 and much higher than in Table 18.1. The coefficients of $\Delta\pi$ fall somewhat but they are not significantly different from one. This fall casts more doubts about the empirical relevance of the tax effect for the period under consideration. The variable for economic activity (ΔG in this case) proves to be significant, at least at the 5 per cent level, for all the periods considered. Thus a higher level of economic activity in

Table 18.3 Regression results with changes in economic activity for equation (11)

Period	α_0	*b*	*c*	$\bar{R}^2$	*D-W*	*SEE*
1959 II–1981 I	−0.0602 (0.027)*	+0.8013 (0.113)**	+0.1002 (0.035)**	0.593	1.725	0.164
1966 II–1981 I	−0.0755 (0.035)**	+0.8347 (0.129)**	+0.1145 (0.044)*	0.633	1.862	0.179
1969 II–1981 I	−0.0589 (0.040)	+0.8804 (0.141)**	+0.1192 (0.049)*	0.670	1.981	0.189
1971 II–1981 I	−0.0381 (0.047)	+0.9112 (0.150)**	+0.1351 (0.054)	0.695	2.203	0.199

Notes:
1. Parentheses enclose standard errors.
2. * indicates significance at the 5 per cent level.
3. ** indicates significance at the 1 per cent level.

the second half of a year as compared with the first half brings about a significant increase in the difference between the rate paid on 12-month securities and that paid on 6-month securities. Finally, the estimates of α_0 fall somewhat as compared with those in the other two tables but again, they are negative and at least for the longer periods they are statistically significant.

SUMMARY AND CONCLUSIONS

Whether or not nominal interest rates adjust fully for the effect of expected inflation is still a matter of controversy and an issue of considerable policy significance. On the basis of estimates of the coefficient of π significantly lower than one, some writers (for example, Summers 1982) have rejected the validity of the Fisher effect. The testing of that effect is, however, very difficult. If the 'real rate' were constant, as Fama had argued in 1975, then the testing would be simple and the coefficient of the expected inflation variable easy to interpret. However, several recent studies have found that the 'real rate' is not constant over the years. What is more disturbing is that these studies have pointed to a growing number of factors that may cause the 'real rate' to change. Thus, until we are sure that we have discovered all those factors *and* have taken account of all of them in traditional empirical estimations, we shall not be able to fully interpret the coefficient that we estimate for π. Until that time, the possibility that omitted variables may bias the results cannot be dismissed.

In this paper, I have suggested an alternative method of testing the validity of the Fisher effect that bypasses, to a large extent, the problems described above. The results obtained using this method indicate that inflationary expectations are in fact fully reflected in the nominal rate of interest. Thus, they provide an endorsement of the Fisher effect. They also indicate that the market is efficient in the sense that it brings about a term structure of interest rates consistent with the term structure of the expected rates of inflation.

Here, I have not provided empirical support for the Darby–Feldstein–Tanzi hypothesis. In spite of the attempt made at neutralizing the change in the 'real rate', the coefficients of the inflationary expectations variable, while not significantly different from one, were consistently below one. In no case was a coefficient larger than one found. The possible explanations for this result are several. First, as argued by the author in earlier work (Tanzi 1980), there is the possibility that for much of the period covered, individuals (just like legislators) may have suffered from fiscal illusions in the sense that they may not have distinguished between real and nominal interest income for tax purposes. Second, there is the possibility that the tax effect is not significant empirically for some of the reasons indicated earlier. It is possible that the magnitude of θ is so close to that of T that the tax effect largely washes out in the expression $\frac{(1-\theta)}{1-T}$. Furthermore, if θ is significant, so that the tax effect is small to start with, a Mundell–Tobin effect, perhaps aided by some fiscal illusion, could wipe out the tax effect. Finally, it is possible that the test proposed in this paper is not sensitive enough to detect a (potentially small) tax effect, or that, as indicated earlier, measurement errors in the Livingston data may have biased the coefficients.

The analysis in this paper has reaffirmed to some extent the importance of changes in economic activity for the determination of interest rates. There seems to be a relationship between changes in economic activity and changes in 'real rates'. If reconfirmed by other studies, this relationship would be important enough to deserve greater attention than it has so far received in macroeconomic work.

While I have focused on the Fisher effect here, the analysis has obvious implications for the literature on the term structure of interest rates. In particular, it has been shown that changes in inflationary expectations may be an important determinant of the term structure of interest rates. This is not really a new idea as one reads often in the financial press that higher inflationary expectations for the periods covered by bonds of long maturity, than for shorter periods, account for the higher interest rates on bonds than on the former. This paper has provided some empirical support for that view. It has also provided some (but by all means not definitive) support for the view that changing economic activity would also play a role in explaining the differences in interest rates for securities of different maturities.

Notes

* I wish to thank Mario Blejer, Arturo Brillembourg, Ke-young Chu, Jacob Frenkel, Leonardo Leiderman, and Andrew Feltenstein for valuable comments on earlier drafts, and Mrs. Chris Wu for statistical assistance.

1. For a discussion of what is meant by 'real rate', see below.
2. For the theory, see Darby (1975), Feldstein (1976), and Tanzi (1976), and for empirical tests, see Tanzi (1980), Peek (1982), Ayanian (1983), Mehra (1984). On the issue of fiscal illusion, see also Melvin (1982), Tanzi (1983), and Peek and Wilcox (1984).
3. See, for example, Gibson (1972) and Pyle (1972).
4. This is consistent with the conclusion reached in Tanzi (1980). In that paper changes in economic activity, which are not necessarily related to inflation, were the main determinant of changes in the 'real rate'. It was concluded that if the economy had been on a steady course, interest rates would have increased in line with inflation. See also the discussion in Tanzi (1982).
5. This happens when the value of b in (4) is different from one.
6. Of course, if inflationary expectation π is replaced by actual inflation, P_t, we would get still another, *ex post*, definition of the 'real rate'.
7. Several of these studies are listed in the references given below.
8. As several writers have pointed out it also depends on whether the individual is more concerned with capital-value risk or with income risk. See Woodward (1983), McCulloch (1975), and Pesando (1975).
9. But see below for some qualifications especially in relation to the role of economic activity that is known to change cyclically.
10. These are the data as revised by Carlson (1977). These data were kindly made available by the Federal Reserve Bank of Philadelphia.
11. This issue of rationality of inflationary expectations is, however, far from settled. See, on this aspect, Jones and Roleyh (1983) and Fishe (1984).
12. Notice that the concept of 'real rate' used here is the first of the two discussed above. In other words, $(R^{12} - \pi^{12})$ has been correlated with $(R^6 - \pi^6)$.
13. Those coefficients were 0.2057 for 6-month rates and 0.1969 for 12-months rates (see Tanzi 1980, Table 3, p. 18).

14. In any case for the reasons mentioned earlier it is very difficult to test for this tax effort.
15. There are several reasons to expect that $T > \theta$ so that some tax effect would remain. One important reason is the possibility of buying a home which allows the investor to largely escape income taxes on the (implicit) return from that investment. Another is the possibility of investing abroad. Still another is the purchase of durables, etc.
16. These points are discussed in Tanzi (1984).
17. For other contributions to the issue of whether securities of longer maturity carry a 'risk premium', see Kessel (1965), Meiselman (1962), Modigliani and Sutch (1967), Modigliani and Shiller (1973), and Malkiel (1966).
18. It was shown that for Treasury bills the 'real rate' rises by about 1 percentage point when G_t increases by 4. Thus a change in the gap from a positive value of 4 to a negative value of 8 could bring about a change in interest rates of about 3 percentage points. The variation in the level of economic activity in recent decades has been even greater than that.

References

1. Ayanian, R. (1983) 'Expectations, taxes, and interest: the search for the Darby Effect', *American Economic Review*, vol. 73.
2. Begg, D. K. H. (1982) *The Rational Expectations Revolution in Macro-economics: Theories and Evidence* (Baltimore: Johns Hopkins University Press).
3. Blinder, A. A. and Fisher, S. (1981) 'Inventories, rational expectations, and the business cycle', *Journal of Monetary Economics*, vol. 8.
4. Brenner, M. and Landskroner, Y. (1983) 'Inflation uncertainties and returns on bonds', *Economica*, vol. 50.
5. Carlson, J. A. (1977) 'A study of price forecasts', *Annals of Economic and Social Measurement*, vol. 1.
6. Darby, M. R. (1975) 'The financial and tax effects of monetary policy on interest rates', *Economic Inquiry*, vol. 13.
7. Fama, E. F. (1975) 'Short-term interest rates as predictors of inflation', *American Economic Review*, vol. 13.
8. Feldstein, M. (1976) 'Inflation, income taxes, and the rate of interest: a theoretical analysis', *American Economic Review*, vol. 66.
9. Fishe, R. P. H. (1984) 'On testing hypotheses using the Livingston price expectation data', *Journal of Money, Credit and Banking*, vol. 16, no. 4.
10. Garbade, K. and Wachtel, P. (1978) 'Time variation in the relationship between inflation and interest rates', *Journal of Monetary Economics*, vol. 4.
11. Gibson, W. E. (1972) 'Interest rates and inflationary expectations: new evidence', *American Economic Review*, vol. 62.
12. Hicks, J. R. (1946), *Value and Capital*, 2nd edition (Oxford: Clarendon Press).

13. Hudson, J. (1982), *Inflation: A Theoretical Survey and Synthesis* (London: George Allen and Unwin).
14. Jones, D. S. and Roleyh, V. V. (1983) 'Rational Expectations and the expectations model of the term structure', *Journal of Monetary Economics*, vol. 12.
15. Keynes, J. M. (1930), *Treatise on Money*, Vol. II (New York: Harcourt Brace).
16. Makin, J. and Tanzi, V. (1984) 'Level and volatility of interest rates in the United States: roles of expected inflation, real rates, and taxes', in Vito Tanzi (ed.), *Taxation, Inflation, and Interest Rates* (Washington: IMF).
17. McCulloch, J. H. (1975) 'An estimate of the Liquidity Premium', *Journal of Political Economy*, vol. 83.
18. Mehra, Y. (1984) 'The tax effect and the recent behavior of the after-tax 'real rate': is it too high?', *Economic Review*, vol. 70 (Federal Reserve Bank of Richmond, July/August).
19. Meiselman, D. (1962), *The Term Structure of Interest Rates* (Englewood Cliffs: Prentice-Hall).
20. Melvin, M. (1982) 'Expected inflation, taxation, and interest rates: the delusion of fiscal illusion', *American Economic Review*, vol. 72.
21. Modigliani, F. and Sutch, R. (1978) 'Debt management and the term structure of interest rates', *Journal of Political Economy*, vol. 86.
22. Modigliani, F. and Sutch, R. (1980) 'Inflation expectations and money growth in the United States', *American Economic Review*, vol. 70.
23. Mundell, R. A. (1963) 'Inflation and real interest', *Journal of Political Economy*, vol. 71.
24. Nelson, C. R. and Schwert G. W. (1977) 'On testing the hypothesis that the "real rate" of interest is constant', *American Economic Review*, vol. 67.
25. Peek, J. (1982) 'Interest rates, income taxes, and anticipated inflation', *American Economic Review*, vol. 72.
26. Peek, J. and Wilcox, J. A. (1984) 'The degree of fiscal illusion in interest rates: some direct estimates', *American Economic Review*, vol. 74.
27. Pesando, J. (1975) 'Determinants of Term Premiums in the market for United States Treasury bills', *The Journal of Finance*, vol. 30, no. 5.
28. Pyle, D. H. (1972) 'Observed price expectations and interest rates', *Review of Economics and Statistics*, vol. 54.
29. Summers, L. H. (1982) 'The non-adjustment of nominal interest rates: a study of the Fisher Effect', *Working Paper*, No. 836 (Cambridge, Mass.: NBER).
30. Tanzi, V. (1976) 'Inflation, indexation and interest income taxation', *Banca Nazionale del Lavoro Quarterly Review*, vol. 29.
31. Tanzi, V. (1980) 'Inflationary expectations, economic activity, taxes, and interest rates', *American Economic Review*, vol. 70.
32. Tanzi, V. (1982) 'Inflationary expectations, taxes, and the demand for money in the United States', *IMF Staff Papers*, vol. 29.
33. Tanzi, V. (1983) 'Expected inflation and interest rates: comment', *American Economic Review*, vol. 73.

34. Tanzi, V. (ed.) (1984), *Taxation, Inflation, and Interest Rates* (Washington, DC: International Monetary Fund).
35. Tobin, J. (1965) 'Money and economic growth', *Econometrica*, vol. 33.
36. Wilcox, J. A. (1983) 'Why real interest rates were so low in the 1970's', *American Economic Review*, vol. 73.
37. Woodward, S. (1983) 'The Liquidity Premium and the Solidity Premium', *American Economic Review*, vol. 73.

19 Investment Demand: A Survey

Akira Takayama*

INTRODUCTION

Keynes's *General Theory* (1936) has inspired many interesting studies in a number of areas, one of which is investment. Like many new frontiers of research inspired by this work, investment has been attracting a great deal of both attention and confusion. An example of this confusion is the relation between the neoclassical marginal productivity (NMP) theory and Keynes's marginal efficiency of capital (MEK). Throughout the 1960s, Jorgenson's theory of investment, which attracted considerable attention, claimed that the MEK was inconsistent with neoclassical theory, but since then this claim has been seriously attacked on the grounds that it ignored the adjustment costs associated with new investment. This criticism in turn gave rise to the adjustment cost approach to investment. Since the late 1970s, Tobins' q theory has also been attracting much attention. Despite initial criticisms, the q theory has been shown to be compatible with the intertemporal choice behaviour of the firm, and that it can be obtained from the adjustment cost approach.

This paper surveys these developments. However, unlike some other surveys, I am *not* interested in detailed accounts of the important contributions. Rather, I am more concerned with tracing the general trend of thought in these developments. Also, throughout the paper, I rule out the problems associated with uncertainlty and 'animal spirit'.

A brief summary is now in order. In the next section, I show that Keynes's MEK rule is equivalent to the NMP rule, *provided* the 'supply price of capital' (p_K) is equal to the price of new investment goods (p_I). In the following section, I explain Jorgenson's theory, clarify two of its weaknesses, discuss briefly the relationship between his theory and Keynes's, and expound the gist of the adjustment cost approach. In the final section, I discuss the q theory of investment, and argue that, despite its important merits, it cannot serve as a theory of investment.

THE MEK AND THE MARGINAL PRODUCTIVITY RULE

At the outset of his discussion on investment in his *General Theory*, Keynes writes:

> When a man buys an investment or capital-asset, he purchases the right to the series of prospective returns, which he expects to obtain from selling its output, after deducting the running expenses of obtaining that output, during the life of the asset. This series of annuities $Q_1, Q_2 \ldots Q_n$ it is convenient to call the *prospective yield of the investment* . . . More precisely, I define the marginal efficiency of capital as being equal to that rate of discount which would make the present value of the series of annuities given by the returns expected from the capital-asset during its life just equal to its supply price. (p. 135)

By the *supply price* of the capital-asset, he means 'the price which would just induce a manufacturer mainly to produce an additional unit of such assets, i.e. what is sometimes called its *replacement cost*', and 'it is not the market-price at which an asset of the type in question can actually be purchased in the market' (p. 135).

Let p_K be the current supply price of capital (K), and assume that K has a finite fixed life of T periods.[1] Let s be an expected scrap value of a unit of K at the end of the Tth period. Then MEK (denoted by ρ) can be defined by:

$$p_K \equiv \sum_{t=1}^{T} \frac{Q_t}{(1+\rho)^T} + \frac{s}{(1+\rho)^T} \tag{1}$$

Given $Q_1, Q_2, \ldots, Q_T$, s, and p_K, (1) is assumed to determine the value of ρ uniquely.[2]

However, consider an income stream, which consists of the annuities of income $Q_1, \ldots, Q_T$ dollars for T periods and s dollars at the end of the Tth period. The present value (PV) of such an income stream is equal to:

$$PV \equiv \sum_{t=1}^{T} \frac{Q_t}{(1+i)^t} + \frac{s}{(1+i)^T} \tag{2}$$

where i is the current rate of interest. Viewing ρ defined in (1) as the rate of return, one can see that the rate of investment will, via arbitrage, be pushed to the point at which the marginal efficiency of capital is equal to the market rate of interest (*General Theory*, p. 137). Namely, the desired stock of capital is determined by $\rho = i$. Putting this differently, the desired K is, via arbitrage, determined by:[3]

$$p_K = \sum_{t=1}^{T} \frac{Q_t}{(1+i)^T} + \frac{s}{(1+i)^T} \tag{3}$$

In his discussion, Keynes emphasizes the role of expectations in determining $Q_1, Q_2, \ldots, Q_T$, and the distinction between p_K and the (current) market price of capital (denoted by p_I). Clearly these factors are important in his theory, but it has led to a considerable confusion in the literature. Let me explain the above theory by stripping these factors, and showing the relation between the MEK theory and the neoclassical rule of equating the marginal product of capital to its rental rate. Needless to say, one obtains neither the Keynes theory *per se*, nor investment theory via an 'animal spirit', but the discussion should help us in understanding his theory as well as clarify some confusion in the literature.

Let Y_t and p_t, respectively, denote the output of the firm and the price of output in period t. Letting N_t be the labour employment in t, one can write the production function for the firm as:

$$Y_t = F(N_t, K)$$

where the decision with regard to capital investment (i.e. the size of K) is made at the beginning of the current period. Let w_t be the wage rate in period t. Assume a competitive market so that the firm cannot affect the p_t, p_I, w_t, and s which would prevail in the market. Further assume static expectations, i.e.

$$p_1 = p_2 = \ldots = p_T \equiv p \quad \text{and} \quad w_1 = w_2 = \ldots = w_T \equiv w$$

The firm chooses N_t, $t = 1, 2, \ldots, T$ and K so as to maximize its profit

$$\sum_{t=1}^{T} \frac{pY_t - wN_t}{(1+i)^t} + \frac{sK}{(1+i)^T} \tag{4}$$

subject to $Y_t = F(N_t, K)$, $N_t \geq 0$, $t = 1, 2, \ldots, T$, and $K \geq 0$.

Assuming an interior solution, the first-order conditions of this problem can be written as:

$$pF_{N_t} = w, \quad t = 1, 2, \ldots, T \tag{5}$$

$$p_I = \sum_{t=1}^{T} \frac{pF_k}{(1 + i)^t} + \frac{s}{(1 + i)^T} \tag{6}$$

where $F_{N_t} \equiv \partial F/\partial N_t$ and $F_K \equiv \partial F/\partial K$. Letting $Q = pF_K$, (4) can be rewritten as:

$$p_I = \sum_{t=1}^{T} \frac{Q}{(1 + i)^t} + \frac{s}{(1 + i)^T} \tag{7}$$

(5) states that the amount of labour is determined by the usual marginal productivity rule (note N_t is constant for all t as long as ρ and w are constant), whereas (7) corresponds to the Keynesian MEK rule, i.e. (3), with our current assumption of $p_I = p_K$. Also, from (7), it is clear that the income stream Q is a 'marginal concept' (i.e. the addition of revenue per one unit increase in capital stock). Moreover, it is clear that Q does not incorporate interest cost.

Suppose instead that capital is *rented* with rent r per period. The firm chooses N_t, $t = 1, 2, \ldots, T$ and K such as to maximize its profit:

$$\sum_{t=1}^{T} \frac{pY_t - wN_t - rK}{(1 + i)^t}$$

subject to $Y_t \leq F(N_t, K)$, $N_t \geq 0$, $t = 1, 2, \ldots, T$, and $K \geq 0$. The first-order conditions are written again under the assumption of an interior solution as follows:

$$pF_{N_t} = w, \quad t = 1, 2, \ldots, T \tag{8}$$

$$pF_K = r \tag{9}$$

(8) and (9) are the usual NMP rules.

One now invokes the intertemporal arbitrage condition, which enforces:

$$p_I = \sum_{t=1}^{T} \frac{r}{(1 + i)^t} + \frac{s}{(1 + i)^T} \tag{10}$$

Combining (8) and (9), one again obtains (7), the (neoclassical version of) the Keynesian MEK rule. Note that $Q = r$; hence, given the above assumptions, the Keynesian MEK rule is nothing other than the neoclassical marginal productivity principle. Setting aside the question of uncertainty, the crucial difference between the Keynesian theory of investment and the neoclassical theory is the distinction between p_K and p_I, where Keynes (see the above quote) explicitly emphasizes the distinction between p_K and p_I.

Also note that the above neoclassical version of the MEK rule as represented by (5) and (6) or (5) and (7) does *not* determine the desired rate of investment, i.e $I(i)$, rather the desired *stock* of capital, say $K(i)$, in addition to the labour demand for each period (N_t).[4]

That the investment function cannot be determined by the above rule may be discomforting. However, this is precisely what neoclassical theory admits. For example, following Lerner (1944), Haavelmo writes: 'What we should reject is the naive reasoning that there is a 'demand schedule' for investment which would be derived from a classical scheme of producer's behaviour in maximizing profit' (1961, p. 216).

JORGENSON'S DISCUSSION OF INVESTMENT

Jorgenson was apparently disappointed with Haavelmo's conclusion, and also felt that the Keynesian theory of investment demand lacked a neoclassical foundation. Thus, he argued that 'it is possible to derive a demand function for investment based on purely neoclassical considerations' (1967, p. 133). He then published a series of articles and books on the investment function. His method involves the technique of calculus of variations which incorporates the intertemporal nature of investment decisions, substantiated by a number of empirical studies by himself and his associates.[5]

Let me begin by discussing Jorgenson's version of the 'neoclassical theory of investment'. Assume that depreciation follows the following rule.[6]

$$\dot{K}_t = I_t - \delta K_t \tag{11}$$

where δ is the rate of depreciation ($0 < \delta < 1$). Also assume a constant rate of discount, i, and define the present value of the sum of cash flows, R_t, for all the future time, W, by:[7]

$$W = \int_0^{\infty} e^{-it} R_t dt$$

where $R_t \equiv p_t Y_t - w_t N_t - p_{I_t} I_t$, p_t is the price of Y, w_t is the wage rate and p_{I_t} is the current market price of capital goods. The production function constraint is:

$$F(N_t, K_t) - Y_t = 0 \tag{12}$$

The firm chooses the time stream of N_t and I_t so as to maximize W, subject to (11) and (12), $N_t \geq 0$ for all t. Assume that the firm is competitive, i.e. it is a price taker, and, for simplicity, assume that all these prices are constant, i.e. $p_t = p$, $w_t = w$, and $p_{I_t} = p_I$, for all t.

The current value Hamiltonian of the above problem is written as:

$$H \equiv [pF(N_t, K_t) - wN_t - p_I I_t] + \lambda_t(I_t - \delta K_t) \tag{13}$$

Then the following conditions are necessary for optimum.[8]

$$\dot{K}_t = \partial H/\partial \lambda_t, \quad \text{i.e.} \quad \dot{K}_t = \mathrm{I}_t - \delta K_t \tag{14a}$$

$$\dot{\lambda}_t = i\lambda_t - \partial H/\partial K_t, \quad \text{i.e.} \quad \dot{\lambda}_t = (i + \delta)\lambda - pF_K \tag{14b}$$

$$(\text{where } F_K \equiv \partial F/\partial K_t)$$

$$\lim_{t \to \infty} \lambda_t e^{-it} K_t = 0 \tag{14c}$$

and that H is to be maximized with respect to N_t and I_t. The maximization of H with respect to N_t yields the familiar rule:

$$F_N = w/p \ (\text{where } F_N \equiv \partial F/\partial N_t) \tag{14d}$$

assuming an interior solution (i.e. $N_t > 0$ at the optimum).

Since the H defined in (13) can be rewritten as:

$$H = pF(N_t, K_t) - wN_t - \delta\lambda_t K_t + (\lambda_t - p_I)I_t \tag{13'}$$

the maximization of H with respect to I_t yields:

$$I_t \to \infty, \text{ if } \lambda_t > p_I; \ I_t - \infty, \text{ if } \lambda_t < p_I \tag{15}$$

and the value of I_t is indeterminate when $\lambda_t = p_I$. The rule indicated by (15) confirms the Lerner–Haavelmo contention that capital is adjusted to the desired level instantaneously and that there is no such thing as a 'demand schedule' for investment. Also (15) presupposes that investment, or the rate of adjustment of K, is unbounded. This has been criticized by the adjustment cost school. Its weakness is summarized by Tobin:

> Jorgenson's investment demand schedule cannot serve the analytical purposes for which such a schedule is desired, and one must look elsewhere for a determinant theory of investment. At the level of a single firm, this may be derived from frictional or adjustment costs. (1967, p. 158)

Jorgenson's analytical difficulty is simple. Instead of (15), he obtains:

$$\partial H/\partial I_t = 0, \text{ or } p_I = \lambda_t$$

This is not correct given the specification of H as expressed in (13′), in which the Hamiltonian H is linear with respect to I_t, a control variable.

The apparent difficulty of unbounded I_t in (15) can be avoided by imposing an additional constraint, $I_{min} < I_t < I_{max}$, in the original maximization problem. Assuming non-constant returns to scale technology, one can at once see from (13′) that $I_t = I_{max}$ if $\lambda_t > p_I$ and $I_t = I_{min}$ if $\lambda_t < p_I$. In this case, it can be shown that K_t approaches the long-run desired K, K^*, defined by:[9]

$$F_N(N^*, K^*) = w/p \tag{16a}$$

$$F_K(N^*, K^*) = (i + \delta)p_I/p \tag{16b}$$

Here $(i + \delta)p_I$ signifies the rent for capital; hence (16a) and (16b) are nothing but the familiar marginal productivity rules. To see that $(i + \delta)p_I$ is the rent for capital, suppose that one unit of the capital good is rented with rent c. The physical quantity of one unit of a capital good at time t will decay to $e^{-\delta t}$. Therefore, if the capital good is rented for an infinite future, the present value of rent over all future time will be:

$$\int_0^\infty ce^{-it}e^{-\delta t}dt = \int_0^\infty ce^{-(i+\delta)t}dt = \frac{c}{(i + \delta)} \tag{17}$$

Intertemporal arbitrage relation will equate this with the price of a unit of capital:[10]

$$p_I = \frac{c}{(i + \delta)}, \quad \text{or} \quad c = (i + \delta)p_I \tag{18}$$

Suppose that inflation takes place in the future. To ease the exposition, suppose that the rate of inflation (π) is constant (in which case the nominal rental payment is $ce^{\pi t}$). Modifying (17) accordingly, one can revise (18) as:

$$c = [(i - \pi) + \delta]p_I \tag{18'}$$

where $(i - \pi)$ is the real rate of interest.

The c discussed above plays a key role in the literature on investment; Jorgenson calls it the *user cost* of capital.[11] It signifies 'the cost that a firm has to bear to obtain one unit of service from the capital good'. With the possibility of capital rental, it is the rent of capital (c), which in turn equals $(i - \delta)p_I$ as shown in (18). When the firm wishes to purchase the capital good and install it instead of renting it, the above definition of user cost still applies in the long-run state as (16b) indicates. Note that in these cases, the cost of installation as well as other costs involved in renting or purchasing the capital good are assumed away. Note also that in obtaining (16b) and (18), the price variables such as p, p_I, and i are assumed to be constant. In the real world, these prices change from time to time. This in turn makes the emphasis on user cost in the sense of $(i - \delta)p_I$ dubious for empirical studies.

Suppose that the firm is in the long-run steady state (N^*, K^*) *à la* (16). Then, by (17) and (18), one immediately realizes that (16b) can be rewritten as:

$$p_I = \int_0^\infty pF_K^* e^{-(i + \delta)t}\, dt \tag{19}$$

where $F_K^* = \partial F/\partial K_t$ evaluated at (N^*, K^*). Ignoring the distinction between p_K and p_I, this corresponds to the Keynesian MEK rule which states that the demand for the K is determined by the equality between the unit price of capital and the present value of all future income from an additional unit of capital. It is a continuous time version of (7). Since (16b) and (19) are equivalent, the Keynesian MEK rule coincides with the NMP rule, if the firm is on path (N^*, K^*), and if $p_I = p_K$. Since a similar observation has already been made with reference to the discrete time model with depreciation by 'sudden death', I therefore disagree with Jorgenson's conclusion that: 'Keynes' construction of the demand function for investment must be dismissed as inconsistent with the neoclassical theory of optimal capital accumulation' (1967, p. 152). Keynes does not explicitly impose some of the above assumptions; thus he obtained a rule which is much less explicit than (19), i.e.:

$$p_K = \int_0^\infty Q_t e^{-(i + \delta)t} \, dt$$

where, as we have assumed, p_K and p_I are different, and Q_t is the '*expected* rate of return' on capital at t: Q_t is the expected revenue minus the expected operating cost (not including the depreciation cost) per additional unit of capital.

It is important to observe that the values of N^* and K^* are equal to the ones determined by maximizing the 'short-run' (or instantaneous) profit:

$$pF(N, K) - wN - cK$$

In other words, the 'long-run' solution (N^*, K^*) for the dynamic optimization problem is reduced to the one for the static optimization problem. In this case, the myopic rule is optimal after all from the long-run view point.

THE ADJUSTMENT COST APPROACH

In the above analysis, it is assumed that the firm can obtain any amount of investment I_t without affecting its price p_{I_t}. This is criticized on the grounds of capital 'fixity'. What then is capital fixity? Following many studies, I interpret it to mean that the costs per unit of gross investment *rise* with the investment rate. This cost behaviour can be rationalized, for example, by introducing the internal costs of investment which are the sum of the purchase (with either perfect or imperfect factor markets) and installation costs. Eisner-Strotz (1963), Lucas (1967a), and Gould (1967) suggested the following form to replace $p_I I_t$:[12]

$$C_t = C(I_t)$$

where $C(I_t) > 0$, $C'(I_t) > 0$, $C''(I_t) > 0$, for $I_t > 0$, and $C(0) = 0$.[13]

$C''(I_t) > 0$ means that adjustment costs will, on the average, be greater the greater the rate of investment.

The firm is now to choose N_t and I_t so as to maximize:

$$\int_0^\infty e^{-it}[pF(N_t, K_t) - wN_t - C(I_t)]dt \tag{20}$$

subject to (11), $N_t \geq 0$, and a given K_0. The current value Hamiltonian of this problem is written as:

$$H \equiv [pF(N_t, K_t) - wN_t - C(I_t)] = \lambda_t(I_t - \delta K_t)$$

where N_t and I_t are the control variables and K_t is the state variable. The rest is routine analysis in optimal control theory. The set of necessary conditions is given by:[14]

$$\dot{K}_t = I_t - \delta K_t, \quad \dot{\lambda}_t = (i + \delta)\lambda_t - pF_K \tag{21a}$$

$$\lim_{t \to \infty} \lambda_t K_t e^{-it} = 0 \tag{21b}$$

$$F_N = w/p, \quad C'(I_t) = \lambda_t \tag{21c}$$

Note that the introduction of C enables one to avoid the aforementioned difficulty of unbounded investment. Since a further analysis is pure routine,[15] I leave it to the interested reader. The basic conclusion when F is homogeneous of degree one is that λ_t and I_t are constant, i.e. $\lambda_\tau = \lambda^*$ and $I_t = I^*$ for all t, and one has:

$$C'(I^*) = c/(i + \delta)(\equiv \lambda^*) \tag{22}$$

If one defines $\hat{K}$ by $\hat{K} \equiv I^*/\delta$, one obtains:

$$\dot{K}_t = \delta(\hat{\mathrm{K}} - K_t) \tag{23}$$

by recalling (11). (23) states that K_t adjusts to its long-run desired stock $\hat{K}$ monotonically, when its response parameter is equal to the rate of depreciation. $\hat{K}$ is often interpreted as the 'long-run desired stock of capital'.

(23), at least in this form, is similar to the response function,

$$\dot{K}_t = \alpha(K_t^* - K_t) \tag{24}$$

used by Jorgenson and his associates. However, these two are quite different: (24) is based on the recognition that the actual stock K_t is, in general, different from the desired stock K_t^*, and the α in it signifies the speed of adjustment.

Jorgenson and his associates, having obtained K_t^* according to the procedure mentioned earlier, undertook empirical studies, and obtained good statistical fits.[16] However, apart from the earlier theoretical criticism, there is another difficulty associated with K_t^*: in obtaining the desired capital stock, it is assumed that the adjustment is instantaneous and frictionless; hence the imposition of a response function for empirical estimation is a theoretical inconsistency, for it implies that the adjustment to the desired capital stock is neither instantaneous nor frictionless. If the adjustment is not instantaneous and involves some friction, this should be incorporated in the maximization behaviour of the firm.[17]

TOBIN'S q, THE VALUE OF THE FIRM AND KEYNES'S MEK

In 1969, Tobin introduced the criterion for investment decisions which became known as 'Tobin's q'. In this article, he denotes the price of *currently* produced goods by p and the market price of *existing* capital goods by qp (p. 326), where all goods are assumed to be homogeneous; i.e., q is the ratio of the two prices. He then pushes this concept a bit further by stating that 'the *rate* of investment – the speed at which investors wish to increase the capital stock – should be related, in anything, to q, the value of capital relative to its replacement cost' (p. 330). He argues that the 'long-run equilibrium' condition 'requires that capital be valued at its reproduction cost, i.e. $q = 1$' (p. 331).

Tobin expressed the public's real physical assets by qK (e.g. p. 327). Namely, q here is an *average* q. However, it has been recognized that the q which is relevant for investment decisions is a *marginal* q, the ratio of the market value of an *additional* unit of capital to its replacement cost. As is implied in the previous paragraph, Tobin (1969) is somewhat confusing on the distinction between the two qs. However, the importance of the marginal q is made explicit in Tobin and Brainard (1977), who state the gist of the q theory in the following way:

The neoclassical theory of corporate investment is based on the

> assumption that the management seeks to maximize the present net worth of the company, the market value of the outstanding common shares. An investment project should be undertaken if and only if it increases the value of the shares. The securities markets appraise the project, its expected contributions to the future earnings of the company and its risks. If the value of the project as appraised by investors exceeds the cost, then the company's shares will appreciate to the benefit of existing stockholders. That is, the market will value the project more than the cash used to pay for it. If new debt or equity securities are issued to raise the cash, the prospectus leads to an increase of share prices . . . Clearly it is the q ratio *on the margin* that matters for investment: the ratio of the increment of market valuation to the cost of the associated investment. The crucial value for marginal q is 1, but this is consistent with average q values quite different from 1. A firm with monopoly power, or other sources of diminishing returns to scale, will have an average q ratio higher than its marginal q. (1977, pp. 242–3, emphasis in original)

By the late 1970s, the q theory became quite popular, and Hall (1977, p. 85) called it 'the major competitor to Jorgenson's theoretical framework', while contending that it was basically a neoclassical theory *à la* Jorgenson and his associates. However, Lovell added that: 'Neither approach works out the dynamics of the adjustment process within the context of a carefully articulated optimization framework that would specifically incorporate the process of expectation formation and adjustment costs' (1977, p. 399).

Then followed a series of works, notably by Abel (1979), Yoshikawa (1980), Hayashi (1982), and Abel-Blanchard (1983), which clarifies that the q theory can indeed by derived from an intertemporal choice theoretic framework which explicitly takes account of the adjustment costs associated with investment. This framework is thus similar to the one discussed earlier.

Since Hayashi's work is aimed at an empirical investigation, it becomes necessarily tedious. For one thing, he allows for a 'depreciation allowance' per dollar of investment for tax purposes (his D function). It is further complicated by allowing for a non-constant discount rate and corporate taxes. Although these generalizations are important, I shall assume them away so as to capture the gist of his theory. Again, I assume all prices to be constant over time.

Hayashi incorporates the adjustment costs of investment into the

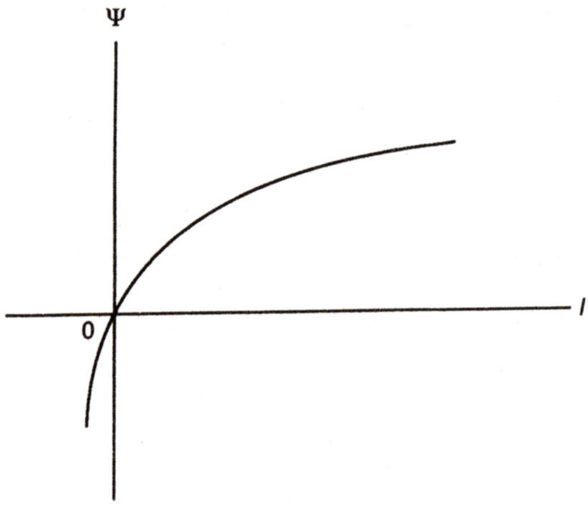

Figure 19.1 An Illustration of the Ψ function

capital accumulation equation, i.e. instead of using (11), he modifies it as follows.[18]

$$\dot{K}_t = \Psi(I_t, K_t) - \alpha K_t \tag{25}$$

As Hayashi (1982, p. 216) puts it: 'In this formulation, I units of gross investment do not necessarily turn into capital: only Ψ [times] 100 percent of investment does . . . Ψ is increasing and concave in I, Ψ drops sharply as I changes form 0 to negative, reflecting the irreversibility of investment'. The Ψ function thus captures the spirit of the adjustment cost approach discussed above. He calls it the 'installation function', which is illustrated in Figure 19.1, where, following him, one can assume:

$$\Psi_I > 0,\ \Psi_{II} < 0, \text{ for all } (I, K);\ \Psi(0, K) = 0, \text{ for all } K$$

where $\Psi_I \equiv \partial\Psi/\partial I$ and $\Psi_{II} \equiv \partial^2\Psi/\partial I^2$. Furthermore, it can also be assumed that:

$$0 < \Psi_I < 1 \text{ if } I > 0,\ \Psi_I = 1 \text{ if } I = 0, \text{ and } \Psi_{II} > 1 \text{ if } I < 0$$

for all K.

The firm is to choose the time paths of N_t and I_t so as to maximize:

$$\int_0^\infty e^{-it}[pF(N_t, K_t) - wN_t - p_I I_t]dt$$

subject to (25), $N_t \geq 0$, and a given value of K_0. The current value Hamiltonian of this problem can be written as:

$$H \equiv [pF(N_t, K_t) - wN_t - p_I I_t] + \lambda_t[\Psi(I_t, K_t) - \delta K_t]$$

The following conditions are necessary for optimum, and are also sufficient if F is concave:

$$\dot{K}_t = \Psi(I_t, K_t) - \delta K_t \tag{26a}$$

$$\dot{\lambda}_t = (i + \delta)\lambda_t - pF_K - \lambda_t \Psi_K, \quad \text{where} \quad \Psi_K \equiv \partial\Psi/\partial K_t \tag{26b}$$

$$\lim_{t \to \infty} \lambda_t K_t e^{-it} = 0 \tag{26c}$$

$$F_N = w/p \tag{26d}$$

$$p_I = \lambda_t \Psi_I \tag{26e}$$

If there were no adjustment costs, the market value of the firm would increase by λ for an additional unit of investment. But the capital stock actually increases by only Ψ_I. Thus (26e) states that the price of currently produced investment goods (p_I) is equal to the marginal benefit of installing one unit of new investment goods.

The crucial assumption introduced by Hayashi (1982) is that the functions F and Ψ are homogeneous of degree one. This is in turn equivalent to specifying,

$$F(N, K) = F_N N + F_K K, \quad \text{for all } N \text{ and } K \tag{27a}$$

$$\Psi(I, K) = \Psi_I I + \Psi_K K, \quad \text{for all } I \text{ and } K \tag{27b}$$

Next, one observes:

$$\frac{d}{dt}[\lambda_t K e^{-it}] = [\dot{\lambda}_t K_t + \lambda_t \dot{K}_t - i\lambda_t K_t]e^{-it} \tag{28}$$

Using (26b), (26a), (27a), (26d), and (26e) in succession, one observes:

$$\begin{aligned}
&\dot{\lambda}_t K_t + \lambda_t \dot{K}_t - i\lambda_t K_t, \\
&= \{(i + \delta)\lambda_t K_t - pF_K K_t - \lambda_t \Psi_K K_t\} + \lambda_t(\Psi - \delta K_t) - i\lambda_t K_t
\end{aligned}$$

$$= -[(pF - pF_N N_t) + \lambda_t\{\Psi_K K_t - (\Psi_I I_t + \Psi_K K_t)\}]$$
$$= -(pF - wN_t - p_I I_t)$$

Thus, along an optimal path, one has:

$$\frac{d}{dt}[\lambda_t K e^{-it}] = -[pF - wN_t - \mathrm{p}_I I_t]e^{-it}$$

Integrating this from 0 to ∞ and using (26c), one obtains:

$$\lambda_0 K_0 = V^*, \quad \text{where} \quad V^* \equiv \int_0^\infty (pF - wN_t - p_I I_t)e^{-it}\,dt \quad (29)$$

where V^* signifies the *value of the firm*. Thus, under the homogeneity of F and Ψ, Hayashi was successful in obtaining this remarkably simple formula.[19]

Whether or not V^* has such a simple expression, depends (among other things) on K_0. Then $(\partial V^*/\partial K_0)$ measures an increase in V^* by an additional unit of K_0. If it exceeds p_I, the firm is encouraged to push investment further. Otherwise, the firm will be discouraged. The magnitude of $(\partial V^*/\partial K_0)$ corresponds to what Keynes (1936, p. 135) calls the 'supply price of capital-asset', referred to at the beginning. Tobin's *marginal q* (denoted by q_M) is then defined by:

$$q_M \equiv \frac{\partial V^*}{\partial K_0}\frac{1}{p_I} \quad (30)$$

His investment criterion is determined simply by whether or not q_M exceeds unity. Thus Tobin and Brainard write:

> Economic logic indicates that a normal equilibrium value for q is 1 for reproducible assets which are in fact being reproduced, and less than 1 for others. Values of q above 1 should stimulate investment, in excess of requirements for replacement and normal growth, and values of q below 1 discourage investment. (1977, p. 238)

In contrast to q_M, Tobin's *average q* can be defined as:

$$q_A = V^*/(p_I K_0) \quad (31)$$

Hence *if* Hayashi's homogeneity assumption (27) is satisfied, one may obtain the following remarkable result from (29), (30) and (31):

$$q_M = q_A \tag{32}$$

I call this *Hayashi's theorem*. Using (29), one may also note that $p_K = \lambda_0$, i.e. the Keynesian supply price of capital is equal to Pontriyagin's multiplier, which is in turn the shadow price of the capital accumulation associated with (25).

What is relevant for investment decisions in Tobin's theory is the *marginal*, not average q, but it is only the latter that one can observe; hence Hayashi's statement that 'Empirical works based on the "q" theory have utilized average q as a proxy for marginal q' – see von Furstenburg (1977).[20] Thus, Hayashi's theorem provides a remarkable bridge between theoretical and empirical studies. Using his theorem, Hayashi proceeds with an empirical study. However, there is one difficulty with his procedure: nowhere does he empirically test his homogenity assumption. If this is not warranted, his empirical study has little meaning. Thus there is a dilemma in Hayashi's testing: to pursue his empirical investigation, he needs this assumption in order to obtain the measure of marginal q, yet the validity of his results depends on the empirical validity of his assumption.

In fact, there may even be a theoretical difficulty in his homogeneity postulate. Let me pursue this by assuming that his premise is indeed satisfied so that F and Ψ are homogeneous of degree one. Using the homogeneity of Ψ, one may define the function ψ by:[21]

$$\psi(z_t) = \Psi(z_t, 1)K_t, \quad \text{where} \quad z_t \equiv I_t/K_t \tag{33}$$

and, again, let $F(N_t, K_t) \equiv N_t f(kt)$. Then (26a)–(26c) can be rewritten as:

$$\dot{K}_t = [\psi(z_t) - \delta]K_t \tag{34a}$$

$$\dot{\lambda}_t = [(i + \delta) - \psi(z_t) + z_t\psi'(z_t)]\lambda_t - pF_K \tag{34b}$$

$$\lim_{t \to \infty} \lambda_t e^{-it} K_t = 0 \tag{34c}$$

$$F_N = w/p, \quad p_I = \lambda_t \psi'(z_t) \tag{34d}$$

$$p_I = \lambda_t \psi'(z_t) \tag{34e}$$

Since $F_N = f(k) - kf'(k)$, and $F_K = f'(k)$, k and pF_K are constant.
Solving $p_I = \lambda_t \psi'(z_t)$ for z_t to obtain $z_t = g(\lambda_t)$, where

$$g'(\lambda_t) = -\psi'/(\lambda_t \psi'') > 0$$

Substituting this into (34a) and (34b), one obtains the system of differential equations which defines the time path of (K_t, λ_t), given boundary conditions (34c) and K_0. After a tedious but routine analysis, one can show that either K_t increases without limit or shrinks to zero – see Semba (1989); i.e. either Hayashi's firm expands without limit, or disappears. It can be shown that this difficulty vanishes if the Ψ function is not homogeneous of degree one. However, lest I be misunderstood, I should point out that there is nothing wrong with the concept of the 'value of the firm' and the definitions of marginal and average q in (30) and (31).

Next, let us obtain V^* and its implication for the adjustment cost model discussed in the previous section. Recall the optimality conditions (21a)–(21–e), and $k_t = k^*$, $I_t = I^*$, $c \equiv pF_K(1, k^*)$, and that K^*, I^* and c are constant. Then simply observe that:

$$\begin{aligned}
V^* &= \int_0^\infty [pF(N_t, K_t) - C(I^*)]e^{-it}\,dt \\
&= \int_0^\infty [pF_K(1, k^*)K_t - C(I^*)]e^{-it}\,dt \\
&= \int_0^\infty [c\{I^*(1 - e^{-\delta t})/\delta + K_0 e^{-\delta t}\} - C(I^*)]e^{-it}\,dt \\
&= (cI^*/\delta)\int_0^\infty e^{-it}\,dt - c(I^*/\delta - K_0)/(i + \delta) \\
&\quad - C(I^*)\int_0^\infty e^{-it}\,dt \\
&= [cI^*/\delta - C(I^*)]/i - c(I^*/\delta - K_0)/(i + \delta) \\
&= \frac{c}{i + \delta} K_0 + \frac{c\delta}{i + \delta}\hat{K} - C(I^*)/i
\end{aligned}$$

where $\hat{K} \equiv I^*/\delta$.

From this, one can compute an increase in V^* by an additional unit of K_0 as:

$$\frac{\partial V^*}{\partial K_0} = c/(i + \delta)(= \lambda^*) \tag{35}$$

Thus, as in Hayashi's case, $\lambda^* = \lambda_0$ (Pontryagin's multiplier) is equal to $(\partial V^*/\partial K_0)$, which is turn signifies the Keynesian supply price of capital p_K. Recalling (22), the optimal investment rule can also be characterized by:[22]

$$\frac{\partial V^*}{\partial K_0} = C'(I^*) = c/(i + \delta) \tag{36}$$

The first equality of (36) states that investment (I^*) is pushed to the point at which the marginal increase in the value of the firm by an additional unit of capital is equal to the marginal adjustment cost of investment. Letting $(\partial V^*/\partial K_0) = p_K$, one can obtain from (36):

$$p_K = \int_0^\infty ce^{-it}\, dt\ [= c/(i + \delta)] \tag{37}$$

Since one unit of capital produces the income stream of $c = pF^*_K$, and since one unit of capital acquired at $t = 0$ will decay to $e^{-\delta t}$ at time t, the RHS of (37) signifies the present value of the total income stream obtained from one unit of capital acquired at $t = 0$. Thus, (37) signifies the true *Keynes MEK rule*, which equates the supply price of capital (p_K) with the present value of all future income streams. It is important to distinguish (37) from (19): p_I in (19) is replaced by p_K in (37). From (37), one can conclude that the true Keynesian MEK rule is consistent with the adjustment cost approach, from which one also obtains a proper understanding of the supply price of capital.

Substituting (21a) and (21b) into (28) and recalling the homogeneity of function F and (21d), one also observes:

$$\begin{aligned}\tfrac{d}{dt}[\lambda_t K e^{-it}] &= [\{(i + \delta)\lambda_t - pF_K\}K_t + \lambda_t(I_t - \delta K_t - i\lambda_t K_t]e^{-it} \\ &= [-pF_K K_t + \lambda_t I_t]e^{-it} \\ &= -[pF - wN_t - \lambda_t I_t]e^{-it}\end{aligned}$$

Integrating this from 0 to ∞, one gets:

$$\lambda_0 K_0 = \int_0^\infty [pF - wN_t - \lambda^* I^*]e^{-it}\, dt \tag{38}$$

where, as before, $\lambda_0 = \lambda_t = \lambda^* = c/(i + \delta)$ and $I_t = I^*$ for all t. Notice that, contrary to Hayashi (1982), the RHS of (38) is *not* V^*.[23] In the present case, the marginal and average qs are *not* equal.

One can now examine whether 'Tobin's q rule' is tenable as an investment criterion. The rule states that investment is pushed up to the point at which marginal q is equal to unity. Recalling (30) and (36), one obtains:

$$q_M = C'(I^*)/p_I = c/[p_I(i + \delta)] \tag{39}$$

When $q_M = 1$, one gets:

$$p_I = c/(i + \delta) = C'(I^*) \tag{40}$$

However, it is plausible to suppose that:

$$C'(0) = p_I \tag{41}$$

That is, the marginal cost of adjustment is equal to the purchase price of capital when the rate of investment is zero. Since $C'' > 0$ for all I, (40) and (41) are inconsistent with each other, except for the uninteresting case of $I^* = 0$. These considerations suggest the need for further investigation of the q theory. One way out of this difficulty might be to abandon the premise that investment is pushed to the point at which $q_M = 1$. Then, from the first relation of (39), one can conclude that I^* will be positive, negative or zero depending on whether q_M is, respectively, greater than, less than or equal to unity, but this relationship obviously does *not* determine the magnitude of investment. Therefore, contrary to popular belief, the q rule is not satisfactory as a theory for determining the *magnitude* of investment demand. A similar argument can also be made in terms of the installation function (Ψ) approach.

The q theory has become so popular recently that it has been introduced into textbooks – see, for example Branson (1989), who duly notes (pp. 305–7) that the link between the marginal and average qs can be 'complex' and can move in the opposite direction. However, despite its popularity, there is *no* empirical support for it.

Notes

* This paper is based on my lecture notes on macroeconomics courses given at various universities over the past two decades.

1. This form of depreciation is called 'depreciation by sudden death'. An

alternative specification is known as 'depreciation by evaporation'. These two specifications do not create a significant difference in conclusions. The colourful terms were coined by Hahn and Matthews (1964).

2. In fact, this assumption is wrong unless the $Q_t s$ and s are all positive. This was discussed a long time ago by, for example, Pitchford and Haggar (1958), who offered the following example. Let $T = 5$, $Q_1 = 15$, $Q_2 = -25$, $Q_3 = Q_4 = 0$, $Q_5 = 30$, $s = 0$, and $p_K = 2.2$. Then ρ can be computed as $\rho = 1.27$ and 0.76, i.e. the value of ρ is not uniquely determined. However, if the $Q_t s$ and s are *all positive*, ρ can uniquely be determined, if one assumes that $(1 + \rho)$ is real and positive. To see this, define the function $f(x)$ by:

$$f(x) = Q_1 x + Q_2 x^2 + \ldots + Q_T x^T + s x^t$$

where $x \equiv 1/(1 + \rho)$. Noting that $f'(x) > 0$ for all $x > 0$ if $Q_1, \ldots, Q_T, s > 0$, and that $f(0) = 0$, one can obtain a unique value of x^* (hence ρ) such that $f(x^*) = p_K$. However, one should also note that $f(x) = p_K$ is, in general, a Tth order polynomial equation, which, in general, has T roots, some of which may be negative and complex numbers. Thus the statement that (1) determines the value of ρ uniquely is in general false. This error is still observed in the literature – see, for example, Uzawa (1984, p. 212).

3. Namely, by the arbitrage condition, the rate of investment is pushed to the point which is determined by (3). I call this rule (3) Keynes's MEK rule, or simply the MEK rule. Note that this rule is established *without* going through that ill-defined ρ; see previous note.
4. Keynes used his MEK rule in explaining investment demand. However, the above consideration indicates that the Keynesian rule explains the *stock* demand for capital, not its flow demand, investment. This is noted and succinctly summarized by Witte (1963, pp. 188–9) where he asserts that 'The firm's demand is for stock rather than for flow of capital'.
5. Jorgenson also published a series of survey articles on investment in 1971, 1972 and 1976.
6. This is the case of 'depreciation by evaporation'.
7. The constant discount rate i may be interpreted as the *current interest rate* by which one can borrow or lend any amount. Here it is assumed that i is constant and that the lending rate is equal to the borrowing rate. The latter assumption is often referred to as that of a perfect capital market. If i is not constant but varies over time, the e^{-it} in W should be replaced by: $e^{-\int_0^t i_s d_s}$.
8. If the function F is concave, then, due to Mangasarian's (1966) theorem, these conditions are sufficient for a global optimum.
9. For a full discussion of this problem, see Takayama (1985, pp. 658–95).
10. If the capital good is rented for a finite period of time, say T, then the intertemporal arbitrage relation is:

$$p_I = \int_0^T c e^{-(i+\delta)t} dt + p_I e^{-(i+\delta)T}$$

This yields the same relation as before: $c = (i + \delta)p$.

11. The concept of 'user cost' is introduced in Keynes's *General Theory*. As a 'preliminary' definition, he stated that 'the amount which he [an entrepreneur] pays out to other entrepreneurs for what he has to purchase from them together with the sacrifice which he incurs by employing the equipment instead of leaving it idle' (p. 23). Later on (pp. 52–3), he gives a more 'precise' definition. Apparently still dissatisfied with his own definition, he wrote the 'Appendix on user cost' (pp. 66–73). Although he states that 'a little reflection will show that all this is no more than common sense', I find his exposition quite confusing. He could (or should) have explained this concept in a much more streamlined way. It requires a great deal of reading and rereading of the relevant portion of the *General Theory* to understand what Keynes meant (or should have meant).
12. Alternatively, one may view adjustment costs as the internal cost of forgone output, and alter the production function to: $Y_t = G(N_t, K_t, I_t)$. A special case of this is: $Y_t = F(N_t, K_t) - C(I_t)$; see Lucas (1967b).
13. Thus, C is a convex function. As a specific form of $C(I_t)$, one can consider $p_I(I_t)I_t$, where $p_I(I_t) > 0$, $p'_I(I_t) > 0$, $p''_I(I_t) > 0$ for $I_t > 0$ and $p_I(0) = 0$. The convexity of C is sometimes challenged – see, for example, Rothchild (1971).
14. Given the convexity of C and concavity of F, (21) also constitutes a set of sufficient conditions.
15. See Takayama (1985, pp. 697–712).
16. Even this may be suspect – see, for example, Eisner and Naidiri (1968) and Clark (1979). However, one should note the counter-criticism by Bischoff (1969).
17. This logical inconsistency gives rise to a sharp criticism by Uzawa: 'It goes without saying that the investment function . . . which is derived from logically completely inconsistent assumptions, cannot have any economic and empirical significance, no matter how good the statistical fit of that function may be' (1969a; my translation).
18. Hayashi (1982, p. 216) refers to Uzawa's (1968; 1969b) 'Penrose function' in justifying his Ψ function.
19. It should be noted that, prior to Hayashi, Yoshikawa (1980) developed a formulation of the q theory. It can be shown that both analyses will yield essentially the same result. For a general theorem that unifies both analyses, see Rose (1981).
20. Other empirical studies of the q theory include Ciccolo (1975), Tobin and Brainard (1977), Abel (1979), Brainard *et al.* (1980), and Oulton (1981).
21. One can assume:

$$\psi' > 0,\ \psi'' < 0,\ \forall\ z;\ \psi'(0) = 1,\ 0 < \psi' < 1,\ \forall\ z > 0,\ \psi' > 1,\ \forall\ z < 0.$$

22. Suppose that $C(I) = p_I(I)I$ with $p_I(I) > 0, p'_I(I) > 0, p''_I(I) > 0$, for $I > 0$ and $p_I(0) = 0$, as specified in footnote 13. Then $C'(I^*)$ is obtained as:

$$C'(I^*) = p_I(I^*) + p'_I(I^*)I^*.$$

Namely, the marginal adjustment cost is equal to the purchase price of an additional unit of investment goods plus installation and other costs.

23. If C is homogeneous of degree one, $C = C'I = \lambda I$ by (21c), and the RHS of (38) does signify the value of the firm. However, C cannot be homogeneous of degree one, because then $C(\theta I) = \theta C(I)$ for any $\theta > 0$. Letting $\theta = 1/I$, one then obtains $C(I) = C(1)I = aI$, where $a \equiv C(I)$, and this violates the strict convexity of C. In this case, $C' = a$ and (22) cannot determine the unique value of I^* uniquely.

References

1. Abel, A. (1979) *Investment and the Value of Capital* (New York: Garland).
2. Abel, A. and Blanchard, O. (1983) 'An intertemporal equilibrium model of saving and investment', *Econometrica*, vol. 51.
3. Arrow, K. J. (1968) 'Optimal capital policy with irreversible investment', in J. N. Wolfe (ed.), *Value, Capital, and Growth: Papers in Honour of Sir John Hicks* (Edinburgh: Edinburgh University Press).
4. Bischoff, C. (1969) 'Hypothesis testing and the demand for capital goods', *Review of Economics and Statistics*, vol. 51.
5. Blanchard, O. J. and Fischer, S. (1989) 'Consumption and investment: basic infinite horizon models', in their *Lectures on Macroeconomics* (Cambridge, Mass.: MIT Press).
6. Brainard, W., Shoven, J. and Weiss, L. (1980) 'The financial valuation of the returns to capital', *Brookings Studies on Economic Activity*, No. 2. (Washington DC: Brookings Institution).
7. Branson, W. H. (1989), *Macroeconomic Theory and Policy* (New York: Harper & Row).
8. Ciccolo, J. (1978) 'Money, equity values, and income', *Journal of Money, Credit and Banking*, vol. 10.
9. Ciccolo, J. and Fromm, G. (1979) 'q and the theory of investment', *Journal of Finance*, vol. 34.
10. Ciccolo, J. and Fromm, G. (1980) 'q, corporate investment, and the balance sheet behavior', *Journal of Money, Credit and Banking*, vol. 12.
11. Eisner, R. and Strotz, R. H. (1963) 'Determinants of business investment', in D. B. Suits *et al.* (eds.), *Impacts of Monetary Policy* (Englewood Cliffs: Prentice-Hall).
12. Eisner, R. and Nadiri, M. I. (1968) 'Investment behavior and the neoclassical theory', *Review of Economics and Statistics*, vol. 50.
13. Fisher, I. N. (1920) *The Theory of Interest* (New York: Macmillan).
14. Furstenburg, von G. (1977) 'Corporate investment: does market valuation matter in the aggregate?', *Brookings Papers on Economic Activity*, No. 2.
15. Gould, J. P. (1968) 'Adjustment costs in the theory of investment of the firm', *Review of Economics Studies*, vol. 35.
16. Gould, J. P. (1969) 'The use of endogenous variables in dynamic models of investment', *Quarterly Journal of Economics*, vol. 83.

17. Haavelmo, T. (1961) *A Study in the Theory of Investment* (Chicago: University of Chicago Press).
18. Hahn, F. H. and Matthews, R. C. O. (1964) 'The theory of economic growth: a survey', *Economic Journal*, vol. 74.
19. Hall, R. E. (1977) 'Investment, interest rates, and the effects of stabilization policies', *Brookings Papers on Economic Activity*, No. 1.
20. Hall, R. E. and Jorgenson, D. W. (1971) 'Application of the theory of optimum capital accumulation', in G. Fromm (ed.), *Tax Incentives and Capital Spending* (Washington DC: Brookings Institution).
21. Hayashi, F. (1982) 'Tobin's marginal and average *q*: a neoclassical interpretation', *Econometrica*, vol. 28.
22. Hestenes, M. R. (1966) *Calculus of Variations and Optimal Control Theory* (New York: Wiley).
23. Hirshleifer, J. (1970) *Investment, Interest and Capital* (Englewood Cliffs: Prentice-Hall).
24. Jorgenson, D. W. (1963) 'Capital theory and investment behavior', *American Economic Review*, vol. 53.
25. Jorgenson, D. W. (1965) 'Anticipations and investment behavior', in E. Kuh, G. Fromm and L. R. Klein (eds.), *Brookings Quarterly Econometric Model of the United States* (Amsterdam: North-Holland).
26. Jorgenson, D. W. (1967) 'The theory of investment behavior', in R. Ferber (ed.), *Determinants of Investment Behavior* (New York: National Bureau of Economic Research).
27. Jorgenson, D. W. (1969) 'The demand for capital services', in K. A. Fox, J. K. Sengupta and G. V. L. Narasimham (eds.), *Economic Models, Estimations, and Risk Programming: Essays in Honor of Gerhard Tintner* (Berlin: Springer-Verlag).
28. Jorgenson, D. W. (1971) 'Econometric studies of investment behavior: a survey', *Journal of Economic Literature*, vol. 9.
29. Jorgenson, D. W. (1972) 'Investment behavior and the production function', *Bell Journal of Economics and Management Science*, vol. 3.
30. Jorgenson, D. W. and Siebert, C. D. (1968a) 'A comparison of alternative theories of corporate investment behavior', *American Economic Review*, vol. 58.
31. Jorgenson, D. W. and Siebert, C. D. (1968b) 'Optimal capital accumulation and corporate investment behavior', *Journal of Political Economy*, vol. 76.
32. Jorgenson, D. W. and Stephenson, J. A. (1967) 'Investment behavior in US manufacturing, 1947–60', *Econometrica*, vol. 35.
33. Jorgenson, D. W. and Stephenson, J. A. (1969) 'Issues in the development of the neo-classical theory of investment behavior', *Review of Economics and Statistics*, vol. 51.
34. Jorgenson, D. W., Hunter, J. and Nadiri, M. I. (1970a) 'A comparison of alternative economic models of quarterly investment behavior', *Econometrica*, vol. 38.
35. Jorgenson, D. W., Hunter, J. and Nadiri, M. I. (1970b) 'The predictive performance of econometric models of quarterly investment behavior', *Econometrica*, vol. 38.

36. Keynes, J. M. (1936), *The General Theory of Employment, Interest and Money* (London: Macmillan).
37. Lerner, A. P. (1944), *The Economics of Control: Principles of Welfare Economics* (New York: Macmillan).
38. Lerner, A. P. (1965) 'On some recent developments in capital theory', *American Economic Review*, vol. 55.
39. Lovell, M. C. (1977) 'Comments and discussion of von Furstenberg's paper', *Brookings Papers on Economic Activity*, No. 2.
40. Lucas, R. E. (1967a) 'Optimal investment policy and the flexible accelerator', *International Economic Review*, vol. 8.
41. Lucas, R. E. (1967b) 'Adjustment costs and the theory of supply', *Journal of Political Economy*, vol. 75.
42. Lutz, F. and Lutz, V. (1951) *The Theory of Investment of the Firm* (Princeton: Princeton University Press).
43. McLaren, K. and Cooper, R. (1980) 'Intertemporal duality: application to the theory of the firm', *Econometrica*, vol. 26.
44. Malkiel, B. (1979) 'The capital formation problem in the United States', *Journal of Finance*, vol. 34.
45. Mangasarian, O. L. (1966) 'Sufficient conditions for the optimal control of nonlinear systems', *Journal of SIAM Control*, vol. 4.
46. Niho, Y. and Musacchio, R. A. (1983) 'Effects of regulation and capital market imperfections on the dynamic behavior of a firm', *Southern Economic Journal*, vol. 49.
47. Oulton, N. (1981) 'Aggregate investment and Tobin's *q*: the evidence from Britain', *Oxford Economic Papers*, vol. 33.
48. Penrose, E. T. (1959) *The Theory of the Growth of the Firm* (Oxford: Blackwell).
39. Pitchford, J. D. and Haggar, A. J. (1958) 'A note on the marginal efficiency of capital', *Economic Journal*, vol. 68.
50. Pontryagin, L. S., Boltyanskii, V. G., Gamkrelidze, R. V. and Mischchenko, E. F. (1962) *The Mathematical Theory of Optimal Processes* (New York: Interscience), translated by K. N. Trirogoff.
51. Rose, H. (1981) 'Shadow prices in intertemporal plans under constant returns to scale', *Economics Letters*, vol. 8.
52. Rothchild, M. (1971) 'On the cost of adjustment', *Quarterly Journal of Economics*, vol. 85.
53. Semba, K. (1989) 'Reconsideration of investment theory', *Aoyama Gakunin Seikei Ronshu*, vol. 14 (in Japanese).
54. Söderstrom, H. T. (1976) 'Production and investment under costs of adjustment: a survey', *Zeitschrist für Nationalökonomie*, vol. 36.
55. Takayama, A. (1971) 'A note on marginal efficiency of capital and marginal productivity of capital', *Lecture Notes* (Indiana: W. Lafayette).
56. Takayama, A. (1985) 'The neoclassical theory of investment and adjustment costs – an application of optimal control theory', in his *Mathematical Economics* (New York: Cambridge University Press), 2nd ed. (1st ed. 1974).
57. Takayama, A. (1987) 'Investment Demand', Chapter 7 in his *Lecture Notes* (Southern Illinois University).

58. Thompson, R. G. and George, M. D. (1968) 'Optimal operations and investment of the firm', *Management Science*, vol. 15.
59. Tobin, J. (1967) 'Comment', in R. Ferber (ed.), *Determinants of Investment Behavior* (New York: National Bureau of Economic Research).
60. Tobin, J. (1969) 'A general equilibrium approach to monetary theory', *Journal of Money, Credit and Banking*, vol. 1.
61. Tobin, J. and Brainard, W. (1977) 'Asset markets and the cost of capital', in B. Balassa and R. Nelson (eds.), *Economic Progress, Private Values and Public Policy: Essays in Honor of William Fellner* (Amsterdam: North-Holland).
62. Treadway, A. B. (1969) 'What is output? Problems of concept and measurement', in V. Fuchs (ed.), *Production and Productivity in the Service Industries* (New York: Columbia University Press).
63. Treadway, A. B. (1971) 'On the rational multivariate flexible accelerator', *Econometrica*, vol. 39.
64. Treadway, A. B. (1974) 'The global optimal flexible accelerator', *Journal of Economic Theory*, vol. 7.
65. Uzawa, H. (1968) 'The Penrose Effect and optimum growth', *Economic Studies Quarterly*, vol. 19
66. Uzawa, H. (1969a) 'A new theory of the investment function', *Nihon Keizai Shimbun*, July (in Japanese).
67. Uzawa, H. (1969b) 'Time preference and the Penrose Effect in a two class model of economic growth', *Journal of Political Economy*, vol. 77.
68. Uzawa, H. (1984), *Reader's Guide to Keynes' General Theory* (In Japanese) (Keynes Ippan Riron o Yomu) (Tokyo: Iwanami).
69. Witte, J. (1963) 'The microfoundations of the social investment function', *Journal of Political Economy*, vol. 71.
70. Wright, J. F. (1963) 'Notes on the marginal efficiency of capital', *Oxford Economic Papers*, vol. 15.
71. Yoshikawa, H. (1980), 'On the '*q*' theory of investment' *American Economic Review*, vol. 70.
72. Yoshikawa, H. (1984) *Studies on Macroeconomics* (in Japanese) (Tokyo: University of Tokyo Press).

20 On the Political Economy of Regime Choice

Koichi Hamada*

INTRODUCTION

History provides us with various experiences of reforms and changes in the international monetary regime. If one looks back on even the recent development of the monetary regime after The Second World War, there have been a series of significant events. The gold-exchange standard of the Bretton Woods regime was transformed gradually to the dollar-exchange standard by a process of delinking the dollar from gold. The New Economic Policy of President Nixon completely cut the tie between gold and the dollar, and obliged Japan to abandon the practice of keeping a fixed parity as many European countries had done. Then there was a short interlude of fixed exchange rates with a wider band of permissible exchange fluctuations . . . The Smithsonian period. Since 1973, however, most of the major industrial countries have floated their floated exchange rates, even though some of them engage in substantial interventions to make the regime as managed rather than pure float exchange rates. European countries started controlling the magnitude of relative fluctuations in exchange rates by the formation of the European Monetary System (see Dam 1982 for the historical development of the monetary system), and now they are looking forward to the monetary as well as economic union in 1992.

Depending on the nature of the prevailing monetary regimes . . . in other words, depending on the nature of ongoing rules and conventions regarding international transactions . . . economic outcomes of the interaction of national policies and government actions may significantly differ. On the other hand, changes in the economic and noneconomic environment give rise to the necessity and often the realization of a reform in the international monetary regime. Unsatisfactory functioning of the prevailing system may as well be the cause of the reform or the abolition of itself. Thus international economic activities are conditioned by the international monetary regime, the rules of the game. The rules of the game themselves in turn evolve from the influence of economic outcomes that are derived from the interaction of policy and private behaviour under the current rule. Thus, the evolution of rules and the economic interplay under the ongoing rules always proceed simultaneously.

If we look back at the experience of (partly managed) floating exchange rates among the industrial countries for more than a decade, we find that it has taught us several important lessons. Many good things can be said for the partly managed flexible exchange rate regime, because this regime has not succumbed to major international monetary crises as was the case under the adjustable peg system. Pressures in foreign exchange markets did not as often as in the old IMF regime result in increasing controls on capital flows or trade flows. Thus, on the one hand, the ongoing system can be regarded as supportive of relatively active international transactions. On the other hand, movements in real as well as nominal exchange rates have been quite volatile. Many economists wonder if the observed degree of volatility was necessary to accommodate smooth resource allocation through trade and capital movements.

This kind of consideration probably lies behind the Tokyo Summit proposal in May 1986 when the Finance Ministers of the Group of Seven (G-7) countries were asked to review their economic objectives and forecasts collectively using various economic indicators. The world is now regrouping for a better system design of international monetary relations.

The purpose of this paper is: to contrast political and economic approaches to regime choice; to clarify some conceptual issues involved in the discussion of regime choice; to ask how recently developed theoretical tools of economics help us understand the nature of regime choice; and finally to provide an example of simple feedback rules pertinent to the current discussions of regime choice facing policy makers in the world.

To begin with, what do we mean by 'regime'? I follow the definition of Cooper (1975) that a monetary regime is a particular set of rules and conventions governing monetary and financial relations between countries. 'Regime' is in a sense more general than 'system' or 'order', because the latter implies some systematic and consistent rules and conventions. In fact, the ongoing floating exchange rates regime can be properly named as 'non-system' (Corden 1983). Rules or conventions in an international regime thus may allow considerable freedom of action by participating agents or countries. On the other hand, 'regime' is distinguished from 'agreement', because one does not regard a once-for-all ad hoc international agreement as a regime. The words 'regime', and 'rules' or 'conventions' suggest a situation where agents themselves interact repeatedly following some specific patterns of behaviour. Therefore, the analysis of a regime possesses a strong bearing on the discussion of repeated plays, commitment to rules and reputation building that are popular among recent game-theoretic literature.

Some political scientists define regime in a slightly different fashion. Many authors in Krasner (1982) take a consensus view: a regime is 'a set of implicit or explicit principles, names, rules, and decision-making procedures around which actors' expectations converge in a given area of international relations'. Here principles are defined as 'beliefs of fact causations, and rectitude'. Norms are 'specific prescriptions or proscriptions for action'. Decision-making procedures are 'prevailing practices for making and implementing collective choice' (Krasner 1982, p. 2).

I am not perfectly comfortable with the strong distinction made by Krasner (1982, p. 3) between principles and norms, on the one hand, and, rules and decision-making procedure, on the other. He claims that principles and norms provide the basic defining characteristics of a regime and that changes in rules and decision-making procedures are changes within regimes while changes in principles and norms are changes of the regime itself. Most of the economists consider, as I observe, that a basic change in rules of interventions in exchange markets, say from fixed exchange rates to floating exchange rates is a change in regimes. Thus, even though one has to distinguish regime changes from 'one shot' arrangements, basic changes in rules of the game should be regarded as regime changes – for a similar view see Keohane (1984, p. 59).

The latter half of the above definition by Krasner suggests the importance of expectations held by actors involved in a particular regime. In a sense, a regime describes a situation where the expectations of actors are more or less self-fulfilled by the realization. Even though I do not find it necessary to amend Cooper's definition by adding complexity with such qualifications as the convergence of expectations, it is worth noting that expectations, particularly credible expectations held by actors can be an important ingredient of a stable regime.

In the next section, I briefly sketch out and contrast political analysis and economic analysis of the regime choice. In the third section, I examine some conceptual as well as theoretical issues and try to relate them to some theoretical framework of economics. In the fourth section, I look back on the evolution of international monetary regime since the Second World War and ask how the conceptual framework in the previous section can explain some facets of the development of international monetary regimes. Finally I consider the issue of choice among alternative monetary regimes that the present (non-socialist) world is facing. I focus on the two popular proposals, i.e. the proposal for stabilizing global money supply by McKinnon (1974, 1984) and the proposal for exchange market interventions to keep the exchange rate within a target zone. I report the main results of a companion paper (Fukuda and Hamada 1986) that suggests prospective directions towards finding appropriate ways to implement the recent summit's proposal for monetary coordination and mutual review of national policy objectives.

POLITICAL AND ECONOMIC APPROACHES TO REGIME CHOICE

Since political scientists, particularly those in the field of international relations, conduct extensive studies on international regime, it would be helpful to sketch out their works briefly before we trace some of the economists' approaches to regime choice, even though constraints of being an economist myself prevent me from providing a well-balanced and extensive survey.

According to Krasner (1982),[1] the attitudes of political scientists can be roughly classified into three categories. One group of scholars (e.g. Puchala and Hopkins 1982, and Young 1982) emphasize the importance of international regime following the Grotian, natural-law, interpretation of international law and regard it more than a composite of sovereign states limited only by the balance of power. They point out the pervasiveness of international regimes. Behaviour of private actors and governments are strongly influenced by principles, norms and rules involved in the regime. Interestingly enough to economists, those authors regard a market as a regime because a market must be embedded in a broader social environment in order to sustain itself (Ruggie 1982). This view in general does not seem, however, to conform well to economists' traditional atomistic thinking that social phenomena and, in some cases, even their evolution can be analysed by the aggregation of individual behaviour.

A completely opposite view, a structuralist view, is strongly set forth by Strange (1982). According to her, regime is a misleading concept that obscures basic economic and power relationships. The study of regime is based on an imprecise definition of the concept, loaded with a value judgement that implicitly supports the status quo, confined to static analysis, and occupied by state-centred paradigm. She suggests, instead, a quite different way of analysing international organizations, for example, looking at international relations from the dimensions of politics (authorities) and markets.

Between these two extreme views, there are many political scientists labeled as 'modified structural'. They recognize that international relations are outcomes of state behaviour that maximize power in an anarchic environment. At the same time, they recognize that international regimes may have a significant impact on realizing Pareto-improving outcomes compared to the state that would have been obtained by individual behaviours in an anarchic environment. This view sounds quite congenial to the economists' conventional view, although to some economists regime would not matter at all as will be explained shortly.

Among many political scientists along this middle line, the work of Keohane (1982; 1984) attracts my attention because his methodology is very similar to that of most economists. He (1984, pp. 32ff) points out the insufficiency of the traditional theory of hegemonic stability (e.g. Kindleberger 1973). Hegomony is usually defined as the preponderance of material resource. In particular, hegemonic power must have controls over raw materials, over sources of capital, over markets and comparative advantages in the production of highly valued goods. This is a rather crude definition, and a more reasonable definition would be 'a situation in which one state is powerful enough to maintain the essential rules governing interstate relations, and willing to do so'. The crude definition may help the analysis of changes in international cooperation and discord, and the latter version helps the interpretation of a specific era where a nation has leadership. A more important question is, Keohane argues, to ask under what conditions a country has incentives to behave as a hegemon, and under what conditions the other countries have incentives to follow (or confront) the leader. International cooperation develops if participants believe that the cooperation facilitates the realization of their own objectives. Since international regimes refer to more or less long-term patterns of behaviour, the theory of rational choice helps us understand the creation, maintenance and evolution of international regimes.[2] Then he introduces many ideas familiar to economists: the Coase theorem and the unimportance of regime choice in an ideal world where the appropriate assignment as well as enforcement of property rights were possible (Conybeare 1980), the existence of economic and 'political' externalities that create market failure and necessitate policy cooperation or the creation of cooperative regime, the role of international regimes to reduce transaction costs, the need for insurance regimes to cope with uncertainty, the strategic nature of coordination problems that can be formulated as variants of the prisoners' dilemma, and the role of bounded rationality.

Now let us turn to the economic analysis of regime choice. First, there can be a position that tends to minimize the importance of regime choice. The application of the Coase theorem by political scientists cited above would be one aspect of the irrelevance of the regime in an ideal situation. In this case, however, the institutional framework for assigning and policing property rights can be regarded as a regime itself. Even in a situation where the specific assignment of property rights does not matter, stability of the assignment does matter.

More importantly for the case of international monetary regimes, there are an increasing number of economists who believe that the world is most properly analysed by postulating the neutrality of money. Only real factors such as taste, real endowments, relative prices, real interest rates and real exchange rates determine resource allocations. In fact in many real models, this type of neutrality of money is assumed. From this viewpoint, the choice between flexible and fixed exchange rates is not an important matter. There could be some difference in the second order in the world under uncertainty where the degree of variations in prices or consumption influence real economic activities may affect the demand for money. But they are of the importance of the second order. Moreover, this reasoning is reinforced if one believes in the neo-Ricardian world. There, reshuffling of the central bank portfolio by interventions would be taken into account by private agents because they foresee the effect of net gain of the central bank through the government's budget constraint.[3]

More eclectic views are held by many others. Following up his illuminating analysis of international interdependence (Cooper 1968),

Cooper (1975) considered systematically the political economic process of choosing an international monetary regime and the relevance of cost–benefit analysis to this problem. According to him, the difficulty of applying the theoretical analysis, and, furthermore, the difficulty of attaining international consensus stem from (1) disagreements on the desirability of distributional consequences of alternative regimes, (2) different weights attached to competing criteria, (3) differences in national circumstances, (4) disagreement over the effectiveness of alternative means to achieve a particular objective, and uncertainty about trustworthiness of other countries within any chosen regime. He applied the apparatus of game theory and pointed out the relevance of Prisoner's dilemma situation.

Along a similar line of approach, and also under the influence of the logic of collective action (Olson 1965), I focused my attention on the fact that there are always two layers of the game being played simultaneously (Hamada 1985, chapter 1–3). The game of agreeing on the rules of the game, or agreeing on an alternative regime is played while policy interactions continue under a given regime. Thus I characterized the logical structure of this gaming situation as a two stage game: the first stage being a game of choosing an international regime and the second stage being the policy interplays. Then I applied the principle of optimality of the dynamic programming (see Table 20.1). If there is a reasonable policy outcome for each policy game under a given regime, then one could solve it by the backwards induction in the game of choosing an international regime. I was not fully aware of the deeper implication of this backward induction process.[4] Unless the outcomes of the policy game were credible, the game of choosing a regime would not be equivalent to the choice among these outcomes. Here one needs to require a criterion which is essentially the same as the requirement of subgame perfectness (Selten 1975, Kreps and Wilson 1982).

The first stage game has a pay-off structure similar to the battle of the sexes (Luce and Raiffa 1957). Unless participants agree on a new regime, the ongoing set of rules will prevail as indicated in Tables 20.1 and 20.2 (for the scenario attached to the battle of the sexes and how the game tree can be written, see Hamada 1985, Ch. 2). From this rather elementary analysis, one can draw at least two interesting implications. First, in order for a new regime to be adopted, the ongoing regime is to be in an impasse serious enough to make the pay-off structure of a new regime attractive for prospective participants. Initially, the values of a, b or c, d in Table 20.2 may not be

Table 20.1 Payoff matrix of the 'Battle of the sexes'

		Girl	
		Fight	Ballet
Boy	Fight	(3, 1)	(0, 0)
	Ballet	(0, 0)	(1, 3)

Table 20.2 Payoff matrix of alternative monetary systems

		Europe	
		Gold Standard	Dollar Standard
US	Gold Standard	(a, b)	(0, 0)
	Dollar Standard	(0, 0)	(c, d)

positive, assuming a normalization device to make status quo as (0, 0). Only a crisis may make them positive. Monetary reform is more likely to come as inevitable reactions to crisis rather than as a realization of a well planned blueprint. Secondly, as the battle of the sexes can be resolved by the coordination of the choice of attractions for dating, conflicts in the game of regime choice may be reconciled by making the rules of the game a composite of various characteristics. Thus one could explain the adoption of adjustable-peg regime after the war, a hybrid regime between the fixed and adjustable exchange rates. In fact Keynes lamented the hybrid system that replaced his thoroughbred plan of clearing union (Keynes 1947).

One can effectively apply this calculus of participation to the question of incentives to join a monetary union or a monetary system (Hamada 1985, Ch. 3). Even though a single currency for the whole world may be ideal, the immediate costs involved in fixing exchange parity makes the adoption of a fixed exchanged rate arrangement quite difficult.

The public good nature of international regime was further explored by Bryant (1980). He compared the monetary regime to 'supranational traffic regulations'. The limitation of the power of the international legal system – international public goods 'without international government' as Kindleberger (1986) put it – enhances the need for policy coordination. At the same time, Bryant emphasizes the catalytic role of supranational institutions such as IMF or GATT in facilitating national governments to realize potential opportunity for coordination.

PROPERTIES OF DESIRABLE REGIMES

Let us now consider some conceptual issues in the choice of regimes. The functioning of alternative regimes and the probability of their realization depend on various factors.

Well-defined rules

In order for a regime to function well, the content of principles, norms and rules of the game involved in the regime should 'normally' be well defined. There are variable degrees in the tightness of the rules of the game. Under the adjustable peg system monetary authorities are required to intervene. On the other hand, under the ongoing floating rate system, or non-system, monetary authorities are free to choose a wide range of behaviour. Usually it is better for the regime that the rules of the game are well defined and well documented. For example, the key concept of 'fundamental disequilibrium' in the old IMF regime was not defined. This concept caused a lot of confusion and thus was not an operational criterion for bringing about prompt exchange-rate adjustment. Of course, some custom laws, or the common law, emerge from actual practice, as the practice of managed float among industrial countries was christened but codified only after several years of its experience by the Jamaica agreement in 1976. I added the qualification 'normally' above, because under certain circumstances the ambiguity of the content of agreement may even help reduce the tension of potential conflict of interest.[5]

Internal consistency

A regime should possess a set of internally consistent rules. For example, in the managed float system, all the countries involved (say the number of country is n) cannot engage in independent interventions. At least one country should remain as a passive agent. This so-called $(n - 1)$ problem illustrates the need for the internal consistency of rules. The present amended Articles of the IMF do not satisfy this condition.

Flexibility to various shocks

Regimes, inclusive of the international regimes, are subject to various kinds of shocks: Real shocks such as changes in productivity and in taste, energy crises, and monetary shocks such as financial innovations and disintermediation in some countries. A desirable international monetary regime should be able to cope with these expected as well as unexpected shocks. The adjustable peg system under the Bretton Woods regimes was very vulnerable to speculative attacks whenever the credibility of the ongoing exchange parity was eroded by some reason. The Bretton Woods regimes became unsustainable under such changes of circumstances as the excess absorption of the USA after the Vietnam war and the inflationary pressures in the commodity market beginning from the late 1960s. (Of course, this inflexibility was not so much due to the pegging as due to its non-adjusting.) One merit of the ongoing flexible or managed float regime is that it somehow survived two major waves of oil crises without incident of closed international exchange market as was the case under the adjustable peg system. Fukuda and Hamada (1987), whose results will be summarized in the last section, can be regarded as an exercise, though limited, to compare the relative vulnerability of fixed and flexible exchange rates with regard to different types of shock.

Simplicity of the rules and information requirements

It would be desirable for a regime to have a simple set of rules and conventions. Simpler rules have a strong advantage in that they can be more easily explained to monetary authorities and more easily understood by them. Also, the rules that do not require extensive processing of information are usually preferred. Thus simpler rules with lower information requirements will be more easily implemented – implementability is another characteristic. I will consider below. Incidentally, the rules considered in the last section of this paper possess the desirable characteristics of simplicity. Needless to say, the information benefit derived from the simplicity of the rules should be contracted by the possible cost of instability due to the simplicity.

Overall desirability and optimality

One could judge, at least in principle, by examining a regime from these viewpoints just mentioned above, what kind of system design is optimal. In order to discuss optimality, one has to define the objective function to be maximized, for example, income stability, price stability or the balance of payments stability. Abundant literature exists on the optimal system design in the international monetary system (see, e.g., Mundell and Swoboda 1969). Thus I do not want to repeat the discussion here. One of the main purposes in my book (Hamada 1985) was to fill the intellectual gap between so many active discussions on the ideal monetary regime and so few systematic attempts to analyze the plausibility of realizing a desirable regime. I regard the discussions of political economic aspects that follow as equally important as the discussions of ideal monetary regimes.

Implementability

However ideal a proposed regime may be, it will not be realized unless it is implementable. The traditional theory of hegemonic stability argues that a leader country, i.e. a hegemone, is necessary to provide the initiative to realize a desired regime. A hegemon is suited to supply the public good. What is required for the leader is political entrepreneurship to inform and persuade the prospective participants of the potential gain of building or reforming a regime, and not the ability to exploit its monopolistic advantage given by the size of the country. According to Olson's theory of collective action (Olson 1965), a larger country has less incentives to diverge from the socially optimal behaviour. From this viewpoint, there is some ground for the theory of hegemonic stability. But I agree with Keohane (1984) in that this theory should be replaced by the analysis of individual incentives for the leader as well as for other participants in the regime.

Enforceability

In the absence of the international government (Kindleberger 1986), most of the norms and the rules of the game are hardly sustained by international sanctions. There are exceptions. Bryant (1980) refers to Article IV of the amended IMF Article of Agreement and the ancillary guidelines for the surveillance that suggest the possibility of interference by the IMF. However, like international law in general, most of the rules are supported only by the willingness of participating nations. Here one finds also the difficulty of enforcing the property right solution even if one could assign appropriate property rights. This gives reasons to study the incentive compatibility.

Incentive compatibility

There are two levels of questions with regard to incentive compatibility. The first question concerns whether there is sufficient inducement to agree on a new regime or to reform the ongoing regime. The second question concerns how the rational behaviours of participating nations interact with their economic policies. In Hamada (1985), I focused attention on these two related issues of incentive compatibility. To implement or reform a regime, not only the leader (or the supplier of the regime) but also other participants should have sufficient incentives to join in a new or reformed regime. The logic of collective actions applies here so that there is a tendency to generate only insufficient amounts of collective actions as public goods. It is important to notice that incentives to implement (or reform) a regime depend on a credible outcome of the chosen regime, the object of the second question.

There has been a rapid development in economic analysis of the second question (see, e.g. many articles in Buiter and Marston 1985). Instead of reviewing the results for the second question, I would like to mention a few important issues with respect to the first question of regime choice and to the relationship between the first question and the second. As is the game at the second stage of policy interaction, the pay-off structures in regime choice problems resemble the prisoner's dilemma. A natural question is how to avoid the Pareto inferior equilibrium and to realize the Pareto superior cooperative solution. Also one might ask if there is some mechanism in the real world to let participants cooperate in order to keep away from the non-cooperative impasse.

One way to realize the Pareto-superior outcome is to change the pay-off structures of the rules of the game in such a way as to ensure incentive mechanism to let participants cooperate. A simple example in the fixed exchange rate is that the appropriate allocation of SDRs as outside money to the world may improve the incentive structure of policy games to keep the world inflation rate within a desirable range – see Hamada (1985, chapter 5). Some analogies can be drawn here between the peace-research and the optimal design of an international monetary regime.

Another interesting finding in game theory is that non-cooperative behaviour may sustain the 'cooperative' outcome if the prisoners' dilemma game is repeated. The 'folk theorem' tells us that if the prisoners' dilemma game is played infinitely many times with no discount factor for payoffs, then any Pareto-efficient configurations can be sustained by non-cooperative behaviour (Auman 1981, see also Friedman 1986 for related issues). Axelrod (1984) engaged in interesting experiments on how cooperation emerges in actual gaming. The reason why the international trade regime and monetary regime are maintained in such a way as to sustain the free trade and free capital movements to a considerable degree may be found in the repetitious nature of international transactions and policy interactions.

If the repetition is finite, the above logic will break down. The prisoners' dilemma situation may fall into the trap of the chainstore paradox. The work by Selten (1975) is a quest for incentive mechanisms to realize a cooperative outcome by introducing uncertainty. Kreps and Wilson (1982) also introduced incompleteness in information and analysed the process of reputation building that may sustain the cooperative outcome even in a finite horizon. Those techniques are just being introduced to international economics. The unresolved question pertinent to our problem is what kind of institutional design in fact increases the sustainability of cooperative outcomes in the game of policy interaction.

Finally, a related question is that of time consistency (Kydland and Prescott 1977). Even if a regime is designed ideally at the outset given certain desirable patterns of behaviour under the regime, there may be, and will be in most cases, incentives for players to divert from, or renege on, the prescribed patterns of behavior at a later time period. This possibility prevents the formation of credible expectations on the desired code of behaviour in the second stage game and blocks the adoption of a desirable regime. This dilemma is resolved if there is a mechanism to let participants pre-commit to a desired code of behaviour. In national states, law inclusive of the constitution helps individuals to commit to a certain type of behaviour. In the world without the authority for sanctioning, there is even more difficulty to let participants observe precommitted rules.

DYNAMICS OF REGIME CHANGES

Then what factors induce changes of regimes? Internal contradictions in the regime triggers a regime change. Political scientists emphasize the power structure (Young 1982). Writers, including those in political science, who are strongly influenced by economic analysis, recognize the importance of cost-benefit structure and incentive mechanisms facing the participants (Stein 1982, Keohane 1984). In my opinion, the regime changes take place more likely as a result of unfavorable external disturbances to the ongoing system that make the status quo intolerable to many participants, than as a result of the well calculated plan for the ideal reform.

Let us illustrate these points by examining the postwar history of the international monetary regime, emphasizing the role of incentive structure. The basic principle practices of the Bretton Woods regime that was effective until 1970 were as follows: (a) Exchange rates are normally fixed but subject to change. The IMF had the authority to allow exchange rate adjustments beyond 10 per cent changes of parity if it recognizes the existence of 'fundamental disequilibrium' while smaller adjustments were open to countries without the permission of the IMF. (b) In principle, the dollar was linked to gold with a fixed parity but in practice, the Pink became weaker and weaker. (c) In practice, the adjustment of the balance of payments was primarily conducted by macroeconomic policies of non-reserve countries, i.e. countries other than the USA.

Under fixed rates, the nature of policy interdependence was relatively simple. Under fixed rates the price levels of the countries of the world have a tendency to converge. Therefore the world price level was related to the weighted average of the rate of excess money creation which the balance of payments was related to the difference between this average and the rate of excess money creation of the particular country. The policy game under fixed rates exhibits the structure of prisoners' dilemma: the non-cooperative behaviour of central banks leads to a more inflationary deflationary outcome depending on whether the world liquidity is more or less than the desirable amount (Hamada 1985, chapter 5). Under fixed rates, cooperation of monetary policy was indispensable.

Mundell (1971) applies his celebrated policy classification approach to this system. The USA adjusts its money supply to peg the price level for the world economy, and countries in the rest of the world adjust their money supply to maintain their balance of payments equilibria. When those countries followed these rules, everything worked all right. There were, however, two kinds of difficulties in this mechanism. One is the asymmetry in the adjustment mechanism in the balance of payments. Countries other than the USA were obliged to contract monetary policies when they were in deficit. In this sense, the dollar standard regime had partly an enforcement mechanism. However, countries other than the USA did not have incentives to expand their monetary policies when they were in surplus. Moreover, the USA did not have a strong incentive to play the role of a benevolent world leader by adjusting its monetary policies to keep the stability of the world price level (Hamada 1985).

Thus one of the main reasons why the Bretton Woods regime collapsed was that the rest of the world did not play the game symmetrically and the USA had to be concerned with domestic policy objectives other than world price stability.[6] Various changes in exogenous factors, such as the US' involvement in Vietnam while keeping its objective for welfare states, productivity gains in Japan or Germany, and the reluctance of these countries to reflect the economy, led the Bretton Woods system to an impasse, which necessitated industrialized countries to adopt the flexible or managed float exchange regime not by deliberate calculation but by the immediate need due to a crisis. The flexible exchange-rate regime, or the managed float, was a convenient new regime that did not need much agreement among participating countries. The rules were codified in Jamaica in 1976, three years after the adoption of flexible exchange rates had taken place. Thus the crisis theory of regime changes seems to explain the transition well.

The adoption of flexible exchange rates essentially blocked the parallel movements of price levels, so that the nature of monetary interdependence became more subtle. The strength of monetary interdependence under flexible exchange rates is, so to speak, of the second degree if the strength of the linkage of price levels under fixed rates is of the first degree. Moreover, the direction of spillover effects of monetary policy is not certain. Positive spillover effects are working through the effect of aggregate demand multipliers as well as through the terms of trade effect. However, negative spillover effects may work through interest rates and capital mobility. Thus, in the policy game under flexible rates, the direction of the influence of the monetary policy of other countries may be positive or negative, depending on the nature of interdependence. If positive spillover effects are dominant, non-cooperative behavior will lead to a situation where every country pursues a less expansionary policy than is required to attain a cooperative solution. On the other hand, if the negative spillover effects are stronger, the noncooperative situation will be such that every country pursues a more expansionary policy than is required to attain a cooperative solution (Canzoneri and Gray 1985).

The weaker degree of interdependence under flexible exchange rates enables monetary authorities to enjoy a greater degree of monetary autonomy, because, at least in principle, the direct linkage among price levels across countries that existed under fixed exchange rates is now blocked. Each country has more freedom to choose its own price levels, less affected by the policies by neighbor countries. Each country can secure some minimum standard of macroeconomic stability by itself. In this sense, one may say heuristically that the 'max-min' solution under flexible exchange rates gives relatively attractive situations to participating countries. Thus in the game of choosing or agreeing on a new regime, the pay-off of the status quo solution would be rather difficult to be dominated by pay-offs provided by a new system. Because of this, this cost-benefit structure may give the present system a much longer life span than might be expected.

The dissatisfaction currently expressed regarding the ongoing managed float regime does not seem to justify a return to the old system. Even though the present system seems to welcome some cooperation, the need for cooperation is not crucial. Under the fixed exchange rate cooperation was inevitable. But the incentive structure to realize cooperation was insufficient. The system lacked coherent incentive compatibility, in addition to its vulnerability to speculative attacks.[7]

Then *quo vadis*, international monetary regime? The complaint on the current regime is over the possible misalignment of exchange rates. However, it is very difficult, in the world where one cannot discriminate permanent from transient shocks, to identify the equilibrium exchange rates. All one could do may be to find some devices that increase the stability of exchange rates automatically. Is not there any way to implement some automatic stabilizer to achieve the self correction of the movements in the system? A modest attempt in this direction will be discussed in the final section.

TOWARDS THE IMPLEMENTATION OF THE SUMMIT PROPOSAL

Thus, at present, the major industrialized countries are groping for a scheme, or a regime one may say, which has desirable properties, and to which they can reasonably commit themselves. Alternative regimes under serious and realistic consideration seem to be not the complete return to the fixed exchange rate, but some kind of managed float regime between the fixed exchange rate and the clean floating rate. (The European monetary unification of 1992 along with the experience of unifying the German monetary system may present a stronger case for fixed exchange rates.) The economic declaration of the Tokyo Summit in May 1986 indicates that the leaders of G-7 countries agreed to review at least their economic objectives taking account of various indicators, if not to intervene in exchange markets.

Needless to say, in the world where uncertainty prevails – concerning the nature of economic disturbances we are exposed to and the properties of the economic universe we are placed in – the design of an appropriate regime or the set of desirable rules is not an easy task. Fukuda and Hamada (1987) made an attempt to seek an appropriate and incentive compatible set of rules.

We focused our attention on two popular proposals: one by McKinnon (1984) that the monetary authorities of major countries should provide stable aggregate monetary growth; the other by Williamson (1983) that monetary authorities set target zones for exchange rates towards which they should push real exchange rates by interventions if exogenous forces push the rates out of it. By developing a two-country, stochastic version of Dornbusch's sluggish price model (Dornbusch 1976) as well as its neoclassical variant, we considered the question what kind of simple rules are desirable to stabilize the output variance. The significance of the simplicity of the rules has already been stressed. The method introduced by Aoki (1981), which decomposes the system into that of average variables and that of difference variables, not only facilitates the calculation of the model and clarifies the structural nature of these proposals. The main findings of our paper can be summarized as follows:

(i) The proposal for global monetary target concerns the aggregate or average variable of the system. On the other hand, the proposal for a target zone to correct misalignment concerns difference variables of the system. One should clearly recognize this qualitative distinction between two kinds of proposals. External disturbances can be classified into two types: the aggregate disturbance that affects the aggregate system, and the differential disturbance that affects two countries in an asymmetric way.

(ii) In the average system, the well known result by Poole (1970) for a closed Keynesian model carries through to the optimal feedback rule of money supply. If aggregate disturbances in IS curves are dominant, and if the interest elasticity of money demand is negligible, then the stable money supply rule is appropriate. On the other hand, if aggregate disturbances are in LM curves, then the money supply rule to stabilize the average nominal rate of interest is appropriate. This result is more or less expected because the world as a whole is a closed system even in the two-country situation.

(iii) More surprisingly, in the difference system, a similar analogy prevails. No or little intervention is desirable if differential (or country specific) disturbances are mainly in IS curves and if the interest elasticity of money demand is negligible. Substantial interventions in such a way as to keep stable exchange rates are more desirable if differential disturbances are mainly in LM curves. Moreover, interventions in such a way to reduce the interest differential between the two countries will serve the same purposé if differential disturbances are mainly in LM curves.

(iv) The minimization of the output variance of each country can be achieved by the simultaneous minimization of the variance of average output and that of the variance of difference in output. The optimal design of stabilization can be achieved by letting each monetary authority commit to the desired rule of money supply. Alternatively it can be achieved by a policy assignment suggested by Mundell (1971) that the leader country, or a hegemon, takes actions responding to the average variable while the follower country adjusts the difference variable. This analysis can also be generalized to *n*-country situations. These results in our joint paper are derived in a simplified model where economic structures of the two countries are symmetric, and disturbances are time independent white noises. Therefore we should recognize the gap between such a theoretical exercise and the appropriate policy proposal to implement some desirable regime. Among many necessary modifications and reservations, we may just mention relatively important ones.

First, in the actual world, disturbances are necessarily time independent but serially correlated. Moreover, we do not know exactly which disturbances are permanent and which are transient. Economic agents and monetary authorities engage in guessing games of what are permanent or transient. The simple policy recommendation obtained under the assumption of white noises may be modified. Presumably, more adaptive rules should be implemented when there are serial correlations in disturbances, and less rigid or drastic rules should be applied when we cannot identify the permanent or transient nature of disturbances. Secondly, the optimal rule will depend on the lag structure of the system and the information set on which private agents and monetary authorities take actions and formulate expectations on future variables. Finally, if we are to apply the feedback process to the current world situation, we need to modify our conclusions taking account of the ongoing process of international credit accumulation due to differences in saving behaviors among countries, which could be based on the possible difference in the pattern of time preferences, the technological development and the given historical datum of resource endowment. The two-country model developed in our paper does not take account of these long-run factors so that the stationary state of the model corresponds to the equilibrium where the current account will be equated to zero. In the actual situation, however, equilibium may consist of a path that allows some non-zero and varying current account balance of payments.

Notes

* Paper presented at the Conference on International Regimes and the Design of Macroeconomic Policy at the Centre for Economic Policy Research (CEPR), London, November 1986. I thank Michael Jones for his comments and suggestions.

1. This special issue contains many interesting papers on regime choices.
2. In his earlier work, Keohane (1982) introduced the ideal of the demand for international regime, contrasting it with the (hegemonic) theory of supply of international regime. Since some countries are demanders as well as suppliers of the regime, separation of demand factors from supply factors does not seem to be a convenient device. Therefore, I prefer his recent version which is based on benefits and cost calculations.

3. There is some truth in this kind of approach. For example, the debt or credit accumulation of foreign assets during the process of economic development, an instance of which is the accumulation of current account surplus in recent Japan, can be regarded as the result of the interaction of the saving-investment process and not necessarily the result of the failure of the international monetary regime.
4. A theoretical attempt was made to formulate rigorously the game of rule making as 'metagame' by Howard (1971). However, his analysis is quite complex and I find it extremely difficult to discern some relevant link between his procedure and the issues considered here.
5. This view may reflect my oriental roots. Mushakoji (1967) convincingly argues that while western decision-making is normally based on clearly defined discrete strategies contingent on possible events, oriental decision-making takes the adaptive form by leaving many future options ambiguous as well as undecided.
6. Another reason was, of course, the vulnerability of the adjustable peg regime to speculative attacks, because the regime provided many opportunities for one-sided speculation.
7. Volatility in flexible exchange rates may be inflicting on the economic welfare of private agents. There is a wide research area concerning this question, but I shall not go into it in this paper.

References

1. Aoki, M. (1981) *Dynamic Analysis of Open Economies* (New York: Academic Press).
2. Auman, R. J. (1981) 'Survey of repeated games', in R. J. Auman *et al.*, *Essays in Game Theory* (Manheim: Manheim Bibliographic Institute).
3. Axelrod, R. (1984), *The Evolution of Cooperation*, (New York: Basic Books).
4. Bryant, R. C. (1980) *Money and Monetary Policy in Interdependent Nations* (Washington, DC: Brookings Institution).
5. Buiter, W. H. and Marston, R. C. (eds.) (1985) *International Economic Policy Coordination* (Centre for Economic Policy Research and National Bureau of Economic Research).
6. Canzoneri, M. B. and Gray, J. A. (1985) 'Monetary Policy Games and the Consequences of Non-Cooperative Behaviour', *International Economic Review*, vol. 26, no. 3.
7. Conybeare, J. A. C. (1980) 'International Organization and the theory of Property Rights', *International Organization*, vol. 34, no. 3.
8. Cooper, R. N. (1968) *The Economics of Interdependence* (New York: McGraw-Hill).
9. Cooper, R. N. (1975) 'Prolegomena to the choice of an international monetary system', in C. F. Bergsten and L. B. Krause (eds.) *World Politics and International Economics* (Washington, DC: Brookings Institution).
10. Corden, M. (1983) 'The logic of the international monetary non-system',

in F. Machlup (ed.), *Reflection of a Troubled World Economy* (London: Macmillan).
11. Dam, K. W. (1982) *The Rules of the Game: Reform and Evolution in the International Monetary System* (Chicago: University of Chicago Press).
12. Dornbusch, R. (1976) 'Expectations and exchange rate dynamics', *Journal of Political Economy*, vol. 84.
13. Friedman, J. W. (1986) *Game Theory with Applications to Economics* (Oxford: Oxford University Press).
14. Fukuda, S. and Hamada, K. (1987) 'Towards the implementation of desirable rules of monetary coordination and interventions', in Y. Suzuki and M. Okabe (eds.), *Toward a World of Economic Stability* (Tokyo: University of Tokyo Press).
15. Hamada, K. (1985) *The Political Economy of International Monetary Interdependence* (Mass.: MIT Press).
16. Howard, N. (1971) *Paradox of Rationality: Theory of Metagames and Political Behavior* (Mass.: MIT Press).
17. Keohane, R. O. (1982) 'The demand for international regimes', in S. D. Krasner (ed.), *International Regimes* (Ithaca: Cornell University Press).
18. Keohane, R. O. (1984) *After Hegemony: Cooperation and Discord in the World Political Economy* (Princeton: Princeton University Press).
19. Keynes, J. M. (1947) 'The International Monetary Fund', in S. E. Harris (ed.), *The New Economics: Keynes' Influence on Theory and Public Policy* (New York: A. A. Knopf).
20. Kindleberger, C. P. (1973) *The World in Depression, 1929–1939* (California: University of California Press).
21. Kindleberger, C. P. (1986) 'International public goods without international government', *American Economic Review*, vol. 76.
22. Krasner, S. D. (1982) 'Structural causes and regime consequences: regimes as intervening variables', in S. D. Krasner (ed.), *International Regimes* (Ithaca: Cornell University Press).
23. Krasner, S. D. (ed.) (1982) *International Regimes* (Ithaca: Cornell University Press).
24. Kreps, D. M. and Wilson, R. (1982) 'Reputation and imperfect information', *Journal of Economic Theory*, vol. 27.
25. Kydland, F. E. and Prescott, E. C. (1977) 'Rules rather than discretion: the inconsistency of optimal plans', *Journal of Political Economy*, vol. 85.
26. Luce, D. and Raiffa, F. (1957) *Games and Decisions* (New York; John Wiley).
27. McKinnon, R. I. (1974) 'A tripartite agreement on a limping Dollar standard?', *Essays in International Finance*, no. 106 (Princeton: Princeton University Press).
28. McKinnon, R. I. (1984) 'An International Standard for Monetary Stabilization', *Policy Studies in International Economics*, no. 8 (Washington, DC: Institute for International Economics).
29. Mundell, R. A. (1971), *Monetary Theory: Inflation, Interest, Growth in the World Economy* (California: Goodyear).
30. Mundell, R. A. and Swoboda, A. K. (eds.) (1969) *Monetary Problems of the International Economy* (Chicago: University of Chicago Press).

31. Mushakoji, K. (1967) *Kokusai Seiji to Nihon* (International Politics and Japan) (Tokyo: University of Tokyo Press).
32. Olson, M. Jr. (1965) *The Logic of Collective Action: Public Goods and the Theory of Groups* (Cambridge, Mass.: Harvard University Press).
33. Poole, W. (1970) 'Optimal choice of monetary instruments in a simple stochastic macro model', *Quarterly Journal of Economics*, vol. 84.
34. Puchala, D. J. and Hopkins, R. F. (1982) 'International regime: lessons from inductive analysis', in S. D. Krasner (ed.), *International Regimes* (Ithaca: Cornell University Press).
35. Ruggie, J. G. (1982) 'International regimes, transactions, and change: embeddel liberalism in the postwar economic order', in Kramer (ed.), *International Regimes* (Ithaca: Cornell University Press).
36. Selten, R. (1975) 'Reexamination of the perfectness concept for equilibrium points in extensive games', *International Journal of Game Theory*, vol. 4.
37. Strange, S. (1982) '*Cave! hic dragones*: a critique of regime analysis', in S. D. Krasner (ed.), *International Regimes* (Ithaca: Cornell University Press).
38. Williamson, J. (1983) 'The exchange rate system', *Policy Studies in International Economics*, no. 5 Washington, DC: Institute for International Economics).
39. Young, O. R. (1982) 'Regime dynamics, the rise and fall of international regimes', in S. D. Krasner (ed.), *International Regimes* (Ithaca: Cornell University Press).

21 Savings, Economic Growth and Balance of Payments: A Marxian Case

Yusuke Onitsuka

INTRODUCTION

The purpose of this paper is to examine the patterns of the balance of payments of a growing economy in the case of Marxian saving behaviour. The literature on the patterns of economic growth in conjunction with the development stages of the balance of payments (DSBOP)[1] can be divided into two groups. The first utilizes the optimal growth approach; Hamada (1968), Onitsuka (1970), Bazdarich (1978), Yano (1980) and Akiyama-Onitsuka (1985) belong here. The second is descriptive in nature in that it does not explicitly address the optimality problem; Frenkel-Fischer (1972a; 1972b; 1974), Onitsuka (1974; 1975), Hori-Stein (1977) and Ruffin (1979) belong here. Some of these works show that, if the time preference is low, an open economy is likely to experience six DSBOPs, from a young debtor to a mature creditor, and that it tends to remain a mature creditor if its time preference also remains constant.[2] These contributions, however, do not tackle the case where different classes in an economy have different time preferences or saving ratios.

This paper extends the latter group by analysing the pattern of economic growth and the balance of payments of an open economy where the capitalist class has a high propensity to save but the worker class does not save at all.

THE MODEL

The production technology is characterized by the following production function which is homogeneous of degree one:

$$Q = F(K, L) \qquad (1)$$

where Q is aggregate output and (F) is the well-behaved production function. K and L are, respectively, the capital stock and labour force. One kind of output can be used as both consumption and capital goods. It is assumed that there is no technological progress other than that embodied in new capital stock.

The investment behaviour is of the following nature because of Penrose-type adjusment costs:[3]

$$\frac{I}{K} = \phi(z), \qquad \phi'(z) > 0; \phi''(z) > 0 \qquad (2)$$

where I is total net investment, ϕ is net investment per unit of capital stock, and z is the rate of growth of capital stock or an increase of capital stock per unit of capital stock:

$$z = \frac{dK}{dt}\frac{1}{K} = \frac{\dot{K}}{K} \qquad (3)$$

z has the following properties:

$$z = z(i, r); \qquad z_1 < 0 \quad \text{and} \quad z_2 > 0$$

where i and r, respectively, are the rates of interest and profit. z_1 and z_2 stand, respectively, for the derivative of z with respect to the first and second variables (i and r). Hence one also has $\phi_1 < 0$ and $\phi_2 > 0$, where $\phi_1 = \partial\phi/\partial i$ and $\phi_2 = \partial\phi/\partial r$.

The saving behaviour is expressed by:

$$S = sYc$$

where S, s and Yc are, respectively, aggregate savings, the saving ratio and income of the capitalist class. Yc is defined as the sum of the income arising from the ownership of domestic and foreign securities issued by domestic and foreign firms. The securities are consols or other perpetuity types, and equities and bonds are not distinguishable from each other. The income of the capitalist class can be expressed as:

$$Yc = rK + iB \qquad (4)$$

where r is the marginal product of real capital and B is the net foreign assets or debt. The worker class is assumed to spend all its wage income on consumption. The net capital outflow or current account surplus is expressed as:

$$\frac{d\dot{B}}{dt} = S - I = s(rK + iB) - \phi(i, r)K \tag{5}$$

It is assumed that the open economy is small and its capital market is completely integrated into the international capital market. Therefore, the domestic and international rates of interest are identical.

The labour force is assumed to grow at a constant rate:

$$\frac{dL}{dt} = nL \tag{6}$$

The three dynamic equations that describe the growth paths given by (3), (5) and (6) can be reduced to two equations, (7) and (8), by introducing per-capita variables. Let k and b, respectively, be per capita capital stock ($k = K/L$) and net foreign assets ($b = B/L$). Noting that $\dot{B}/L = \dot{b} + nb$, where $\dot{B}$ and $\dot{b}$ are, respectively, dB/dt and db/dt, one gets:

$$\dot{b} = (si - n)b + srk - \phi(z)k \tag{7}$$

$$\dot{k} = z(i, r)k \tag{8}$$

Let θ be the share of profits in total output, i.e. $\theta = rk/f(k)$, where $f(k) = F(k, 1)$. Then equation (7) can be rewritten as:

$$\dot{b} = (si - n)b + s\theta f(k) - \phi(z)k \tag{7'}$$

From now on, discussion is confined to the case where θ is constant.

In order to examine growth paths it is useful to draw phase diagrams. The $\dot{b} = 0$ curve in Figure 21.1 stands for the locus of a point (k, b) that makes the RHS of (7′) equal to zero. Likewise, the $\dot{k} = 0$ line stands for the stationary state where k is not growing. The $\dot{b} = 0$ curve is expressed by:

$$(b)_{\dot{b}=0} = -\frac{\theta f(k)}{si - n}\left(s - \frac{a}{\theta}\right) \tag{9}$$

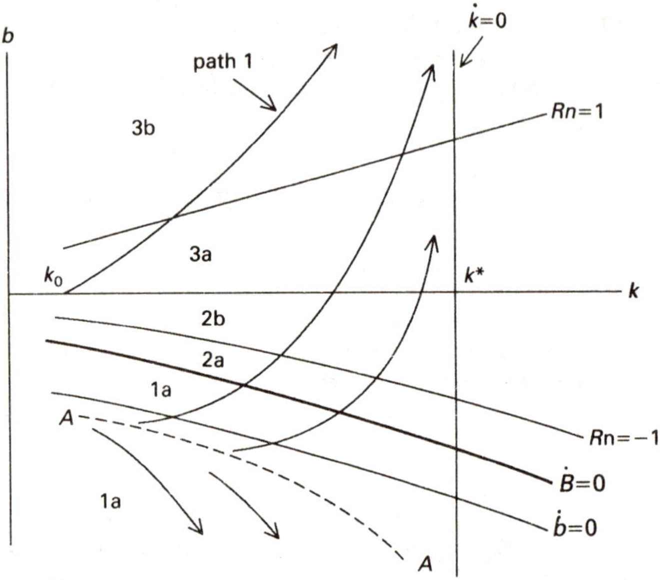

Figure 21.1

where a is the investment–output ratio, i.e. $a = \theta k/f(k)$. The slope of the $\dot{b} = 0$ curve is:

$$\left(\frac{db}{dk}\right)_{\dot{b}=0} = -\frac{\theta r}{si - n}\left[s - \frac{a}{\theta} - \frac{\phi}{\theta r}(1 - \varepsilon_{\theta,k} - \theta)\right] \qquad (10)$$

where r equals $f'(k)$ and $\varepsilon_{\theta,k}$ is the elasticity of investment with respect to k, i.e. $\varepsilon_{\phi,k} = (\partial\phi/\partial k)(k/\phi))$.

The basic characteristics of the growth paths crucially depend on the relative magnitudes of the saving ratios. The movement of b is unstable if the saving ratio is sufficiently high, i.e. $si - n > 0$ and stable if $si - n < 0$, as is indicated by (7). The sequence of DSBOP along the growth path also depends on such parameters or variables as a, θ and $\varepsilon_{\theta,k}$ – see (9) and (10). Here, analysis is confined to the high saving case $si - n > 0$, which can be divided into three subcases.[4]

HIGH SAVING RATIO: CASE 1

If s is greater than a/θ, and $a(k)$ decreases as k grows for all k, one has the growth paths shown in Figure 21.1. If $a(k)$ increases at the early

Table 21.1 Economic growth and the balance of payments

Major four DSBOPs	*Stage 4* capital-importer–creditor (CIC) $(B < 0, B > 0)$		*Stage 1* capital-importer–debtor (CID) $(B < 0, B < 0)$		*Stage 2* capital-exporter–debtor (CED) $(B < 0, B < 0)$		*Stage 3* capital-exporter–creditor (CEC) $(B < 0, B > 0)$	
eight sub-DSBOPs	*4a* immature CIC $iB > \lvert\dot{B}\rvert$	*4b* mature CIC $iB < \lvert\dot{B}\rvert$	*1a* immature CID $\lvert iB\rvert > \lvert\dot{B}\rvert$	*1b* mature CID $\lvert iB\rvert > \lvert\dot{B}\rvert$	*2a* immature CED $\lvert iB\rvert > \dot{B}$	*2b* mature CED $\lvert iB\rvert < \dot{B}$	*3a* immature CEC $iB < \dot{B}$	*3b* mature CEC $iB > \dot{B}$
A TA	deficit (X − M < 0)				surplus (X − M > 0)		deficit (X − M < 0)	
B SA	surplus $(iB > 0)$		deficit $(iB > 0)$				surplus $(iB > 0)$	
C CA (A + B)	deficit $(X - M_1 + iB < 0)$				surplus $(X - M + iB > 0)$			
D CaA	surplus $(B < 0)$				deficit $(B > 0)$			
E BP (C + D)	equilibrium $(X - M + iB - B = 0)$				equilibrium $(X - M + iB - B = 0)$			

Notes:
X = exports; M = imports; TA = trade account; SA = services account; CA = current account; CaA = capital account and BP = balance of payments.

stages, the $\dot{b} = 0$ curve can have a positive slope; in Figure 21.1 it lies entirely below the k axis while per capita net foreign asset is increasing above the k axis and decreasing below it.

Let me specify those curves that partition the (k, b) plane into various DSBOPs. Along the $\dot{B} = 0$ curve, the current account is in balance or net capital flows are zero. On the $Rn = 1$ curve, net capital exports (imports) equal interest receipts (payments); $Rn = \dot{B}/iB$. The $Rn = -1$ curve is the locus of (k, b) on which capital exports (imports) equal interest payments (receipts). These curves are summarized in Figures 21.1, 21.2 and 21.4, and the characterization of their development stages is summarized in the Table 21.1 (11)–(13) provide their exact specification:

$$\dot{B} = 0 \text{ curve} \qquad b = -\frac{\theta f(k)}{si}\left(s - \frac{a}{\theta}\right) \tag{11}$$

$$Rn = 1 \text{ curve} \qquad b = -\frac{\theta f(k)}{(1 - s)i + n}\left(s - \frac{a}{\theta}\right) \tag{12}$$

$$Rn = 1 \text{ curve} \qquad b = -\frac{\theta f(k)}{(1-s)i+n}\left(s - \frac{a}{\theta}\right) \qquad (13)$$

Let me consider a developing economy that is closed initially, then opens up by internationalizing its capital market. The typical growth path of this economy is path 1. Due to its high saving ratio, it becomes a capital exporter as soon as it opens its capital market. Note that $\dot{B} > 0$ at k_0. The economy goes through two sub-DSBOPs, immature capital exporter-creditor (DSBOP 3*a*) and mature capital exporter-creditor (stage 3b) In stage 3*b*, which is often called the 'mature creditor stage', interest receipts exceed capital exports, and capital exports and net foreign assets keep on growing forever.[5]

HIGH SAVING RATIO: CASE 2

If the saving ratio is smaller, and provided that $s < a(k)/\theta$ holds for $k < \hat{k}$ and $s > a(k)/\theta$ for $k^* > k > \hat{k}$, the growth paths will look quite different. They are depicted in Figure 21.2, which is drawn on the assumption that $a'(k) < 0$ for all $k < k^*$. $\hat{k}$ is the value of k that

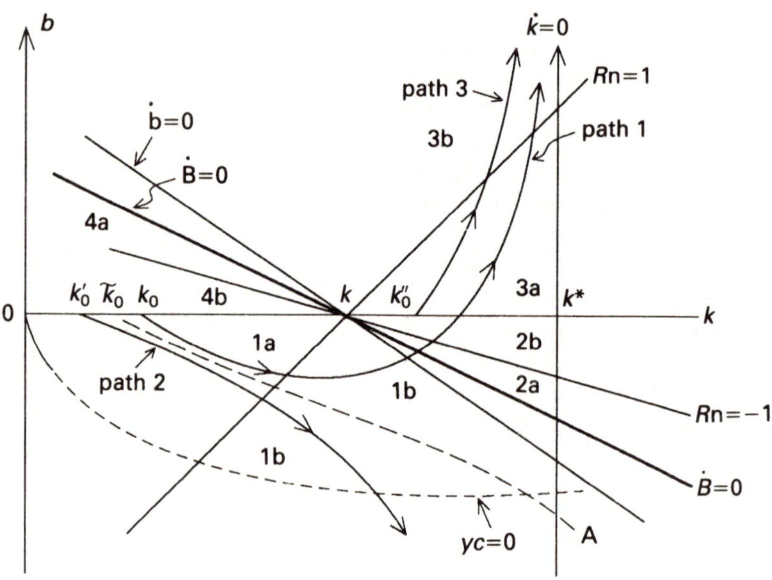

Figure 21.2

makes $a(k)/\theta$ equal s, and k^* is the value of k at the stationary state, i.e. $z(i, r(k^*)) = n$. The representative path (path 1) goes through six DSBOPs, as the theory suggests. Note that this pattern is identical with the high saving ratio case derived from a model that does not distinguish one class from the other (Onitsuka 1974). When the initial condition for k is as large as k_0'', the sequence for the stages is the same as that of path 1 in Figure 21.1.

However, if the initial condition of k is as low as k_0', which is lower than a critical value ($\tilde{k}_0$), the economy starts as a capital importer–debtor (stage 1) and remains one forever, although it does experience two sub-DSBOPs, 1*a*, and 1*b*. This case is indicated by path 2. When the economy reaches the $y = 0$ curve on which the income of the two classes becomes zero ($Y = Q + iB = 0$), capitalist consumption becomes negative. The two classes have to change their consumption habits before the economy reaches the $y = 0$ curve. When the two classes have the same saving ratio, a growth path like path 2 will not exist (Onitsuka 1974). The broken curve $\tilde{k}_0A$ indicates the area of the initial conditions (k_0, b_0) that led the economy into infinite indebtedness.

HIGH SAVING RATIO: CASE 3

Next, consider the case where the investment–output ratio (a) rises from a low level up to a certain k and then declines over time. This particular behaviour of a is witnessed in the history of the economic development of Japan. Most other Asian economies, including Korea, have also shown a rising tendency in the investment–output ratio. The movement of a and its relation to the saving ratio are shown in Figure 21.3.

The corresponding pattern of DSBOP is depicted in Figure 21.4. Path 1 indicates that the economy initially becomes a capital exporter–creditor (stage 3), then moves to that of a capital importer–creditor (stage 4). After reaching stage 4, it goes through six sub-DSBOPs, as suggested by the theory. In other words, after the capital market is internationalized, it experiences ten sub-DSBOPs during its entire process of economic development. These sub-stages are: 3*a*, 3*b*, 4*a*, 4*b*, 1*a*, 1*b*, 2*a*, 2*b*, 3*a*, 3*b*. It is interesting to note that the above sequence does not only consist of the full sequence of the eight stages from 1*a* to 4*b*, but also includes a reversal of the order from 4 and 1 and a partial repetition of stage 3.

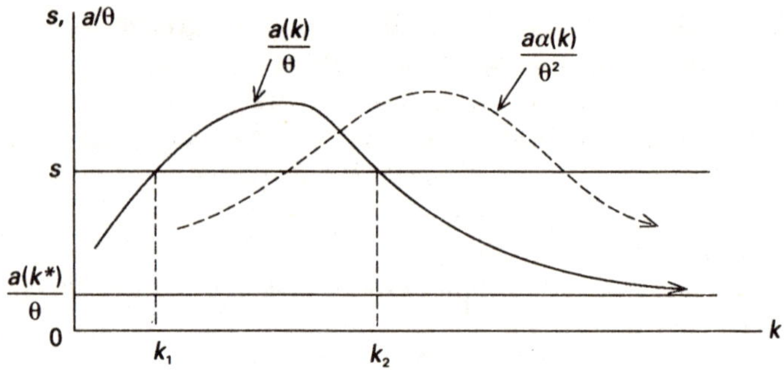

Figure 21.3

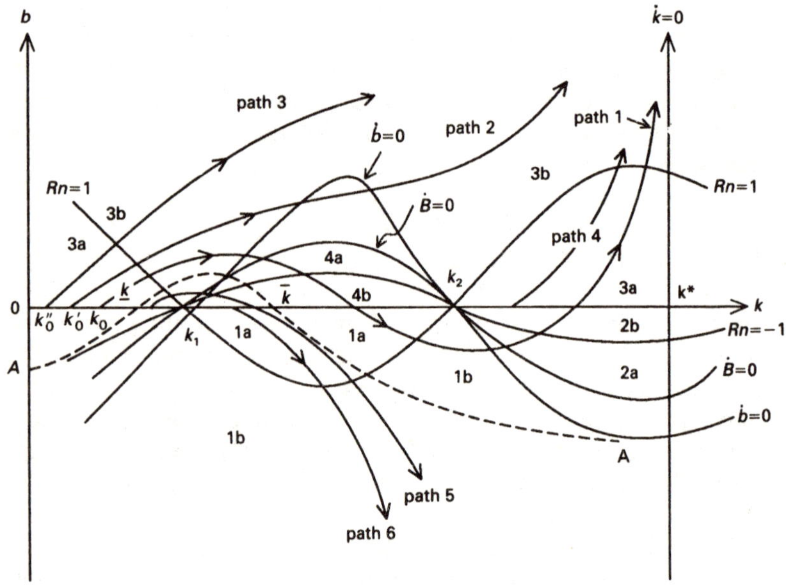

Figure 21.4

If the initial condition is lower than k_0 (say, k_0'), i.e. like path 2, the sequence of DSBOP is:[6] 3*a*, 3*b*, 4*a*, (4*b*), (3*a*) and 3*b*. The characteristic of path 2 is that it always remains in the stages of a creditor, although it can shift to the stages of capital importer temporarily. If the initial condition is still lower than k_0' (say, k_0''), the economy starts as a capital exporter–creditor (stage 3) and remains one forever. This case is identical with the high saving ratio case 1 above. When the initial condition is higher than a certain critical level (k), but less than k_1, the DSBOP sequence becomes 3*a*, 3*b*, 4*a*, 4*b*, 1*a* and 1*b* (see path 5). For the initial condition of k that is larger than k_1, but less than k, the growth path remains in the DSBOP of capital importer–debtor (1*a* and 1*b*). The broken curve $A\underline{k}\bar{k}A$ partitions the (k, b) plane into two areas; an economy with an initial condition (k_0, b_0) in the area below this curve always ends up in a capital importer–debtor position, although it may become a capital exporter–creditor during the early stages (paths 5 and 6).

CONCLUSION

Under the assumption that only the capitalist class saves a large proportion of its income, the patterns of economic growth and balance of payments are often similar to those of an economy where both the worker and capitalist classes have the same high saving ratios ($s > n/i$). There is, however, an important difference. An open economy may become a capital exporter-creditor as soon as its capital market is integrated into the world capital market, and may not experience the stages of capital importer-debtor at all. Moreover, it can experience as many as ten sub-DSBOPs that consist of capital exporter-creditor (stage 3) and capital importer–creditor (stage 4), followed by the full sequence of the classical pattern described by the conventional theory of DSBOP (stages 1, 2 and 3). This pattern also indicates that a partial reversal and repetition of stages can occur, provided the investment–output ratio initially rises before it starts falling. This may suggest some clues for a partial resolving of the anomalous sequences of DSBOP that have been observed in the history of many countries other than the USA and UK.

Notes

1. For a textbook description of the theory of DSBOP, see Samuelson (1970) and Kindleberger (1968). For an empirical discussion, see Crowther (1957) and Kindleberger (1985).
2. See Onitsuka (1970; 1974; 1975), Bazderich (1978), Akiyama-Onitsuka (1985) and Blanchard (1986).
3. See Lucas (1967) and Uzawa (1969) for this type of adjustments costs.
4. For the case where $si - n < 0$ holds but the two classes have the same

saving ratios, see Frenkel-Fischer (1972a;b and 1974) and Onitsuka (1974; 1975).

5. As (7) indicates, the growth rate of per capita net foreign assets converges $si - n$, which is positive. This implies that the economy will eventually become a large one that holds the greater part of bonds issued in the world in the long run. I confine my analysis to the case where the economy is infinitestimally small at the beginning, and the population growth rate and the saving ratio are such that $si - n$ is very small. The present analysis is an approximation of a high saver that is valid up to a certain level of economic development, including that of the early part of stage 3*b*.
6. The numbers of the stages in parentheses indicate those stages that may be skipped along the path.

References

1. Akiyama, T. and Onitsuka (1985) 'Current account, capital export and the optimal patterns of development stages of balance of payments', *Discussion Paper*, no. 85–7 (Yokohama: Yokohama National University, Japan).
2. Bazdarich, M. J. (1978) 'Optimal growth and stages in the balance of payments', *Journal of International Economics*, vol. 8.
3. Blanchard, O. J. (1986) 'Debt, deficits and finite zones', *Journal of Political Economy*, vol. 93.
4. Crowther, G. H. (1959) *Balance and Imbalance of Payments* (New Haven: Harvard University Press).
5. Fischer, S. and Frenkel, J. (1972a) 'Investment, the two-sector model, and trade in debt and capital goods', *Journal of International Economics*, vol. 2.
6. Fischer, S. and Frenkel, J. (1972b) 'International capital movements along balanced growth paths: comments and extensions', *Economic Record*, vol. 48.
7. Fischer, S. and Frenkel, J. (1974) 'Economic growth and the stages of the balance of payments', in G. Horwith and P. Samuelson (eds.), *Trade, Stability, and Macroeconomics* (New York: Academic Press).
8. Hamada, K. (1966) 'Economic growth and long-term capital movements', *Yale Economic Essays*, no. 6 (New Haven: Yale University).
9. Kindleberger, C. P. (1968) *International Economics* (Homewood, Ill.: Irwin).
10. Kindleberger, C. P. (1985) *International Capital Movements* (Cambridge: Cambridge University Press).
11. Lucas, R. E. (1967) 'Optimal investment policy and the flexible accelerator', *International Economic Review*, vol. 13.
12. Onitsuka, Y. (1970) *International Capital Movements and Patterns of Economic Growth*, unpublished doctoral dissertation, (Chicago: University of Chicago Press).
13. Onitsuka, Y. (1974) 'International capital movements and the patterns of economic growth', *American Economic Review*, vol. 64.

14. Onitsuka, Y. (1975) 'International capital movements, economic growth and the patterns of trade and balance of payments: an extension', *Osaka Economic Papers*, vol. 25.
15. Ruffin, R. J. (1979) 'Growth and the long-run theory of international capital movements', *American Economic Review*, vol. 69.
16. Samuelson, P. A. (1970) *Economics* (New York: McGraw-Hill).
17. Uzawa, H. (1969) 'Time preference and the Penrose Effect in a two-class model of economic growth', *Journal of Political Economy*, vol. 77.
18. Yano, M. (1984) 'Statics and dynamics of trade and balance of payments: a perfect foresight approach', an unpublished paper (Department of Economics: Cornell University).

22 Factor Migration, Trade and Welfare under the Threat of Commercial Policy

Martin C. McGuire*

INTRODUCTION

It has become a common place to observe that economic interdependence among countries has dramatically increased due to the deepening integration of the world economy. The hope is no less common that ensuing economic cooperation among the states of the world might lead to decreasing hostility and conflict. Economic cooperation may take a variety of forms with diverse benefits therefrom and different distributions among participants, and realistically, any agreement to cooperate whether explicit an implicit may break down exposing participants to risks and costs they otherwise would not have borne. These costs will also vary with the form of economic cooperation between nations and prudence will require that any state contemplating a step toward closer economic relations carefully weigh these costs as well as the benefits. The implications of economic cooperation among countries would be better understood, therefore, if we examine the implications of the fact that there are risks that cooperation will fail over the entire spectrum of possible economic relations. At one end of this range lies complete isolation and autarky at the other, complete economic-political unification. Between these extremes, cooperation begins with limited trade in commodities, shades into restricted then free commodity trade, followed by preferential trading agreements, then free trade areas and customs unions, and finally exchange of factors of production including direct foreign investment and labour migration.

Some may disagree as to the ordering of each of these steps from isolation to complete integration – e.g. whether exchange of factors of production should be considered the last step before complete integration or not. However, most would agree that as one proceeds along such a spectrum both the net economic benefits to a cooperating region increase, as well as that the exposure to risk of breakdown in cooperation and the costly consequences of such a breakdown also increase. The purpose of this paper is to lay out certain initial considerations relevant to comparison of the benefits from two general types of cooperation between states versus the costs of a breakdown in such cooperation. The two classes of economic interaction to be compared are trade in commodities on the one hand, and exchange in migration of factors of production on the other.

One of the consequences of international conflict is frequently the disruption of trade among trading partners, or between such partners and the rest of the world. Such losses need not be altogether regrettable if they deter or reduce the frequency of conflict (as there is some evidence to suggest they do – see Polachek 1985). Conflict can cut off or truncate trade between adversaries or among innocent bystanders. It has been recognized at least since the time of Adam Smith that protective measures of trade control taken before trade disruption can limit a country's losses from an autarky imposed by war. Such protectionism may constitute justifiable restriction on free trade.

Smith laboured without the benefit of the factor price equalization (FPE) theorem, however, without knowledge of the one–one correspondence between goods price equalization (GPE) and FPE, and therefore without awareness of the perfect equivalence between factor movements and goods movements across national boundaries in a Heckscher-Ohlin (HO) world. This equivalence, first spelled out by Mundell (1957), has played an important role in modern analyses of the effects of protectionism, of discrimination, and of imperfect competition on the movement of capital, labour or other factors of production across boundaries. This paper begins to merge these two lines of thought to compare the effects factor migration and commodity trade in an *uncertain* world subject to trade disruption.

CLASSICAL PROTECTIONISM IN AN HO MODEL

The classical argument for protection is readily incorporated into a HO trade context with the assumption that factors of production are completely immobile in the short run, both between industries and between countries. Figure 22.1 shows a country's long run production possibilities with a fixed factor endowment as *TT*. With world prices *p*

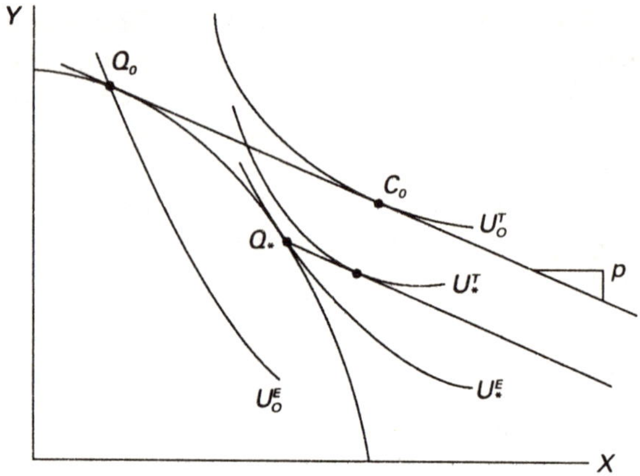

Figure 22.1

and no risk of trade disruption, this country should produce at Q_O and consume at C_O, concentrating in production of Y which it then exports. Now assume trade is disrupted; for simplicity, assume it is totally curtailed. Having locked its productive factors in at Q_O in the short run, the country must also consume at Q_O. Thus, if the likelihood of trade disruption is, say, $(1 - \pi)$, then *ex ante* the subject country will enjoy utility level U_O^T during peace or free trade with probability π and U_O^E during emergency with probability $(1 - \pi)$. Its *ex ante* expected utility becomes

$$E(U) = \pi U_O^T + (1 - \pi)U_O^E \tag{1}$$

Now through trade restriction of one sort or another such a country might control the pre-emergency allocation of resources so as to discourage the degree of specialization beneficial under certain free trade. Such control might proceed all the way to maximization of utility under pure autarky by restricting production to point Q_*. Then utility if trade is disrupted becomes U_*^E and if trade is allowed U_*^T, with expected utility:

$$E(U) = \pi U_*^T + (1 - \pi)U_*^E \tag{2}$$

It is notable that U_*^T cannot be achieved in the pre-emergency trading situation unless domestic production is subsidized. A tariff or quota alone will choke peacetime consumption down to U_*^E – an outcome approximately observed in autarkic socialist economies. The two pairs of outcomes just identified as $U^j_K(j = T, E; k = 0, *)$ are merely two points on a continuum. For a fixed probability some intermediate restrictions on free trade specialization may be optimal. In the two good small country case, suppose the world terms of trade between X and Y were given by p, and the small country transformation function by $Y = F(X)$. Then assuming Y is exported and X imported, maximization of expected utility is derived from:

$$E(U) = \pi U[\{X + M\}, \{F(X) - pM\}] + (1 - \pi)U[X, F(X)] \quad (3)$$

where M represents imports of X and pM represents exports of Y. The results are:

$$\frac{U_x^T}{U_y^T} = p \quad (4)$$

(i.e. MRS = world price in a trading world)

$$\frac{dF}{dx} = \frac{\pi U_x^T + (1 - \pi)U_x^E}{\pi U_y^T + (1 - \pi)U_y^E} \quad (5)$$

(i.e MRT = 'probability weighted average' of free trade and emergency MRS).

This result can be visualized easily with supply–demand curves as in Figure 22.2, showing the situation for import good X. In the absence of trade restriction with no disruption to trade, X_O^P is produced, X_O^C consumed, and the difference imported, while X_O^P is both produced and consumed if trade is discontinued. As a result of trade stoppage consumer surplus in the amount of areas 3 to 7 is lost. Now suppose government interference takes the form of a subsidy, σ, to producers of X, then: production increases to X_*^P, peace time consumption remains at X_O^C, and area 5 is lost from producer surplus in peace but areas 3 and 4 are gained when an emergency comes up. Since the marginal subjective valuation MRS^T arises with likelihood π and MRS^E with likelihood $(1 - \pi)$ the optimum value of σ and therefore supply price $F_x = dF/dX$, occurs where F_x equals the probability weighted average $\pi MRS^T + (1 - \pi)MRS^E$, assuming constant marginal utility $U_y^T = U_x^T$ for illustration. Table 22.1 gives a summary of these outcomes.

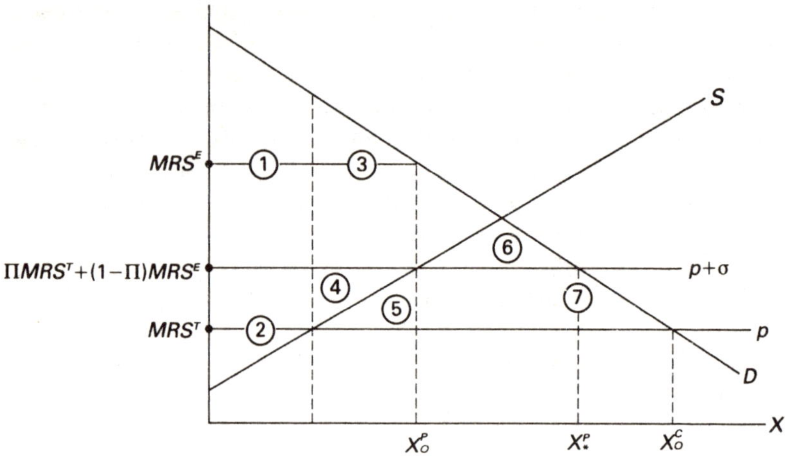

Figure 22.2

Table 22.1 Producer/consumer surplus outcomes

		State of the world	
		Emergency autarky	*Peace and free trade*
Policy chosen	No trade restrictions	1,2	1,2,3,4,5,6,7
	Welfare-maximizing trade restriction	1,2,3,4	1,2,3,4, ,6,7
	Gain/loss from optimum policy	$(3+4) \times (1-\pi)$	$-5 \times \pi$

One advantageous feature of this supply–demand presentation is to clarify how gains and losses from trade impairment can actually be measured as areas under supply–demand curves. Estimates of supply and demand schedules for exports and imports are all that is needed to determine how gains and losses depend on the probability of disruption. For each of various guesses as to the likelihood of trade disruption, an optimal trade restriction can then be identified.

FACTOR MIGRATION

Every country espouses an objective of national self-sufficiency at least to a degree adequate to national survival. Accordingly, all countries take some measures to limit their vulnerability to trade disruption. Among the alternatives to tariffs or subsidies, etc., for controlling the degree of specialization must be counted preferential trading agreements and customs unions on the international front, and stockpiling, emergency planning or stand-by production base capacities on the domestic front. An important extension of the national defence argument for protection must include these alternatives to protection. Another instrument for influencing a country's vulnerability to trade disruption would seem to be capital/labour migration or movements of other factors into and out of the home country. Although analyses of factor movements have appeared with increasing popularity of late, these all have been with reference to free trade or second best restricted trade conditions – and not the war–peace dichotomy which forms the texture of this paper.

For purposes of the analysis of factor migration as it relates to national self-sufficiency and defense, one theorem of importance is that in a world governed by HO assumptions a country can protect itself completely from the costs of trade disruption by infinitely many alternative changes in its stock of factors of production. Such changes in labour or capital will come about by in-migration or out-migration. Figure 22.3 shows the relationships between (1) the Edgeworth box of factor of production endowments, contract curves, and relative wages and (2) product transformation curves in an HO world. With world price 'p' for each value of capital K_i alternative values of L generate a Rybczinski-line R_i^L in product space $X - Y$. One such line, R_I^L, is labelled in Figure 22.3b and the set of product transformation curves it identifies is included. Movement along R_I^L to the south-east designates production points consistent with increasing immigrations of labour given p. Figure 22.3c shows two entire families of Rybczinski lines, R_i^L and R_j^K, where the latter group refers to effects of variations in the capital stock when labour is held constant at L_j. The orientation of R_i^L and R_j^K derives from the assumption that good X is relatively labour-intensive and good Y is relatively capital intensive irrespective of overall economywide proportions of labour and capital. Panel 3c also adds the income expansion path between goods X and Y for a given p. This income expansion path will intersect successively with new combinations of R_i^L and R_j^L. Each corresponding combination of K_i and K_j indicates a different set of factor endowments which would completely insulate the small country in question from potential disruption of trade embargos. Thus, Figure 22.3 demonstrates that through factor migration (immigration or emmigration) a country can completely protect itself from trade

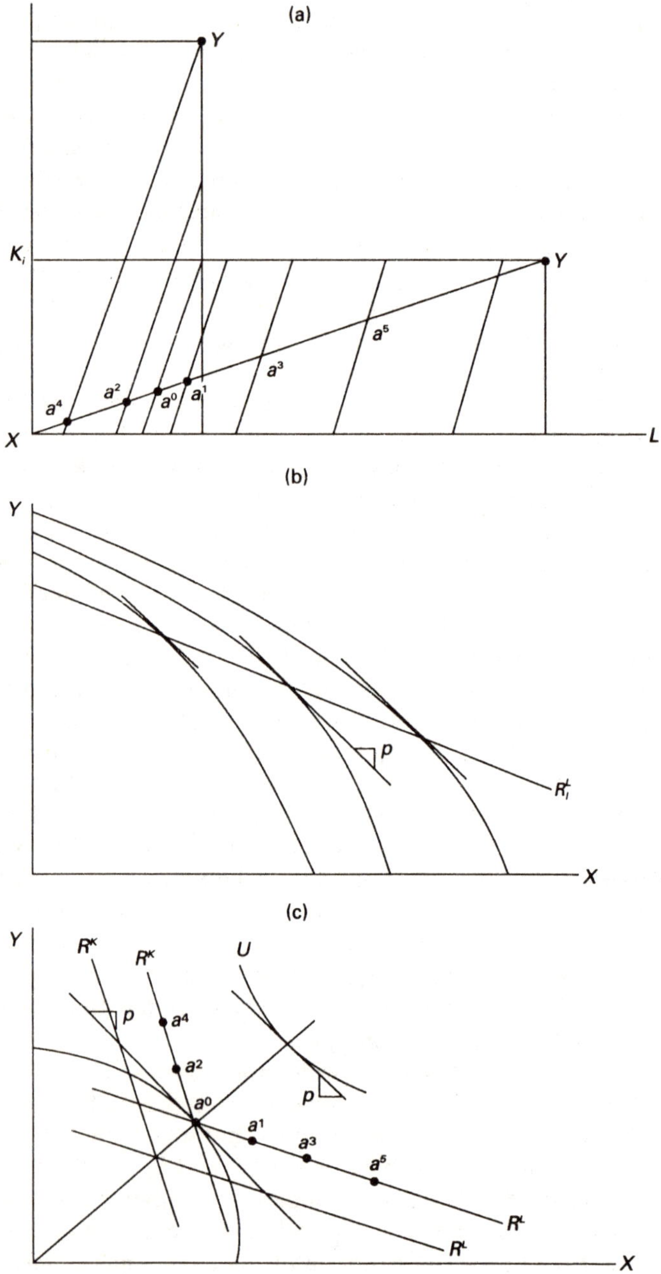
(a)
Y
K_i
Y
a^5
a^3
a^2
a^0
a^1
a^4
X
L
(b)
Y
p
R_i^L
X
(c)
Y
R^K
R^K
U
p
a^4
a^2
a^0
p
a^1
a^3
a^5
R^L
R^L
X

Figure 22.3

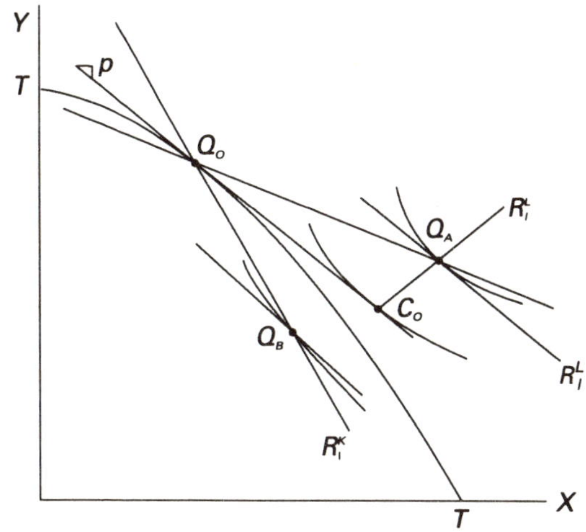

Figure 22.4

disruption. (This proposition is valid only under the stringent assumptions of the HO model.) Figure 22.4 continues the argument with an example of a small country with indigenous factor endowment (L_l, K_l), and a set of demands such that it would produce Q_O but consume at C_O importing X and exporting Y. This country can achieve complete autarky and therefore insulate itself totally from trade disruption either by importing labour or by exporting capital. Labour imports move it along R_l^L until, at point Q_A, demands for all products can be produced at home. Capital export shrinks the economy along R_l^K until, at Q_B again, all 'domestic' demand is met from domestic production. These alternatives are perfect substitutes due to the equivalence between imports of L or exports of K and exports of X or imports of Y; or similarly due to the equivalence between imports of K or exports of L and exports of Y or imports of X.

Thus, one is driven to the conclusion that factor migration can protect a country completely from the losses which would arise when its trade is disrupted without causing any offsetting loss under peace time free trade. If this is true, why do we see so little migration of labour and exchange of capital relative to huge trade volumes – trade which is subject to disruption with familiar consequences of economic upheaval? Part of the answer to this question is that the conclusion (viz. that factor migration can insulate a country from losses due to trade disruption) is valid only under the assumption that factor migration is *welfare-neutral* for the migrating factor and for the society of origin or destination as well. But this may be a fallacious assumption. Thus, in Figure 22.4 the conclusion that in-migration of L insulates the country from disruption just as would out-migration of K only follows if the home country 'natives' are indifferent as to where their capital produces and consumes and are indifferent whether they live-work-consume at home or with foreigners abroad. However, a country may not be indifferent about where 'its' citizens work, live, consume, and locate capital. Similarly, a country and its government may not be indifferent when foreign capital or foreign nationals enter its borders even if such entry reduced vulnerability to trade stoppage. In this case, factor migration and goods trade may be equivalent only if taxed or subsidized, or not at all. In more technical terms, there may be *public good* considerations affecting the utility of migrant labour in both the country of origin and of destination or there may be *externalities* transmitted or received by visiting labour. Along another dimension, when factors migrate across countries *irreversibilities* may be anticipated; that is, extracting capital or workfore from a foreign location, whether under peacetime normal conditions or more especially under emergency or war conditions may be difficult to impossible. In the latter case, capital may be expropriated, workers and their assets seized, and in the extreme, held hostage. Still another explanation for limits on capital/labour migration short of the prediction of an HO model may be that the model itself is inaccurate in its assumptions. Thus, decreasing returns to scale may limit factor migration or diverse, specific, immobile factors may contribute to production in different countries causing an ultimate decline in marginal returns to mobile factors. Furthermore, the HO model may be inaccurate in its assumptions of competitive organization, of full information, of free mobility of factors of production, or of exhaustively and appropriately defined property rights.

As a beginning to deal with these possibilities, we can now extend our model of the expected utility maximizing national security argument for protection, to analyze the case for autarky inducing factor movements. Again, we make the initial assumption that good X is imported and Y exported by a small country facing a world price of p, in a HO framework. With indigineous endowments of labour $\bar{L}$ and capital $\bar{K}$, the country will allocate these factors among industries so that the wage rate w and rental rate r of capital are equalized across countries at levels which depend on world factor prices. Now suppose we introduce the possibility that capital may enter or exit from this country in an amount $\hat{K}$. $\hat{K}$ is measured positively for foreign capital inflows and negatively for capital outflows so that the entire capital stock of the country becomes, $K_T = \bar{K} + \hat{K}$. If capital flows in, output of the capital intensive industry (assume to be X) will increase, and of the labour intensive industry will decrease. Here one might assume that this capital inflow, K, if positive, all becomes located in industry X. Our assumption, however, will be that any inflow of capital is uniformly mixed with the pre-existing capital and is divided among industries in the same proportions as domestic capital. Evidently, how the in-migrating capital is intermingled with existing domestic capital (which is native to the recipient country) may influence whether foreign capital can be identified and its return taxed adversely or in the extreme confiscated altogether. Here, we are choosing an assumption that domestic and foreign capital are as thoroughly mixed – and therefore probably as indistinguishable – as possible.

If capital is allowed to immigrate, the receiving country's total product increases in value from $w\bar{L} + r\bar{K}$ to $w\bar{L} + r\bar{K} + r\hat{K}$. The amount of that product available for home consumption becomes $w\bar{L} + r\bar{K} + t\hat{K}$ allowing for the possibility that entry of foreign capital imposes an extra cost of t per unit, a cost which we assume is diffused throughout the domestic society. (If capital immigration generated an extra external benefit, then t would be negative.) The domestic share, s, of total product then becomes:

$$s = \frac{w\bar{L} + r\bar{K} - t\hat{K}}{w\bar{L} + r\bar{K} + t\hat{K}} \tag{6}$$

The amounts of goods X and Y produced depend simply on factor allocations:

$$X = f(L_x, K_y); \quad Y = (L_x, K_y) \tag{7}$$

subject to factor limits

$$L_x + L_y = \bar{L}, \tag{8}$$

$$K_x + K_y = \bar{K} + \hat{K} \tag{9}$$

But these amounts are not all available to the native citizenry to consume or trade. Instead, we assume sX and sY are available. These amounts can be traded in world markets at terms of trade, given by p.

With the model now set up, we can explore the interaction between factor movement and trade in commodities under several scenarios.

OPTIMUM IMMIGRATION: NO RISK OF TRADE DISRUPTION

In a world of complete certainty, the policy problem of choosing a level of factor migration which maximizes domestic national welfare then becomes:

$$\text{Maximize } U[(sX + M), (sY - pM)] \qquad (10)$$
$$\{M, s(\hat{K}), X(\hat{K}), Y(\hat{K})\}$$

The generic solution requires

$$p = \frac{U_x}{U_y} = \frac{\phi_L}{f_L} = \frac{\phi_K}{f_K} \qquad (11)$$

and

$$(pX + Y)\frac{ds}{d\hat{K}} = -rs \qquad (12)$$

as first order conditions. Interpretation of the first is one of straightforwad efficiency in production and exchange. The second condition requires that capital be imported or exported until marginal diversion of total product to foreign immigrant capital equal the average domestic capture of capital product. In this case of no uncertainty and no risk of trade disruption, the optimal capital import or export, $\hat{K}^{opt}$, depends crucially on the value of t, the externality parameter in (6). For $t = 0$, (12) solves identically, indicating that, provided the chance of trade disruption is zero, any value of $\hat{K}$ is as good as any other since commodity trade can substitute perfectly for goods trade. For $t > 0$, $\hat{K}^{opt} = -\infty$ for $t < 0$, $K^{opt} = +\infty$. A determinate, interior solution – indicating that some definite amount of capital is most preferred (i.e. national welfare maximizing) – requires a non-linear externality term in the sharing function of (7). Thus, if t instead of a parameter were itself related to $\hat{K}$ – say $t = a\hat{K}$ to signify an increasing quadratic external cost imposed by the immigrating factor in the recipient society – an interior, determinant amount of capital in-migration could be shown to be optimal.

CAPITAL MIGRATION UNDER RISK OF AUTARKY

The maximand in the above problem assumes a riskless outcome. We can incorporate risk in the model as in the analysis of free trade restrictions by assuming a known chance $(1 - \pi)$ of trade disruption. Then, expected utility becomes:

$$E(U) = \pi U[(sX + M), (sY - pM)] + (1 - \pi)U[sX, sY] \quad (13)$$

with the constraints the same as in the riskless case. This maximand represents a hazard that trade will be disrupted and the country forced into autarky.

A crucial feature of these trade disruption scenarios, which might be modelled in diverse ways, concerns the status of the foreign, imported factors of production once trade stops. This status is reflected in the form of $(1 - \pi)U[C_x, C_y]$ where C_x and C_y denote domestic native consumption opportunities once trade is curtailed. Various alternative dispositions which might arise include

$$C_x = sX; \quad C_y = sY \quad (14)$$

which would indicate that foreign factor owners maintain all their claims on production during war or emergency just the same as in peace. As an alternative we might write

$$C_x = X; \quad C_y = sY \quad (15)$$

to indicate that all foreign assets (including workers) are siezed (workers drafted) along with their production. Still another alternative is:

$$C_x = f[L_x, (\frac{\bar{K}}{\bar{\bar{K}} + \hat{K}} K_x)]; \quad C_y = \phi[Y_y, (\frac{\bar{K}}{\bar{\bar{K}} + \hat{K}} K_y)] \quad (16)$$

Foreign capital (or workers as the case might be) is repatriated and

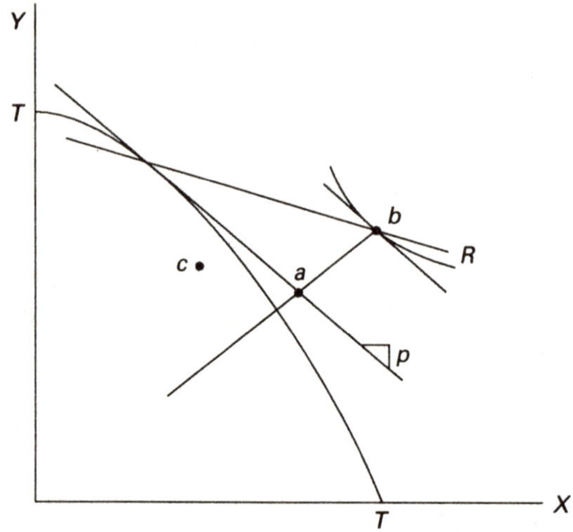

Figure 22.5

factor inputs in domestic production are proportionately reduced. These possible production outcomes are illustrated as points *a*, *b* and *c* in Figure 22.5.

As a case in point, assume that foreign factor owners are not discriminated against in the event of trade disruption (i.e. (14) above), then the relevant objective function becomes:

$$E(U) = \pi U[sX + M), (sY - pM)] + (1 - \pi)U[sX, sY] \quad (17)$$

with the same set of constraints as in the risk free scenario. First order conditions for a welfare maximum are

$$\frac{U_x^T}{U_y^T} = p; \quad \frac{U_x^T + \frac{1-\pi}{\pi}U_x^E}{U_y^T + \frac{1-\pi}{\pi}U_y^E} = \frac{\phi_L}{f_L} = \frac{\phi_K}{f_K} \quad (18)$$

These first-order conditions imply that when entry of foreign capital generates non externality (positive or negative) migration should proceed until it just substitutes for trade such that all loss from trade disruption is eliminated and:

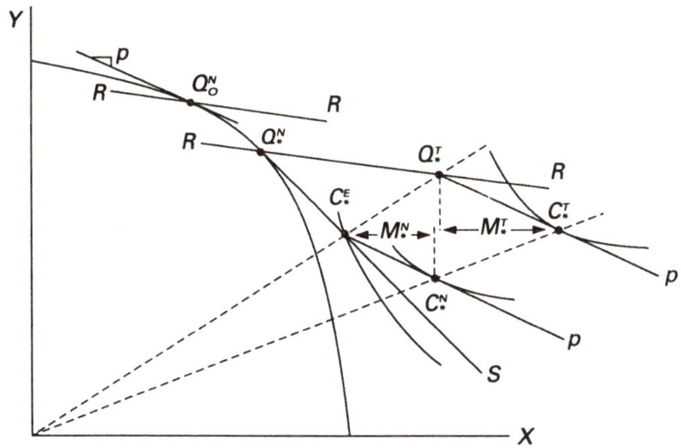

Figure 22.6

$$\frac{U_x^T}{U_y^T} = \frac{U_x^E}{U_y^E} = p \tag{19}$$

This outcome is illustrated in Figure 22.5 (point b).

If society must pay a premium for foreign capital (by way of internal adjustment costs of one form or another), the effect is the same as a tariff on the importable or subsidy on domestic production of the import competing industry. Figure 22.6 both illustrates this optimum and demonstrates that a tariff or subsidy *lowers* the gains from factor movement which was undertaken as protection against the risk of trade disruption (as shown by Bhagwati 1979). With imported capital generating an external diseconomy, 'domestic native' production shifts from Q_O^N to Q_*^N, where relative marginal costs include the external effect. Capital migration then is allowed to proceed to Q_*^T which generates a total of C_*^T of 'domestic' (native plus immigrant) consumption in peacetime with imports M_*^T. In contrast to M_*^T the amount M_*^N is imported for native consumption. Domestic native consumption during peace is shown at point C_*^N with immigrant's consumption the difference between C_*^T and $C - N_*$. C_*^E represents domestic native consumption in an emergency when trade is disrupted. The optimum mix between factor imports and commodity imports is also readily illustrated in a supply-demand curve diagram as in Figure 22.7. The demand curve D_N refers to demands by

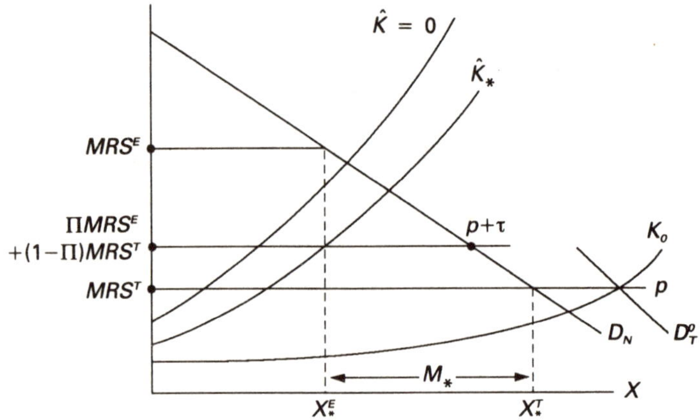

Figure 22.7

domestic natives, while D_T includes all demands, native and immigrant. The optimal amount of capital import under conditions of no external cost is assumed to be $\hat{K}_O$ with marginal product curve as shown. Now assume that external cost t raises the relative price of good X by τ. The optimal capital import then yields supply curve $\hat{K}_*$. Consumption during peacetime is X_*^T including imports M_*; consumption during trade stoppage when imports are blocked is X_*^E. $\hat{K}_*$ is the optimal supply of capital; for this amount of capital inflow, probability weighted marginal benefits $[\pi MRS^E + (1 - \pi)MRS^T]$ just equal externality inclusive marginal cost of production (i.e. $p + \tau$).

MIGRATION AND WELFARE

In essence, the preceding model of factor migration as a substitute for trade in goods identifies protection from effects of trade disruption as a primary benefit from factor movement within a HO world. Another significant possible benefit is that factor growth through migration will *increase* free trade welfare. This could occur if the home country is specialized completely in the production of its export good. Then immigration of the factor which is used intensively in the import industry will increase the free trade welfare of the native population. Alternatively, outmigration of the factor used intensively in the export sector will increase the free trade welfare of those left behind. In

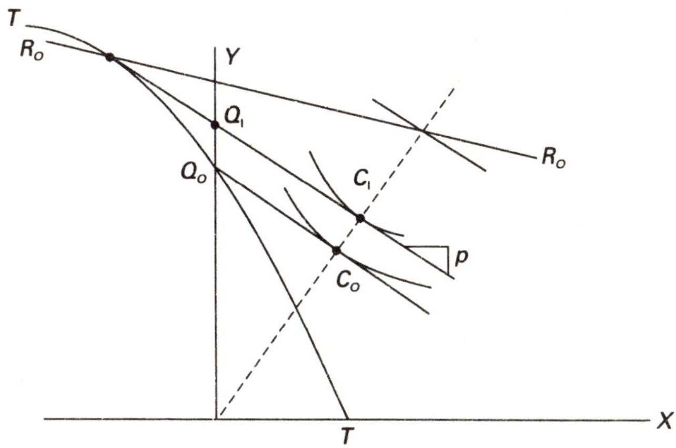

Figure 22.8

Figure 22.8, under free trade, production is specialized at Q_O, which is beneath R_O due to labour shortage; consumption is shown at C_O. If labour is accepted into this economy, native production under free trade can move to Q_1, native consumption to C_1.

More than protection from trade disruption, factor immigration may actually make autarky following on disruption preferable for the domestic native population. Factor immigration beyond that needed to insulate from disruption may reverse the trade pattern with the result that domestic native utility is *greater* at U^E than U^T. Here is a conclusion to suggest a positive benefit from factor movement beyond protection from trade disruption.

If factor movement can substitute for trade, and if costly vulnerability to trade disruption is thereby averted, factor movement may save a country the costs of forestalling (or reducing the probability of) emergency embargo through defense or security efforts, or through other measures such as stockpiling and standby production. And if the amount of trade vulnerability a country allows actually invites embargos (as Bhagwati and Srinivasan (1976) have argued) – such that more trade makes disruption more likely – then factor movements to diminish commodity trade would actually reduce the likelihood of the embargos or similar emergencies.

All of these arguments in favour of free factor migration to reduce a country's vulnerability to disruption seem to raise the question whether any discernible *disbenefits* of factor migration can be identified within the HO framework, or must recourse be made to other effects to explain limitations on factor movements in the real world. The answer to this question might depend in part on distinguishing between migration of people and migration of other factors, e.g. capital.

Exchange of factors of production both depends on the risks of emergency (up to and including war) and also will influence the magnitude of such risks. On the one hand, a high risk of trade disruption will reduce factor movement. On the other hand, exchange of factors between states or regions will provide each with incentives to limit conflict. The exchange of factors of production could extend to potentially adversarial states. In this case, such exchanges would probably limit the chances of hostilities breaking out, since once a state of hostility exists previous factor exchanges become similar to an exchange of hostages. For example, as between Israel and its mid-Eastern neighbours, exchange of factors (because of the potential loss if war breaks out) might limit risks of war. On the other hand, such trades might appear so dangerous as to be rejected. The difference between capital and labour as objects of inter-country migration may be crucial at this point. Labour migration seems more risky than capital movement. Human hostages will command more powerful allegiance from governments and therefore expose the immigrant's homeland to stronger pressures to escalate or settle if conflict among neighbouring states arises. On the other hand, capital, if exchanged, may be less vulnerable to expropriation because identity of ownership may be more easily concealed and capital may be stored and replaced.

Once we step outside the HO world of identical technologies and homogeneous production functions across all countries, numerous other reasons to explain limits on factor migration are accessible. These alternative explanations include decreasing returns to scale in production, existence of specific immobile factors in different countries, noncompetitive elements in market structures, diverse technologies across countries and so on. Although all these alternatives can change the optimal quantity of factor migration, and may be indeed necessary to invoke an interior limited solution for welfare maximizing factor exchange, none would appear to undermine the usefulness of the idea of factor exchange as protection against costly consequences of trade stoppage, nor to soften the risks of loss which such exchange may induce.

CONCLUSION

The connections between a country's economic position in the world economic system and its strategic position in the world geo-political system must become a topic of growing interest and importance as political and economic dependencies among states continues to increase. This paper addresses a particular rather narrowly defined question from the larger context of how economic relationships may reduce conflict or generate it. In the larger context, the question may be asked whether commercial intercourse among countries reduces or exacerbates their conflicts. Voluntary commercial exchange will always entail mutual accrual of benefits, but the redistribution of power brought on by trade or economic integratation within the world political system need not be reciprocal let alone symmetric. Just as economic strength must form the basis for a country's winning its conflicts, political conflict if it induces military competition is a form of economic warfare among adversaries (Wolfson 1985). Moreover, where countries compete outside their own borders for third markets, their economic rivalry may easily spill over into the political sphere. And every exchange of goods between trading partners insofar as it is a dynamic process can cause dislocation, pain and resentment in both countries. Adding to these relationships the fact that some trade in goods or factors of production may have special importance to the distribution of military strength, the situation becomes still more complex. Thus, the idea that some countries might wish to insulate themselves partially from their growing dependence on trade with particular rivals and each other is not unintelligible. By allowing factors of production to emigrate and to consume their wages/rents, etc., in the country of destination, nations reduce their vulnerability to trade disruption. However, the cost of such insulation must be reckoned if accomplished by factor in migration as a dilution of national unity, possibly as a necessary compromise in the character of national public goods, possibly as less secure central command over the economy in time of emergency. On the other hand, if insulation from trade disruption were accomplished by means of factor out migration, then not only is the domestic economy smaller and therefore expectedly less robust in time of war, but domestic interests have become hostage to foreign power, creating a situation which might increase the demands on security from the state.

In the light of the rather general considerations raised in this paper, and our models of trade, protection and migration, it is clear that policy makers faced with the opportunities have no easy task in selecting the best instruments for advancing economic cooperation and possibly some degree of political conciliation. The structure of this paper, however, does suggest that any exchange of capital, workers, technical knowledge, or personnel should be coordinated with commodity trade policy. The costs and benefits of varying degrees of economic cooperation could depend decisively on the risks of trade disruption, the risks of more serious hostilities, the reversibility of commodity-factor exchange agreements, and the potential for loss when cooperation is tested.

Note

* Research leading to this paper was sponsored by the Japanese Fulbright Commission and the Faculty of Economics, Osaka University. The paper is a derivative from and uses constructs contained in the work of H. Shibata (1985) and H. Shibata and M. McGuire (1986).

References

1. Arad, R. W. and Hillman, A. L. (1979) 'Embargo threat, learning and departure from comparative advantage', *Journal of International Economics*, vol. 9.
2. Bergstrom, C., Loury G. C. and Persson, M. (1985) 'Embargo threats and the management of emergency reserves', *Journal of Political Economy*, vol. 93.
3. Bhagwati, J. (1979) 'International factor movements and national advantage', *Indian Economic Review*, vol. 14, no. 2 (N.S.).
4. Bhagwati, J. and Tironi E. (1980) 'Tariff change, foreign capital and immiserization', *Journal of Development Economics*, vol. 7
5. Bhagwati, J. and Brecher, R. A. (1980) 'National welfare in an open economy in the presence of foreign-owned factors of production', *Journal of International Economics*, vol. 10.
6. Bhagwati, J. and Brecher, R. A. (1981) 'Foreign ownership and the theory of trade and welfare', *Journal of Political Economy*, vol. 89.
7. Bhagwati, J. and Srinivasan, T. N. (1976) 'Optimal trade policy and compensation under endogenous uncertainty: the phenomenon of market disruption', *Journal of International Economics*, vol. 6.
8. Bhagwati, J., Brecher, R. A. and Srinivasan, T. N. (1983) 'On the choice between capital and labour mobility', *Journal of International Economics*, vol. 14.

9. Cheng, J. (1985) 'Intermittent trade disruptions and optimal production', unpublished paper (Gainesvile: Department of Economics, University of Florida, FL 32611).
10. Grossman, G. M. and Razin, A. (1984) 'International capital movements under uncertainty', *Journal of Political Economy*, vol. 92.
11. Helpman, E. and Razin, A. (1978) *A Theory of International Trade under Uncertainty* (New York: Academic Press).
12. Hillman, A. L. and Ngo Van Long (1983) 'Pricing and depletion of an exhaustible resource when there is anticipation of trade disruption', *Quarterly Journal of Economics*, vol. 98.
13. Kemp, M. C. and Liviatan, N. (1973) 'Production and trade patterns under uncertainty', *Economic Record*, vol. 49.
14. Loury, G. C. (1983) 'The welfare effects of intermittent interruptions of trade', *American Economic Review*, vol. 73 (Papers and Proceedings).
15. MacDougall, G. D. A. (1960) 'The benefits and costs of private investment from abroad: a theoretical approach', *Economic Record*, vol. 36.
16. Markusen, J. R. (1983) 'International factor movements and commodity trade as complements', *Journal of International Economics*, vol. 13.
17. Mayer, W. (1977) 'The national defense tariff argument reconsidered', *Journal of International Economics*, vol. 7.
18. McGuire, M. and Shibata, H. (1985) 'National self-sufficiency protection and defense', unpublished paper (Osaka: Faculty of Economics, Osaka University, Japan).
19. Mundell, R. A. (1957) 'International trade and factor mobility', *American Economic Review*, vol. 47.
20. Polachek, S. W. (1980) 'Conflict and trade', *Journal of Conflict Resolution*, vol. 24.
21. Shibata, H. (1985) 'A note on trade and security expenditure and defense cost-share arrangements', unpublished paper (Osaka: Faculty of Economics, Osaka University, Japan).
22. Svensson, L. E. O. (1984) 'Factor Trade and goods trade', *Journal of International Economics*, vol. 14.
23. Tolley, G. S. and Wilman, J. D. (1977) 'The foreign dependence question', *Journal of Political Economy*, vol. 85.

23 Explaining the Pattern of Factor Flows between the North and the South

Arvind Panagariya*

INTRODUCTION

Suppose we divide the world into two regions, a rich region called the North and a poor region called the South. Within this scheme, the pattern of international factor flows during the past three decades may be viewed as being characterized by the following stylized facts:

(i) On a net basis, capital has flowed from the North to the South. This is especially true of direct foreign investment.
(ii) Unskilled labour has moved from the South to the North. Often the North has imposed severe restrictions on such movements. The result has been substantial illegal immigration of unskilled labour into that region.
(iii) Skilled labour has also flowed from the South to the North. An important characteristic of this category of labour, emphasized in the present paper, is that it is employed overwhelmingly in nontraded goods sectors. For example, 33 per cent of legal immigrants into the US in 1977 reported their occupation to be related to services, construction or transportation. Looking from emigrating countries' viewpoint, 36 per cent of all emigrants holding Indian passports during 1960–1967 were nurses, veterinarians, doctors or teachers. A similar pattern has been observed for the Philippines where 44 per cent of all emigrants in the early 1970s were individuals working in nontraded goods sectors.[1]

My purpose here is to explore conditions which may give rise to stylized facts (i)–(iii) within a simple international trade model. Although the existing literature contains a rich analysis of a variety of issues related to international factor mobility, so far we do not seem to have a model which is simultaneously consistent with the pattern of migration described above. Much of the conventional literature on the subject relies on the Heckscher–Ohlin (HO) model which treats capital and labour symmetrically and, moreover, makes no distinction between skilled and unskilled labour.[2] The literature on brain drain, as exemplified in various contributions in Bhagwati (1976), distinguishes between the two types of labour, but its main focus is on the welfare implications of emigration of skilled workers from less developed countries. A recent paper by Ethier (1985) also distinguishes between skilled and unskilled labour but his main concern is to explain temporary migration of the latter into some of the European countries.

As in other areas of trade theory, in recent years, emphasis in the area of factor mobility has shifted from the HO model to the specific-factors model. For example, Caves (1971) has employed the standard specific-factors model to explain two-way capital flows referred to as 'cross-hauling'. His main conclusion is that in the specific-factors model, an exogenous inflow of one type of capital will lead to an outflow of the other type of capital. More recently, Jones *et al.* (1983) have considered a two-sector, specific-factors model of a small open economy in which the location of both types of capital is determined endogenously. Assuming that one sector produces a nontraded good, exogenous shocks such as a change in tastes in this model lead to cross-hauling.[3]

As my objective here is to explain the pattern of movement of as many as three factors, I must inevitably employ a model characterized by factor specificity. The particular model I have chosen allows for three sectors of which two produce traded goods while the third produces a nontraded good, labelled 'services'. Each sector employs 'unskilled labour' and a sector-specific factor. I refer to the factor specific to the nontraded goods sector as 'doctors' and identify it with the factor described in category (iii) above. The specific factor employed in one of the two traded goods sectors is labelled 'capital' while the remaining specific factor may be called 'land' or another type of physical or human capital. Finally, the model allows for two countries, distinguished by their relative factor endowments.

In its production structure, the model resembles one of the three 'Dutch-disease' models considered by Corden and Neary (1982). The difference is that I employ a two-country framework whereas they assumed a small-country context. Moreover, my concern is with international migration while their interest was in explaining the

Dutch-disease phenomenon. The analysis presented below also differs from Jones *et al.* (1983) in that it employs a two-country model and deals with simultaneous flows of *three* factors.

It is worth noting at the outset that the analysis here is entirely static in nature. As such, the process of capital accumulation, whether in machines or in human beings, is outside the model. Indeed, endowments of physical and human capital (doctors) which play a central role in the analysis are taken as exogenously given. A more complete model should, of course, attempt to endogenize the process of capital accumulation.

In the following section, I present the basic assumptions of the model, and in the next, I derive the conditions for obtaining the migration pattern described in (i)–(iii). The paper finishes with some concluding remarks.

THE MODEL

Let there be two countries, North and South. Assume that these countries are identical in all respects except in their relative endowments of various factors. Precise differences in endowments will be spelled out shortly.

Let us distinguish all variables relating to the South by an asterisk (*) so that unasterisked variables relate to the North. Assume that each country produces three goods, 1, 2 and 3. Quantities of output, unskilled labour, and the sector-specific factor in sector i in the North are denoted X_i, L_i and V_i, respectively.

It is assumed throughout that goods 1 and 2 are traded while 3 is non-traded, and is referred to as 'services'. Factor V_3 is to be identified with human capital specific to the production of 3, e.g. doctors, nurses, teachers, etc., but I call it 'doctors'. Factor V_1 is labelled as physical capital specific to sector 1. Finally, V_2 may be viewed as either land or another type of human or physical capital.

The relative endowment differences are somewhat tricky to specify in a model with four factors of production. For the purpose at hand, I need two assumptions:

Assumption 1 Relative to the North, South's endowment of labour is at least as large as its endowment of sector-specific factors.

More precisely,

$$(L^*/L) \geq \sum(L_i/L)(V_i^*/V_i) \quad i = 1, 2, 3 \tag{1}$$

where L and L^* stand for the total supplies of unskilled labour in, respectively, the North and South.

Assumption 2 At the goods prices prevailing in the North, the South has a larger share in the world supply of doctors than its share in the world income.

In symbols:

$$V_3^*/(V_3 + V_3^*) > Y^*(Y + Y^*) \tag{2}$$

where Y and Y^* stand, respectively, for nominal incomes in the North and South, both measured at goods prices prevailing in the North.

A few comments regarding these assumptions are in order. According to (1), the relative supply of labour in the South must exceed a weighted sum of its relative supplies of the three specific factors where the weights sum to unity. The weight associated with a given sector's specific factor is the allocative share of labour in that sector in the North. This weighting is somewhat unsatisfactory in that it makes use of allocative shares of labour which themselves depend on equilibrium values of the L_i. But in the specific factors model, this weighting scheme turns out to be the only convenient way of defining international differences in endowments of the mobile factor relative to specific factors. A sufficient but not necessary condition for (1) to hold is $L^*/L \geq V_i^*/V_i$ for each i. It is worth noting that the definition of labour abundance employed by Amano (1977, p. 134) to analyse the patterns of trade in the standard specific-factors model is equivalent to that employed in Assumption 1. To demonstrate this fact, subtract unity from either side of (1). Then, denoting the proportionate difference between the endowments of the North and South of a given factor by a circumflex, e.g. $(L^* - L)/L = \hat{L}$ etc., one can obtain:

$$\hat{L} \geq \sum \lambda_{Li}\hat{V}_i \quad i = 1, 2, 3 \tag{1'}$$

where $\lambda_{Li} = L_i/L$ is the allocative share of unskilled labour in sector i in the North. The definition of labour abundance implied by (1′) is the same as that employed by Amano.

Assumption 2 requires that if one measures incomes in both countries at the goods prices prevailing in the North, the share of the South in world income be less than its share in the world supply of doctors. This assumption seems to be reasonable at least with respect to the countries between which such migration has taken place, e.g. India and the Philippines on the one hand and US on the other. For future reference, it is worth noting that condition (2) is equivalent to $V_3^*/V_3 > Y^*/Y$, which, after subtraction of unity from each side, may be written as:

$$\hat{V}_3 > \hat{Y} \tag{2'}$$

The essential approach here is to specify the conditions determining an equilibrium in the North and then perform comparative statics around this equilibrium to determine how its values for various endogenous variables differ between the North and South. Of particular interest are the real factor prices which allow us to predict the direction of factor flows between the two countries. It is worth noting that although the comparative statics technique allows one to consider only infinitesimally small differences in factor endowments, the results here will remain essentially valid for large differences in endowments.

To proceed with formal analysis, let a_{Li} for ($i = 1, 2, 3$) denote the amount of labour per unit of output in sector i and a_{Vi} represent the quantity of the specific factor per unit of output in that sector in the North. Remembering that X_i stands for output, the usual full-employment conditions in the North will be given by $a_{Vi}X_i = V_i$ and $\Sigma\, a_{Li}X_i = L$. Total differentiation of these conditions yields:

$$\hat{X}_i + \hat{a}_{Vi} = \hat{V}_i \quad i = 1, 2, 3 \tag{3}$$

$$\sum \lambda_{Li}\hat{X}_i = \hat{L} - \sum \lambda_{Li}\hat{a}_{Li} \quad i = 1, 2, 3 \tag{4}$$

As noted in connection with inequality (1′), $\lambda_{Li}(= L_i/L)$ denotes labour's allocative share in sector i.

Per unit cost of production facing an individual firm is given by $a_{Li}w + a_{Vi}r_i$ where w is the economy-wide wage rate and r_i is per unit price of the services of factor V_i. Assuming that production functions are linear homogeneous and factor markets are perfectly competitive, cost minimization by firms implies:

$$\theta_{Li}\hat{a}_{Li} + \theta_{Vi}\hat{a}_{Vi} = 0 \quad i = 1, 2, 3 \tag{5}$$

where θ_{Li} and θ_{Vi} denote labour's and the specific factor's income share in sector i. Perfect competition in the goods market leads to average-cost pricing, i.e. $a_{Li}w + a_{Vi}r_i - p_i$, where p_i denotes the price of commodity i. Totally differentiating this equation and taking (5) into account, one gets:

$$\theta_{Li}\hat{w} + \theta_{Vi}\hat{r}_i = \hat{p}_i \quad i = 1, 2, 3 \tag{6}$$

A final condition on the supply side relates factor prices to the input-output coefficients through the elasticity of substitution, σ_i. More precisely, one has:

$$\hat{a}_{Vi} - \hat{a}_{Li} = \sigma_i(\hat{w} - \hat{r}_i) \quad i = 1, 2, 3 \tag{7}$$

Relationships (4)–(7) specify completely the supply side of the model. Let me therefore turn to the demand side. Here the most significant assumption I make is that of unit income elasticity of demand for services. Homotheticity of preferences, usually assumed in international trade models, is sufficient to validate this assumption. Besides, the recent estimates of income elasticity of demand for services provided by Kravis *et al.* (1983) are fairly close to unity. The main reason for this assumption here is that it makes the price of the nontraded good depend on relative factor endowments only.

Let $D_3 = D_3\,(p_1, p_2, p_3, Y)$ represent the demand for good 3 in the North. In this equation, Y represents the nominal income and is equal to $\Sigma\, p_i X_i$ as well as $wL + \Sigma\, r_i V_i$. Differentiating D_3 totally and making appropriate substitutions, one can write:

$$\hat{D}_3 = \sum e_{3i}\hat{p}_i + \sum \phi_i \hat{X}_i|; \quad i = 1, 2, 3 \tag{8}$$

where e_{3i} is the compensated elasticity of demand for good 3 with respect to p_i and ϕ_i is the value share of the output of sector i in Y. Note that good 3 being non-traded, ϕ_3 represents the income as well as the expenditure shares. As defined, e_{33} is necessarily negative and $\Sigma e_{3i} = 0$.

Equilibrium in the non-traded goods sector requires:

$$\hat{D}_3 = \hat{X}_3 \tag{9}$$

As noted earlier, my intention is to compare the equilibrium values of real factor prices between the North and South at an equilibrium characterized by free trade in goods 1 and 2 but no trade in good 3. It follows that the relative price of good 1 in terms of good 2 will be the same between the two countries so that choosing good 1 as the numeraire good, one can set $\hat{p}_1 = \hat{p}_2 = 0$. It is then easily verified that the system (3)–(9) consists of 15 linear equations in exactly 15 endogenous variables, namely, $\hat{X}_i$, $\hat{a}_{Li}$, $\hat{a}_{Vi}$, $\hat{r}_i$, $\hat{w}$, $\hat{p}_3$ and $\hat{D}_3$ ($i = 1, 2, 3$). These equations can be solved for changes in factor prices and other variables in response to changes in factor endowments. This task is performed in the next section.

SOLUTION OF THE MODEL AND RESULTS

The model can be solved in a fairly straightforward fashion. The first step is to obtain a solution for the relative price of services. For this purpose, one can combine equations (3)–(5) to obtain:

$$\sum \phi_i \hat{X}_i = \theta_L \hat{L} + \sum \theta_i \hat{V}_i \quad i = 1, 2, 3 \tag{10}$$

where θ_L and θ_i are the shares in *total income* in the North for, respectively, labour and the ith specific factor, e.g. $\theta_L = wL/Y$. Setting $\hat{p}_1 = \hat{p}_2 = 0$ in (8), and making use of (10), one gets:

$$\hat{D}_3 = e_{33}\hat{p}_3 + \theta_L \hat{L} + \sum \theta_i \hat{V}_i \tag{11}$$

Next, one solves (3)–(7) for $\hat{X}_3$ in terms of changes in the price of good 3 and factor endowments. As one also needs solutions for factor prices, it is useful to display some intermediate steps. Using (5)–(7), one can eliminate the $\hat{r}_i$ and solve for the $\hat{a}_{Li}$ and $\hat{a}_{Vi}$ in terms of $\hat{w}$ and $\hat{p}_i$. In particular, one has:

$$\hat{a}_{Li} = -\sigma_i(\hat{w} - \hat{p}_i), \quad \hat{a}_{Vi} = \alpha_i \theta_{Li}(\hat{w} - \hat{p}_i), \quad i = 1, 2, 3 \tag{12}$$

where $\alpha_i (= \sigma_i/\theta_{Vi})$ represents the elasticity of demand for labour in sector i.

Next, one can eliminate the $\hat{a}_{Li}$, $\hat{a}_{Vi}$ and $\hat{X}_i$ from (3), (4) and (12), and solve the resulting equation for $\hat{w}$. One gets:

$$\hat{w} = -(1/\Delta)[\hat{L} - \sum \lambda_{Li} \hat{V}_i - \sum \lambda_{Li} \alpha_i \hat{p}_i] \tag{13}$$

where $\Delta(= \Sigma\lambda_{Li}\alpha_i)$ is the elasticity of the total demand for labour with respect to the wage rate. For notational convenience, I define $\hat{L} - \Sigma\lambda_{Li}\hat{V}_i = \hat{\gamma}$ and rewrite (13) as:

$$\hat{w} = -(1/\Delta)[\hat{\gamma} - \sum \lambda_{Li}\alpha_i\hat{p}_i] \qquad (13')$$

Note that in terms of the definition given earlier, $\hat{\gamma} > 0$ implies an increase in labour abundance. Since the South is assumed to be labour abundant, $\hat{\gamma}$ shall be positive in the rest of this paper.

One can now combine (3), (12) and (13′) to obtain the solution for $\hat{X}_i$:

$$\hat{X}_i = (\alpha_i\theta_{Li}/\Delta)[\Delta\hat{p}_i - \sum \lambda_{Li}\alpha_i\hat{p}_i + \hat{\gamma}] + \hat{V}_i \quad i = 1, 2, 3 \qquad (14)$$

Recall that I am setting $\hat{p}_1 = \hat{p}_2 = 0$ to ensure identical prices of traded goods between the two countries. Therefore, for $i = 3$, one can rewrite (14) as:

$$\hat{X}_3 = \sigma_{33}\hat{p}_3 + \sigma_{L3}\hat{\gamma} + \hat{V}_3 \qquad (14')$$

where $\sigma_{33}(= \alpha_3\theta_{L3}/\Delta)(\lambda_{L1}\alpha_1\lambda_{L2}\alpha_2)$ and σ_{L3} $(= \alpha_3\theta_{L3}/\Delta)$ denote the respective elasticities of X_3 with respect to p_3 and L. Both σ_{33} and σ_{L3} are positive. Since the market for services must be cleared domestically in each country (see (9)), (11) and (14′) can be combined to yield:

$$\hat{p}_3 = -(1/E_3)[\hat{\beta} + \sigma_{L3}\hat{\gamma}] \qquad (15)$$

where $\hat{\beta} = \hat{V}_3 - (\theta_L\hat{L} + \Sigma\theta_i\hat{V}_i)$ and $E_3 = (\sigma_{33} - e_{33})$ is the general equilibrium elasticity of excess supply of services and is positive. In order to establish the sign of $\hat{\beta}$, recall that $Y = \Sigma\hat{p}_i\hat{X}_i i$. At constant commodity prices, this equation yields[4] $\hat{Y} = \Sigma\phi_i\hat{X}_i$, in view of (10), which implies $\hat{\beta} = \hat{V}_3 - \hat{Y}$. Given Assumption 2, or more specifically (2′), one immediately obtains $\hat{\beta} > 0$. Indeed, $\hat{\beta}$ is nothing but my measure of the relative abundance of doctors.

(15) allows one to deduce the following important result:

Proposition 1 Given Assumptions 1 and 2, services will be cheaper in the South than in the North.

The importance of Proposition 1 stems from the fact that recent empirical work done by Kravis *et al.* has shown a clear and systematic tendency for service prices to be lower in poor countries. This phenomenon has been explained by them (Kravis *et al.* 1983) in terms of the productivity differential model, by Kravis and Lipsey (1983) and Bhagwati (1984) in terms of a multi-commodity, HO model and by Clague (1985) in terms of a variant of the specific-factors model.[5] Here, I provide an additional model which generates the phenomenon of lower service prices in poor countries. The strength of this model is that it is also able to generate the pattern of international factor flows described in (i)–(iii). None of the existing models of international differences in service prices have been shown to generate this pattern of factor flows.

In order to predict the pattern of factor flows, I need to compare real incomes of a given factor across countries. Since the non-traded goods prices differ between the two countries, one must employ a price index for comparability. The natural index in this context is $p_1^{\gamma_1}p_2^{\gamma_2}p_3^{\gamma_3}$ where γ_i denotes the proportion of income spent on good i by the representative consumer. Remembering that good 3 is non-traded, one has $\gamma_3 = \phi_3$.

Given the assumed price index, the real wage in the North can be written as $w/p_1^{\gamma_1}p_2^{\gamma_2}p_3^{\phi_3}$. Morever, since the traded goods prices are the same between the South and North, the proportionate excess of the real wage in the former over the latter can be written as $\hat{w} - \phi_3\hat{p}_3$. Analogously, the real return to the ith specific factor in the South will exceed that in the North proportionately by $\hat{r}_i - \phi_3\hat{p}_3$.

In the following analysis, it will be assumed that migrating labour and doctors do not own any productive property, e.g. V_1 and V_2, or claims to income from such property. Furthermore, since workers and doctors must move bodily in order to move their services in another country, it will be assumed that they spend their income in the country where they earn it. These assumptions imply that the decision to migrate by labour and doctors will depend entirely on international differences in their real earnings, i.e. $\hat{w} - \phi_3\hat{p}_3$ and $\hat{r}_3 - \phi_3\hat{p}_3$.[6]

As regards the flow of capital (V_1) its owners need not move with it. Therefore, they may spend their income in the country other than where capital owned by them is employed. If they choose this option, the relevant factor price difference is given by $\hat{r}_1$. On the other hand, if they choose to move with their capital, the relevant factor price differential will be $\hat{r}_1 - \phi_3\hat{p}_3$.[7] As we shall see, in the present model, both of these factor price differentials predict the same direction of capital flows.

One can now proceed to look at factor-price differences between the North and South. Remembering that $\hat{p}_1 = \hat{p}_2 = 0$ at the equilibrium under consideration and that $\hat{p}_3 < 0$, it is evident from (13′) that the wage in terms of the traded goods will be lower in the South than that in the North. Intuitively, at the factor prices prevailing in the North, (1) implies excess supply of labour in the South so that the wage must be lower in the latter country. Furthermore, (2) (along with (1)) implies a lower price of good 3 in the South which, via zero-profit conditions, puts further pressure on the wage rate. Given that the traded goods prices are the same in the two countries while nontraded goods prices are different, the fate of labour in terms of traded goods gets tied to the non-traded goods price as well.

Although the wage in terms of traded goods is unambiguously lower in the South, labour's real income need not be. Services are cheaper in the South which causes the purchasing power of income, measured in traded goods, to be understated in that country. This is, of course, one of the main messages emerging out of the *International Comparisons Project* headed by Kravis, Heston and Summers – see Kravis *et al.* (1982). To make the point formally in the context of the present model, subtract $\phi_3\hat{p}_3$ from each side of (13′) and set $\hat{p}_1 = \hat{p}_2 = 0$ to obtain:

$$\hat{w} - \phi_3\hat{p}_3 = -(1/\Delta)\hat{\gamma} + [(\lambda_{L3}\alpha_3/\Delta) - \phi_3]\hat{p}_3 \qquad (16)$$

In general, the RHS of (16) may be positive or negative implying that the model can generate a higher or a lower real income for labour in the South. A sufficient but not necessary condition for a lower real wage in the South is:

$$\lambda_{L3}\alpha_3/\Delta > \phi_3 \qquad (17)$$

Interpretation of this condition is straightforward. $\lambda_{L3}\alpha_3/\Delta$ represents the magnitude of the decline in wages in terms of traded goods due to a 1 per cent decline in the price of the non-traded good. By contrast, ϕ_3 represents the amount by which the real wage increases in response to the price decline. If the former exceeds the latter, *ceteris paribus*, the real wage must fall whenever the price of the non-traded good falls. Note that if $\hat{\gamma} = 0$, condition (17) is not merely sufficient but also necessary for the real wage in the South to be lower than that in the North.

This conclusion can be summarized in:

Proposition 2 Assuming that the South is relatively abundant in labour and doctors and that (17) is satisfied, unskilled labour will choose to migrate from the South to the North.

Next, let me consider capital, V_1. Setting $i = 1$ and $\hat{p}_1 = 0$, (6) can be rewritten as:

$$\hat{r}_1 = -(\theta_{L1}/\theta_{V1})\hat{w} \tag{6'}$$

We have already seen that the wage rate in terms of traded goods is lower in the South. Therefore, the rental on capital will be higher there. Furthermore, since services are cheaper in the South, the earnings of capital in that country will be higher than in the North in terms of every good. One can immediately deduce:

Proposition 3 Assuming that the South is relatively abundant in labour and doctors, at a free-trade equilibrium, capital will have an incentive to migrate from the North to the South.

Finally, let us look at the real income of doctors in the South relative to that in the North. Combining (6) and (13′), one can obtain

$$\hat{r}_3 - \phi_3\hat{p}_3 = (\theta_{L3}/\theta_{V3})[(\hat{\gamma}/\Delta) - \{(1/\theta_{L3}) - (\theta_3\theta_{V3})/\theta_{L3}) - (\alpha_3\lambda_{L3})/\Delta)\}\hat{p}_3] \tag{18}$$

Substituting for $\hat{p}_3$ from (15) and remembering that $(1/\theta_{L3}) = 1 + (\theta_{V3}/\theta_{L3})$ and $\Delta = \Sigma\lambda_{Li}\alpha_i$, one can rewrite (18) as

$$\hat{r}_3 - \phi_3\hat{p}_3 = (\theta_{L3}/\theta_{V3})[(\hat{\gamma}/\Delta) - \{(\hat{\lambda}_{L1}\alpha_1 + \lambda_{L2}\alpha_2)(1/\Delta) + (\theta_{V3}/\theta_{L3})(1 - \theta_3)\}\{(1/E_3)(\hat{\beta} + \sigma_{L3}\hat{\gamma})\}] \tag{18'}$$

The first term inside the square brackets, $\hat{\gamma}/\Delta$, represents the effect of a change in labour abundance on doctors' income. At constant commodity prices, increased labour abundance causes the wage to fall and, hence, the return on doctors' services to rise. The second term in the square brackets captures the effect on doctors' income of a change in the price of the nontraded good. Given $\hat{\gamma} > 0$ and $\hat{\beta} > 0$, this effect is negative.

Given these two opposite effects, in general, the real income of doctors may be higher or lower in the South than that in the North. *Ceteris paribus*, the larger the relative abundance of doctors, the lower is their income. The necessary and sufficient condition for doctors' income to be lower in the South is:

$$\hat{\gamma}/\Delta < \{(\lambda_{L1}\alpha_1 + \lambda_{L2}\alpha_2)(1/\Delta) + (\theta_{V3}/\theta_{L3})(1 - \theta_3)\}(\hat{\beta} + \sigma_{L3}\hat{\gamma}) \quad (19)$$

Note that this condition is necessarily satisfied if $\hat{\gamma} > 0$ or, equivalently, the North and South possess identical amounts of labour relative to the amounts of various sector-specific factors.

To summarize, one has:

Proposition 4 Assuming that the South is relatively abundant in doctors and labour and that condition (19) is satisfied, doctors in that country will have an incentive to migrate to the North.

CONCLUSIONS

In this paper, I have presented a simple model in which capital has an incentive to migrate from the North to the South while skilled and unskilled labour *may* find it attractive to migrate in the opposite direction. It must be noted that the model does not yield entirely unambiguous results and restrictions on parameters are required (see (17) and (19)) in order to obtain the desired pattern of migration. This fact should not be viewed too unfavourably, however, because the model has attempted to explain the simultaneous migration of as many as three factors, two of which are sector specific while the third is mobile among all three sectors. Ambiguity with regard to the real return to the intersectorally mobile factor in the presence of commodity price changes is well known in the literature. (17) is merely a device to resolve this ambiguity.

An interesting question in the context of this paper concerns the welfare effects of emigration on the nonemigrant population. It can be shown that in the present model, ignoring the affects on the terms trade between internationally traded commodities, emigration necessarily hurts the nonemigrant population. The intuitive argument, contained in Kenen (1971) and Rivera-Batiz (1982), is that the non-emigrant population loses the opportunity to trade with the emigrants after emigration takes place. Consequently, the gains from trade accruing to the latter are lost after emigration.

Notes

* A substantial part of the work on this paper was done while the author was on a sabbatical leave from the University of Maryland. Financial support is gratefully acknowledged.

1. I have taken these data from Rivera Batiz who, in turn, draws upon a variety of sources including US Department of Justice (1977), Institute of Applied Manpower Research (1970) and Gupta (1973). Reubens (1976) provides further evidence supporting the assertion that migration of skilled labour from less developed countries to the USA has included a disproportionately large number of workers employed in non-traded goods sectors.
2. See, for example, Mundell (1957), Johnson (1965), Jones (1967), Kemp (1969), Markusen and Melvin (1979), and Bhagwati and Brecher (1980). For additional references, see the recent surveys by Bhagwati (1979) and Ruffin (1984).
3. See Jones *et al.* (1982) and Panagariya (1986a) for additional models of cross-hauling.
4. Note that in the absence of any distortions, for infinitesimally small changes $Y = \Sigma\phi_i X_i$ even if prices are allowed to change. The reason is that $\Sigma X_i dp_i = 0$ for small movements along the transformation curve.
5. The productivity differential model goes as far back as Harrod (1933) and was developed further by Balassa (1964) and Samuelson (1964). Bhagwati (1984) provides a formalization of this model within the HO framework.
6. If migrating labour or doctors own property, two additional issues should be considered. First, the issue of whether they continue to own this property or passes it on to their relatives after they migrate needs to be resolved. Second, in the event they continue to own the property, one needs to know if they can move it with them or not. Note that in the presence of non-traded goods, the real value of the income from such property depends not merely on where it is located but also on where its *owner* resides. Incidentally, the assumption that migrating workers do not own any property turns out to be crucial in evaluating the welfare effects of such migration. For example, see Kenen (1971).
7. The asymmetry between the treatments of migration involving human beings and other factors such as capital has also been discussed by Wong (1983). He does not explicitly mention the assumption that labour does not own any capital but it is obviously implicit in his analysis.

References

1. Amano, A. (1977) 'Specific factors, comparative advantage and international investment', *Economica*, vol. 44.
2. Balassa, B. (1964) 'The Purchasing-Power Parity Doctrine: a reappraisal', *Journal of Political Economy*, vol. 72.
3. Bhagwati, J. N. (1976) *The Brain Drain and Taxation: Theory and Empirical Analysis* (Amsterdam: North-Holland).
4. Bhagwati, J. N. (1979) 'International factor movements and national advantage', *Indian Economic Review*, vol. 14.
5. Bhagwati, J. N. (1984) 'Why are services cheaper in the poor countries?', *Economic Journal*, vol. 94.
6. Bhagwati, J. N. and Brecher, R. A. (1980) 'National welfare in an open economy in the presence of foreign-owned factors of production', *Journal of International Economics*, vol. 10.
7. Caves, R. E. (1971) 'International corporations: the industrial economics of foreign investment', *Economica*, vol. 38.
8. Clague, C. C. (1985) 'A model of real national price levels', *Southern Economic Journal*, vol. 51.
9. Corden, W. M. and Neary, J. P. (1982) 'Booming sector and de-industrialization in a small open economy', *Economic Journal*, vol. 92.
10. Ethier, W. J. (1985) 'International trade and labour migration', *American Economic Review*, vol. 75.
11. Gupta, M. L. (1973) 'Outflow of high-level manpower from the Philippines', *International labour Review*, vol. 107.
12. Harrod, Sir Roy F. (1933) *International Economics* (Cambridge Economics Handbook)(London: Nisbet & Cambridge University Press).
13. Institute of Applied Manpower Research (1970) *The Brain Drain Study*, Report No. 4 (New Delhi).
14. Johnson, H. G. (1965) *International Trade and Economic Growth* (Cambride: Harvard University Press).
15. Jones, R. W. (1967) 'International capital movements and the theory of tariffs and trade', *Quarterly Journal of Economics*, vol. 81.
16. Jones, R. W., Neary, J. P. and Ruane, F. P. (1983) 'Two-way capital flows', *Journal of International Economics*, vol. 14.
17. Jones, R. W., Neary, J. P. and Ruane, F. P. (1983) 'Two-way capital flows: cross hauling in models of foreign investment', *Collabourative Paper*, No. 82–37 (Laxenburg, Austria: International Institute for Applied Systems Analysis).
18. Kemp, M. C. (1969) *The Pure Theory of International Trade and Investment* (Engelwood Cliffs: Prentice-Hall).
19. Kenen, P. B. (1971) 'Migration, the terms of trade and economic welfare in the source country', in J. N. Bhagwati (ed.), *Trade, Balance of Payments and Growth* (Amsterdam: North-Holland).
20. Kravis, I. B. and Lipsey, R. E. (1983) 'Towards an explanation of national price levels', *Princeton Studies in International Finance*, No. 52.
21. Kravis, I. B., Heston, A. and Summers, R. (1982) *World Product and Income: International Comparisons of Real GDP* (Baltimore: Johns Hopkins University Press).

22. Kravis, I. B., Heston, A. and Summers, R. (1983) 'The share of services in economic growth', in F. G. Adams and B. Hickman (eds.), *Global Econometrics: Essays in Honor of Lawrence R. Klein* (Cambridge, Mass.: MIT Press).
23. Markusen, J. R. and Melvin, J. R. (1979) 'Tariffs, capital mobility, and foreign ownership', *Journal of International Economics*, vol. 9.
24. Mundell, R. A. (1957) 'International trade and factor mobility', *American Economic Review*, vol. 47.
25. Panagariya, A. (forthcoming) 'Increasing returns, dynamic stability and international trade', *Journal of International Economics*.
26. Reubens, E. P. (1976) 'Some dimensions of professional immigration into developed countries from Less Developed Countries, 1960–1973', in J. N. Bhagwati (ed.), *The Brain Drain and Taxation: Theory and Empirical Analysis* (Amsterdam: North-Holland).
27. Rivera-Batiz, F. L. (1982) 'International migration, non-traded goods and economic welfare in the source country', *Journal of Development Economics*, vol. 11.
28. Ruffin, R. R. (1984) 'International factor mobility', in R. W. Jones and P. B. Kenen (eds.), *Handbook of International Economics*, Volume I (Amsterdam: North-Holland).
29. Samuelson, P. A. (1964) 'Theoretical notes on trade problems', *The Review of Economics and Statistics*, vol. 46.
30. US Department of Justice (1977) *Annual Report, Immigration and Naturalization Service, 1977.*
31. Wong, K.-Y. (1983) 'On choosing among trade in goods and international capital and labour mobility: a theoretical analysis', *Journal of International Economics*, vol. 14.

24 Japan's Land Prices: A Cross-sectional Analysis

Kazuo Sato

INTRODUCTION

If Japan, by now Asia's old economic giant, has an Achilles' heel, it must be found in its land problem. Overcrowded in a small land area, Japan's land prices have stayed on an ascending orbit. Though the stock market crashed, the land market still remains robust (the bubble finally collapsed in 1991). The extraordinary land-price boom since 1987 has elevated Japan's metropolitan land prices to as high as a hundred times over American land prices. Sato (1991) has analyzed Japan's land-price inflation from macroeconomic perspectives by constructing a simple macroeconomic model involving land.

In this paper, I examine Japan's land prices across prefectures at a given point of time – in the mid-1980s just prior to the explosive land-price boom. I show that cross-prefectural variations in land prices can be explained adequately by the basic model I employ in Sato (1991). In particular, I find the elasticity of substitution to be very much above one. When that is the case, the land-use efficiency must vary considerably among prefectures, accounting for much of variations in land prices. I conclude the paper by briefly examining the possible effects of tax policy on land prices.

THE BASIC MODEL

The model we consider is very simple. Let P_L be the current price of land (per m^2) and R the current rent it yields. R is the marginal value product of land which has to be imputed in the case of owner-occupied land. i is the interest rate and π_L^e is the expected rate of land-price inflation. For the current year, the holding cost of land is $P_L i$ where i stands for not only the interest rate but other land-holding costs such as taxes. On the other hand, the total yield on land is

$(R + P_L\pi_L^e)$. If the land market is competitive, the cost and the yield ought to be equated,[1] i.e.

$$P_L i = R + P_L\pi_L^e \tag{1}$$

or

$$P_L = \frac{R}{i - \pi_L^e} \tag{2}$$

As land is immobile, land is exempted from factor-price equalization. Thus, P_L, R, and π_L^e can vary by location.

Let L be the total land area and PY be GNP originating on L in current value. (2) is rewritten as:

$$P_L = \left(\frac{PY}{L}\right)\left(\frac{R}{PY/L}\right)\frac{1}{i - \pi_L^e} \tag{3}$$

which decomposes the land price into three components: the average value product of land, the relative share of land rent, and the real interest rate.

To determine the relative share of land rent, assume that the aggregate production function is a CES function with the following:

$$Y^{-\rho} = (CL)^{-\rho} + \ldots, \qquad \rho = (1 - \sigma)/\sigma \tag{4}$$

where σ is the constant elasticity of substitution. The real land rent is equal to the marginal product of land, i.e.,

$$\frac{R}{P} = \frac{\partial Y}{\partial L} = C^{-\rho}\left(\frac{L}{Y}\right)^{-1-\rho}$$

or

$$\frac{R}{P}\frac{L}{Y} = \left(\frac{CL}{Y}\right)^{-\rho} \tag{5}$$

where P is the product price. Substituting (5) into (3), one gets:

$$\frac{P_L}{P} = C^{-\rho} \left(\frac{Y}{L}\right)^{\frac{1}{\sigma}} \frac{1}{i - \pi_L^e} \tag{6}$$

C is the efficiency coefficient of land. The more efficient land is, its C must be higher. Such land commands higher rent and is accordingly higher priced. For this conjecture to be true, we must have $\sigma < 0$ or $\sigma > 1$. Hence, the elasticity of substitution ought to be larger than 1. One should like to substantiate this conjecture.

A MACROECONOMIC COMPARISON

While the underlying relationship is simple, putting actual numbers into the variables involved is not at all an easy task. Land is extremely heterogenous, and its prices vary widely by location and by use. Land prices – both urban and agricultural – tend to be inordinately high in metropolitan areas like Tokyo, Kanagawa and Osaka. National averages are heavily influenced by these few outliers and are not necessarily representative of the true average situation.

To make things worse, reported land prices – especially, urban land prices – may significantly understate the true market value (see below). The data of land rent is either unavailable (because the majority of urban land is owner-occupied) or heavily distorted under the Land Lease Law and the House Lease Law which overprotect tenants' rights. Finally, there is no direct observation on π_L^e.

Thus, in checking the empirical plausibility of the basic relationship (3), one has to be content with assemblying whatever little information one has. First, land has to be aggregated into a few categories. The categories I consider are farm land and urban land (denoted, respectively, by subscript r and u). Farm land is limited to paddy fields and ordinary fields, excluding forests, pastures, etc. Urban land covers residential, commercial and industrial sites.

In comparing national averages, we take the unweighted geometric means of 43 prefectures excluding Tokyo, Kanagawa, Osaka and Okinawa. This is because information is missing on farm land prices in these four prefectures. But it also serves to reduce the heavy aggregation bias by excluding the three extreme outliers in our sample.

First, in Table 24.1, I compare average land prices (P_L) and the

Table 24.1 Farm-urban disparity (national averages[a])

	(1) Farm (1000 yen/m^2)	(2) Urban (1000 yen/m^2)	(3) = (2)/(1) Urban/farm
P_L	1.005	59.0	59
PY/L	0.176	25.1	143

Notes:
[a] Unweighted geometric averages for 43 prefectures (excluding Tokyo, Kanagawa, Osaka, and Okinawa).

Sources: see Appendix, Statistical Data Sources. P_L is for 1986 and PY/L is for FY 1985.

Table 24.2 Prices, average product, and rent for land (national averages)

		(1) Farm[a]	(2) Non-financial corporations[b]
(A)	$P_L/\frac{PY}{L}$	5.7	1.5
(B)	$R/\frac{PY}{L}$	0.103	0.067
(C)	R/P_L	0.018	0.044

Notes:
[a] Arithmetic averages for 43 prefectures – see Appendix, Statistical Data Sources.
[b] For value added, see *Financial Statements of Corporations*, Ministry of Finance, 1985; for values of land and other assets, see *Annual Report on National Accounts*, Economic Planning Agency.

average value product of land (PY/L) for farm land and urban land in the mid-1980s. There is a wide disparity between farm land and urban land in both of these measures. If P_L is underestimated to one-third of the true value (see fourth section), the disparity is quite comparable in both P_L and PY/L.

To quantify (3), we need information on R. For farm land, tenant rent is reported. Column (1) of Table 24.2 is based on this information. R/P_L is as low as 2 per cent. For urban land, there is no such information. One may make some educated guess, however. Take the non-financial corporate sector. The total (net) value added is reported in Ministry of Finance's *Financial Statements of Corpora-*

tions, which is divided into labour cost and capital cost (for FY 1985, capital cost is 28 per cent of value added). The market value of this sector's assets (land, tangible physical net assets, and financial assets) is reported in Economic Planning Agency's *Annual Report on National Accounts* (as of the end of 1985, land was 0.24 of all assets). If the rate of return (capital cost/assets) was uniform on all assets, it comes to 0.044, which is shown on row (C) of Column (2), Table 24.2. The actual land rent is likely to be less than this figure because the rate of capital gain tends to be higher on land than on other assets and the land rent could be lower by this differential. Hence, 0.044 is an upper bound on R/P_L with respect to urban land.

Thus, R/P_L is a plausibly small number for both farm land and urban land.

URBAN LAND PRICES

The estimation equation is (6). The sample consists of all of the 47 prefectures. P_{Lu} is the average price of urban land (per m^2). PY_u/L_u is GNP originating in the secondary and tertiary sectors, divided by urban land area. C is represented by two variables. The first is the population density in heavily inhabited districts (Pop_c/L_c) as defined in the 1985 *Population Census*. The second is the relative weight of heavily inhabited districts in the prefecture's total inhabitable land area (L_c/L). It is apparent that both the variables ought to be positively related to C. Finally, as to $(i - \pi_L^e)$, assume that i is common to all prefectures but π_L^e varies with place and is positively connected to the actual rate of land-price increase in the immediate past – an assumption which is acceptable if the actual inflation rate π_L is more or less steady.

Since the data are obtained from various sources (though most of them are taken from *Japan Statistical Yearbook*), they are not necessarily strictly comparable. In particular, P_{Lu} which is defined as 'prices judged appropriate by the prefectural governments based on the prices evaluated by real estate appraisers' (*Japan Statistical Yearbook* 1985, p. 480) may significantly understate the true market values.[2] However, so long as the underestimation is uniform over all prefectures, it is not likely to bias the elasticity estimates.

My cross-prefectural regression equation, in double log form, is as follows:

Table 24.3 Standard deviation of variables of (7)

	(1) *Standard deviation*	*(2)* *coefficient*	*(3)* *= (1) × (2)*	*(4)* *% of (3)*
$\log PY_u/L_u$	0.191	0.554	0.106	31
$\log Pop_c/L_c$	0.096	0.576	0.055	16
$\log L_c/L$	0.357	0.340	0.121	36
π_{Lu}	0.058	0.958	0.052	17
$\log P_{Lu}$	0.313		0.338	100

$$\log P_{Lu} = \underset{(.208)}{0.554} \log PY_u/L_u + \underset{(.225)}{0.576} \log Pop_c/L_c$$

$$+ \underset{(.079)}{0.340} \log L_c/L + \underset{(.346)}{0.958} \pi_{Lu} + \text{constant},$$

$$R^2 = 0.9346, \quad N = 47 \tag{7}$$

In this regression, all coefficient estimates are significant. The elasticity of substitution is 1.8. The population density and the geographical extent of population concentration have both strong positive effects on land prices.

I take special note that the effect of π_{Lu} is strong. A one percentage point increase in π_{Lu} leads to an increase in P_{Lu} from 1.00 to 1.25. There is thus a strong element of self-prophecy in land-price formation, assuming that π_{Lu} is a predictor of π^e_{Lu}. If people perceive of a higher land-price inflation in the future, the land price now is to be raised by a considerable margin. This in fact is what made Tokyo land prices extremely high already in the mid-1980s. It is not known how exactly π^e_{Lu} is related to π_{Lu}. But suppose that the coefficient of π_{Lu} applies to π^e_{Lu} as well. Then, in order to have this much strong effect on P_{Lu}, it is seen that $(i - \pi^e_L)$ is about 0.05.

Based on (7), one can decompose the variance of P_{Lu} into those of the explanatory variables – see Table 24.3. The largest contribution comes from L_c/L, followed by PY_u/L_u. Not unexpectedly, prefectures with heavy population concentration witnessed particularly high urban land prices.

Table 24.4 Standard deviation of variables of (8)

	(1) Standard deviation	(2) coefficient	(3) = (1) × (2)	(4) % of (3)
log PY_r/L_r	0.114	0.102	0.012	13
log Pop_{nc}/L_{nc}	0.186	0.425	0.079	95
log L_c/L	0.267	–0.342	–0.090	–105
log P_{Lu}	0.190	0.398	0.076	87
π_{Lr}	0.018	0.646	0.012	14
log P_{Lr}	0.132		0.087	100

FARM LAND PRICES

For farm land prices, we run a regression parallel to (7) substituting rural variables for urban variables. One significant modification is the addition of P_{Lu} as an explanatory variable. The argument goes as follows. Prices of farm land are affected positively by the prospect of its conversion to urban uses. When this conversion is made, the land price jumps up hundred-fold. Thus, the stronger the prospect, the higher farm land prices. This prospect is positively related to the current urban land price since a prefecture with strong demand for urban land must already have higher urban land prices.

The data for P_{Lr} is available for 43 prefectures. Four prefectures are missing. Their omission lowers R^2 because the three of them – Tokyo, Kanagawa and Osaka – are extreme outliers. The regression for the 43-prefecture sample is as follows:

$$\log P_{Lr} = \underset{(.167)}{0.102} \log PY_r/L_r + \underset{(.157)}{0.425} \log Pop_{nc}/L_{nc}$$

$$- \underset{(.152)}{0.342} \log L_c/L + \underset{(.180)}{0.398} \log P_{Lu} + \underset{(1.387)}{0.696} \pi_{Lr}$$

$$+ \text{constant}, \ R^2 = 0.3815, \quad N = 43 \tag{8}$$

PY_r/L_r and π_{Lr} are both not significant though both coefficients are positive in sign. R^2 is much lower.

The decomposition of the standard deviation of log P_{Lr} is shown in Table 24.4. The simple correlation between log Pop_{nc}/L_{nc} and log L_c/L is 0.48. It suggests that these two variables offset each other, leaving log P_{Lu} as the most influential explanatory variable.

THE ELASTICITY OF SUBSTITUTION

The most significant finding of our simple empirical exercise is the fact that the elasticity of substitution is significantly above unity in both the cases of farm land and urban land. In this connection, it is useful to note that σ turns out to be less than unity unless the variables are included for efficiency differences C. In fact, if P_{Lu} is regressed on PY_u/L_u alone, one gets:

$$\log P_{Lu} = \underset{(.087)}{1.521} \log PY_u/L_u + \underset{(.029)}{0.407}, \quad R^2 = 0.8710, \quad N = 47 \tag{9}$$

in which σ is 0.67.

Also, if farm land and urban land are not separated, one can get σ close to unity. Since P_L and PY/L are both low in agricultural prefectures and both high in metropolitan prefectures, the two variables vary more or less in proportion if land is aggregated.[3]

When σ is above unity, P_L ought to vary far less than PY/L does. But P_L varies far more than PY/L does. This is the reason why C has to vary considerably over prefectures. Thus, the land price in Tokyo is the highest in the nation, not because PY/L is the highest there but because C is the highest.

THE EFFECTS OF TAX POLICY

Consider the land tax, which is imposed on the land value. Let τ be the land tax rate on the market value of land. Then (1) is modified to

$$P_L(i + \tau) = R + P_L\pi_L^e \tag{10}$$

or

$$P_L = \frac{R}{i + \tau - \pi_L^e} \tag{11}$$

If landowners are strictly interested in the after-tax rate of return alone, there will be no tax shifting. This is seen by computing the after-tax rate of return, which is:

Table 24.5 The effect of the land tax on land prices (assuming $i - \pi_L^e = 0.02$)

τ	P_L/R
0	50
0.01	33
0.02	25
0.03	20

$$\frac{R - P_L\tau}{P_L} = i - \pi_L^e \tag{12}$$

It is independent of τ. The land price, however, responds very sensitively to the tax rate: see Table 24.5.

On the other hand, imagine that landowners are interested in the absolute amount of land rent after tax, which is:

$$R - P_L\tau = (i - \pi_L^e)\, P_L = \frac{i - \pi_L^e}{i + \tau - \pi_L^e}\, R \tag{13}$$

A rise in τ lowers after-tax rent. To compensate for this loss, R must be increased. It involves substituting other factors for land. If the compensation is fully made, the land price itself will remain unchanged.

Which of these two possibilities is more plausible? It is an empirical question.[4,5]

There are other taxes which also work on the land price. Consider the corporation income tax. When this tax is raised, the after-tax return on net capital assets declines. If this rate of return is to be restored to a predetermined level (e.g. the interest rate), then the capital input must be reduced and other factors including land must be increased (at a given level of output). With the elasticity of substitution greater than 1, this factor substitution must have a sufficient scope.

Thus, tax policy has an important bearing on land-price formation.

APPENDIX: STATISTICAL DATA SOURCES

(1) Land prices

P_{Lu}: Urban land prices, average for all uses, 1 July 1986, from 'Average prices of housing land by use and prefecture (per m^2)', *Japan Statistical Yearbook, 1987* (Table 14–13, p. 495; originally from the National Land Agency).

P_{Lr}: Farm land prices, average of prices of paddy fields and ordinary fields, 31 March 1986, from 'Farm rent, prices of farm land, and sales prices of paddy fields or fields converted to other use by prefecture', *Japan Statistical Yearbook, 1987* (Table 5–16, p. 157; originally from the Japan Real Estate Institute and the National Chamber of Agriculture). Prices are weighted by areas of paddy fields and ordinary fields as reported in *Japan Statistical Yearbook, 1988* (Table 1–9, p. 9 for 1986).

π_{Lu}, π_{Lr}: Annual rates of change in P_{Lu} and P_{Lr} from 1982 to 1986.

(2) Value added

PY_u: GNP originating in the secondary and tertiary sectors, in current value, for Fiscal Year (FY) 1985.

PY_r: GNP originating in the primary sector, in current value, for FY 1985.

Both series from *Japan Statistical Yearbook, 1987*, (Table 16–12, p. 564 (originally from the Economic Planning Agency).

(3) Land areas

L_u: Urban land area, privately owned, 1 January 1986.

L_r: Farm land area, privately owned, the sum of paddy fields and ordinary fields, 1 January 1986.

Both series from *Japan Statistical Yearbook, 1988*, (Table 1–9, p. 9.

(4) Densely inhabited districts

L: Inhabitable area, 1982

Pop: Total population, 1985.

The two series from Economic Planning Agency, *Keizai Yoran*, 1986, p. 68.

L_c: Densely inhabited districts, 1985.

Pop_c: Population in densely inhabited districts, 1985.

Two series from *Japan Statistical Yearbook, 1986*, Table 2–6, pp. 30–31.

$L_{nc} = L - L_c$

$Pop_{nc} = Pop - Pop_c$.

Notes

1. Because of various rigidities, not all economic agents may act so as to establish (1). For example, some agents may perceive of the yield in excess of the cost but do not buy additional land. But, the equality (1) must hold for those who actually buy or sell land. Then, (1) is the equilibrium condition for clearing the land market.
2. P_{Lu} may be compared with sales prices of farm land converted to urban uses. To be as much comparable as possible, we take P_{Lu1} (prices of residential sites in city planning zones) for the former and P_{Lr1} (sales prices of farm land for residential sites). For the year 1986, one has:

$$\log P_{Lu1} = \underset{(0.095)}{0.915} \log P_{Lr1} + \underset{(.111)}{0.530}, \ R^2 = 0.6704, \ N = 47$$

The unweighted geometric mean is \$136 300/m^2 for P_{Lr1} and \$45 800/m^2 for P_{Lu1}. Thus, P_{Lu1} was more or less uniformly one-third of P_{Lr1}.
3. By running a cross-prefectural land-price regression (pooling time series), Boone and Sachs (1990) accept the unitary elasticity of substitution. Their dependent variable, however, is the average land price for all kinds of land. This commits a fallacy of composition as I pointed out above.
4. An empirical study by Ando *et al.* (1990) shows a negative effect of property tax on land prices. This seems to support the first possibility. The effective land tax rate in Kanagawa Prefecture (which they studied) was 0.18 per cent on housing land and 0.00045 per cent on farm land. They find from cross-section time-series regressions that 'Doubling the property tax on the housing land and farm land lowers the land price by about 7.5 and 8.5 per cent respectively'.
5. Following the same line of argument, one may say that the inheritance tax tends to raise the land price if land owners try to keep after-tax inheritance (consisting mostly of land) intact.

References

1. Ando, I., Iwata, K., Yamazaki, F., Hanazaki, M., Ishikawa, T., Ebina, K. and Kawakami, Y (1990) *Econometric Analysis of Property Tax on Land – A Case Study for the 13 Cities in Kanagawa Prefecture, 1976–1986* (Tokyo: Economic Planning Agency).
2. Boone, B. and Sachs, J. (1990) *Is Tokyo Worth Four Trillion Dollars? An Explanation for High Japanese Land Prices* (Tokyo: Economic Planning Agency).
3. Economic Planning Agency (Japan) (1990) 'Structural problems in the Japanese and World economy', *Papers and Proceedings of the Seventh International Symposium* (Tokyo: Economic Planning Agency, March).
4. Sato, K. (1991) 'Tochi to Makuro Keizaigaku – Nihon Keizai o Taisho to shite' (Land and macroeconomics: the case of the Japanese economy), *Nihon Keizai Kenkyu*, no. 21, May.

25 Asia–Pacific Cooperation: Issues and Prospects

Peter Drysdale*

INTRODUCTION

Vigorous expansion in trade, investment and other economic ties within the East Asian and Pacific economy have been critically important to the region's extraordinary growth in recent decades. East Asian economies have experienced stronger sustained growth in this period than the world has previously known.

Despite the revolution now taking place in the Eastern bloc and the former Soviet Union, there is little doubt that East Asian industrialization is bound to be a primary influence on world trade and economic growth in the next quarter century and beyond just as it was around Japan's emergence as a great industrial power in the last. This is a time of great challenge and opportunity for all those countries which are a part of this process of industrialization and trade growth in the Asia–Pacific economy.

My first purpose is to explain the priority attaching to Asia–Pacific economic cooperation in international economic diplomacy and the opportunities for countries in the East Asian and Pacific economy and then to outline the emerging role of Asia–Pacific economic diplomacy. East Asian economies have grown more rapidly for longer than any others in world economic history. East Asia's production has, in the last three decades, grown from less than one quarter of North America's to rough equality with that of North America and almost one quarter of the world's. In this time, East Asia has been a main source of dynamism in international and especially long distance international trade. It has become the most important source of world savings (larger than North America or Europe) and overwhelmingly the largest source of surplus savings for international investment.

The shift in the world's economic centre of gravity towards East

Asia has brought with it large changes in the international economic and geo-political system, as well as in the analytic and ideological prisms through which people all over the world now view reality. These developments are of particular and strategic importance in the conduct of international economic diplomacy.

EAST ASIA'S GROWTH RECORD

From the mid-1950s, Japan grew at a rate that more than doubled output each decade, until, by the time of the first oil shock, its production per capita was close to the frontiers of the world industrial economy. The four Asian newly industrializing economies (NIEs) started their high growth later, in the early 1960s, and from a lower base than Japan, but on average have been growing even more rapidly. Three of them, Taiwan Singapore and Hong Kong, have already surpassed the average per capita output in lower-income OECD countries. Korea, starting from a lower base still, seems likely to attain the living standards of OECD laggards in the near term. Over the past decade, China joined the ranks of the high-growth East Asian economies. Up to now, it has exceeded the goal that it set itself, to double output each decade. In the principal ASEAN economies other than Singapore (Indonesia, the Philippines, Thailand and Malaysia) growth has been less consistent and more modest, but has comfortably exceeded average performance for world developed and developing economies alike since the late 1960s. Japan's growth since it broadly 'caught up' with productivity levels elsewhere in the OECD in the mid-1970s has been less spectacular, but has remained above the average of advanced economies.

In the early postwar period, when the multilateral trading system around the GATT was being established, North America accounted for one half of world GNP, and East Asia, devastated by war and civil strife, for only a few per cent. By the early 1960s, the North American share of world production was still extremely large, around 40 per cent, but East Asia's share had increased to 9 per cent. By the early 1980s, North America's share of world GNP had fallen to around 28 per cent and East Asia's had more than doubled to almost 20 per cent. These trends continue, and in the 1990s East Asia will contribute more than North America to world GNP, with the two regions accounting for over one half of world output.

Despite uncertainties, generated by the setback in China and political change in other parts of the region, these shifts in the focus of world economic power are entrenched. They have implications on a global scale for the leadership and management of the international trade and economic system. They have particular implications for a country like Australia, whose prosperity has become closely linked with successful East Asian industrialization and the Pacific economy in the last few decades.

The weight and role of the different economies in East Asia are, of course, undergoing very dramatic change. Japan has become a mature industrial economy with relatively less dependence per unit of domestic production on raw materials, and the NIEs have pursued strong outward-looking economic development strategies. But the transformation of the Australian postwar trade relationship with Japan into a broader trade, capital and technology relationship with East Asia and the Pacific and the critical nature of this change to Australia's underlying resource and industrial competitiveness in the world economy are, for example, key interests for Australia, as well as for other resource-supplier economies, in their approach to economic diplomacy and corporate strategy in the future.

A significant characteristic of industrial transformation in East Asian countries is that their trade growth has required the taking over of market shares from established exporters, first in labour-intensive manufactured goods, as Japan did from Britain and Europe in both the prewar and postwar periods and as other NIEs in East Asia have done from Japan and, in recent decades, from one another.

Hence the ascension of Japan to the ranks of the relatively high-income economies is reducing the relative importance of basic raw materials trade with that market, and also shifting raw materials markets to other East Asian countries and opening new opportunities for industrial cooperation, investment and specialization in technologically sophisticated goods and services within the region, with stronger intra-industry trade growth, especially among the adjacent economies of Northeast Asia.

ASIA–PACIFIC ECONOMIC INTEGRATION

The scale of the changes taking place in consequence of successful economic growth in East Asia is reflected in the immense shifts in regional trade flows. In the period between 1965 and 1988, the share of the Pacific (here including East Asia, North America and Australasia) in world trade grew from around 30 per cent to 37 per cent – see Table 25.1. East Asian and Pacific countries transact 64 per cent of their trade with each other. In 1965 intra-regional trade was less than 50 per cent of Pacific trade. The proportion of intra-regional trade is now approaching that in Europe: in 1988, intra-regional trade amounted to 71 per cent of Europe's total trade. These developments have been influenced by three sets of factors: the relatively rapid growth of Japan and the rest of East Asia in world production, the extent of complementarity of trade in the region, and a group of geographic, political and historic factors such as locational proximity and the dissolution of colonial blocs after the Second World War.

The process of East Asian and Pacific economic integration will intensify as Japanese corporations follow, in the 1980s and 1990s, the pattern of overseas expansion set by US multinationals in the 1950s and 1960s. Japanese direct investment abroad rose a further 40 per cent in 1988 to $US41 billion, compared with US direct investment abroad of over $US300 billion. Roughly half the exports of Japanese overseas affiliates are directed to Japan, although it is noteworthy that the bulk of manufactured goods imported from East Asia by Japan in recent years have come from independent enterprises in Korea, Taiwan and elsewhere.

EAST ASIA'S ECONOMIC FUTURE

But what is the outlook for the East Asian and Pacific economy in the decades ahead?

The key point is that East Asia's share of world production and trade will continue to rise through the 1990s and beyond:

(a) The Japanese economy can expand more rapidly than other industrial countries if structural changes allow increasingly scarce labour and skills to be channelled to the most productive industries. Japan too has much to gain from deepening commitment to trade and economic liberalization.
(b) Chinese growth depends on the timing of the resumption of reform, with an average growth in excess of 7 per cent likely if there is solid progress on reform early in the decade, and 4 to 5 per cent otherwise.
(c) The Republic of Korea and Taiwan can be expected to double output in the 1990s, although this will require continued learning

Table 25.1 Asia-Pacific and world trade shares, 1965 and 1988 (per cent)

Partner / *Reporter*		*Australia & NZ* *1965*	*Australia & NZ* *1988*	*Japan* *1965*	*Japan* *1988*	*Other North-east Asia* *1965*	*Other North-east Asia* *1988*	*ASEAN* *1965*	*ASEAN* *1988*	*China* *1965*	*China* *1988*	*North America* *1965*	*North America* *1988*
Australia & NZ	X	6.1	7.7	14.3	25.3	2.4	12.4	1.3	7.4	4.5	3.1	13.3	13.3
	M	5.6	7.3	9.3	19.8	1.2	8.1	2.0	5.4	0.6	2.0	25.7	23.3
Japan	X	4.8	3.0	–	–	8.7	13.9	8.5	8.3	3.1	3.7	34.7	37.3
	M	7.8	6.2	–	–	3.0	15.0	6.8	11.7	2.9	5.1	34.6	26.1
Other North-east Asia[a]	X	3.1	2.1	15.4	13.2	3.5	9.9	6.6	5.9	0.8	9.1	31.6	35.1
	M	2.2	2.8	26.3	27.7	3.2	5.0	3.8	7.2	16.2	12.9	22.3	20.0
ASEAN	X	3.7	2.4	23.5	19.1	5.4	11.6	2.9	17.4	2.1	2.5	28.7	21.8
	M	2.1	3.3	27.3	23.6	4.2	8.3	4.9	16.1	4.4	3.5	23.3	17.0
China	X	2.1	0.8	15.9	16.9	28.8	38.4	7.1	5.9	–	–	1.1	8.0
	M	13.3	2.8	19.0	20.6	1.1	22.4	3.1	5.7	–	–	7.5	15.8
North America[b]	X	3.1	2.0	6.8	10.1	1.9	10.0	1.5	3.1	0.3	1.6	29.4	34.2
	M	1.7	1.1	9.0	18.1	1.8	8.3	2.0	4.2	0.1	1.8	36.1	28.5
Asia–Pacific total[c]	X	3.7	2.5	7.4	10.0	3.8	12.4	2.9	6.5	1.1	3.5	28.3	31.9
	M	3.6	2.9	9.6	17.0	2.1	9.7	3.0	7.1	1.5	4.0	32.7	24.9
Western Europe	X	2.2	0.8	0.8	2.0	0.6	2.0	0.7	1.2	0.5	0.6	9.5	9.0
	M	2.2	0.7	1.2	4.8	0.5	2.2	0.6	1.4	0.4	0.7	13.5	8.1
Middle East	X	3.0	1.2	13.6	21.1	0.8	5.5	0.9	7.1	0.4	0.8	7.9	14.7
	M	1.5	1.8	5.4	10.0	1.0	6.2	0.2	3.1	0.9	1.4	18.1	13.6
Mexico	X	0.4	0.3	8.1	5.2	1.0	1.6	0.4	0.5	0.3	0.5	63.7	79.7
	M	1.3	0.4	2.5	6.5	0.1	2.0	..	0.3	..	0.1	68.4	77.1
Latin America[d]	X	0.2	0.4	4.0	6.0	0.3	2.1	0.2	1.0	0.8	1.8	38.2	47.0
	M	0.6	0.6	3.8	6.6	0.3	2.8	0.2	0.4	..	0.4	42.0	47.9
Rest of world	X	0.7	0.5	3.2	6.3	0.5	2.9	0.5	1.8	1.0	2.8	5.9	11.4
	M	1.4	1.4	6.0	8.0	0.9	4.3	0.8	3.0	1.1	3.5	15.9	9.7
World	X	2.3	1.5	3.8	6.2	1.5	6.4	1.3	3.6	0.8	2.0	16.5	20.1
	M	2.4	1.6	4.5	10.3	1.0	5.5	1.3	3.8	0.8	2.2	21.1	16.6

		Asia–Pacific total		Western Europe		Middle East		Mexico		Latin America		Rest of world	
		1965	*1988*	*1965*	*1988*	*1965*	*1988*	*1965*	*1988*	*1965*	*1988*	*1965*	*1988*
Australia & NZ	X	45.1	72.2	44.2	16.9	1.6	3.6	0.5	0.3	1.2	1.4	7.9	5.9
	M	45.4	66.5	45.2	27.7	4.6	2.6	0.1	0.2	0.5	1.3	4.3	1.9
Japan	X	60.1	66.3	13.8	21.6	3.7	3.3	0.5	0.7	5.7	3.3	16.7	5.5
	M	55.4	64.4	9.2	15.8	13.7	10.1	1.8	0.8	9.0	4.1	12.7	5.6
Other Northeast	X	61.2	75.3	23.6	16.6	2.4	2.7	2.1	0.3	1.5	1.7	11.3	3.7
Asia[a]	M	74.0	75.6	17.5	14.4	2.1	3.8	0.4	0.3	1.7	2.2	4.7	4.0
ASEAN	X	66.3	75.0	24.6	15.7	0.8	2.9	··	0.1	0.8	0.9	8.2	5.5
	M	66.2	71.8	24.3	17.1	2.9	6.5	0.3	0.1	0.6	1.5	7.6	3.1
China	X	55.1	70.1	23.5	11.1	3.2	4.1	··	··	0.3	0.8	17.9	13.8
	M	44.0	67.3	27.3	18.0	2.0	1.4	0.2	0.3	7.4	4.1	19.3	9.2
North America[b]	X	43.0	61.0	31.2	21.6	3.0	3.1	3.3	4.7	13.2	10.3	9.6	4.0
	M	50.7	61.9	25.1	21.6	1.8	2.5	2.3	4.4	16.8	10.3	5.6	3.7
Asia–Pacific total[c]	X	47.5	66.9	28.9	19.5	2.9	3.1	2.4	2.2	10.0	5.5	10.7	5.0
	M	52.6	65.6	24.3	19.3	3.9	4.3	1.8	2.4	12.2	6.6	7.0	4.2
Western Europe	X	14.3	15.7	64.9	71.3	3.0	3.5	0.5	0.2	4.1	1.9	13.7	7.6
	M	18.5	17.8	57.7	69.8	4.8	2.4	0.3	0.3	5.5	2.5	13.5	7.5
Middle East	X	26.5	50.3	53.6	32.8	9.1	8.1	··	··	1.7	3.2	9.1	5.6
	M	27.1	36.1	47.1	49.1	13.6	7.8	··	··	0.8	2.4	11.4	4.6
Mexico	X	73.9	87.7	9.3	10.1	0.1	0.1	–	–	8.4	2.0	8.3	0.1
	M	72.3	86.3	24.5	11.6	··	··	–	–	2.5	1.8	0.7	0.3
Latin America[d]	X	43.8	58.3	34.6	25.2	0.4	2.0	0.2	0.5	17.0	10.2	4.2	4.3
	M	46.9	58.7	30.0	24.3	1.5	3.5	0.7	0.6	19.3	11.4	2.3	2.1
Rest of world	X	11.8	25.7	42.0	55.7	2.1	2.7	··	··	27.3	1.0	16.8	14.9
	M	26.0	30.0	49.0	51.8	2.3	2.6	0.4	0.1	2.3	2.6	20.4	13.0
World	X	26.3	39.8	48.4	46.4	2.9	3.4	0.9	1.0	10.0	3.7	12.4	6.7
	M	31.1	39.9	45.2	45.9	4.3	3.4	0.7	1.1	7.7	4.5	11.7	6.3

Notes:
X = exports. M = imports. *a* Korea, Taiwan and Hong Kong. *b* United States and Canada. *c* Australia, New Zealand, Japan, Other Northeast Asia, ASEAN, China, North America and the Pacific Islands. *d* Includes Mexico, the Caribbean and other Latin American countries. ·· These figures are positive values less than 0.1.

Source: IMF, *Direction of Trade Statistics*, International Economic Data Bank, Research School of Pacific Studies, Australian National University.

of the conditions for stable industrial relations in a democratic society in Korea, and continued progress on structural reform in Taiwan. The importance of the framework of social and institutional structures to the efficient operation of the labour market is borne out in the North-east Asian experience.

(d) Hong Kong could again double output in a decade if confidence in the post-1997 arrangements were established by the early restoration of the momentum of reform in China, but long delays will weaken Hong Kong's economic capacity and hold growth down to 4 or 5 per cent a year.
(e) Thailand and the rest of Southeast Asia, other than the Philippines, are on the threshold of strong growth and industrialization in the pattern of Northeast Asian economies a decade earlier.
(f) By the end of the decade Japan can be expected to have the highest per capita income among advanced industrial countries, Hong Kong a per capita income in the middle range of industrial economies, Taiwan at the lower end of the range, and Korea not far outside the range.
(g) China could enter the ranks of middle-income developing countries by the end of the century if there is early resumption of reform, but will otherwise remain a low-income developing economy.

East Asia's share of world trade is likely to expand more or less in line with its share of world output and trade growth will continue to be highly complementary with the resource economies in the region. Two decades hence, this observation will also apply more closely to Indonesia, as industrialization proceeds on Java.

Northeast Asia will become a less important source of capital flows to world markets through the 1990s. But:

(a) The stock of foreign assets will continue to grow, in the case of Japan, more than doubling from the current level. Japan is already the world's largest creditor.
(b) The international role of Japanese direct investment will continue to expand after Japan's share of capital flows falls, because of the advantages of direct investment in international business organization.
(c) Deficit countries will need to correct their positions in line with diminished access to Northeast Asian capital flows, to avoid a major dislocation in world financial markets.

Whether East Asia's share of world production continues to expand so rapidly beyond the year 2000 depends partly on whether the Chinese systematic reforms, embraced in principle in the 1980s, have been implemented. There are, I believe, powerful forces impelling China in this direction.

The focus on East Asia does not imply that other regions are unimportant, or in any absolute sense less important, to the future of the global economy. The big issues of world peace and stability for the foreseeable future will be defined for East Asia in terms of alliance relationships with the USA and the resolution of global issues upon which, in the end, everything else depends. The maintenance of an open international trading system, the avoidance of macroenvironmental catastrophes, and the avoidance of thermonuclear war will be resolved in a wider international arena in which the powerful states of East Asia share importance with many others.

But the fact remains: success in utilizing opportunities associated with East Asian economic growth will be fundamental to the success of global economic adjustment in the coming decades and the impact of East Asia's growth will continue to be of an order of magnitude more important to world prosperity than relations with any other region, despite the promise of reform and growth in Eastern Europe and the countries of the former Soviet Union.

CHALLENGES FOR ECONOMIC DIPLOMACY

The growth of deeper and more complex trade and other economic ties within East Asia and the Pacific is reinforcing the common interests of East Asian and Western Pacific countries in trade and economic diplomacy. A key element in this complexity is the development, over the last decade, of tension in the management of USA–Japan economic relations (and to a lesser extent of those between the US and Taiwan and Korea). The immediate cause of this tension was the extreme imbalance in the external positions of both the USA and Japan, in the early 1980s, the former experiencing a large deficit and the latter a large surplus on the current account. While the adjustment of these imbalances had to be through macroeconomic policy changes, business interests and political forces in the USA, in particular, focused sharply on trade and commercial policies practised in East Asia as providing both the cause and the cure of the problem.

The reality, as always, is more complicated. If Japan acquiesces in settlement by bilateral and discriminatory management of the difficulties with the USA, then a broad retreat into sectoral and regional protectionism would likely gather pace, with world-wide ramifications. Not least of these ramifications would be damage to the trade and industrial development ambitions of East Asian countries, in whose trade growth there is such a considerable stake. Japan imposed its first Voluntary Export Restraint on Korean knitwear imports in February 1989. Such developments in trade diplomacy, if they spread, would create serious political complications, especially when China returns to seeking a larger place in the world economy and moves from a planned to a more open market economy.

Specifically, smaller Pacific economies, like those of the ASEAN countries and Australasia, have much to lose from any restriction of open trade growth that results from bilaterally-managed trade and economic settlements between North America and East Asia. This is both directly, through the effect of commodity trade access, and indirectly, through the impact of such arrangements on the growth of the NIEs of East Asia and their demand for imports from the region. More widely, there is a large interest in stability in trans-Pacific dealings and an effective framework for representing East Asian economic interests to the rest of the world.

The immediate dangers (in the form of the US application of 'Super 301' trade penalties on Japan and threatened use against South Korea and other East Asian countries) have eased, but these tensions are embedded in the dynamics of East Asian industrialization and, over the last decade or so, have given Asia-Pacific economic cooperation an increasing priority in international economic diplomacy.

The countries of East Asia and the Pacific now have to shape their approach to international economic policy in an environment in which their actions have an increasing influence on global outcomes. Japan has been catapulted into a position of particular influence and responsibility. In trade, finance, technology and development cooperation, whatever Japan does or does not do bears strongly on other countries in the Pacific and globally.

Only a few decades back, the whole region, including Japan, was under the umbrella of American economic and political power. The western Pacific was a relatively small element in the world economy and world trade. But policy interdependence now typifies the Asia–Pacific and international economy. And defining strategic interests in foreign economic policy and regional development is a paramount concern for East Asian and Pacific countries. This requires the establishment of mechanisms for effective communication of policy interests and priorities. There is an interest in coordinated policy development, both to exploit the potential for trade growth in the Pacific and to project Pacific interests and define East Asian and Pacific responsibilities in the global arena. These matters are at the heart of the change in the international economic regime now being cautiously but purposefully put into place by the Asia–Pacific Economic Cooperation (APEC) group of countries.

The ministerial level meeting on APEC in Canberra, 5–7 November last year, was the signal of a profound change in the whole regime whereby policies will be developed in the Pacific and international economy. The gathering of the most powerful and representative group of ministers responsible for foreign economic policy ever to assemble in Asia and the Pacific (from Japan, Korea, the ASEAN countries, Canada, the US, New Zealand and Australia) testified, above all, to the growing imperative of regional economic cooperation. US Secretary of State James Baker believes that the Asia-Pacific group could become as important in the international economic system as the Bretton Woods institutions. No-one, least of all Baker, imagines this happening in the near term but it is likely to evolve over the next decade or two.

It will be no easy task to build a coalition in the Pacific that will make the achievement of common policy goals more manageable and ease the transition in international economic leadership responsibilities. One effect of economic change, and the domestic and international uncertainties it creates, is to make institutions, and the forums and settlements they make possible, much more important to the success of international economic collaboration.

Here, of course, the countries of the Pacific have neither the example of a recent Armageddon such as that which impelled Europe towards the 1957 Treaty of Rome, nor the close economic, cultural and geopolitical interests which provide a ready basis for cooperation in North America. Yet despite the heterogeneity of Pacific countries, the process of establishing an infrastructure for closer economic cooperation was begun in 1980 through the Pacific Economic Cooperation Conference (PECC).

PECC's forums and task forces, which deal with regional cooperation in trade, agriculture, fisheries, minerals and energy, investment, monitoring macroeconomic trends, and transport, telecommunications and tourism, serve both policy and commercial strategic purposes. In this, their tripartite structure (official, industry, academic participation) and quasi-official status is a considerable advantage. The seventh PECC meeting was held in Auckland last year. An important policy achievement, which grew out of consultations within PECC, was the development of Pacific support for the comprehensive round of multilateral trade negotiations currently under way (the Uruguay Round). Another achievement has been facilitation and broadening of the economic dialogue between China and Taiwan. This will be an important advantage in drawing China, Taiwan and Hong Kong into the high-level APEC dialogues already begun.

COOPERATION ASIA–PACIFIC STYLE

Compared with the elaborate mechanisms for consultation on economic policy matters that have evolved within Europe, or that are enshrined in the OECD, those in the Pacific are as yet quite rudimentary. Nonetheless, they incorporate features quite uniquely suited to the problems of encouraging policy coordination among Asia-Pacific economies.

The essential features are: support for the enhancement of information about policy practices and economic data to assess policy interests; the opportunity for interchange on policy matters among officials of Pacific countries; and encouragement to seek policy convergence through the exploration of common interests and problems. PECC's unique structure and operating modalities, including the 'non-official' but informed character of its deliberations, are essential to its functioning (around the constraints of Pacific diplomacy such as presented by China's relations with the region) and constitute a special strength in its role of policy development through APEC within the Pacific.

In a policy environment that is subject to rapid change and immense political and cultural diversity, the anticipation of new policy issues, the need for new policy approaches, and the need for increased transparency of policy interests, recommend against the representation of policy positions, and their entrenchment, in a formal bureaucratic structure of extensive government-to-government arrangements. Government-level consultations *do not*, however, require elaborate bureaucratic structures.

From this perspective, the APEC meeting in Canberra has been a logical step in a careful and, thus far, successful process of building the consensus on foreign economic policy approaches within the Pacific necessary to preserve and enhance the conditions for continued economic growth. It signified an important change in gear. In the global arena, East Asian and Pacific countries share an immediate concern about the international trade policies, coordination of macroeconomic policy and the management of the exchange rate and international financial system. In these matters, particularly in questions of international trade diplomacy, the interests of Asia–Pacific countries as a group are converging on stronger support for an open economic system. There is a close consistency between regional policy objectives and international economic policy goals.

Asia–Pacific countries have no interest in European-style union or the formation of a discriminatory trading bloc. Any such development would be inimical to the long-term interests of the region which is reliant on rapid trade transformation and global access. Rather, the aims of broadly based Asia–Pacific economic cooperation are: to promote multilateral trade liberalization and sharing of the responsibilities of world trade and economic leadership; to lower tensions between the USA and its East Asian economic partners over trade issues and payments imbalances; to reduce the risks associated with a more inward-looking Europe; to accommodate new problems of competitive strength in East Asia; to manage whatever challenge the emergence of China, with its partially reformed centrally planned system, brings when it returns as a major player in Pacific economic relations; and to define a new relationship with the former Soviet bloc. The agenda of regional interests is huge and complex. This fact has defined the unique character and development of Asia–Pacific economic consultative mechanisms to date and for the future.

Anxieties about organizational structures and being able to maintain effective representation of interests alongside the two regional economic giants have been expressed within the ASEAN countries. They are present also within Australasia and all the smaller Asia–Pacific economic partners. They dictate the precepts which condition the future course of Asia–Pacific economic cooperation. The central ideas are: *openness* in international economic policy and diplomatic approach; *evolution* in the practice of high level consultation; and *cooperation and equality* in managing a growing economic partnership.

A central element for the smaller partners (ASEAN and Australasia included) is the framework that the APEC meetings at ministerial level offer for effective representation of interests through the leverage that joining forces provides. This is no North–South dialogue talk-fest in the making. A notable feature is the absence of emphasis on development assistance issues. Success requires there be no threat to existing institutions, such as those of ASEAN. It requires building up and drawing upon the established 'non-official' institutions like PECC, with its valuable tripartite structure, in an evolutionary development of the infrastructure for the higher level regional dialogues that have now begun. It also implies a significant and constructive redefinition of the framework within which foreign demands on Japan can both be focused and qualified so as to make them more reasonable and digestible to the Japanese and international polities alike. This interest, in providing a 'frame of reference' within which Japan increasingly shares responsibilities for regional and international economic leadership, has long been an important rationale behind efforts to develop broader dialogue on policy matters among the countries of East Asia and the Pacific and to re-orient the USA–Japan partnership into a broader Pacific partnership.

The message here is that an increasing (not dominant) leadership role for Japan is to be found within a pluralist structure of Asia–Pacific and world economic power, encompassing the effective representation of broader Pacific and global economic interests.

FUTURE TASKS AND CHALLENGES

The powerful forces of East Asian industrialization raise a number of difficult questions and involve some uncertainties. These questions focus on the approach to international economic policy and to the regime necessary to sustain and smooth the transformation of international competitiveness within East Asia and between East Asia and the rest of the world.

The whole world has been forced to respond to East Asia's internationally oriented economic growth. The entire framework of international trade has changed in this process and is still to find a new stability. Europeans have been motivated to accelerate integration; East Europeans and those in the former Soviet Union to throw off the shackles of closure and command. US political and intellectual thinking is heavily burdened by ambivalence, in the realization that the very success of postwar American international economic policies and political commitment has inevitably reduced the relative economic power and weight of the US itself.

Western Pacific countries must also respond to these shifts in their international environment, as well as to the powerful direct implications of East Asia's economic growth. The emergence of East Asia as a major centre for world economic activity has greatly reduced the region's relative isolation from the countries of industrial power, a continuing factor as East Asian growth and economic integration proceed south. At the same time, the growth of deeper trade and economic ties in East Asia and the Pacific is reinforcing the common interests of East Asian and Western Pacific countries in trade and economic diplomacy. Significantly, these involve commitment to an open, non-discriminatory international trading system.

Just as the alliance framework within East Asia and the Pacific must continue to respond to Japan's new stature as a world economic power, the struggle with openness and economic modernization in China, and the new circumstances in East–West relations, so too must Western Pacific priorities in economic diplomacy change gear, if not course.

In brief, Western Pacific countries have a particularly vital interest in policy approaches supportive of stability in the East Asian and Pacific economy and trans-Pacific dealings.

An international economic diplomacy which gives utmost priority to Asia–Pacific economic cooperation and consultation on international economic policy approaches supportive of an open and liberal international trading and economic system has now acquired a double urgency.

It was natural, although not inevitable, that Australia took some initiative in establishing the infrastructure to serve these purposes, through PECC and the important step of convening the first APEC ministerial level meeting last November. Meetings of both bodies seem now likely to progress in loose tandem: the next meetings of both will take place in Singapore, where PECC has established its central secretariat.

The emergence of stronger regional institutions is of great importance in maintaining a liberal trading environment supportive of sustained growth in East Asia and, thereby, the Western Pacific region's own trade prospects; in constraining the tensions between the USA and East Asia and their resolution through the use of narrow bilateral power; in advancing direct trading interests in East Asia; and, now more importantly than ever, in providing coherence in the response from this part of the world to the changes in the countries of the former Soviet Union and the Eastern bloc.

There is no question that the challenge for future Asia–Pacific economic cooperation, currently surrounded with most uncertainty, is the accommodation of China. While any sustained attempt to turn back the clock on reform in China would inevitably lead to a decline in the legitimacy of Communist Party rule and temporarily, at least, to national political disintegration, there is a huge task in mending the fracture in confidence in the reform process, both inside and outside China.

In this context, it is particularly important to engage China and all its parts in all the regional endeavours of Asia–Pacific economic consultation. The uncertainty surrounding the immediate future of Chinese reform (and similar events that are bound, from time to time, to disrupt the progress of East Asian industrialization over its long haul) should not divert the inevitable involvement, and substantial strategic interest, in the process.

In the short term, the important aim is to consolidate regional countries' willingness to make substantial liberalizing commitments at the GATT, in the context of a successful outcome from the Uruguay Round. In the long term, the aim is broader, involving the building of commitment to specific moves towards free trade on a multilateral basis, by identifying and negotiating packages of liberalizing commitments in sectors that are important to East Asian and Pacific trade. The achievement of these objectives will emerge only from high quality professional analysis, prior to substantive discussion of liberalization. This is best done not through the establishment of a new bureaucracy, but through the marshalling and coordination of work in established institutions, including *inter alia* through the national secretariats as well as the task forces of the PECC. Economic ministers and their bureaucracies will need to establish an efficient coordinating mechanism, however informal, for making sure that the work is done between APEC meetings.

Indeed, it is important to avoid the domination by the currently large and affluent economies that highly bureaucratic and expensive structures for regional cooperation would entail. There is no Paris in the Pacific and the setting up of a substantial, new central secretariat to undertake all the analytical support for APEC would lead to complex and unproductive negotiations about formulae for its establishment and domination of the organization and its agenda by the largest partners. It is proving much more effective to marshal the analytic skills and make progress in policy dialogue in less formal and more imaginative ways. Using existing mechanisms, such as the range of PECC task forces, as well as support from other organizations such as the Asian Development Bank and the ASEAN Secretariat, has the added advantage of avoiding bureaucratic entrenchment of policy positions (characteristic of inter-governmental institutions) in an environment of extremely rapid change requiring flexible policy responses.

The central interest of Asia–Pacific countries is in maintaining, strengthening and expanding the rules for an open international economy and, in the short term, increasing the chances of substantial progress in trade liberalization in the Uruguay Round. They can do this best by helping to build on the region's recognized interest in and commitment to liberalization, to reinforce each other's resolve, and to provide leadership to the rest of the world.

A second interest is to address issues that are especially important to cooperation among neighbouring states with large economic relationships but which so far are not part of the constructive agenda of multilateral negotiations: among others, transport and communications systems and infrastructure educational standards, content and accreditation and aspects of commercial law. This would be a context in which Asia–Pacific economies, for example, could test interest in the exchange of liberal approaches to the granting of civil aviation landing rights.

A third interest is to broaden the USA–Japan dialogues and ease associated tensions over trade and other economic policies. The current constructive focus on institutional barriers to trade adjustments is of importance and interest to all Asia–Pacific countries. While the evidence of recent adjustments in imports and production in Japan, Korea and Taiwan is impressive, aspects of these adjustments depend on unfamiliar institutional arrangements. It is in the interests of exporters and importers that these be better understood. It is in the interests of all countries that action based on this understanding be multilateral, and not bilateral and discriminatory. None of these interests can be advanced effectively in such existing institutions as the GATT and the OECD at this time, although progress with the first of them would advance the interests of these two institutions.

The second and third interests outlined above would overlap with subjects which have been considered within the OECD by a different set of countries. The series of meetings, which began the dialogue between the OECD, Hong Kong, Korea, Taiwan and Singapore in January 1988, is productive in enhancing the dialogue on, and correcting some simplistic interpretations of, the dynamic Asian economies' (DAEs) international trade and monetary policies. Yet there remains an important distance between the central interests of the OECD and those which are driving broader Asia–Pacific dialogues.

Expansion of the OECD to include one or more additional Pacific states could be useful in informing European governments and communities of the character of East Asian economic growth. However, given the growing strength and broadening base of regional interests witnessed over the past few decades, expansion of the coverage of the OECD provides no adequate substitute for mechanisms to enhance dialogue on substantive economic cooperation in the Asia–Pacific region. A strategic interest will be in building up productive associations between the OECD and the new institutions that are now emerging to serve regional economic cooperation interests in the Asia–Pacific economy.

A key conclusion is that the Pacific belongs to no single nation: not Japan, despite its new-found economic power, nor China, despite the scale of its industrial promise, nor, any longer, to the USA, despite its continued and pivotal role in the international economy. The responsibilities of Asia–Pacific economic policy leadership are bound to be developed as shared responsibilities. The huge and rewarding task of establishing a degree of intimacy among the heterogeneous nations of East Asia and the Pacific upon which confident policy strategies can be promulgated and executed in support of international systemic objectives is a challenge to which Asia–Pacific countries are now (fortunately) at last beginning to turn.

Note

* Hirofumi Shibata's work has been an inspiration to me ever since, as a student, I read his seminal paper on the equivalence of tariffs and quotas. This intellectual inspiration has been enriched by close personal association through our work together in the Faculty of Economics, Osaka University, and exchanges with my own university. It is a special privilege to offer this essay in recognition of Hirofumi Shibata's immense contribution to the profession, his wonderful intellectual openness, and his warm friendship.

References

1. Drysdale, P. (1989) *International Economic Pluralism: Economic Policy in East Asia and the Pacific* (Sydney: Allen and Unwin; New York: Columbia University Press).
2. Drysdale, P. (1990) 'Australia's Asia–Pacific economic diplomacy', *Current Affairs Bulletin*, vol. 66.
3. Drysdale, P. and Garnaut, R. (1989) 'A Pacific free trade area?', in *Free Trade Areas and US Trade Policy* (Washington, DC: Institute for International Economics).
4. Drysdale, P., Viviani, N., Yamazawa, I. and Watanabe, A. (1989) *The Australia–Japan Relationship: Towards the Year 2000* (Canberra: Australia–Japan Research Centre; Tokyo: Japan Center for Economic Research).
5. Garnaut, R. (1989) *Australia and the Northeast Asian Ascendency* (Canberra: Australian Government Publishing Service).
6. Harris, S. (1989) 'Regional economic cooperation, trading blocs and Australian interests', *Australian Outlook*, vol. 43.

26 Output-neutral Quotas on Imports

Brian Hindley

INTRODUCTION

When one firm controls domestic production of a good, a quota on competing imports may cause a decline in the output of that firm. If the free trade level of imports is imposed as a quota, the quota necessarily provides the domestic firm with an incentive to reduce its output.

In Figure 26.1, *MC* is the marginal cost curve of the single domestic producer, and *DD* is the domestic demand curve. Supply from the rest of the world is infinitely elastic at a price of P_W. In the absence of a quota, therefore, domestic output is *OH* and imports are *HT*.

Without a quantitative restriction on imports, the fact that there is only one domestic producer is neither here nor there. That producer is a perfect competitor in the world market. He can sell nothing at a price higher than P_W – any attempt to raise his price above that level will result in the replacement of his sales by a flood of imports.

A quota on imports, however, converts him into a monopolist in the domestic market. No flood of imports can then follow an increase in his price. The demand curve facing the domestic producer is no longer $P_W P_W$ but *DD* less *HT*. This demand curve is represented in Figure 26.1 by $D_V D_V$. The domestic producer will now maximize his profits by producing at *M* (necessarily less than *H*), and charging a price of P_V (necessarily more than P_W).

As a consequence of imposing the free trade level of imports as a quota, the importing country must suffer a welfare loss given by the dotted area in Figure 26.1. Whether that is the only welfare cost, from a national point of view, depends upon the destination of the rents generated by the quota. These rents are represented by the brick-shaded area in Figure 26.1. If they accrue to domestic residents, as will be the case when rights to import under the quota are given to domestic residents, they do not represent a national welfare loss.

Many current quotas, however, take the form of voluntary export

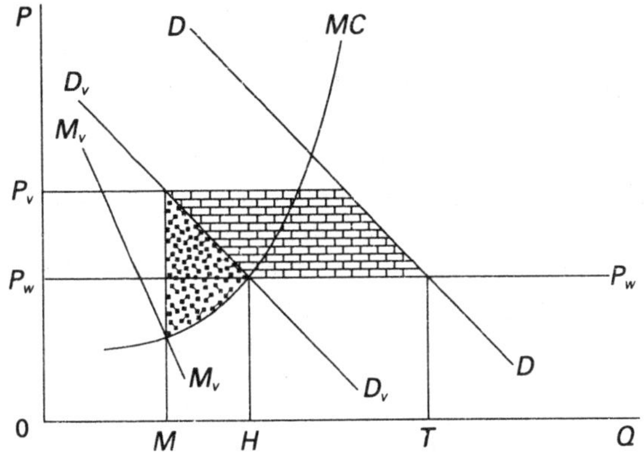

Figure 26.1

restraints (VERs), which are arrangements under which the foreign government accedes to a request by the home government to restrict exports. When the restriction on imports takes the form of a VER, it is the foreign producers who obtain the quota rents. In that event, the entire shaded area in Figure 26.1 represents the domestic welfare cost of imposing the free trade level of imports as a VER.

The demand curve facing the domestic producer is *DD* less the amount of the quota. Hence, a more restrictive quota on imports will shift the demand curve facing the domestic producer to the right. If the quota on imports is zero (that is, imports are banned), *DD* itself will be the demand curve of the domestic producer. In general, a decrease in permitted imports will cause the domestic producer to expand his output from *OM*, towards *OH*, the output he would have under free trade.[1] Thus, a sufficiently restrictive quota may cause him to produce exactly the same output under the quota as he would produce in the absence of the quota. I shall call such a quota 'output-neutral'.

All of the propositions noted above are well known.[2] So far as I know, however, there has been no *quantitative* assessment of the conditions under which a quota will cause a domestic firm or firms to contract or expand output. Hence, a number of questions lack answers, even in terms of plausible magnitudes. For example, how restrictive must a quota be before it provides a single domestic producer with an incentive to expand output above the free trade level? What is the welfare cost of expanding output and employment in the industry by this means? Might there be no quota on imports that will provide him with an incentive to expand output? In this paper, I exploit the simplest available model to make a start on filling these gaps.

Lack of earlier interest in exploring such magnitudes might be explained by a belief that protection of a single domestic producer by quotas on imports is not sufficiently frequent to be relevant to any problem in the real world. That is a mistake, however. Before turning to the characteristics of output-neutral quotas, the empirical relevance of the analysis deserves brief discussion.

EMPIRICAL RELEVANCE

The clearest case of protection of a single domestic producer by VER is provided by the agreement on video-cassette recorders between the European Community (EC) and Japan, entered into in February, 1983. At that time there were two indigeneous EC producers: Philips and Grundig. In February 1983, however, Philips owned 25 per cent of the shares of Grundig. It later acquired a majority holding. Hindley (1986) discusses this case in some detail.

Several other developed-country industries protected by VERs are sufficiently concentrated that they might respond to a VER as would a single producer. Steel and motor cars, for instance, have been protected by VERs in the United States and the EC (in the case of motor cars, by individual member states of the EC).

Moreover, the incentives that may lead a single domestic producer to reduce output will push a trade union in the same direction. Just as protection by quota reduces the cost (in terms of units sold) of an increase in the price charged by the domestic producer, protection by quota reduces the cost of an increase in wage rates (in terms of lost employment) for a single trade union. Thus, a VER or quota protecting a multi-firm industry with a single trade union will provide that union with an additional incentive to raise wage rates and thus (by pushing the marginal cost curve upwards) to reduce output and employment.

Finally, protection by quota, as opposed to VER, is more prevalent in developing than in developed countries. Many developing-country markets are small, and it is likely that some of these quotas protect industries consisting of one or two local producers. In such cases, the analysis is likely to apply directly.

A SINGLE DOMESTIC PRODUCER PROTECTED BY QUOTA

The demand for a homogeneous product in country A is separable and is given by:

$$Q = A\pi^{E} \qquad E < -1 \tag{1}$$

Foreign producers are perfectly competitive and their supply to the A market is perfectly elastic. Hence, before the quota, the marginal revenue and the marginal cost of the domestic producer is equal to the world price.

Before the quota, foreign suppliers have a market share of Θ. The effect of the quota is to place an upper limit on their share of $\alpha\Theta(1 \geq \alpha \geq 0)$.

AN OUTPUT-NEUTRAL QUOTA

What are the characteristics of a quota that causes the domestic producer to choose to hold his output constant at q? Denoting quantities before and after the quota with subscripts 0 and 1:

$$q = Q_0(1 - \Theta) \tag{2}$$

and

$$q = Q_1(1 - \alpha\Theta) \tag{3}$$

Hence, under the assumption of constant domestic output:

$$\frac{Q_1}{Q_0} = \frac{1 - \Theta}{1 - \alpha\Theta} \tag{4}$$

and from (1):

$$\frac{\Pi_1}{\Pi_0} = \left[\frac{Q_1}{Q_0}\right]^{\frac{1}{E}} \tag{5}$$

Thus, substituting (4) into (5):

$$\frac{\Pi_1}{\Pi_0} = \left[\frac{1 - \Theta}{1 - \alpha\Theta}\right]^{\frac{1}{E}} \tag{5'}$$

The post-quota demand curve of the domestic producer is obtained by substitution of (3) into (1):

$$\Pi = \left[\frac{q}{A(1 - \alpha\Theta)}\right]^{\frac{1}{E}} \tag{6}$$

and if *MRD* is the marginal revenue of the domestic producer, it follows from (6) that under the quota:

$$MRD_1 = \Pi_1 \left(1 + \frac{1}{E}\right) \tag{7}$$

In the pre-quota position, $MRD_0 = \Pi_0$. Since domestic output is constant, so is marginal cost and the quota will give the domestic firm an incentive to expand output if:

$$MRD_1 > MRD_0 \tag{8}$$

From (5′) and (7), however:

$$\frac{MRD_1}{MRD_0} = \left[1 + \frac{1}{E}\right]\left[\frac{1 - \Theta}{1 - \alpha\Theta}\right]^{\frac{1}{E}} \tag{9}$$

The output-neutral quota occurs when $MRD_1 = MRD_0$, or when:

$$\left[\frac{1 - \Theta}{1 - \alpha\Theta}\right]^{\frac{1}{E}} = \frac{E}{1 + E} \tag{10}$$

(10) can be used to calculate, for particular values of the market share of imports Θ and elasticity of demand E, the quota restriction α that is output-neutral. Some results of such a calculation are displayed in Table 26.1. A quota that is less restrictive than the numbers displayed in the table will reduce domestic output. To provide the domestic producer with an incentive to expand output, a more severe restriction is necessary.

The contents of Table 26.1 are rather remarkable. Protection by quota of a single domestic producer provides that producer with an

Table 26.1 Output-neutral values of permitted imports (expressed as a fraction of pre-quota imports)

		Elasticity of demand				
		1.500	*2.000*	*3.000*	*4.000*	*5.000*
Share	0.850	0.260	0.470	0.580	0.620	0.640
	0.800		0.250	0.410	0.460	0.490
of	0.750	Domestic		0.210	0.280	0.320
	0.700	output falls			0.070	0.120
imports	0.65	even if imports are banned				

incentive to reduce output unless the share of imports is very high. Even if the share of imports is high, moreover, a very severe quota restriction is required to give an incentive to expand output. It seems likely, therefore, not merely possible, that protection by quantitative restriction of a single import-competing producer will cause a reduction of domestic output.

WELFARE COSTS OF AN OUTPUT-NEUTRAL QUOTA

What economic welfare costs must be absorbed before a quota expands output (that is, before the output-neutral point is reached)?

Two components of welfare loss require consideration. The first is lost consumer surplus. This can be approximated by:

$$LCS = \int_{Q_1}^{Q_0} \left[\frac{Q}{A} \right]^{\frac{1}{E}} dQ - \Pi_0(Q_0 - Q_1) \qquad (11)$$

and denoting total sales of the product in the protecting country before and after the quota by R_0 and R_1:

$$\frac{LCS}{R_0} = \frac{1 - \frac{R_1}{R_0}}{1 + \frac{1}{E}} - 1 + \frac{Q_1}{Q_0} \qquad (12)$$

The second component of welfare loss (from the standpoint of members of the country imposing the quota) is the increased rents of foreign producers. The total rent created by the quota is:

$$T = (\Pi_1 - \Pi_0)Q_1 \qquad (13)$$

or, expressed as a fraction of the pre-quota sales of the industry:

$$\frac{T}{R_0} = \left[\frac{R_1}{R_0} - \frac{Q_1}{Q_0}\right] \tag{14}$$

In the case of a VER, a fraction $(1 - \alpha\Theta)$ of T goes to the domestic producer and the rest to foreign producers.

Summation of (12) and (14) gives the total welfare loss to members of the protecting country other than the owners of the protected firm:

$$\frac{W}{R_0} = \frac{1 + \frac{R_1}{R_0}}{1 + \frac{1}{E}} - 1 + \frac{R_1}{R_0} \tag{15}$$

Multiplication of (4) and (5), and substitution of the resulting expression for R_1/R_0 into (15) gives:

$$\frac{W}{R_0} = \frac{-1}{1+E}\left[1 - \left(\frac{1-\Theta}{1-\alpha\Theta}\right)^{\frac{E+1}{E}}\right] \tag{15'}$$

and substituting (10) into (15′) gives:

$$\frac{W}{R_0} = \frac{-1}{1+E}\left[1 - \left(\frac{E}{E+1}\right)^{E+1}\right] \tag{15''}$$

Hence, the gross loss of welfare is independent of market shares. Table 26.2 gives the welfare losses entailed in reaching the output-neutral point.

To convert the figures in Table 26.2 into net welfare losses, it is necessary to deduct from them the increase in the profits of the domestic producer. From (14), these increased profits, D, are:

$$\frac{D}{R_1} = (1 - \alpha\Theta)\left[\frac{R_1}{R_0} - \frac{Q_1}{Q_0}\right] \tag{16}$$

Table 26.2 Welfare loss of an output-neutral VER to members of the country other than the protected producer (expressed as a fraction of total pre-quota sales of the product)

$-E$	1.500	2.000	3.000	4.000	5.000
W/R_0	0.845	0.500	0.277	0.193	0.147

Table 26.3 Increase in the profits of the quota-protected domestic producer at the output-neutral point (expressed as a fraction of total pre-quota sales of the product)

		Elasticity of demand				
		1.500	*2.000*	*3.000*	*4.000*	*5.000*
Share of imports	0.850	0.300	0.150	0.075	0.050	0.038
	0.800		0.200	0.100	0.067	0.050
	0.750	Domestic		0.125	0.083	0.060
	0.700	output falls			0.090	0.075
	0.650	even if imports are banned				

Table 26.4 Net welfare loss of a quota at the output-neutral point (expressed as a fraction of total pre-quota sales of the product)

		Elasticity of demand				
		1.500	*2.000*	*3.000*	*4.000*	*5.000*
Share of imports	0.850	0.545	0.350	0.200	0.143	0.109
	0.800		0.300	0.177	0.126	0.097
	0.750	Domestic		0.152	0.110	0.085
	0.700	output falls			0.103	0.072
	0.650	even if imports are banned				

and by substitution of (4), (5) and (10), this becomes:

$$\frac{D}{R_0} = -\frac{(1 - \Theta)}{(1 + E)} \qquad (16')$$

Table 26.3 gives calculated values of this sum.

The net welfare loss to the country using the VER is now obtained by deducting a figure in Table 26.3 from the corresponding column in Table 26.2. The results are displayed in Table 26.4.

CONCLUDING COMMENT

It is widely recognized that VERs are an expensive means of protection, though the very high welfare losses possible under imperfect competition may be less widely appreciated. Also, it may be less widely recognized that VERs may cause the output of a protected industry to decline when that industry is imperfectly competitive. Nevertheless, the preliminary results presented here suggest that outcome is probable, not merely possible.

Of course, the model presented here is very simple. It can be extented in many ways. Explicit consideration of the effects of protection by VER on a domestic duopoly, and of the effects of a VER on an industry in which firms with monopoly power face a single union, are among the more obvious extensions.

Notes

1. A shift to the right of the demand curve facing a monopolist does not necessarily imply an expansion in output. A sufficient condition for that result is that the second derivative of price with respect to quantity is greater than zero.
2. Bhagwati (1969) puts forward the basic proposition. This paper results in part from a comment by Shibata (1968) on an earlier paper by Bhagwati. Shibata suggested the applicability of the analysis to voluntary export restraints.

References

1. Bhagwati, J. (1969) 'On the equivalence of tariffs and quotas', in J. Bhagwati (ed.), *Trade, Tariffs and Growth* (London: Weidenfeld and Nicolson).
2. Hindley, B. (1986) 'European Community imports of VCRs from Japan', *Journal of World Trade Law*, March/April.
3. Shibata, H. (1968) 'A note on the equivalence of tariffs and quotas', *American Economic Review*, vol. 58.

27 1992 and EC Public Utilities*

Ali M. El-Agraa

INTRODUCTION

The classic examples of public utility goods and services are defence, education, energy, health, transport and telecommunications. In the European Community (EC), education is largely the prerogative of national governments, but the EC is playing an increasing role in this area, both in terms of ERASMUS (European Community Action Scheme for the Mobility of University Students) and the recently agreed strategy on the mutual recognition of degrees and qualifications within the EC. Also, although the others are presently not entirely subject to the internal market arrangements, sooner or later, they are bound to follow, especially with regard to defence. The aim of this paper is to point out the possible gains from extending the internal market only to defence, energy, telecommunications and transport, since education and health are most likely to continue on a national (regional) basis. Obviously, one needs to appreciate what the internal market means, and the overall gains expected from it before discussing these issues; hence the paper begins with these considerations.

WHAT IS 'THE INTERNAL MARKET'?

When the Heads of State or Government of the EC met in Milan in June 1985 and endorsed the aims of the White Paper which was presented to them by the EC Commission, they committed the EC to complete a 'frontier-free market' by 31 December 1992. When the member nations of the newly-enlarged EC met in Luxembourg in December 1985 and signed the so-called Single European Act (SEA), they incorporated the internal market in this first major reform of the EC constitution. However, the SEA is more than that since it commits the EC member states to the achievement of five other aims:

increased economic and social cohesion so that weaker nations may participate fully in the freer market; a common scientific and technological development policy; further development of the European Monetary System (EMS); the emergence of an EC social dimension, including further action to promote health and safety at work; and coordinated action towards improving the environment. In addition, the SEA brings foreign policy into scope in terms of foreign policy coordination and provides it with a more effective support structure than it had in the past, including its own secretariat which is housed in the EC Council building in Brussels. Also, there are institutional changes: it was agreed that the Council would take decisions by qualified majority vote in relation to the internal market, research, cohesion and improved working conditions, and that in such cases, the European Parliament should share in decision making.

For the purposes of this paper, all one needs to know is that the internal market seeks to eliminate all non-tariff barriers (the only tariffs that exist today are temporary due to the transition periods granted to the new member nations) to the movement of goods, services and factors of production within the EC by the end of December 1992.

THE EXPECTED BENEFITS

Benefits without growth

According to the *Cecchini Report*, which summarizes the findings of a study carried our on behalf of the EC Commission (see Commission 1988 a popular version is to be found in Cecchini 1988), the completion of the internal market will regenerate both the goods and services sectors of the EC. The study estimates the total potential gain for the EC as a whole to be in the region of 200 billion ECU, at constant 1988 prices. This would increase EC GDP by 5 per cent or more. The gains will come not only from the elimination of the costs of barriers to intra-EC trade, but also from the exploitation of economies of scale which are expected to lower costs by about 2 per cent of EC GDP. Also, the medium-term impact of this on employment is to increase it by about two million jobs. These estimates are considered to be minimal since the study points out that if the governments of the member nations of the EC pursue macroeconomic policies that recognize this potential for faster economic growth, the total gains could reach 7 per cent of EC GDP and increase employment by about five million jobs. Hence, if these predictions become a reality, the EC will gain a very substantial competitive edge over non-participating nations.

Growth benefits

Although these expected gains have generated tremendous enthusiasm for the internal market, they are not really substantial enough to cause countries like Japan and the USA to react in a panic so as to avoid missed opportunities. However, new estimates by Baldwin (1989) may have sown the seeds for such a response. Baldwin argues that the gains may be about five times those given in Cecchini.

Baldwin's approach differs from that of Cecchini in one significant respect. He questions Cecchini for not making allowance for an increase in the long-term rate of growth. He contends that the methodological background to the estimates in Cecchini is based on traditional growth theory which assumes that countries become wealthier because of technological change, and that the dismantling of barriers to trade and increasing the size of markets will not permanently raise the rate of technological progress. Thus, both Cecchini and the traditional methodology are built on the premise that the liberalisation of markets cannot permanently raise the rates of growth of the participating countries.

Cecchini addressed the question of how the internal market will alter the *level*, not the *rate*, of growth of output. Thus, he reached the conclusion that the creation of the internal market will squeeze more output from the same resources, for reasons such as the lower costs due to economies of scale and enhanced competition, giving the predicted benefits reported in the previous section. Note, however, that although these expected gains will take some time to realize, the underlying methodology envisages them as a step-increase – see line 1 in Figure 27.1.

Baldwin's claim that this approach underestimates the gains rests on two distinct arguments. The first endorses the traditional approach, but asks about what the expected rise in output will do to savings and investment. He argues that if they stay as constant percentages of national income, they will both rise in absolute terms. Consequently, the stock of physical capital will also increase, leading to a further rise in output which will raise savings and investment again; thus a virtuous cycle will set in.

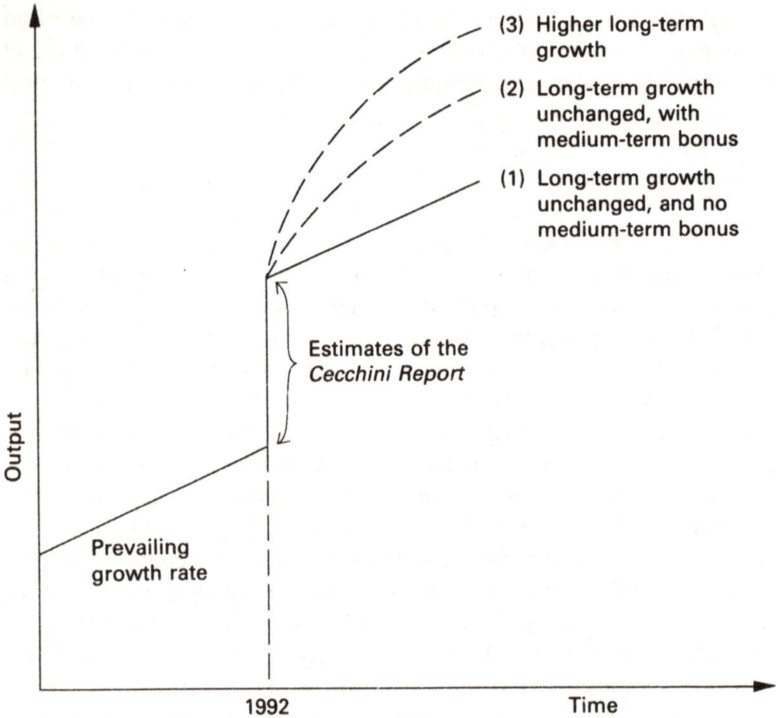

Figure 27.1 Baldwin's possible growth paths for the European Community after the end of 1992

Orthodox economists will challenge the assertion that this burst of faster growth will continue indefinitely. They will argue that as the capital stock rises, a larger percentage of each year's investment will simply replace existing capital due to depreciation. Thus the capital stock will grow at a diminishing rate, and sooner or later, investment will match depreciation bringing to a halt any further increase in the capital stock. The economy then reaches a new equilibrium with a larger capital stock and a higher level of output than initially, but the economy once more growing at the earlier long-term rate. Therefore, it follows that even if there is no permanent rise in the growth rate, Cecchini must have missed this vital element: the expected rise in GDP of about 6.5–7 per cent will raise the levels of savings and investment and increase the capital stock, making the EC grow faster while this process continues. Baldwin thinks that half of this adjustment might take about ten years. He labels this a 'medium-term growth bonus' – see line 2 in Figure 27.1. Converting this into an equivalent change in the level of output, and relying on conservative assumptions, Baldwin concludes that the gains from the internal market will be in the region of 3.5–9 per cent, as against the 2.5–7 per cent predicted in Cecchini.

However, Baldwin is not content with this. He declares that the medium-term bonus may be augmented by a permanent rise in growth, giving a 'long-term growth bonus – see line 3 in Figure 27.1. This is because, unlike orthodox theory (which argues that there is a 'steady state' in which the capital stock grows at the same rate as the labour force, thus with the constant labour force assumed by Cecchini, there will be a constant capital stock), he follows the model proposed by Romer (Chicago University) which is built on the premise that the capital stock can rise indefinitely. This leads him to believe that the increase in EC investment after 1992 will raise the growth rate for the EC permanently by something in the range of a quarter to three-quarters of a percentage point. Expressed as an equivalent increase in the level of output, the total bonus (the combined bonuses from the medium- and long-terms) would be about 9–29 per cent of GDP. Adding this estimate to that by Cecchini, one gets an overall figure of 11–35 per cent increase in GDP.

There are serious reservations regarding the estimates by both Cecchini and Baldwin, but, given our immediate task, these should be left to the conclusion. However, at this juncture, it is appropriate to provide a simple theoretical framework for the expected benefits.

Theoretical illustration

Let me consider two cases. The first is one in which comparative advantage can be exploited by trade. The second concerns the case of enhanced competition where there is no comparative advantage between countries. The basic model behind the diagrams used below is fully set out in standard trade theory books – see El-Agraa (1989b). Therefore, no explanation will be provided here.

The first case is illustrated by Figure 27.2. Due to the removal of certain market barriers and distortions, the relative price of a particular commodity is equalised throughout the entire EC market at the lower P_2 in the EC member country under consideration. As we have seen, this is because it is assumed that the presence of these barriers is costly, leading to the higher price level P_3 in that country. Since this country is a net importer from the rest of the EC, comparative

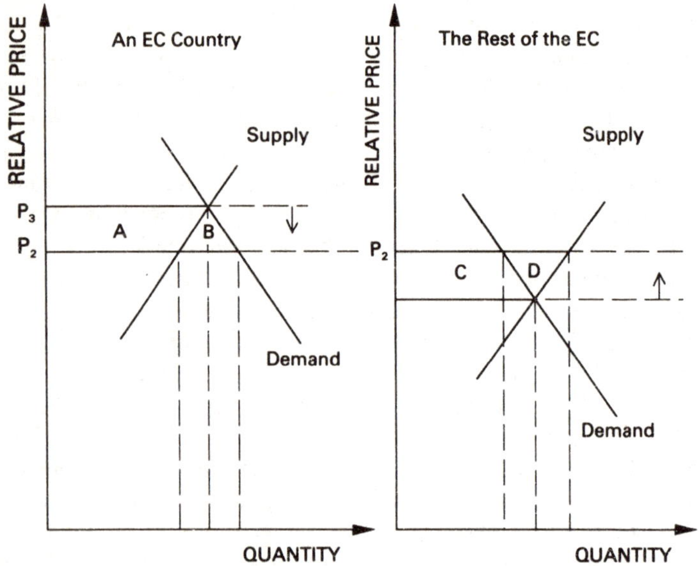

Figure 27.2 Effects of Eliminating Market Barriers and Distortions for a Given Commodity (the Case in which Comparative Advantage can be Exploited by Trade)

Source: Adapted from Emerson *et al.* (1988)

advantage lies with the EC or, alternatively, this country has a comparative disadvantage. In this member country, the removal of the barrier increases consumers' surplus by areas *A* and *B* and reduces producers' surplus by area *A*, giving a net benefit of area *B*. In the rest of the EC, there is an increse in producers' surplus of areas *C* and *D* and a reduction in consumers' surplus of area *C*, resulting in a net benefit of area *D*. Therefore, the total benefit to the EC as a whole is the sum of the two net benefits, i.e. areas *B* plus *D*. In short, the analysis in the case of the member country is the reverse of the one for tariffs while the analysis for the rest of the EC is exactly the same as that for general protection, especially with regard to the agricultural surpluses resulting from the EC's Common Agricultural Policy – see El-Agraa (1990).

The second case is illustrated by Figure 27.3. As barriers are removed, importers are able to reduce their prices from P_2 by the amount of direct costs saved. Domestic producers respond by reducing their own prices through reductions in their excess profits and

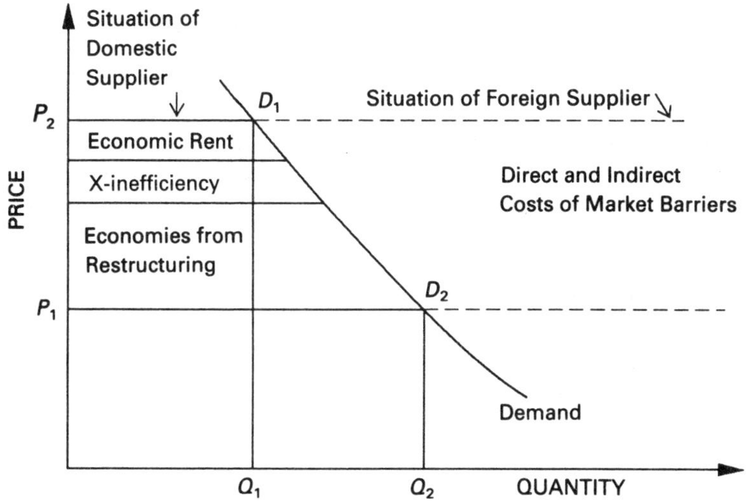

Figure 27.3 Effects of Eliminating Cost-increasing Barriers (the Case of Enhanced Competition where there are no Comparative Advantages between Countries)

Notes:

(a) Economic rent consists of the margin of excess profits or wage rates that result from market protection.

(b) X-efficiency consists of, for example, the costs of overmanning, excess overhead costs and excess inventories (i.e. inefficiencies not related to the production technology of the firm's investments).

(c) Economies from restructuring include, for example, the greater economies of scale or scope obtained when inefficient production capacity is eliminated and new investments made.

(d) Direct costs are those such as delays at frontiers and the cost of differing technical regulations that would immediately fall if the market barriers were eliminated.

(e) Indirect costs are those that would fall as foreign suppliers adjust to the more competitive situation with more efficient production and marketing.

Source: Adapted from Emerson *et al*. (1988)

wages or by eliminating inefficiencies of various types (overhead costs, excess manning and inventories, etc.). As prices fall, demand increases beyond Q_1 and this induces investment in productive capacity in this industry which results in economies of scale and further price reductions. However, this is not the end of the story since this more competitive market environment is supposed to make industries reconsider their business strategies in a fundamental way, leading to restructuring (mergers and acquisitions, liquidations and investment) over a number of years until output increases to Q_2.

As can be seen from the diagram, there is an increase in consumers' surplus equal to area $P_2D_1D_2P_1$, but what happens to producers' surplus is not so clear. On the one hand, they may be able to compensate for price cuts in terms of cost reductions, but they will lose some economic rent. On the other hand, since they have become more competitive, they may be able to sell outside the EC, thus increase their output and profits. For the EC economy as a whole, it can be said that there is a net benefit since the gains to the EC consumer are in excess of the losses incurred by the EC producers. However, in the light of the discussion in El-Agraa (1989a and 1990, chapter 4), it must be emphasized that this analysis is extremely simple.

EC PUBLIC UTILITIES

Transport

Road transport

The total volume of international surface transport in the EC is estimated to be 730 million tonnes – see Emerson *et al.* (1988). In terms of tonnage, the shares of the different modes of transport in 1982 were 32 per cent for sea, 31 per cent for road haulage, 28 per cent for inland waterways and 9 per cent for rail.

In the road transport sector, the movement and operation of vehicles throughout the EC is partly restricted, and competition is considerably distorted by different national regulations on capacity and access to the road haulage industry and tariff control. A system of licenses requires hauliers to apply for a limited number of permits in order to move goods between given member countries. In addition, there is a general prohibition on 'cabotage', i.e. the possibility for non-resident hauliers to collect and deliver loads within the borders of another member state.

There is a variety of regimes regulating road haulage within the member countries. All countries apply qualitative controls (e.g. safety regulations). A survey of six EC countries indicates that some countries also apply quantitative restrictions on market entry, through the restrictive issuance of permits. This is the case in France,

Germany, Italy and the Netherlands; Belgium and the UK do not apply such restrictions. Tariffs (price controls) also exist in some countries, notably France, Italy and the Netherlands. However, France plans to eliminate tariff regulations by 1991, and in Italy it is believed that there is considerable illegal undercutting of minimum prices as well as illegal cabotage.

Following the judgment by the EC Court of Justice of 22 May 1985 on the Common Transport Policy, the EC Council has committed itself, by Decisions in November 1985 and June 1986, to suppress all quantitative restrictions by 1992 at the latest and in the meantime to increase the total number of EC-wide permits by 40 per cent each year and suppress gradually the remaining distortions of competition. The EC Commission has made appropriate proposals to this effect, but Council decision is still pending. A proposal on liberalisation of cabotage was discussed but not adopted by the Council in December 1987.

A liberalized regime of international road haulage in the EC, including permission for cabotage, would also imply pressure in favour of regulatory reform in the more heavily restricted national markets. As the US example quoted below suggests, this might well lead to very substantial reductions in transport costs for industry and commerce, going well beyond cost savings for international traffic.

The special nature of the rail transport system largely precludes competition or free market access in international rail transport services. Tariffs on international routes are negotiated bilaterally and the revenue from international rail traffic is shared between the participating national rail companies. The White Paper does not propose measures of liberalisation for rail transport.

The restrictions in the road transport sector inhibit competition and are likely to prevent an efficient use of transport equipment. As a result, transport costs are undoubtedly higher than would be the case in an unrestricted market, and there are possibilities for monopolistic profits for the holders of limited licenses. While comprehensive information on the likely magnitude of these costs is not available, some quantitative indications are available from a number of sources.

The present permit system and prohibition of cabotage is reflected among other things in the cost of empty moves. A study by Ernst and Whinney (1989) has estimated, at the EC level, the cost of empty moves at about 1–2 billion ECU, of which about 20 per cent may be related to regulatory restrictions. A study by DRI Europe (1986) has suggested that the potential market for consecutive cabotage (cabotage on the return leg of an international journey) could be about 1–5 per cent of present domestic traffic.

The shortage of international road transport licenses is suggested by the existence of a black market for permits in some countries and the complaints made by road transport organizations. The shortages are particularly marked for multilateral EC permits. A study by Cooper *et al.* (1987) found that in the UK the black market price of an annual multilateral EC permit was 17 000 ECU, which corresponds to 23 per cent of a truck's typical annual costs.

The experience of the USA in deregulating the truck sector in 1980 provides an interesting point of reference since the previous licensing system there was analogous to that still prevailing in the EC. A number of studies provide evidence of increased capacity utilisation, lower rates and better service. In a study by Delaney (1987), the savings from improved transportation efficiency have been estimated to amount to $26 billion in 1985, compared with transport costs of some $260 billion. Further cost savings are estimated to result from reduced inventories made possible by increased efficiency in the trucking industry.

Note that the overall gains given at the beginning were calculated on the assumption that the road haulage prices will fall by only 5 per cent.

Inland waterways and sea transport

By contrast with road transport, restrictions on inland waterway transport in the EC are of less overall importance given the fact that Rhine navigation, which accounts for 80 per cent of the goods carried between the member countries, has been liberalised. However, cabotage still has to be fully liberalised in this sector. Sea transport services are subject to certain restrictions on marine cabotage. For both modes of water transport, the Commission has put forward proposals to establish free competition by 1992.

Air transport

Civil aviation is a major and fast-growing industry. In Western Europe, the revenue of 17 major scheduled airlines amounted in 1985 to 31.3 billion ECU, of which 42 per cent was intra-EC traffic. In the context of the internal market, the provision of efficient and low-cost air services is important both to the consumer for his/her direct uses, and for businesses engaged in the European market as a whole. The economic interests of the geographically peripheral regions of the EC are particularly concerned, since uncompetitive air transport aggravates their locational disadvantages, and competition from other modes of transport is less intense.

Since the 1946 Bermuda Agreement on international air transport, with the exception of deregulation in the USA in the late 1970s, the economic model of international air services has been mainly one of licensed duopolies. In Europe, a system of about 200 separate bilateral agreements between 22 countries has emerged, in which designated carriers provide services whose cost, capacity and conditions are either directly or indirectly regulated. Rights by an EC carrier to offer services between two other member countries (the so-called fifth freedom rights) are effectively prohibited: of about 400 routes operated within the EC, only 44 tolerate the fifth freedom, of which only one has been granted to an EC airline. In 1987, only 5 per cent of European routes had multiple designation, i.e. more than one airline per country per route. In a number of cases, the revenues on city pair routes are pooled and split 50:50 between both carriers. Price competition is limited, despite various possibilities for discount fares. The larger scale ban on new entrants in Europe, except for transatlantic services and charter flights, has meant that even the 'contestable markets' model of oligopoly has not prevailed in the sector.

The White Paper envisages that the EC should move to a more liberalized regime, notably with respect to tariffs, capacity controls and access to the market. After lengthy negotiations, the Council agreed in December 1987 to an initial 3-year package covering air fares, capacity access to the market and the application of the competition rules of the Treaty to civil aviation. As regards bilateral capacity control, the ranges accepted by the Council move from the initial 50:50 rules to 45:55 range in the first two years, followed by 40:60 in the third year. On fares, the package ensures that regulatory authorities at one end of a route will no longer be able to reject arbitrarily lower fares put forward by innovative airlines; a range of new discount and cheap discount fares and conditions are to be introduced. On market access, greater competition will be achieved by allowing a greater number of airlines compete especially on dense traffic routes; links between hubs and regions will be expanded considerably, and certain fifth freedom rights will be exercised by airlines within the EC.

Within the context of the internal market for services, it is regrettable that intra-EC tariffs should be based on outdated IATA exchange rates, whereas periodically adjusted exchange rates based on the ECU would reduce many existing distortions in demand patterns. Within the context of 1992, the next stage would achieve greater competition by limiting significantly the interventions by governments on fare approvals, capacity constraints and route licensing. In addition, the development of an EC air transport market will require a common approach to negotiations with third countries on air transport issues, including traffic rights.

The main result of the regulatory regime prevailing so far has been inefficiencies in resource utilisation and a loss of consumers. While the nationalised European firms have recorded profit levels far below those of private industry, costs were far higher for US airlines during the early 1980s. Almost half of available seats have been flown empty, except over the North Atlantic, and relatively small aircraft (though the situation may be changing) offer lower-scale economies, widely employed. A study by Pryke (1987) provided many instances of the unproductive use of staff and equipment by European airlines compared to US companies, even after corrections have been made for such objective differences as fuel costs, size of aircraft and length of haul. Continued high costs are attributed to a lack of pressure on scheduled airlines to cut costs because of a lack of competition. During the period 1978–82, the costs of international services in Europe were, on average, 60 per cent higher than international services in North America. Data also show that corrected costs for European carriers per available tonne/kilometre were over 50 per cent higher than for US carriers' domestic services. Unadjusted maintenance costs were 119 per cent higher, administrative overheads 365 per cent higher and ground and passenger service costs 315 per cent greater. Five leading US carriers flew their narrow-bodied aircraft 8.33 hours per day, compared to 6.7 hours for five top European carriers. Salaries of cabin crew in regulated European airlines were also relatively higher than in the USA. European civil aviation is characterised more by inefficiences on the cost side than high profitability. In 1985, a relatively good year financially for the airlines, the average operating profitability ratio of (operating) revenue to expenditure excluding interest for 17 leading European airlines was only 5.1 per cent.

A report on air transport in Europe by *The Economist* of London (1986) estimated the variable costs of flying a similar route length to be 20 per cent higher in Europe than in North America, while ticket costs were, on average, 35–40 per cent higher in 1986. The conclusion was that an increase in competition in Europe would allow a reduction in Tariffs by 15–20 per cent.

Note that the overall gains given at the beginning were calculated on the assumption of a 10 per cent reduction in civil aviation costs and prices under conditions of a competitive civil aviation market in Europe. Although this is a substantial figure, it is modest in comparison with what has just been stated.

Lower prices would help increase load factors in the industry. The often unquestioned argument that demand for business travel is inelastic seems quite questionable, especially for smaller businesses whose trading activities beyond national frontiers should be particularly stimulated by the completion of the internal market. The following example was quoted by Emerson *et al.* to demonstrate this:

> In May 1986, the Irish Department of Tourism and Transport designated a new private airline to offer service on the Dublin/London route. A substantial reduction in the fare to just below IRA 100 return, which was matched by the main carrier, had the effect of an increase in traffic on the route by some 29 per cent, or 200,000 extra passengers between May and December 1986, a considerable number of these being small businessmen. A survey conducted in autumn 1986 showed that some 30 per cent of passengers on this route indicated they were travelling entirely as a result of the lower fare. (Emerson *et al.* 1988, p. 117).

Telecommunications services

The telecommunications services sector plays an increasing role in determining the competitiveness of marketable services and manufacturing industry in a modern society. EC PTT revenue from the service sector totalled over four times that for equipment in 1985, at 63 billion ECU. By comparison, in the USA the sector is twice as big as in the EC. Voice telephony accounted for 85–90 per cent of total PTT telecommunications revenue in 1985, with up to 10 per cent deriving from facsimile and up to 5 per cent from telex.

With the arrival of the new digital signalling and switching systems, telecommunications are increasingly converging with the digital technology of electronic data processing. The process will be greatly enhanced with the imminent introduction of the integrated services digital networks (ISDNs), sometimes called the 'global digital highway'.

As von Weizsacker (1987) observes, digital telecommunications are now doing for the computer what the railway network did for the steam engine: they likewise do for information transfer what transport infrastructure does for trade in physical goods. Thus, telecommunications will play a major role in promoting the integration of the EC economy by the end of 1992.

The change over to digital forms of traffic will not only allow the interlinkage of a wide range of monitors, computers and high-speed printers, but will have a major effect on the structure of the telecommunications system itself. In the opinion of many sectoral experts, growth of data, text and image transmissions should continue to increase at a multiple of that for voice transmissions so that it should bypass the value of the former within 20 years. The traditional market structure that was suitable for voice telephony is not the most suitable for the newly emergent network services known as 'value-added services' or VANs, such as data banks, electronic mail and electronic data interchange. International voice telephony services are provided jointly by national administrations. Except for transit traffic, there has been little effective international trade of a competitive nature in these services. However, the new value-added services now open up the way to international trade and specialisation based on cost advantage, efficiency, innovation and, to a lesser extent, economies of scale in the national network.

Just as with equipment, the typical structure of the operating authority is one based on the 'natural monopoly' model due to high fixed investment in the network. Recently in the UK, USA and Japan a degree of competition, deregulation on long-distance services, and privatisation has been introduced. Generally in Europe, however, national PTTs maintain their monopoly on access to the network, determining what range of services is provided and forbidding large subscribers who rent 'leased lines' from arbitraging any spare capacity to another user. For example, in one EC country the national broadcasting and railway authorities have substantial spare capacity on their leased lines but are contractually prevented from selling this to other firms.

In exchange for a legal monopoly on service traffic, the PTTs shoulder social obligations, such as the provision of universal services. The cost of linking outlying rural regions to the network is traditionally subsidised by profits on heavy routes and on long-distance calls. But there are a number of developments which now make the traditional market structure less suitable. New technology has considerably reduced the cost of long-distance traffic and the introduction of new value-added services is being severely handicapped by current restrictions on network use. The new range of sophisticated equipment and possibilities may only be achieved under less restricted market structures. Finally, rival economies, especially the USA, are liberalising their services sectors to stimulate greater international competitiveness and innovation.

Telecommunications are similar to computers in that they constitute a classic case of a learning industry where competitive structures unburdened by taxes are most conducive to market growth. Von Weizsacker (1987) argues that such distortions in tariff structures act as an indirect tariff on inter-EC trade and are incompatible with the aims of the EC. The introduction of a more rational tariff-based policy (i.e. cost-based policy), would also reduce the likelihood of 'cream skimming' of the most profitable traffic by new entrants in case of liberalisation, a possibility frequently advanced as an argument against network liberalization.

If the telecommunications services sector is to maximize its contribution to the integration and competitiveness of EC industry, it is becoming increasingly apparent that a more appropriate institutional structure is needed. Existing restrictions on network-user and service-producer freedom must be reduced to a minimum, and the current policy of cross-subsidisation at the expense of long-distance traffic revised. A comparison of long-distance rates shows that in many instances, intra-EC cross-border traffic can cost more than longer distance calls within a country. In any community, charges should be related to duration and distance and treated as if part of the domestic system.

The main objective of the EC as set out in the Green Paper (EC Commission 1987) is to ensure that EC industry derives the maximum benefit in terms of cost, quality and variety from the full development of the sector. To this end, a number of actions have been initiated, in particular: RACE (Research in Advanced Communication Techniques for Europe) which has now been adopted; the proposals for introduction of common ISDN standards within the EC; STAR (EC programme for the development of certain less-favoured regions by improving access to advanced telecommunication services); directives on mutual recognition of type approval and on the first phase of opening up access to public contracts; a European Telecommunications Standards Institute; and conditions for open network provision.

The Green Paper accepts that the role of national administrations in the provision of network structures, especially voice telephony, should be maintained. However, a distinction is drawn between such 'reserved services' as voice telephony and 'competitive services', especially value-added services. Unrestricted provision of such competitive services between member countries is proposed, as well as requirements for interoperability and access to transfrontier service providers. Liberalization should be introduced in such a fashion as to minimize the risk of 'cream skimming' referred to above. The Commission believes that the general principle that tariffs should be cost-related can be achieved by the end of 1992.

An attempt to quantify the costs of non-Europe (the term depicting the lack of a single market) in telecommunications services has been made in the study by Muller (1989). In order to place current policy options in perspective, he analysed three senarios: (i) a status quo scenario, where it is assumed that the recommendations of the Green Paper were not made but other developments still take place; (ii) a scenario based on the current provisions of the Green Paper; and (iii) a scenario of full network competition in long-distance and international transmission, but excluding competition in the local loop (e.g. that for local calls). A number of telecommunications costs are considered:

(a) Open competition for equipment procurement could lead on its own to a reduction in tariff levels of between 2 and 3 per cent depending on current national procurement policies. If, on average, tariffs were reduced by 5 per cent, the effects of extra network demand could lead to increasing economies of scale and fill (i.e. using available network to a higher capacity) which could yield savings of 750 million ECU per annum.
(b) More competitive conditions for the 'non-reserved services' would offer several kinds of benefit. Harmonisation of standards for terminal equipment and networks should reduce the barriers to entry, increase market growth, stimulating learning and scale effects. A liberalised equipment certification programme, with mutual recognition of standards, could also increase network use. Resource savings of 500–700 million ECU would be possible. Further liberalisation of the value-added services market, as proposed in the Green Paper, would stimulate additional service offerings and further network use. It would also reduce the importance of geographic space as a barrier to the spreading of

the new service industries in the EC. Benefits resulting from extra network use are estimated to be between 300 and 500 million ECU by the end of 1992. The availability of open network provision could further encourage the growth of VANs and increase the above benefits by 200 million ECU by the end of 1992.

(c) Moving tariff structures closer to costs would cause users to make more allocatively efficient decisions and increased network utilisation. The static welfare losses of the current tariff structure are estimated at up to 10 per cent of call revenue or 4 billion ECU. These estimates do not allow for the effects of current tariff restrictions on user and producer freedom regarding arbitrage and 'cream skimming' which Muller estimates to be considerable.

Alternative analyses rely upon comparisons between some EC countries and between the EC and Canada, and these confirm that there are big differences between levels and rates of growth of productivity not explained by scale. If scale network competition or improved regulatory policies could reduce such '*X*-inefficiencies', Muller estimates that productivity growth rates, currently of the order of about 2 per cent per annum, could accelerate by a further 0.5–1 per cent per annum, which could imply cumulating gains of 600 million ECU per year.

The conclusions of the detailed estimates contained in the Muller paper are briefly summarized in Table 27.1. These indicate that the potential economic gains of the Green Paper scenario could be up to 2 billion ECU. Extending the estimates to cover a more ambitious, but technically feasible, degree of network competition for long-distance and international traffic, a further 4 billion ECU of economic gains might be achieved.

Energy

In 1985, fuel and power products as defined in the national accounts (coal, coke, oil and oil products, natural gas, nuclear fuels and electricity) accounted for about 8 per cent (509 billion ECU) of EC total production. Therefore, energy is a major sector, which raises important issues of internal market policy. Consumption patterns in terms of energy sources differ considerably between countries. For example, in 1986 nuclear energy accounted for 21.7 per cent and 32.8

Table 27.1 Effects of regulatory reforms for European telecommunications services

Measures	*Minimum green paper effect (in ECU billion)*	*'Full network competition' effect*[1]
1. Lower equipment costs lead to lower tariffs and thereby economies of scale and fill in the network use	0.75 savings[2]	Slightly larger
2. More competitive 'non-reserved services':		
a. Easier CPE certification, increased product	0.5–0.7 savings	Not estimated
variety, lower CPE prices, larger network use	0.3–0.4 savings by 1990	Large, owing to fewer network restrictions
b. Liberalization of VANs		
c. Open network provision	0.2 savings by 1990	Not estimated
3. Tariff reforms (closer to cost)	Not estimated	4 billion ECU per annum

Notes:
1. For long-distance and international traffic.
2. These include the direct savings on equipment purchases.

Source: Muller, J. (1989).

per cent of total energy consumption in Belgium and France respectively, whereas it was only at 1.8 per cent in Italy and the Netherlands. For internal market considerations, a rough distinction can be made between energy distributed via networks (electricity and natural gas) and fuels, which are more or less freely traded on the market place (oil and solid fuels). Whereas the first category is characterized by the existence of monopoly suppliers, in the second case the economic environment is usually more competitive.

However, there are examples of obstacles to competitive trade even in the latter case. For instance, with regard to oil, some countries still operate national marketing monopolies, although on a diminishing scale, and others retain price controls or import licensing systems. Different national specifications for oil products, concerning sulphur and lead content, or other technical characteristics such as the viscosity and density of the products, are also an element of extra

Table 27.2 Cross-frontier transfers of electricity (including trade with some European non-EC countries)

Country	*Balanced exchanges*[1] *(TWh)*[2] *(1)*	*Net import (+) /exports (−) (TWh) (2)*	*Electricity demand (TWh) (3)*	*(2) as % of (3)*
Belgium	5.3	−0.2	53.9	0.3
Denmark	0.7	+1.4	28.8	4.5
France	7.6	−25.5	316.8	7.6
Germany	14.5	+4.6	383.7	1.1
Greece	0.3	+1.2	27.3	4.0
Ireland	–	–	11.3	–
Italy	1.8	+22.1	199.9	10.3
Luxemburg	0.4	+3.5	3.8	78.0
Netherlands	0.0	+2.3	66.9	3.3
Portugal	1.0	+1.9	21.1	8.6
Spain	2.9	+1.2	119.7	0.9
UK	–	+4.2	282.8	1.4
EUR 12	61.6	+14.2	1 516.3	0.8

Notes:
1. TWh = kWh × 10^9.
2. Balanced interchanges consist of equal quantities exported and imported at different times. The one-way quantities of these exchanges are given in column (1). The additional net import or export quantities are given in column (2).

Source: Emerson *et al.* (1988) p. 97.

by the removal of the existing trade barriers in the energy sector is a difficult task given the issues at stake. A detailed study on this question has not been undertaken, but would be warranted. The following indications should therefore be viewed as an initial rough impression of the orders of magnitude involved. For oil products, the adoption of common specifications at the EC level would reduce refineries production costs. Refiners are at present forced to supply different ranges of products, varying from one EC country to another. The potential cost reductions might be around 500 million ECU. For coal, direct state aids to coal production totalled 3.3 billion ECU in 1986 (for the EC of twelve). This figure only reflects direct costs for taxpayers, and does not take into account the costs of other forms of protection. These may, however, be viewed as implicitly included in some degree in the possible benefits from more extensive

Table 27.3 Ratio of elasticity prices to the unweighted average price (EUR 12 = 1) for the 12 capital cities of EC countries[1] for typical domestic and industrial consumers (January 1985) (including taxes, except VAT where deductible)

Country	*Consumer domestic*[2]	*Sector industrial*[2]
Belgium	1.13	0.94
Denmark	1.02	1.12
France	1.03	0.77
Germany	1.05	0.97
Greece	0.87	1.16
Ireland	0.88	1.13
Italy	1.64	1.24
Luxemburg	0.81	0.84
Netherlands	1.08	1.10
Portugal	0.89	0.98
Spain	0.79	0.89
UK	0.81	0.86

Notes:
1. Prices were collected in Dusserldorf, Milan and Rotterdam for Germany, Italy and the Netherlands, respectively.
2. Domestic consumer with annual consumption of 3500 kWh of which 1300 kWh at night. Industrial consumer with annual consumption of 10 GWh, maximum demand of 2500 kW and a load factor of 4000 hours.

Source: Eurostat.

linkages between electricity grids and gas networks beyond national boundaries. The latter would favour a growth in trade of electricity and gas, and an improved use of production equipment. Although such development would affect only parts of the market, it would nevertheless create an increased, competitive price discipline, including the sources of finance for power-generating utilities. Resulting cost reductions might amount to around 8 billion ECU for electricity and gas supplies. To give another perspective on these figures, if electricity prices in countries presently experiencing above EC average prices (see Table 27.3) were to be reduced to that average price, savings would total about 6 billion ECU, that is about 5 per cent of the value of total EC production.

Defence

Presently, although the EC countries form a European sub-set of NATO, reflected in the Eurogroup and the Independent European Programme Group (IEPG), defence is still outside the EC's remit. Nevertheless, the EC is often criticized for wasteful duplication of its weapons industries, with member countries purchasing defence equipment from their national suppliers. The result is a diversity of weapons operated by the European members of NATO, with each nation buying relatively small quantities. This lack of standardization has implications for the size of defence budgets and EC industrial policy. One study estimated that within NATO, wasteful duplication amongst the Europeans amounted to the whole of European R&D expenditure plus 25 per cent of its procurement outlays, giving a total development and production waste of $4.4 billion at 1975 US prices (Callaghan 1975). In addition, rising weapons costs mean that a given defence budget purchases smaller quantities of equipment. For example, the production cost of a strike aircraft (e.g. Tornado) exceeds £10 million per unit at 1981 prices and, in real terms, Hartley (1983) argues that it is probably four times as costly as its predecessor. Within each nation, the result is rising R&D costs per unit and fewer opportunities for economies of scale in production; hence government support for a small scale weapons industry, typical of most European nations, is costly. A glance at the data will show that the equipment expenditure of each European nation is considerably below that of the USA, although a combined EC procurement agency would greatly reduce the scale differential. Nor would the potential benefits of an EC involvement in weapons policy be confined to defence. Weapons industries are amongst the technological leaders; they manufacture civil products (e.g. aerospace, electronics, nuclear power, telecommunications) and they are substantial employers. In other words, EC efforts to develop a common industrial policy and technology policy cannot ignore the defence industries.

Since this is a large field, it suffices to quote some examples from Vredeling (1987):

(a) Armoured vehicles – Europe has a solid technological base but the desire of many countries to make their own tanks means short production runs and high unit costs.
(b) Conventional munitions – the USA benefits from large-scale

production and low unit costs, although the level of technological sophistication of US products is similar to that in Europe.

(c) Guided missiles – Europe's position is weakened by the technology gap in electronics and the fragmentation of the markets, which extends from development to production.

(d) Aircraft and helicopters – the excellent performance of the European industry makes it vital to develop collaborative programmes covering the full range of military aircraft.

CONCLUSIONS

I hope it is apparent that the estimates of the gains from the internal market, both overall and from the public utilities considered in this paper, rest on crucial assumptions. Thus, it is appropriate to conclude by highlighting the limitations of these premises.

The main reservation is that the estimates given in the *Cecchini Report* should not be taken at face value. First, in spite of the endorsement of the SEA by all the member nations, there does not seem to be a philosophy common to all of them to underpin the internal market. Second, these estimates do not take into consideration the costs to be incurred by firms, regions and governments in achieving them. Third, the internal market aims at the elimination of internal barriers to promote the efficient restructuring of supply, but it remains silent on the question of demand; thus the internal market seems to be directed mainly at the production side. Fourth, putting too much emphasis on economies of scale, when their very existence has to be proved, will encourage 'concentration' rather than 'competition', and there is no evidence to support the proposition that there is a positive correlation between increased firm size and competitive success. Finally, the estimates are for the EC as a whole, thus it is likely that each member nation will strive to get the maximum gain for itself with detrimental consequences for all, i.e. this is like the classical oligopoly problem where the best solution for profit maximization purposes is for oligopolists to behave as a joint-monopolist, but if each oligopolist firm tries to maximize its own share of the joint profit, the outcome may be losses all round. Note that a rigorous specification of these reservations is fully set out elsewhere – see El-Agraa (1990, chapters 4 and 5) and El-Agraa (1989a).

Apart from the criticisms given in the relevant section, Baldwin's estimates are also subject to these reservations since they start from

Cecchini's. Hence, there is no need to dwell on them. Here, it is sufficient to reiterate that such potential benefits may prove rather elusive since the creation of the appropriate environment does not necessarily guarantee the expected outcomes. However, this does not mean that the EC should not be congratulated for its genuine attempts at creating the necessary competitive atmosphere, only that one should not put too much emphasis onto estimates which can easily be frustrated by the realities of every day EC economic life.

Irrespective of the seriousness of these reservations, one should admit that at least a considerable amount of benefit can be gained from subjecting EC public utilities to a single EC market. Given the dramatic changes in East–West relations, the developments in Eastern Europe and German reunification, it may not be too long before this happens.

Note

* The sections on most of the public utilities rely heavily on Emerson *et al.* (1988).

References

1. Baldwin, R. (1989) 'The growth effects of 1992', *Economic Policy*, no. 9, October.
2. Callaghan Jr., T. A. (1975) *US–European Economic Cooperation in Military and Civil Technology*, Center for Strategic and International Studies (Georgetown University Press).
3. Cecchini, P. (1988) *1992: the European Challenge* (London: Gower).
4. Commission of the European Communities (1985) *Completing the Internal Market (White Paper* from the EC Commission to the EC Council) – COM(85)310.
5. Commission of the European Communities (1987) *Green Paper on the Development of the Common Market for Telecommunications Services Equipment*, COM(87) 290 final.
6. Commission of the European Communities (1988) *Completing the Internal Market: an Area Without Internal Frontiers* (COM(88)650), Brussels.
7. Commission of the European Communities (1989) *Research on the Cost of Non-Europe: Basic Findings* (the *Cecchini Report*), Brussels, 16 volumes.
8. Cooper, J., Browne, M. and Gretton, D. (1987) 'Freight transport in the European Community: making the most of UK opportunities', paper

presented to the Transport Study Group, Polytechnic of Central London.
9. Delaney, R. V. (1987) 'The disunited States: a country in search of an efficient transport policy', mimeo (Washington DC: CATO Institute).
10. DRI Europe (1986) *European Road Freight Deregulation – Intentions and Proposals* (London: MacGraw-Hill).
11. El-Agraa, A. M. (ed.) (1983) *Britain within the European Community: the Way Forward* (London: Macmillan; New York: Crane Russack).
12. El-Agraa, A. M. (1988) *Japan's Trade Frictions: Realities or Misconceptions?* (London: Macmillan; New York: St. Martin's).
13. El-Agraa, A. M. (1989a) *The Theory and Measurement of International Economic Integration* (London: Macmillan; New York: St. Martin's).
14. El-Agraa, A. M. (1989b) *International Trade* (London: Macmillan; New York: St. Martin's).
15. El-Agraa, A. M. (1989c) 'Japanese business and the European Community', *Kinyu Journal*, vol. 30, no. 1.
16. El-Agraa, A. M. (ed.) (1990) *The Economics of the European Community* (Hemel Hempstead: Simon and Schuster; New York: Prentice Hall International). Third edition. First two editions were published by Philip Allan, Oxford and St. Martin's Press, New York.
17. Emerson, M. (1988) *The Economics of 1992: the EC Commission's Assessment of the Economic Effects of Completing the Internal Market* (Oxford: Oxford University Press).
18. Ernst & Whinney (1989) 'An illustration in the road haulage sector', in Vol. 1 of the complete *Cecchini Report* – see Commission (1989).
19. Hartley, K. (1983) 'EC defence policy', in A. M. El-Agraa (ed.), *Britain within the European Community: the Way Forward* (London: Macmillan; New York: Crane Russack).
20. Muller, J. (1989) *The Benefits of Completing the Internal Market for Telecommunication Equipment and Services*, Vol. 10 of the complete *Cecchini Report* – see Commission (1989).
21. Pryke, R. (1987) 'The competition among international airlines', *Thames Essay* (London: Trade Policy Research Centre).
22. von Weizsacker, C. (1987) 'The economics of value-added networks', mimeo.
23. Vredeling, H. (1987) *Report of a Group of Independent Experts Presided by H. Vredeling* (Brussels: NATO).

Author Index

Subject Index

cost for refiners which could be reduced with the adoption of common standards at the EC level.

The coal sector is subject to EC (ECSC) rules governing state aids to the coal industry. These rules aim to limit such aids strictly in terms of volume, purpose and duration. The coal policy guidelines, set out in a decision (No 2064/86/ECSC of June 1986 establishing rules for state aids to the coal industry, *OJL* 177, 1. 7. 1986), allow state aid to the coal industry when it contributes to the following aims:

(a) improvement of the competitiveness of the coal industry, contributing to assuring a better security of supply;
(b) creating new capacities provided that they are economically viable; and
(c) solving the social and regional problems related to developments in the coal industry.

Thus, the current principles for national aids to the coal sector recognize the need to take account of the major adjustment problems of the industry, and the social and regional consequences of that adjustment, but are also based on the view that the need for aids should be progressively reduced by taking steps to restore the industry to a state of economic viability. In fact, the financial situation of the coal industry has steadily deteriorated during the past decade. Losses and the aid required have risen appreciably. In 1985, the aid granted totalled 3 billion ECU, and in 1986 it amounted to 3.3 billion ECU. In recent years, the fall in oil prices, the world market price for coal, and the exchange rate of the US dollar have been major factors behind these trends.

The problems are of different nature in the sub-sectors relying on distribution networks, i.e. the electricity and gas industries. There is a wide variety of organizational structures for the electricity supply industries in EC countries. These vary from very large, publicly owned undertakings, which account for all or most of the electricity supplied, to systems which rely on a number of large and small public, semi-public or privately owned companies. In their geographic areas, these enterprises usually enjoy a monopoly of supply. The purpose of such monopolies is, generally, to provide to customers the most economic conditions of supply. The relative lack of trade between regional networks, both within countries and across frontiers, does, however, hinder achievement of that goal. Electricity costs can vary widely between one EC country and another for equivalent categories of consumers. In addition, the choice of fuels for power stations can be affected by national policies, for instance embargoes on nuclear power, or measures to favour the use of nationally produced coal in the electricity sector. There is, therefore, scope for offsetting these problems, at least in part, by greater recourse to drawing supplies from neighbouring undertakings, including those across borders, and such possibilities should be considered as a serious option alongside indigenous production. This is, of course, only feasible if supplies from other countries can offer the same degree of security as domestic production. This can be achieved by contractual arrangements, established in a climate of confidence between trading partners along lines of recognized EC principles.

Cross-frontier transfers of electricity already take place between EC countries, although a substantial part of it consists of equal quantities exported and imported at differing times – see Table 27.2. Net imports or exports are important in the case of some EC nations (France, Italy, Luxembourg and Portugal).

An efficient allocation of resources requires that electricity prices reflect true costs in supplying each category of users and avoid discrimination between different types of consumer – an agreed EC pricing principle (see Council *Recommendation* of 27 October 1981 on electricity tariff structures in the EC, *OJL* 337, 24. 11. 1981). In practice, pricing policies are such that the distribution of costs between households and industrial consumers differs widely between individual EC nations. Some countries tend to favour industry relative to the household consumer, whereas the reverse appears to be the case for other EC nations. The further integration of the electricity industry in the EC requires both increased price transparency and more consistent pricing policies, as well as increased trade through grid interconnections. In the case of natural gas, modifications of the monopoly rights of companies which transport and distribute gas could encourage a certain degree of dissociation between their area of operation and national frontiers. The resulting increase in price competition could benefit consumers, especially in neighbouring regions, while gas utilities could also benefit from larger markets for their investment planning. As a consequence, energy-consuming industries in certain EC nations would cease to be penalized in terms of competitiveness *vis-à-vis* their foreign rivals who can rely on cheaper energy inputs.

An accurate estimate of the economic gains that could be obtained